Traces of Dreams

TRACES OF DREAMS

Landscape, Cultural Memory,
and the Poetry of Bashō

Haruo Shirane

STANFORD UNIVERSITY PRESS
STANFORD, CALIFORNIA

Stanford University Press
Stanford, California
© 1998 by the Board of Trustees of the
Leland Stanford Junior University
Printed in the United States of America
CIP data appear at the end of the book

Frontispiece: Painting by Morikawa Kyoriku (1656–1715), a disciple and Bashō's painting instructor. 42.1 x 12.2 in. The calligraphy and the poem—*kareeda ni/karasu no tomarikeri/aki no kure* (on a leafless branch a crow comes to rest—autumn nightfall)—are by Bashō, who probably inscribed this around 1692-93. (Courtesy Idemitsu Art Museum)

For Tomi and Seiji

Acknowledgments

I am grateful for the many hours spent with Ogata Tsutomu, whose immense learning and encouragement have made this book possible. I am indebted to many friends, colleagues, and teachers, all of whom I cannot mention here. Among them, I thank Andrew Pekarik, Karen Brazell, Paul Rouzer, Thomas Rimer, Paul Varley, Howard Hibbett, Lewis Cook, Chris Drake, Henry Smith, Dan Bromberg, and the anonymous reader for Stanford University Press, each of whom read chapters or drafts and provided invaluable feedback. Special thanks to William Higginson for his haiku imagination and many comments. I am indebted to Horikiri Minoru, Hori Nobuo, and Kawamoto Kōji, who gave me precious advice while I was in Japan. Many thanks to Watanabe Masaru and Sakaguchi Akiko for carefully checking the manuscript and offering numerous suggestions. Donald Keene kindly lent me his Bashō library, and Edward Seidensticker paved the way. Yasuko Makino of the Starr East Asian Library at Columbia University procured numerous books and documents for me. Anne Commons helped with references. Jamie Newhard assisted with the index. John Ziemer and John Feneron were exemplary editors. I acknowledge support for research from the Columbia University Council on Research and Faculty Development, the Japan Foundation, the National Endowment for the Humanities, and the Social Science Research Council. I would like to thank Paul Anderer, who has been a superb colleague and friend. I have been blessed with an extraordinary group of graduate students at Columbia. Most of all, I could not have done without Tomi Suzuki, who has always been my warmest supporter and most incisive critic.

H.S.

Contents

References and General Notes

Translations. All translations are mine unless otherwise noted. The word-for-word literal translations, which follow the English translations, reveal only the most basic meaning. "Acc." indicates the accusative particle *o* (*wo*); "nom." represents the nominative particle *ga*.

Dates, seasons, Bashō's life. In dating Bashō's hokku, I have followed Kon Eizō's *Bashō nenpu taisei,* the most authoritative chronology of Bashō's hokku. I give the solar date alongside the original lunar date; for example, the figures in parentheses in the expression "January 31, 1687 (12.18.Jōkyō 3)" indicate the 18th day, Twelfth Month, in the third year of the Jōkyō era. The First to Third Months of the lunar calendar (roughly the equivalent of February through April) were spring, the Fourth to the Sixth (roughly May through July) summer, the Seventh through the Ninth (roughly August through October) autumn, and the Tenth through Twelfth (November through January) winter.

Those English readers not familiar with the facts of Bashō's life, particularly as they relate to his poetry and haikai career, should consult Makoto Ueda's *Matsuo Bashō* (New York: Twayne, 1970; reissued by Kōdansha, 1982) and his *Bashō and His Interpreters* (Stanford: Stanford University Press, 1991); the latter provides an excellent chronology and collection of translations.

Terms and titles. Whenever possible, a Japanese term or title is translated at its first appearance in this study. A glossary of key Japanese literary terms appears as an appendix; all primary sources are listed by title, with the original Japanese, in the Selected Bibliography.

Personal names. I have followed the normal Japanese order for names, with the family name first, followed by the given name. Haikai poets are given by their haikai names (*haigō* or *haimyō*). Thus, Matsuo Bashō is referred to as Bashō, his *haigō*, and not Matsuo, his family name.

Texts. All of Bashō's hokku are drawn from Kon Eizō's *Bashō kushū* (Collected hokku of Bashō, 1982), one of the most authoritative editions of Bashō's hokku available today. All hokku by Bashō cited in this book are listed in the Index of Cited Hokku in alphabetical order. Unless otherwise noted, all references to Bashō's prose texts are to *Matsuo Bashō shū*, ed. Imoto Nōichi, Hori Nobuo, and Muramatsu Tomotsugu, NKBZ 41 (Shōgakukan, 1972), a readily available single-volume edition. All references to Dohō's *Sanzōshi* and Kyorai's *Kyoraishō*, two key poetic treatises of the Bashō school, are from *Rengaron shū, Nōgakuron shū, Hairon shū*, ed. Ijichi Tetsuo, Omote Akira, and Kuriyama Riichi, NKBZ 51 (Shōgakukan, 1973). Citations are followed by an abbreviation of the series title, the volume number, and the page. For example, "NKBZ 51: 525" refers to p. 525 of vol. 51 of the *Nihon koten bungaku zenshū*.

Abbreviations

KBZ   Kōhon Bashō zenshū
KHT   Koten haibungaku taikei
NKBT   Nihon koten bungaku taikei
NKBZ   Nihon koten bungaku zenshū
HT   Haisho taikei
SNKBT   Shin Nihon koten bungaku taikei
SNKS   Shinchō Nihon koten shūsei

Poems rise not so much in response to present time, as even Rilke thought, but in response to other poems.

—Harold Bloom, *The Anxiety of Influence*

Every creative imitation mingles filial rejection with respect, just as every parody pays its own oblique homage.

—Thomas Greene, *The Light in Troy*

A work of art is perceived against the background of, and by way of association with, other works of art. The form of a work of art is determined by its relationship with other forms existing prior to it. . . . Creation as a parallel with and contrast to some model is a description applicable not just to parody but to any work of art in general. New form comes about not in order to express new content but in order to replace an old form that has already lost its artistic viability.

—Victor Sklovsky, "Theory of the Formal Method"

CHAPTER 1

Introduction

Refiguring Cultural Memory

> jumping in
> and washing off an old poem—
>   a frog   —Buson

Interest in Matsuo Bashō (1644–94), perhaps the best known Japanese poet in both Japan and the West, is driven by a large population—by some estimates as high as five million—of active haiku practitioners (*haijin*) in Japan, many of whom look to Bashō's poems for technique and inspiration. In contrast to the Anglo-European tradition of poetry, which has been in precipitous decline over the last century, Japanese poetry, particularly in the form of the 31-syllable *tanka* and 17-syllable *haiku*, remains an integral element of contemporary Japanese culture, and Bashō, as the putative founder of haiku, remains a central figure. In the West Bashō's poems and travel literature, especially *Narrow Road to the Interior* (*Oku no hosomichi*), have repeatedly been translated into English and other Western languages, and much has been written about his work, especially in the context of the English haiku movement. His popularity is such that a book containing a hundred different English translations of the frog poem has been translated.[1] For many American schoolchildren, haiku—or some English variant of it—is their first exposure to poetry, if not to creative composition. In this global age, haiku may in fact be Japan's most significant literary export.

This book is a study of *haikai*, popular linked verse—which eventually gave birth to haiku—and of what I refer to as "haikai imagination." My working assumption is that haikai is both a specific poetic genre, which was widely practiced in the Tokugawa period by commoners and samurai, *and* a particular mode of discourse, an attitude toward language, literature, and tradition, an approach that is most prominently displayed in haikai linked verse, the seventeen-syllable *hokku* (later called haiku), *haibun* (haikai prose), and *haiga* (haikai painting) but that also pervaded much of early modern Japanese culture and literature. This haikai imagination emerged from the interaction between the new popular, largely urban, commoner- and samurai-based cultures that came to the fore in the seventeenth century *and* the residual classical traditions, which haikai and other popular genres parodied, transformed, and translated into contemporary languages and forms.

Haikai imagination, which took pleasure in the juxtaposition and collision of these seemingly incongruous worlds and languages, humorously inverted and recast established cultural associations and conventions, particularly the "poetic essence" (*hon'i*) of classical poetic topics. For haikai poets, as for their classical predecessors, these literary and cultural associations were largely embodied in nature, in historical objects, and in geographic places, in landscape broadly defined, which possessed what Walter Benjamin has called "aura"[2] and which preserved the cultural memory and became the source of authority and legitimacy as well as the contested ground for haikai re-visioning and re-mapping. This cultural memory, hitherto the preserve of a limited number of social groups, was appropriated, vernacularized, reconstructed, and spread by "town teachers" such as Bashō and by the emerging print technology, creating a new sense of communality among widely divergent commoners and samurai and laying the ground for what Benedict Anderson has referred to as the "imagined community."[3] While addressing broader issues of language, landscape, and cultural memory, this study explores the poetry and prose of Bashō in the context of the social practices of the time, especially the communal, dialogic process by which haikai spread and worked.

One of the most dramatic transformations in Japanese history occurred in the seventeenth century, in the transition from the medieval period (thirteenth–sixteenth centuries) to the early modern era (1600–1867), when vast alterations in literary and cultural paradigms gave birth to a whole new body of vernacular literature, the foremost of which was haikai, or popular linked verse. The seventeenth century witnessed the emergence of the urban commoners (*chōnin*) as an economically and culturally powerful class; the spread of mass education, especially through domain (*han*) schools for samurai and the temple schools (*terakoya*) for commoners; and the advent of printing—all of which led to the widespread production and consumption of popular literature, which became a commodity for huge markets. At the same time, traditional Japanese and Chinese literary texts were printed, distributed, and widely read for the first time.[4]

Until the seventeenth century, literary texts had been transmitted only in hand-written manuscripts of limited quantities and were almost entirely the possession of a small elite group of aristocrats, priests, and high-ranking samurai. In the medieval period traveling minstrels (*biwa hōshi*) had chanted military epics such as the *Tale of Heike* to a populace that could often neither read nor write. The average samurai was illiterate, as were farmers and craftsmen. With the emergence of a new socioeconomic structure, the government promotion of education, and the spread of print capitalism in the seventeenth century, this situation changed drastically. By the middle of the seventeenth century, almost all samurai, now the bureaucratic elite, were able to read, as were the middle to upper levels of the farmer, merchant, and artisan classes. This newly literate populace transformed haikai, which had been practiced in the medieval period among a limited range of social groups, into a vastly popular form. In the second half of the seventeenth century, haikai books—over

650 separate titles—were second in popularity only to Buddhist texts among Kyoto publishers, who published an estimated 300,000 volumes in first editions alone. *Sequel to Mountain Well* (*Zoku yama no i*), a haikai seasonal almanac published in 1667, ends with the note: "967 authors, 48 provinces, 5,035 verses."[5]

The seventeenth century witnessed not only a dramatic rise in the standard of living for almost all levels of society but a striking change in the nature of cultural production and consumption. In the medieval period, provincial military lords (*daimyō*) were able to learn about the Heian classics from traveling renga (classical linked verse) masters such as Sōgi (1421–1502), but the acquisition of classical texts was limited to a relatively small circle of poet-priests, powerful warriors, and aristocrats, who were deeply rooted in the traditional culture of Kyoto. A monopoly—epitomized by the *Kokin denju*, the secret teachings of the *Kokinshū* (Collection of old and new Japanese poems; ca. 905)—had been established over the study of classical texts, the study of which was often passed on through carefully controlled lineages, in one-to-one transmissions to the elected few. In the seventeenth century, by contrast, anyone who could afford to pay for lessons could receive instructions from "town teachers" (*machi shishō*) in any one of many arts or fields of learning. The transmission of learning was not dependent, as it had been in the medieval period, on the authority of poetry families or the patronage of large institutions such as Buddhist temples or powerful military lords. The haikai teacher, or *haikai sōshō*, was one of many available "town teachers" who competed for clients and depended on their individual popularity to make a living. Cultural activities such as poetry, Noh singing (*utai*), and tea ceremony not only became available to commoners but also became highly commercialized, leading to the commodification of culture.

These commoners, however, did not possess a textually based cultural tradition as aristocrats, priests, and some samurai had earlier: one consequence was a sharp contrast between their cultural past, which was closely associated with aristocratic, religious, or foreign (Chinese) authority, and contemporary life and culture. This sharp dualism formed the basis for one of the most salient aspect of haikai and Tokugawa popular culture: the constant interaction of a vertical axis, based on a perceived notion of a cultural past that had expanded to include Yoshitsune, Benkei, the Soga brothers, and other popular medieval legends, with a horizontal axis, based on contemporary, urban commoner life and a new social order.

In kabuki theater, which emerged together with haikai in the urban centers in the late seventeenth century, these two axes took the form of two simultaneous plots—which were later called the *sekai* (literally, "world" or "sphere"), or "vertical" plot, and the *shukō* (originally, "intention"), or contemporary counterpoint—in which a new "horizontal" plot, based on the present, was superimposed on a familiar, "vertical" plot drawn from the past. In the noted kabuki play *Sukeroku*, for example, the eponymous townsman protagonist is identified as one of the Soga brothers, a medieval samurai hero, thus resulting in a double identity across time. Haikai similarly emerged from the interaction of socially and temporally disparate worlds, from the intersection of a seemingly unchanging, idealized past (that included China) with a constantly, rapidly changing present, the centripetal force of the former serving to hold in check the centrifugal force of the latter. The pleasure and the humor of haikai, like that of kabuki, often derived from the combination of these disparate worlds, from the twist imposed by the horizontal, contemporary axis on the vertical axis. In Bashō's *Narrow Road to the Interior* (*Oku no hosomichi*), to give an example from haikai prose, the "I" or the traveler has a double identity: he is simultaneously a contemporary haikai poet *and* a seventeenth-century incarnation of Saigyō, the late Heian waka poet/traveler. Haikai required "newness" (*atarashimi*), but, like kabuki, that novelty lay not so much in the departure from or rejection of the perceived tradition as in the reworking of established practices and conventions, in creating new counterpoints to the past. In Edo culture the ability to create the new out of the old was generally a more highly regarded form of newness than the ability to be unique or individual.

Haikai, or popular linked verse, opened with the seventeen-syllable (5/7/5) hokku—which later became the haiku—to which was added a fourteen-syllable (7/7) second verse (*wakiku*), which was capped in turn by a seventeen-syllable (5/7/5) third verse (*daisanku*), and so forth, until a sequence of 36 (*kasen*), 44 (*yoyoshi*), 50 (*gojūin*), 100 (*hyakuin*), or 1,000 verses (*senku*) was completed. Although haikai, like renga, could be composed by a single individual, as a solo composition (*dokugin*), it was usually a communal activity, in which two or more participants took turns adding verses to create a sequence. Each added verse (*tsukeku*) was joined to the previous verse (*maeku*) to form a new poetic world, even as it pushed off from the poetic world created by the combination of the previous verse and the penultimate verse (*uchikoshi*). The following sequence (nos. 22, 23, 24) appears in a *kasen* called *Beneath the Cherry Trees* (*Ko no moto ni*) in *Gourd* (*Hisago*; 1690), a Bashō-school haikai anthology edited by Shadō (d. 1737).

> "I want to see Kumano,"
> she wept   —Bashō
>
> Kumano | mitaki | to | nakitamaikeri
> Kumano | want-to-see | said | wept
>
>   bow in hand
>   the barrier guard at Ki
>   unyielding
>   —Chinseki
>
> tatsukayumi | Ki | no | sekimori | ga | katakuna | ni
> handheld-bow | Ki | 's | barrier-guard | as-for | unyielding | ly
>
> the bald head probably
> from too much drinking
>   —Kyokusui[6]
>
> sake | de | hagetaru | atama | naruran
> sake | with | having-become-bald | head | is-probably

The first verse, which is in classical Japanese, uses an honorific verb (*nakitamaikeri*) to suggest the high status of the traveler (presumably a woman) who is weeping because she is anxious to visit Kumano, a popular site for religious pilgrimages in the Heian and medieval periods. The next verse by Chinseki (otherwise known as Shadō) joins with the previous verse by Bashō to reveal that the traveler is weeping because a guard holding a bow is refusing to let her pass through the barrier at Ki Province. The third verse, which pushes off from Bashō's verse and combines with Chinseki's verse, humorously transforms the barrier guard into a tippler, whose head has grown bald, or so it appears, from excessive drinking. In contrast to classical linked verse, which maintained a harmonious tone and preserved classical content and diction, haikai drew on different languages, especially the vernacular, and moved radically, as it does here, from one social world to another: the aristocratic, seemingly tragic, somber world of the first two verses is unexpectedly transformed into the lighthearted, commoner world of the last two verses. The manner in which the added verse reworked, transformed, and twisted, usually in humorous fashion, the world and language of the previous verse / penultimate verse was directly related to the manner in which haikai parodied classical texts and conventions: both involved recontextualizing existing texts or established worlds so as to create new meanings and perspectives. Haikai, as we shall see, was a hybrid form that emerged in a transformational relationship to established texts, genres, and languages, which haikai "translated" or transformed into the vernacular and into popular, contemporary forms.

Haikai can be considered both a specific poetic genre—popular linked verse, practiced widely by commoners and samurai—and a particular mode or approach to language, literature, and tradition infused with what I call "haikai imagination." What, then, was haikai in this broad sense? How does haikai imagination manifest itself in different aspects of Bashō's poetry and prose?

The style and approach to haikai changed significantly from period to period and from movement to movement, but certain characteristics recur. First, haikai implied the interaction of diverse languages and subcultures, particularly between the new popular cultures and the elite traditions, and the humor and interest that resulted from the sociolinguistic incongruity and difference, especially as a result of the witty or sudden movement from one world to another. Second, haikai imagination meant taking pleasure in recontextualization: in defamiliarization, in dislocating habitual, conventionalized perceptions; and in refamiliarization, in recasting established poetic topics into new languages and material cultures. Haikai imagination was also marked by a constant search for "newness," for both new perspectives and new sociolinguistic frontiers in contemporary Japan as well as in reconstructed versions of the Japanese and Chinese past. Last but not least, haikai imagination implied the ability to interact in a playful, lively dialogue that resulted in the communal production of culture and art and a sense of bonding across class and family lines.

Of particular interest here is the complex relationship between haikai and the construction of tradition, especially the refiguring of cultural memory. As is well known, Bashō looked to classical and medieval poets, especially Nōin (998–1050?), Saigyō (1118–90), and Sōgi (1421–1502), for poetic and spiritual inspiration and was heavily influenced by Chinese poetry and poetics, especially that of Li Po (701–62) and Tu Fu (712–70). At the same time, Bashō was a poet of haikai, which, by its very nature, was parodic, oppositional, and immersed in popular culture. What kind of literary past did Bashō envision and construct and for what reasons? In what ways were his poetry and prose manifestations of haikai spirit? How was it possible to be both haikai-esque, working against the established canon, and traditional at the same time? What implications does this have for reading Bashō's poetry and prose and for understanding the larger cultural milieu?

A salient characteristic of Tokugawa culture was the intense interaction of diverse languages—urban and provincial, Kamigata (Kansai region) and Edo (Kantō region), samurai and urban commoners (*chōnin*), aristocratic and commoner, classical and vernacular, Chinese and Japanese—to mention only the most prominent. In previous periods, regional and social differences had also generated contrastive languages, but the cultural center had always been in

Kyoto or with those closely associated with its cultural milieu. The awareness of linguistic and sociocultural differences was enhanced by a number of factors: the shift of the political center to the East, to Edo, which became a major metropolis; the emergence of two distinctive cultural regions (Kansai and Kantō); and the institution of the *sankin kōtai* (alternate-year residence) system, which brought the provincial daimyō and their large entourages to Edo and generated substantial intercourse between the urban center and the provinces. With the spread of education, the rise of Neo-Confucian ideology, and the increase of popular interest in Chinese literature, the Chinese language (and its Japanese variants) also became important.

As Inui Hiroyuki has shown, haikai, which emerged in the medieval period and came to the fore in the Tokugawa period, thrived at the intersection of these languages, especially between classical diction—a highly encoded, self-enclosed language that bore the taste and values of a refined, aristocratic past—and various types of popular languages, which had a strong sense of immediacy and referentiality, closely tied to everyday, commoner life and material culture. Bashō composed the following poem, which appears in *Backpack Notes* (*Oi no kobumi*), in May 1688 (4.20.Genroku 1).

Lodging for the night at Akashi

octopus traps—
fleeting dreams beneath
a summer moon

takotsubo|ya|hakanaki|yume|o|natsu|no|tsuki
octopus-trap|:|fleeting|dream|(acc.)|summer|'s|moon

The octopus traps were lowered in the afternoon and raised the next morning, after the octopus had crawled inside. The octopus in the jars—and implicitly the troops of the Heike clan that were massacred on these shores at the end of the twelfth century and whose ghosts subsequently appear before the traveler in *Backpack Notes*—are having "fleeting dreams," not knowing they are about to be harvested. The reader's mind jumps between an elegant, classical phrase, the "summer moon" (*natsu no tsuki*), which the poetic tradition deemed to be brief as the summer night and which was associated in classical literature with ephemerality, and "octopus traps" (*takotsubo*), an everyday, vernacular word, representing commoner life. In a haikai-esque transformation, the vernacular injects new life into a classical cliché—the theme of impermanence—and the classical phrase, with its established overtones, transforms the "haikai word" (*haigon*) into poetry. The resulting poem is both humorous and tragic at the same time.

One result of this cohabitation of contrastive languages and subcultures was the emergence in the seventeenth century of the culture of *mitate* (literally, "to view and construct"), in which one image was superimposed on or equated with another. The literature, drama, and art of visual allusion moved back and forth between two starkly different worlds, between that of Japanese and Chinese classics and that of the new commoner society, each providing a lens or filter to view the other. The audience simultaneously "saw" the world of classical/medieval Japan or China alongside or through a redone contemporary version. Haikai, which may be considered the ultimate literature of double vision, flourished in this cultural space, which required both a familiarity with the "classics"—some of which were newly constructed—as well as an ironic distance from them. In contrast to allusive variation (*honkadori*), the medieval poetic technique of "borrowing" (*toru*) from a classical "foundation poem" (*honka*), which assumed a common base of diction, tone, and subject matter with classical poetry, the Tokugawa *mitate* was characterized by startling, dramatic, and often witty changes that it imparted to the target text. Artists such as Hishikawa Moronobu (1618–94), a pioneer of ukiyoe prints and a contemporary of Bashō, used the technique of *mitate* in the visual arts, both alluding to and radically transforming the topics and imagery of the classical tradition into contemporary, commoner form.[7]

Bashō's haikai was unorthodox, reacting against the rapidly growing, often flamboyant, material culture of the new cities. One consequence was that Bashō's haikai differed in significant ways from the *mitate* found in Moronobu's ukiyoe prints and from the poetry of Saikaku (1642–93), another contemporary haikai poet. The popular culture found in Bashō's poetry and prose was not the stylish men and women of the floating world (*ukiyo*), of the great urban centers, but rather the mundane, everyday lives of farmers and fishermen in the provinces. The new popular literature and drama, including haikai, emerged out of urban, *chōnin* society and culture, especially the three major metropolises of Kyoto, Osaka, and Edo—Teitoku (1571–1653), the leader of Teimon haikai, was based in Kyoto, Sōin (1605–82) and Saikaku, the leaders of Danrin haikai, in Osaka—but Bashō was a socially marginal figure born in Iga, a small province to the southeast of Kyoto. His family, which came from the lowest rung of the samurai class, had, by Bashō's time, fallen to the level of farmer, and ultimately belonged to no particular class or group. Bashō's poetry and prose are pervaded by liminal figures, the beggar, the old man, the outcast, the traveler—no doubt reflecting his own socially marginal origins. The natural world of Bashō's poetry likewise tends to be off-center, dominated by subdued, withered images, *shigure* (winter rains), *susuki* (pampas-grass or miscanthus), *obana* (pampas grass in ear), *karasu* (crow), *kō-mori* (bat), *dokuro* (skull). His allusions were not to the sensuous Heian classical figures of Ariwara Narihira, Ono Komachi, and the shining Genji—the famous lovers so often alluded to in contemporary ukiyoe and frequent sources of parody for haikai—but rather to spartan medieval traveler-poets such as Saigyō and Sōgi or Chinese recluse-poets such as Tu Fu and Li Po. The difference is perhaps most evident in Bashō's treatment of Noh drama, or rather the librettos for Noh (*utaibon*), which, by the late seventeenth century, had become extremely popular, serving as new classics for Tokugawa commoners. In contrast to the typical ukiyoe *mitate* print, which alluded to the more erotic and elegant aspects of the Noh, especially the "women plays" (*kazura-mono*), Bashō focused on the muted image of the *waki*, or the traveling monk, and the fate of tragic heroes of the "warrior" plays (*shura-mono*).

In the seventeenth century, as in previous centuries, a sharp distinction was maintained between the traditional forms—such as *waka*, classical linked verse, Chinese poetry, Noh drama—and the new, popular genres—such as *kyōka* (comic waka), haikai, *kana-zōshi* (vernacular fiction), *jōruri* (recitation to music), and *kabuki*. The popular genres frequently parodied their high counterparts by borrowing the elegant, aristocratic forms of traditional literature and giving them popular, vulgar, or erotic content. *Preface to Young Men of Old and New* (*Kokin wakashū no jo*), *Fake Tale* (*Nise monogatari*), *Dog Essays in Idleness* (*Inu tsurezure*), *Dog Poems of a Hundred Poets* (*Inu hyakunin isshu*) were word-for-word parodies, often in erotic form, of the *kana* preface to the *Kokinshū*, the *Tales of Ise*, *Essays in Idleness* (*Tsurezuregusa*), and *Poems of a Hundred Poets* (*Hyakunin isshu*), respectively. Sometimes the reverse phenomenon occurred: what initially appeared to be low turned out to be high, the vulgar refined, the profane made spiritual. This literature of reversal often inverted—no doubt to the delight of commoner audiences—the strict social hierarchy in which the samurai were the elite and the commoners occupied the lowest rung. In the kabuki play *Sukeroku*, the dashing young *chōnin* protagonist turns out to be Soga Gorō, the younger of the famous samurai Soga brothers (who died in 1193), in a contemporary Edo setting. In a parallel movement, which was unusual for haikai, Bashō sought out the spiritual and poetic in seventeenth-century everyday, commoner culture, endowing contemporary language and topics, particularly those drawn from provincial life, with the kind of nuances and sentiments hitherto found only in classical or Chinese poetry.

Cultural Memory and Seasonal Landscape

Haikai humor typically resulted from raising the expectation of X and then giving Y, by emphasizing a difference that ran counter to established conventions and expectations. In haikai, that incongruity was often caused by a pun that unexpectedly linked contrastive words or cultures. Sometimes established roles were suddenly altered or shifted; for example, when a human being acted like a god, animal, or inanimate object, or when nature took on human characteristics. Most of all, however, the incongruity came from the juxtaposition of classical and contemporary, popular cultures, from the exaggeration, inversion, and displacement of established literary associations and cultural conventions, particularly the "poetic essence" (*hon'i*) of poetic topics. For Bashō, as for most previous poets, these literary conventions and expectations were largely embodied in nature, in historical objects, and in poetic places, that is to say, in landscape broadly defined, which became the contested ground for haikai re-visioning.

Much of the *Kokinshū*, which, by the Kamakura period, formed the core of what came to be considered the Heian classics, was arranged in a temporal progression that embodied nature as it unfolded through the four seasons. Even today, most collections of modern haiku are arranged not by author, genre, or historical period but by the cycle of the seasons. To compose poetry was to participate in this larger communal body of seasonal and toponymic associations, which embodied the cultural memory and which haikai poets like Bashō both inherited and worked to remap and enlarge. Haikai not only recuperated and reconstructed the classical landscape in vernacular, popular form, but also sought to expand the topographical, social, and material borders. The result was often a double vision in which the reconstructed or imagined past intersected with the immediately observed present.

Haikai generally worked against a specific horizon of expectations—especially that created by the seasonal topic—creating what Kenneth Burke has called "perspective by incongruity."[8] A good example is Bashō's famous frog (*kawazu*) poem, which was written in 1686 and which appears in *Spring Days* (*Haru no hi*).

> an old pond ...
> a frog leaps in,
> the sound of water

furuike | ya | kawazu | tobikomu | mizu | no | oto
old-pond | : | frog | jumps-in | water | 's | sound

Since the ancient period, the frog had been admired for its singing, its beautiful voice, as in the following waka (vol. 10, no. 2165), which appears in a section on frogs in the *Man'yōshū* (Collection of ten thousand leaves; 759).

kami tsu se ni	On the upper rapids
kawazu tsuma yobu	a frog calls for his love.
yū sareba	Is it because,
koromode samumi	his sleeves chilled by the evening,
tsuma makamu toka	he wants to share his pillow?

In the Heian period, "frog," a seasonal word for spring, also became associated with the blossoms of the *yamabuki*, the bright yellow globeflower (*Kerria japonica*), and with limpid mountain streams, as in the following anonymous poem from *Kokinshū* (Spring II, no. 125).

kawazu naku	At Ide, where the frogs cry,
Ide no yamabuki	the yellow globeflowers
chirinikeri	have already scattered.
hana no sakari ni	If only I had come when
awamashi mono o	they were in full bloom!

As a result of a noted phrase in the *kana* preface to the *Kokinshū*, "Listening to the voices of the warbler that sings in the flowers or the frog that lives in the water, we ask, what of all living things does not create poetry," the frog also became associated with the "composition of poetry" (*utayomi*). *Gathered Gems* (*Renju gappeki shū*; 1476), an influential Muromachi classical renga handbook, lists the classical associations (*yoriai*) of the frog: "When it comes to the frog, one thinks of Ide, globeflower [*yamabuki*], lodging together [*aiyadori*], beneath the fire-burning hut [*kaiya ga shita*], water for the rice seedling bed [*nawashiro mizu*], living in water, and classical poetry [*uta*]."[9] Sōkan (d. ca. 1539–40), the legendary founder of haikai, parodied this last association.

> hands to the floor
> formally reciting a poem—
> a frog

te | o | tsuite | uta | mōshiaguru | kawazu | kana[10]
hand | (acc.) | pressed-to-floor | poem | recite | frog | !

According to one source, Kikaku (1661–1707), one of Bashō's disciples, suggested that Bashō use *yamabuki ya* (globeflower!) in the opening phrase, which would have left Bashō's hokku within the circle of classical associations. Instead Bashō worked against what was considered the "poetic essence" (*hon'i*), the established classical associations, of the frog. In place of the plaintive voice of the frog singing in the rapids or calling out for his lover, Bashō gave the sound of the frog jumping into the water. And instead of the elegant image of a frog in a fresh mountain stream beneath the globeflower (*yamabuki*), the hokku presented a stagnant pond. Almost eighty years later, in 1769, Buson (1716–83), an admirer of Bashō, offered this poetic meta-commentary.

> jumping in
> and washing off an old poem—
> a frog

> tobikonde | furu-uta | arau | kawazu | kana[11]
> jumping-in | old-poem | wash | frog | !

Bashō's frog, leaping into the water, washed off the old associations of the frog with classical poetry, thus establishing a new perspective. At the same time, Bashō's hokku gave a fresh twist to the seasonal association of the frog with spring: the sudden movement of the frog, which suggests the awakening of life in spring, stands in contrast to the implicit winter stillness of the old pond.

Dialogic Poetry

Bashō composed haikai with two or more poets in a communal situation in which the participants gathered to link verses, usually at the invitation of a host and under the guidance of a haikai master. In contrast to modern haiku, which is often monologic, a single voice describing or responding to a scene or experience, haikai was inherently dialogic, either a response to the previous verse in a linked verse sequence or part of a witty verbal or visual dialogue with other participants. Such haikai is by implication always open-ended and unfinalized, waiting to be augmented, altered, or consumed by the addressee. Yamamoto Kenkichi, the modern pioneer in the study of poetic salutations (*aisatsu*), has argued that each hokku implicitly ends with the phrase "Isn't it?" Ogata Tsutomu believes that the famous frog poem is not only a poem about a frog, but also an invitation to Bashō's haikai partners, suggesting something like: "The frog has always been regarded as a creature that sings, especially in fresh streams, in the spring, but I want to look at the frog differently. Wouldn't you be interested in doing this together?" Kikaku responded to Bashō's hokku with this second verse (*wakiku*):

> a spider's nest
> hanging on young reeds
>
> ashi | no | wakaba | ni | kakaru | kumo | no | i
> reed | 's | young-leaf | on | hangs | spider | 's | nest
>   (KBZ 3: 335)

Kikaku's *wakiku* is linked to the hokku both by scenic extension, focusing on the edge of the water, and by connotative equivalence: the sense of spring implied by the young leaves on the reeds (*ashi no wakaba*), a seasonal word for spring. Other disciples "answered" Bashō's hokku by composing their own frog poems at a poetry competition at Bashō's hermitage in the spring of 1686 (Third Month, Jōkyō 3). "Frog Competition" ("Kawazu awase"), which was edited and published by Senka, another of Bashō's disciples, opens with:

> First round:
> Left side
>
>   an old pond ...
> a frog leaps in,
>   the sound of water
>
> Right side
>
>   endearingly
> a frog crouches on
>   a floating leaf
>   —Senka

itaike|ni|kawazu|tsukubau|ukiha|kana[12]
endearing|ly|frog|crouch|floating-leaf|!

Like Kikaku's *wakiku*, Senka's hokku extends the scene of Bashō's hokku: the frog that jumped into the old pond has swum to a floating leaf, on which it now crouches. The exchange, which continued to juxtapose and exchange various points of view, extended for 24 rounds and involved 41 poets.

Bashō's hokku worked against the established conventions of the frog topos, but, ironically, as Bashō's frog poem became canonized, it became the frequent object of parody, as in this hokku by Ryōkan (1758–1831), the noted Zen priest-poet.

> a new pond—
> not even the sound of
> a frog jumping in

ara|ike|ya|kawazu|tobikomu|oto|no|nashi[13]
new|pond|:|frog|jumps-in|sound|'s|nothing

The American haiku poet Bernard Einbond,[14] who catches the subtle overtones of Bashō's poem even as he twists it, writes:

> frog pond . . .
> a leaf falls in
> without a sound

Sketch of a Life

Since the haikai imagination manifested itself in many ways and forms—poetry, prose, painting, lifestyle, language, travel, perspective—and changed significantly over the course of Bashō's career, this study aims at elucidating different aspects of this complex issue while focusing on selected historical points in Bashō's career. I have made a deliberate choice not to cover Bashō's entire life or poetic career or to follow the chronological or biographical format used by most studies of Bashō. Nevertheless, it is necessary to review the main outline of his career, to grasp the spatial configuration of his travels, and most of all, to understand the nature of his interactions with other poets, without whom his poetry or prose would not have come into being.

Bashō was born in 1644 (Kan'ei 21) in the castletown of Ueno, in a mountain-clad basin in Iga Province, approximately thirty miles southeast of Kyoto in what today is the northwestern part of Mie Prefecture.[15] Bashō's grandfather and great-grandfather belonged to the samurai class, but for reasons that are uncertain—they may have been devastated by Oda Nobunaga's (1534–82) forces during the struggles preceding the founding of the Tokugawa shogunate—they were disenfranchised, apparently losing most or all of their property. By Bashō's generation, the family members had fallen so low that they had become farmers with only tenuous ties to the samurai class. Bashō at first served as a domestic employee of the Tōdō house, which had administered the castletown of Ueno from around 1608, presumably to serve as a companion to Toshitada, better known by his haikai name, Sengin, the son of the Tōdō lord. Bashō meanwhile adopted the haikai name of Munefusa, or Sōbō, and became a devotee of the Teimon style of haikai. In 1666, Sengin died prematurely, at the age of 25, apparently forcing Bashō to leave the Tōdō house and severing his tenuous connection with the samurai class.

In the spring of 1672, at the age of 29, Bashō decided to move to Edo, to establish himself as a haikai master (*sōshō*) who could charge fees for his services. Bashō probably chose not to go to nearby Kyoto, the national center of haikai, because it was already saturated with established haikai masters. Osaka, which was soon to rival Kyoto as a haikai center, was also a difficult market to penetrate. Edo, by contrast, was a new metropolis in great social flux, in the midst of a population explosion, with new clientele, especially the provincial samurai, who resided in Edo on a regular basis as a result of the *sankin kōtai* system and for whom haikai became a popular and inexpensive means of diversion. Furthermore, Edo did not have the kind of pyramidal haikai organization (*haidan*) that dominated Kyoto and Osaka, the two main centers of haikai at the time.

In Edo, Bashō, who changed his haikai name to Tōsei, came under the influence of Sōin, the leader of the Danrin school of haikai, with whom he composed in 1675. *Twenty Solo Sequences by Tōsei's Disciples* (*Tōsei montei dokugin nijikkasen*), a poetry collection published in 1680, reveals that by the mid-1670s Bashō had the nucleus of disciples and patrons—notably Kikaku, Ransetsu (1654–1707), Sanpū (1647–1732), and Ranran (1647–93)—who were to play a major role in the formation of what later came to be known as the Bashō school (*Shōmon*).

In the winter of 1680, at the age of 37, Bashō left the residence that he had occupied in the middle of Edo for nine years and retreated to Fukagawa, on the banks of the Sumida River. By moving to the outskirts of Edo, Bashō (who, as a haikai master, was already outside the official four-class system of the samurai, farmer, artisan, and merchant) left behind the commercial marketplace of haikai, thereby becoming an outsider twice removed from the center of Tokugawa society. During the next four years, in the Tenna era (1681–84), Bashō wrote in the so-called Chinese style (*kanshibun-chō*). Bashō's hermitage at Fukagawa acquired the name of the Bashō Hut (Bashō-an), after the *bashō* plant, or Japanese plantain, given to him in the spring of 1681 and from which he took his most famous penname.[16] In January 1683 (12.28.Tenna 2), a fire that enveloped Edo destroyed the Bashō Hut, and Bashō moved elsewhere until around October 1683 when the second Bashō Hut was built in Fukagawa by his friends and patrons.

In the fall of 1684, Bashō departed on the first of a series of journeys that would occupy much (four years and nine months) of the remaining ten years of his life. In his first journey, commemorated in his travel diary *Skeleton in the Fields* (*Nozarashi kikō*), Bashō traveled west, visiting Nagoya in Owari (Aichi), Mino (Gifu), and Ōmi (Shiga), especially Konan, the area south of Lake Biwa—successfully recruiting followers in all three areas—before returning to Edo in the summer of 1685. At Nagoya, he composed linked verse with a local group led by Kakei (1648–1716) that resulted in the *Withering*

Gusts (Kogarashi) *kasen* and the compilation in 1684 of *Winter Days* (*Fuyu no hi*), the first major anthology of the Bashō circle and the beginning of what is now referred to as the Bashō style (*Shōfū*).

In the early winter of 1687, in a journey later commemorated in *Backpack Notes* (*Oi no kobumi*), Bashō, now 44 by the Japanese count, once again left Edo, returned to Iga Province, and then traveled to Yoshino, Nara, Suma, and Akashi, along the Inland Sea. *Backpack Notes* ends with a description of Suma and Akashi in the summer of 1688, but Bashō continued to travel, first to the Ōmi and then to the Mino and Owari regions, composing haikai with various groups. At the end of the journey, in mid-September 1688 (8.15.Genroku 1) Bashō, accompanied by Etsujin (1656–1716?), a disciple from Nagoya, visited Obasuteyama (Abandoned-Old-Women Mountain) in Sarashina (Nagano), the site of the famous autumn moon, before returning to Edo at the end of the month—a journey commemorated in *Journey to Sarashina* (*Sarashina kikō*).

After returning to his hermitage in Fukagawa, Bashō rested for about seven months, but in the spring of 1689, he departed once again, this time with Sora (1649–1710), for Michinoku in the northeast, in a expedition later commemorated in *Narrow Road to the Interior*. The arduous journey began from Fukagawa in mid-May 1689 (3.27.Genroku 2) and ended, a little over five months and almost 1,500 miles (6000 *ri*) later, at Ōgaki in Mino (Gifu), in mid-October (Ninth Month) of the same year. For the next two years, Bashō remained in the Kamigata area, where he commuted back and forth among three main groups of disciples, at Iga (his hometown), at Ōmi (near Lake Biwa), and at Kyoto. In September 1690, he saw the publication of *Gourd* (*Hisago*), a haikai anthology compiled by his disciples at Ōmi that embodied his new poetics of lightness. Together with Kyorai (1651–1704) and Bonchō (d. 1714), two disciples in Kyoto, Bashō then edited *Monkey's Straw Coat* (*Sarumino*), the magnum opus of the Bashō school, which was published in the summer of 1691. Bashō finally returned to Edo in December of 1691, at the age of 48. Bashō, who moved into the third Bashō Hut (built near the previous one) in the summer of 1692, became involved with a new group of Edo poets, centered on Yaba (1662–1740), with whom he pursued the poetic ideal of lightness (*karumi*) and eventually produced *Charcoal Sack* (*Sumidawara*), which was published in 1694.

In June 1694 (5.11.Genroku 7) Bashō departed for his home in Iga, visited Nagoya on the way, and remained in Iga for the remainder of the summer, occasionally visiting disciples in the Ōmi and Kyoto areas. At the end of October, wanting to mediate a conflict between two disciples in Osaka, Bashō departed for Osaka with Shikō (1665–1731). He arrived seriously ill, suffering from a stomach ailment, and died on the afternoon of November 28, 1694 (10.12.Genroku 7), at the age of 51.

Any study of this kind must contextualize itself, which requires an understanding of the reception or, rather, production of Bashō and his literature in the three centuries since his death. This is particularly critical since Bashō was deified in the Tokugawa period and has subsequently become a central figure in the modern canon. Chapter 2 of this work ("Bashō Myth East and West") consequently focuses on the reception of Bashō in both Japan and the West, with particular attention to the issue of objectivity and subjectivity, which has dominated the modern debate on Bashō and haiku. R. H. Blyth and other postwar pioneers of English haiku—no doubt influenced by Masaoka Shiki and other modern Japanese haiku poets—have regarded haiku as a poetry of the "concrete object" and have stressed the "haiku moment," which presents an event as "happening now" and encourages an intersubjective movement in which the poet's spirit becomes one with nature. This has been accompanied by a strong tendency to emphasize the notion of haiku as intuitive rather than intellectual or allusive, as dealing with momentary images rather than with concepts or issues. Western studies of Bashō have similarly tended to be predominantly mimetic or expressive, to read his poetry as momentary reflections of the immediate scene, and have followed highly biographical reading modes based on the notion of Bashō "the man." This study is intended to go beyond

these mimetic and expressive reading modes by exploring the multi-
dimensional aspects of haikai imagination: its intertextual nature,
particularly its relationship to the larger cultural landscape and the
manner in which haikai achieves meaning through reconstruction
and recontextualization; its heteroglossic, multivoiced character; and
its interpersonal, communal, performative dimension. Much of this
haikai imagination was negated or minimalized in modern Japan by
the Western-influenced emphasis on individualism, realism, and a
unified, national language (*kokugo*). Masaoka Shiki and other Meiji
writers, for example, found the notion of *shukō*, of contemporary
counterpoint to the familiar worlds of the past, which lay at the
heart of much Edo popular literature and art, to be contrived and
counter to the modern notion of *shasei* (sketch), of depicting things
"as they are."

Most studies of Bashō's poetry and prose are biographical in na-
ture, examining his poetry in chronological fashion, with special at-
tention to the details of his personal life, of which much is known
from his correspondence and the records of his disciples. One con-
sequence has been that the changes in Bashō's poetic style, which
evolved rapidly from period to period, are interpreted as the result
of changes in Bashō's own life, and Bashō is regarded as a unique in-
dividual rather than as a product of his times. The haikai style estab-
lished by Bashō and his school is generally divided into three main
periods: the Jōkyō (1684–88) era, highlighted by *Winter Days* (1684)
and the poetics of *fūkyō* (poetic madness); the period from Bashō's
journey through the Interior in the spring of 1689 to the publication
of *Monkey's Straw Coat* in 1691, marked by the fusion of classical
and everyday worlds; and the period from Bashō's return to Edo in
the winter of 1691 to his death in 1694, focusing on lightness and
the poetry of commoner life and language. As Chapter 3 ("Haikai
Language, Haikai Spirit") reveals, the developments or changes in
Bashō's style were usually an extension of the larger movements or
trends in the haikai world in which Bashō participated: Teimon
haikai in the 1660s (Kanbun era), Danrin haikai in the 1670s (Enpō
era), the Chinese style in the early 1680s (Tenna era), the renga style

(*renga-tai*) in the mid-1680s (Jōkyō era), and the landscape (*keiki*) style in the late 1680s and early 1690s (Genroku period, 1688–1704).

As we shall see, a fundamental change occurred in the mid-1680s, when the haikai world was swept by the elegant renga style, which did not require "haikai words" (*haigon*), and then quickly followed by the landscape style, which sought to observe the natural world closely, as some classical poetry had earlier. Haikai could no longer be defined by its language, its witty verbal play, or even by its penchant for parody. "Haikai spirit" (*haii*), like the word *haikai* itself, initially referred to the element of comedy and humor, particularly the interest in wordplay and in parody, but in the late 1680s it took on the much wider meaning of discovering new worlds and perspectives, especially that opposed to convention, tradition, and the ordinary. Haikai became more of a general attitude or approach, which could be embodied in different forms, and which, in the case of Bashō, emerged in the form of a haikai persona, the *fūkyō* (poetic madness) character who pursued poetic objects in a seemingly crazy manner and who ultimately drew attention to the haikai-esque lifestyle, thought, and action of a poet who reacted against contemporary socioeconomic trends. Further complicating the situation, Genroku haikai, like other commoner forms, also became a vernacular conveyer of cultural orthodoxy, both literary and ideological. Despite its popular origins and its anti-establishment character, haikai, especially that of Bashō, increasingly became a transmitter of traditional moral, spiritual, and social values. Bashō, who stood at this crossroads in haikai history, attempted the difficult task of creating poetry and prose that had the spiritual, aesthetic, and social implications of traditional Japanese and Chinese poetry even as it retained haikai's popular, heteroglossic character. The result was poetry and prose that was profoundly paradoxical in tone and nature—transgressive yet traditional, humorous yet sorrowful, spiritual yet mundane.

Chapter 4 ("The Art of Juxtaposition: Cutting and Joining") examines the dynamics of textual juxtaposition and the different kinds of links—homophonic, metonymic, and metaphoric—that lie at the

heart of Bashō's haikai. The successive verses in a linked verse se-
quence were read both together and apart, as parts of a larger scene
and as fragments in a collage. The same kind of tension existed
within the seventeen-syllable hokku, which was both split and
joined by the "cutting word" (*kireji*). Kyoriku (1656–1715), one of
Bashō's foremost disciples, argued that the "combination poem"
(*toriawase*), which combined different topics in a single hokku, was
the most important technique of the Bashō school and, furthermore,
that the combination poem should leap beyond the established asso-
ciations of a given topic. One result was the unexpected "combi-
nation" of classical topics and popular subject matter, traditional and
contemporary subcultures, classical diction and haikai words. The
same could be said of the links in Bashō's haikai, which attempted
to avoid the established lexical associations (*yoriai*), based on classi-
cal precedent, on which classical renga had depended. At the same
time, Bashō and his disciples attempted to harmonize these disjunc-
tive elements, to find congruity in incongruity, to integrate these
different languages and subcultures through the poetics of "scent,"
of intersecting overtones, and through a regenerative process that
gave new life to classical clichés and poeticized vernacular phrases.
In short, the art of juxtaposition relied on the larger haikai process
of defamiliarization and recontextualization.

Chapter 5 ("Linking and Communal Poetry") examines a 36-verse
sequence composed by Bashō and a group of Nagoya poets in 1684,
a sequence often thought to mark the beginning of the Bashō style.
Linked verse involved a constant recontextualization of existing
texts and worlds so as to create new, unexpected meanings and per-
spectives. At the same time, the complex rules of linked verse guar-
anteed a sense of continuity amid constant change and movement
and ensured that cultural memory, particularly as embodied in the
seasonal landscape, was passed on, providing the foundation for
linkage and imaginative play. As a communal art, haikai joined the
individual to the other participants, creating a significant bond that
transcended family, class, and blood distinctions. The same commu-
nal form also "linked" the participants to the past, to literary and

historical worlds, including China, that became the basis of linking and through which the participants traveled in the course of the haikai sequence.

As a form of popular literature, haikai reflected the variegated social and economic worlds of the participants, who came from a broad spectrum of society—from high-ranking samurai to merchants, farmers, doctors, and priests—but it also provided an important window onto "imagined worlds," onto the newly discovered "past" of China and Japan, giving the participants a sense of participating in a common history and cultural tradition. Town teachers and haikai masters such as Bashō gave wealthy commoners and high-ranking samurai a sense of cultural identity, of continuity to a hallowed past, which they lacked but were eager to acquire and which came to include Chinese culture and literature. Teitoku, a classical scholar and the founder of Teimon haikai, had even seen haikai as a means (a first stage) of teaching commoners and samurai the literary classics. Bashō, who was very conservative for a haikai poet, had a tendency to move toward classical and Chinese poetry, to join the company of the "ancients," the noted poets of the past, even as his socially and geographically diverse haikai partners served to anchor Bashō in the material culture and variegated languages of the late seventeenth century. The end result was the dynamic interaction of past and present, of classical and contemporary cultures, that lies at the heart of haikai and of Bashō's poetry and prose.

Chapter 6 ("The Poet as Guest") focuses on haikai as a form of poetic dialogue, as a means of communal bonding and exchange, and as a ritualistic, sometimes religious, utterance. More than half of Bashō's hokku were greetings, which had either a social or religious function.

> gazing intently
> at the white chrysanthemums—
> not a speck of dust

shiragiku | no | me | ni | tatete | miru | chiri | mo | nashi
white-chrysanthemum | 's | eye | in | standing | see | dust | even | not-be

This hokku, which Bashō composed at the residence of Sonome, or Madame Sono (1664–1726), one of his disciples, is typical of Bashō's mature style in that it at once describes the purity and elegance of a white chrysanthemum and compliments the host. Even Bashō's famous frog poem has been interpreted (in *Shiwasubukuro*; 1764) as a greeting to the host from the poet (frog) who is lodging at (jumping into) the residence of an old friend (the pond). Bashō's haikai paid homage not only to the haikai partner and social companion but also to the spirits of the past, to the ancient poets and spiritual figures, who came to embody the literary and historical tradition and from whom Edo commoners and samurai participants acquired a sense of cultural identity and belonging. These greetings to the "ancients," like those to the spirits of the land, bridged the gap between past and present, between the new vernacular culture and the elite, classical traditions. At the same time, these poetic salutes to the dead led to a re-visioning of the cultural landscape, a reconstruction of cultural memory in contemporary, vernacular, popular forms and language.

Chapter 7 ("Seasonal Associations and Cultural Landscape") explores the ways in which this cultural memory was embodied in the seasonal and topographical landscape, in seasonal topics and poetic places, which became the object of haikai re-visioning. In Bashō's day, seasonal topics existed on two axes: a vertical axis, which focused on classical topics such as cherry blossoms and the autumn moon, and on a horizontal axis, which embraced such contemporary, popular topics as dandelions and cat's love. The same was true for the poetic topography, which can be divided into *utamakura*, places in classical poetry, and so-called *haimakura*, or haikai places, which haikai poets had newly discovered and written on. Haikai was known for its freedom, its ability to explore the contemporary world, and for the broad expanse of languages and subcultures embodied in the horizontal axis, but ultimately haikai poets, including Bashō, gravitated toward the vertical axis, to traditional poetic topics, which became not only the object of parody and comic inversion but also the arena of haikai recontextualization and refamiliarization, in which seasonal and topographical sites were given new, contemporary form. The traditional seasonal topics and their cultural associations, however, were not simply displaced; instead, as we shall see, they provided the horizon of expectations against which the haikai poem established its newness or implied difference. The brevity of the hokku is in fact possible because each poem is implicitly part of a massive, communally shared poem.

Chapter 8 ("Remapping the Past: Narrow Road to the Interior"), which focuses on *Oku no hosomichi*, Bashō's prose masterpiece, analyzes the manner in which Bashō remapped the cultural landscape of the Interior, or the northern region of Japan, through haibun, or haikai prose, a new genre that combined, in unprecedented fashion, Chinese prose genres, Japanese classical prototypes, and vernacular language and subject matter, thereby bringing together at least three major cultural axes. For Bashō, as for classical and haikai poets before him, the poetic tradition often resided in poetic places (*utamakura*) and in natural objects and human artifacts that bore the traces of the past and that became the carriers of collective memory. Travel, which grew extremely popular in the Edo period, became a means of visiting these places and objects, of communing with the noted poets of the past, a way of renewing that memory and appropriating it for a new vernacular, popular culture. For Bashō, the process took on a medieval tone. In a typical passage in *Narrow Road to the Interior*, the traveler, taking on the persona of the wandering priest in a Noh play, enters into a dream-like state, pays homage to the spirits of the dead, offers a poetic prayer for their salvation, and then, as if returning from another world, presents a new, haikai vision amid the old. Travel, in short, became a means both of recuperating the past and refiguring cultural memory.

Whenever his poetry began to stagnate, Bashō departed on a journey, engaging in poetic dialogue with other poets, often unknown or still young, in different parts of the country. In this relentless drive to seek new poetic ground, Bashō either abandoned or lost, one after another, disciples who had played a major role at one stage but were unable to contribute or participate in Bashō's latest movement. Bashō, in a motion that was highly unorthodox for contemporary haikai poets, moved simultaneously in two fundamental directions. On the one hand, he journeyed into the past, seeking out traces of the "ancients," reshaping and expanding the cultural memory as it was embodied in nature, the seasons, and the landscape. On the other hand, he moved horizontally from disciple to disciple, from region to region, from style to style, in constant pursuit of new languages and perspectives.

Chapter 9 ("Awakening to the High, Returning to the Low: Bashō's Poetics") explores a cluster of poetic ideals that lay at the heart of Bashō's poetics and that emerged beginning in the mid-1680s, particularly after his journey to the Interior in 1689: "awakening to the high, returning to the low" (*kōgo kizoku*), "truth of poetic art" (*fūga no makoto*), "following the Creative" (*zōka zuijun*), "object and self as one" (*butsuga ichinyo*), "the unchanging and the changing" (*fueki ryūkō*), and "lightness" (*karumi*). In one form or another, these poetic ideals or slogans were attempts to come to terms with the fundamental paradox of late-seventeenth-century haikai and of Bashō's haikai in particular, which looked to the past for inspiration and authority and yet rejected it, which parodied the classical (and Chinese) tradition even as they sought to become part of it, and which paid homage to the "ancients" and yet stressed newness. As we shall see, Bashō incorporated various aspects of contemporary Neo-Confucian thought, Taoism (especially *Chuang-tzu*), and Buddhist philosophy—not to mention classical poetics—into his haikai poetics in an attempt to legitimize haikai, hitherto regarded as a lowly form, to make it part of the larger poetic, cultural, and aesthetic tradition, and to give it spiritual depth, making it, in some sense, an art of living. Bashō's movement in this direction led to his canonization. But he also stressed such notions as the "ever-changing," "newness," and "lightness," which clearly distinguished haikai from traditional forms and emphasized its popular, contemporary, everyday, fleeting character. Notions such as "the unchanging and the ever-changing" and "awakening to the high, returning to the low" brought these two vectors together in regenerative fashion.

"Awakening to the high, returning to the low," for example, meant returning to the sociolinguistic roots of haikai, to the variegated languages and worlds of contemporary commoner and samurai life, to those topics left out or overlooked by the traditional genres, and combining them with the heightened spiritual, aesthetic, and poetic awareness achieved by the "ancients," the noted poets and spiritual masters of the past. The ancients were, paradoxically, to be a source of inspiration but not of models to be emulated. The result, it was hoped, was a poetry that could parody and turn away from the established literary associations and conventions even as it renewed the cultural memory, embodied most prominently in the seasonal and topographic landscape, with a never-ending stream of fresh language, new perspectives, and innovative poets.

CHAPTER 2

Bashō Myth East and West

Fan-piece, for Her Imperial Lord
O fan of white silk,
clear as frost on a grass-blade,
You are also laid aside.
      —Ezra Pound, 1913

Modern literary historians have traditionally spoken of three successive major schools of haikai in the latter half of the seventeenth century—the Teimon, Danrin, and Bashō schools—and have identified the Genroku period (1688-1704) with the "Bashō-style." But, as recent Japanese scholarship has shown, Bashō, even at the peak of his career, was only one of a number of prominent haikai masters—Gonsui (1650-1722), Shintoku (1633-98), Onitsura (1661-1738), Raizan (1654-1716), Saikaku (1641-93), Saimaro (1656-1738)—and was far from having the largest or most influential school.[1] The Bashō school did not flourish in the major cities—Kyoto, Osaka, and Edo—which were the centers of haikai activity, and was dominated by other schools, especially by Teimon and Danrin poets and by those who practiced *maeku-zuke* (verse-capping), which ran directly counter to the Bashō style. Bashō first established himself in Edo and later had a base in Kyoto, but his main following emerged in the provinces, particularly in the Owari (Nagoya), Mino (southern Gifu), Ōmi (surrounding Lake Biwa), and Kaga (southern Ishikawa) areas. After Bashō's death, his disciples formed their own individual followings, and his school rapidly faded. And yet within a hundred years of his death, Bashō had been enshrined, deified as the saint of haikai.

Bashō as Deity

How then did this happen? Like other traditional Japanese art forms, haikai was socially governed, at least from the latter half of the seventeenth century, by a master/disciple lineage structure that honored not only the immediate master but also the founder of the particular school. Although Bashō may not have been the most famous or most influential haikai master in the Genroku period, he had the most talented group of disciples—Kikaku (1661–1707), Ransetsu (1654–1707), Kyorai (1651–1704), Jōsō (1662–1704), Shikō (1665–1731), Sanpū (1647–1732), Yaba (1662–1740), Etsujin (b. 1656), Sora (1649–1710), Bonchō (d. 1714), Dohō (1657–1730), and others—many of whom became noted poets and who created the Bashō legacy.

After Bashō's death, a number of these disciples or their disciples established schools in the provinces, often becoming fierce rivals in the process, and promoted Bashō's name, using and enhancing his authority as a way to expand or consolidate their local base of power. These provincial disciples—of whom Shikō, Yaba, and Otsuyū (1675–1739)[2] are probably the most famous—traveled widely, lecturing, teaching haikai, and leading linked verse sessions. Yaba, an Edo disciple who worked with Bashō at the end of his master's life, moved to Nagasaki in 1704 (Hōei 1), journeyed throughout the southwest, drawing large numbers of followers in the Kyūshū and Chūgoku (Okayama, Hiroshima, Yamaguchi, Shimane, Tottori) areas. Even more influential was Shikō, based in Mino Province, who spent most of his life expanding the sphere of his Mino school into the Hokuriku (Toyama, Fukui, Ishikawa, Niigata), Chūbu (Yamanashi, Nagano, Gifu, Shizuoka, Aichi), and Kyūshū areas. In 1704 Shikō joined forces with Ryōto (1659–1717) and Otsuyū (otherwise known as Bakurin), who had established a large school at Ise. The combination of the Mino and Ise schools, referred to by later haikai poets as the "Shibaku followers" (*shibaku no to*)—*shi* from Shikō and the *baku* from Bakurin—formed a broad national movement. Shikō, who had studied with Bashō at the end of his life, taught a simpli-

The painting, the calligraphy—which breaks the poem into six parts—and the poem were all done by Bashō, probably around 1692. 31.5 x 10.4 in. Bashō first composed the poem—*kuzu no ha no/omote/ mise/keri/kesa no/shimo* (showing the face of the arrowroot leaves—morning frost)—in 1691. In contrast to classical poetry, in which the autumn wind turns over the leaves of the arrowroot (*kuzu*), revealing the white backs of the leaves, this hokku focuses on the front or face of the leaves, which a severe frost (*shimo*, seasonal word for winter) has turned white. In this painting, the frost-bitten, dangling leaves of the kuzu vine are mixed with the stiffer leaves of bamboo grass. Signed "Baseo." (Courtesy Tenri University Library)

fied, easy-to-understand style that emphasized everyday language
and had great appeal to commoners, particularly beginners.[3]

Bashō's direct disciples—Kyorai, Kyoriku (1656–1715), Shikō,
Rogan (d. 1693), Dohō, and Hokushi (d. 1718) in particular—were
the first to compile Bashō-related texts and record his teachings,
which also served to promote Bashō's image. Kyorai's *Kyoraishō*
(Kyorai's gleanings; comp. 1704) and Dohō's *Sanzōshi* (Three book-
lets; comp. 1702), the two most noted collections of teachings, imi-
tate the form of the *Analects*; and a group of immediate disciples—
Kikaku, Ransetsu, Kyorai, Jōsō, Kyoriku, Shikō, Sanpū, Yaba, Ho-
kushi, and Etsujin[4]—were canonized by Shikō and later poets as the
"Ten Disciples of Bashō" (*Shōmon jittetsu*) in imitation of the "Ten
Disciples of Confucius" and the "Ten Disciples of Shakyamuni."
But it was not until the 1730s, at the start of what modern scholars
refer to as the Revival (*Chūkō*) movement, led by haikai poets who
aimed to return to the original Bashō style, that many of the major
texts of Bashō's corpus began to be edited and published. For exam-
ple, *Haikai Seven Anthologies* (*Haikai shichibu shū*), which became
the primary form by which Bashō's linked verse was appreciated,
was compiled by Ryūkyo (1686–1748) in 1731 and published as a
single set in 1756. *Haikai Seven Anthologies*, or *Seven Anthologies*
(*Shichibu shū*) as they are now called, brought together the major
haikai collections from each period of the Bashō style—*Winter Days*
(*Fuyu no hi*; 1684), *Spring Days* (*Haru no hi*; 1686), *Desolate Fields*
(*Arano*; 1689), *Gourd* (*Hisago*; 1690), *Monkey's Straw Coat* (*Sarumino*;
1691), *Charcoal Sack* (*Sumidawara*; 1694), and *Sequel to Monkey's
Straw Coat* (*Zoku sarumino*; 1698)—thereby showcasing Bashō's no-
tion of newness and constant change.[5]

The Bashō Revival movement, which came to the fore in the
1760s and climaxed during the 1770s–1780s, during the An'ei (1772–
81) and Tenmei (1781–89) eras, was a remarkable period, led first by
Taigi (1709–71) and then by Buson (1716–83), which witnessed the
blossoming of talented poets from around the country: among
them, Buson, Taigi, and Chōmu (1732–95) from Kyoto, Ryōta
(1718–87) and Shirao (1738–91) from Edo, Kyōtai (1732–92) from

Nagoya, Bakusui (1718–83) and Rankō (1726–98) from Kaga, Chora (1729–80) from Ise. Most of these haikai masters originally came from the provincial Mino/Ise (Shibaku) schools. Another smaller group—Ryōta, Taigi, Buson—had roots in urban haikai, especially that of Kikaku, one of Bashō's early Edo disciples. Disillusioned with the degeneration of both urban and provincial haikai and with the world around them, these poets looked to the literary and historical past, to Chinese literature and painting, but most of all, to the poetry of Bashō, who came to represent an idealized poetic past. Buson, who led this movement, expressed his desire to return to the Bashō style in the following hokku:

> the frog of the ancient pond
> grows old—
> fallen leaves

furuike | no | kawazu | oiyuku | ochiba | kana[6]
old-pond | 's | frog | grows-old | fallen-leaf | !

Bashō's frog, associated with spring, no longer jumps into the old pond. Instead, it "grows old" (*oiyuku*), buried by the fallen leaves (*ochiba*), a seasonal word for winter; that is, people have forgotten about the true Bashō style.

During the Revival period, the question was not whether to return to the Bashō style but, rather, which particular Bashō style or phase to follow: Buson, Kyōtai, and Bakusui, for example, admired the early Bashō style, especially *Empty Chestnuts* (*Minashiguri*; 1683) and *Winter Days*, whereas Ryōta, Chora, Shirao, and Rankō followed the late Bashō ideal of lightness, particularly the spare style of *Charcoal Sack* (1694). The poetic debate in this period was dominated by treatises arguing for the superiority of one Bashō style over another. Buson, who came to the fore around 1770, was drawn to Kikaku, Bashō's Edo disciple, whose *Gathering Flowers* (*Hanatsumi*; 1690) inspired his own sequel *New Gathering Flowers* (*Shin hanatsumi*; published 1797). The Bashō Revival also produced a number of superb Bashō scholars—especially Riichi (1714–1783), Ryōta,

Rankō, and Chōmu (1732–95)—who edited Bashō's texts and wrote biographies of the master.[7]

Not all Revival period poets admired Bashō: Ryōtai (1719–74), better known as the Kokugaku (National Learning) scholar Takebe Ayatari, and Ueda Akinari (1734–1809), a Kokugaku scholar and novelist, severely criticized Bashō. Akinari, for example, believed that Bashō's stance as a hermit-traveler was both hypocritical and anachronistic: in contrast to Saigyō and Sōgi, who lived in periods of turmoil, Bashō had no need to be a wanderer. But after the Revival came to a close in the 1790s—Buson died in 1783 and Kyōtai in 1792—Bashō was increasingly idolized, and even this kind of criticism disappeared. The eightieth anniversary of his death in 1773 (An'ei 2) and the ninetieth anniversary in 1783 (Tenmei 3) became major occasions for celebrating Bashō and his poetry, but the centennial in 1793 was unmatched in scale: hundreds of ceremonies and memorial services (*kuyō*, or offerings to the dead), including the erection of stone monuments, were held across the country.

Soon after his death, Bashō's disciples began building stone memorials (*tsuka*), usually engraved with "Bashō the Elder" (*Bashō ō*), probably in imitation of the inscription on Bashō's gravestone at Gichūji Temple.[8] *Tsuka* engraved with a famous Bashō hokku were even more popular, becoming sites of worship at which visitors could commune with Bashō through the hokku. The spirit of Bashō was ritually transferred from the Gichūji Temple to the new *tsuka*, each of which became a kind of branch temple, and a Bashō memento was buried beneath the stone to retain his spirit. Each year haikai poets would gather at the local *Bashōzuka*, or Bashō gravestone, to pay respects and compose poetry. Although stone memorials with engraved poetry have been erected to other poets in both the modern and premodern period, nothing compares with the Bashō *tsuka*, which numbered close to a thousand by the end of the Tokugawa period. The Shibaku school employed this method of proselytism—its initiation ceremonies for haikai masters usually included the construction of a Bashō *tsuka*—and the practice continued into the Revival period when Chōmu and others transformed the Gichūji Temple into a central temple for Bashō worship. On the hundredth anniversary of his death, a Shintō shrine celebrating Bashō as a deity (Tōsei reijin)[9] was built in Kyūshū, and a similar shrine was constructed in Shinshū (Nagano). Even the Nijō family, which represented the conservative line of classical poetry, posthumously granted Bashō the title of "Grand master of the orthodox lineage" (*Shōfū sōshi*), which implied that Bashō was no longer just a Genroku haikai poet but the symbolic founder and authoritative master of haikai. In 1806 the imperial court, alluding to the famous frog poem, also conferred on Bashō the title "Jumping Sound God" (Hion myōjin).

Bashō's posthumous popularity can be traced in part to his image as a recluse poet and an eternal traveler, an ascetic in search of inner freedom, an image largely constructed by his disciples and poetic descendants. As Ogata Tsutomu has argued, this image of Bashō as an outsider who sought freedom from both social and material bonds probably had considerable appeal to a Tokugawa populace strapped down by the rigid, hierarchical four-class system.[10] The only comparable figure in this regard was Saigyō (1118–90), the late Heian waka poet and priest whom Bashō admired and imitated and whose image eventually overlapped with that of Bashō. Significantly, the Saigyō that Bashō and many of his contemporaries admired was derived largely from the legendary figure found in *Tales of Saigyō* (*Saigyō monogatari*; ca. 1480), which depicts a traveling poet devoted to spiritual awakening.

Whether consciously or not, the image of Bashō was conflated by later poets with those of his poetic and religious predecessors. The *Memorial to Bashō the Elder* (*Bashō ō gyōjō ki*, edited by Rotsū, 1695) notes that Bashō was the "Tu Fu of Japan," "today's Saigyō," the reincarnation of Yoshida Kenkō (1274–1338), and the spiritual twin of Sōgi. The Shikō school envisioned Bashō as a wandering mendicant priest similar to those found in the Ji sect, the popular Pure Land (Jōdo) Buddhist sect founded by Priest Ippen (1239–89), who had traveled through the provinces chanting the *nenbutsu*, the holy name of the Amida Buddha.[11] Chōmu, one of the leaders of the Bashō Revival and a Ji Pure Land priest, deepened this image of a wandering mendicant monk in his *Illustrated Life of Bashō the Elder* (*Bashō ō ekotobaden*; 1792, with paintings by Kanō Shōei), the first major biography of Bashō, given as an offering to the Gichūji Temple on the centennial of Bashō's death. The *Illustrated Life of Bashō the Elder*, which was modeled on the *Illustrated Life of Priest Ippen* (*Ippen hijiri e*) and which had a profound influence on Bashō's subsequent reception, portrayed Bashō as an unceasing traveler who spiritually awakens as a result of a profound awareness of the Buddhist truth of impermanence. Bashō's posthumous image thus came to resemble that of Saigyō and Ippen, both of whom had been popularized during the medieval period by the tradition of pictorial biographies of traveling saints. Bashō's literary and religious predecessors were gradually absorbed into the image of Bashō himself to the point where Bashō became the ultimate embodiment of the Japanese poet-wayfarer as well as a haikai saint. In short, the focal point of Bashō's canonization, at least in the initial stages, was not only his poetry—the frog poem became famous quite early—but the popularized image of Bashō. One result is that Bashō's poetry and prose have continued to be read largely in light of his "life" and his persona, which for many have become the measure by which he is evaluated.

Masaoka Shiki and Modern Reception

Masaoka Shiki (1867–1902), the pioneer of modern Japanese haiku, launched a scathing attack on Bashō in "Chat on Bashō" ("Bashō zōdan"), serialized in the newspaper *Nihon* (*Japan*) in 1893–94.[12] Shiki criticized the Bashō school as a haikai cult that worshiped Bashō as a god and regarded his verses as sacred scripture. In what at the time was a blasphemy, Shiki declared that of Bashō's thousand or so hokku, only a few hundred were even worthy of examination; the rest were failures. Shiki recognized that the remaining poems still represented a sizable achievement, particularly those that evinced "sublimity and grandeur" (*yūkon gōsō*),[13] but Bashō was no longer to be regarded as a haikai saint. Readers should instead focus a critical and skeptical eye on his writings. At about the same time, Shiki discovered Buson, who had largely been ignored by scholars and who opened up for him the possibilities for objective verse outside Bashō. In 1897 (Meiji 30), he began serializing *Haiku Poet Buson* (*Haijin Buson*, published as a book in 1899), in which he placed Buson above the more famous Bashō and defined Buson in Darwinian evolutionist terms as "more advanced."

In "Chat on Bashō," Shiki also condemned haikai linked verse, which he regarded as a trivial social game and declared that only the hokku, the seventeen-syllable opening verse, which he referred to as haiku, had value. "The hokku is literature. Renga and haikai are not." "Linked verse emphasizes change, a non-literary element."[14] Linked verse, with its constant movement and its dependence on what Shiki called "knowledge" (*chishiki*)—as opposed to "emotion" (*kanjō*)—was incompatible with his stress on the modern notions of literary unity and the individual self. By the Meiji period, haikai as linked verse had more or less disappeared, leaving only the independent hokku or haiku. The change in the nature of the literary genre, the shift toward modern literary perceptions, as underscored by Shiki's remarks, combined with the earlier Tokugawa reception of Bashō as a lonely recluse and wayfarer subsequently caused Bashō to be viewed as a solitary haiku poet rather than a communal haikai master.

Shiki also argued that haiku should be based on the notion of *shajitsu* or *shasei*, "sketching from life," on direct, individual observation of the external world, which he believed to be the key to the modernization of haiku. Around 1893–94 (Meiji 26–27), Shiki encountered a group of painters in Western-style painting (*yōga*)—Nakamura Fusetsu being the most prominent—who introduced him to the notion of *shasei*, a painterly ideal of sketching directly from life.[15] Initially, Shiki used *shasei* as a slogan to revive "actual feeling or sensation" (*jikkan*) at a time when traditional haikai was paralyzed by fixed concepts and conventions, but the term became associated with objectivity and mimesis.[16] In *Haiku Poet Buson* Shiki regarded Buson as the discoverer of "objective beauty" (*kyakkanteki bi*) and "active beauty" (*sekkyokuteki bi*), as opposed to Bashō, whom he saw as a "subjective" (*shukanteki*) poet, the pioneer of "passive beauty" (*shōkyokuteki bi*), exemplified by the notion of *sabi* (overtones of quiet, meditative loneliness). Initially, Shiki applied this notion of *shasei* to both nature and human affairs, but toward the end of his life he believed, as he indicated in his essay "Six-Foot Sick Bed" ("Byōshō rokushaku"; 1902), that poetry should apply *shasei* only to nature and leave human affairs to the modern novel—a stance that had a profound impact on the future of modern haiku.

Bashō's fall from exalted status ironically had the effect of opening up the debate on the relative merits of Bashō's work and of arousing the interest of modern writers outside the world of haikai, to which his literary influence had been largely confined during the Tokugawa period. Stripped of his divine status, Bashō came alive as a "human being," capturing the imagination of modern novelists and poets, including *shijin* (Western-style free verse poets) and modern tanka poets. Interest turned to Bashō "the man," the marginalized artist, whose suffering and alienation from society seemed to echo those of the modern individual. For example, Kitamura Tōkoku (1868–94) and Shimazaki Tōson (1872–1943), both *shijin* and prominent members of Bungakukai (a romantic movement that flourished in the 1890s), saw Bashō as an ideal "poet" (*shijin*).[17]

Modern haiku from the mid–Meiji period on gravitated in two fundamental directions: toward the latest movements in contemporary arts and literature, particularly Western-style poetry (*shi*), and toward the reaffirmation of the traditional and historical roots of haiku. In contrast to the first direction, which attempted to assimilate the latest literary or avant-garde movements into haiku, the second looked back to earlier, traditional views of haikai. As Hirai Shōbin has suggested, these two broad movements have frequently come to be symbolized in the modern period by Buson and Bashō, respectively.[18] In contrast to Buson, who was associated with a number of modernist movements and with European poetry, Bashō has been regarded as a "Japanese" poet, whose poetry embodied the original essence of haiku and who came to represent the "Japanese tradition." Kawahigashi Hekigodō (1873–1937), one of Shiki's immediate haiku successors, considered Buson the "best poet of the past and present" (*Haikai Casual Talk*; 1903)[19] and criticized Bashō's frog poem for a lack of objective description: "When one probes into whether this frog is singing or jumping, whether there are many frogs or one, whether it is an afternoon scene or an evening scene, or where the author is, one realizes that this verse is completely unfinished." By contrast, Shiki's other major disciple, Takahama Kyoshi (1874–1959), who opposed the direction of Kawahigashi Hekigodō's New Trend (Shinkeikō) haiku, favored Bashō, particularly the subdued, penetrating *sabi* style of Genroku haikai. In a series of articles in *Hototogisu* (Cuckoo) in 1903–4, Kyoshi drew attention to the "passive" (*shōkyokuteki*), *sabi* character of Genroku poetry, which contemporary poets had rejected in favor of the "active" (*sekkyokuteki*) beauty of the Bashō Revival poets.[20] Kyoshi, who returned from prose to the haiku world in 1912 and dominated it for the next forty years, stressed traditional elements, especially composition on seasonal topics, and did much to revive Bashō's reputation as a haiku poet. Kyoshi, who stressed the development of subjectivity (*shukan*), admired the way in which Bashō managed to combine the subjective and the objective.[21] In 1927, Kyoshi advocated the notion of "composing poetry on blossoms and birds" (*kachō fūei*), which drew on Bashō's poetics and implied that if the poet refrained from directly expressing his or her emotions and concentrated on describing nature in the context of the four seasons, those emotions would naturally emerge through the natural imagery.

Mizuhara Shūōshi (1892–1981), one of Kyoshi's leading disciples, turned against his teacher in leading the New Haiku (Shinkō) movement and in his preference for Buson over Bashō. However, two of Shūōshi's followers, Ishida Hakyō (1913–69) and Katō Shūson (1905–93), broke away from Shūōshi in 1935 to join the Pursuit of Humanity (*Ningen tankyū*) group—under the leadership of Nakamura Kusatao (1901–83)—which sought an inner life appropriate to the contemporary age and looked to Bashō for inspiration.[22] The

Pursuit of Humanity group, which dominated the haiku world from around 1935 through the postwar period, sparked a modern Bashō revival, a period of research and literary re-evaluation. Extensive work was done on the relationship of Bashō's texts to their classical and Chinese precedents; and it was recognized, particular after the discovery of Sora's journal in 1943, that much of Bashō's work— such as *Narrow Road to the Interior*—had highly fictional elements. Yamamoto Kenkichi (1907–88), an influential literary critic and a major Bashō scholar, stressed the notion of haikai-ness, particularly those of play, greeting, and spontaneity. Ogata Tsutomu advocated the notion of poetry as a communal, dialogic activity (*za no bungaku*). These scholars were interested in reconstructing the social and interpersonal context for Bashō's poetry and prose, which they saw as significantly different from the modern emphasis on the self and on mimetic readings, and in this regard they have laid the groundwork for this study.

The Imagists

The Western reception of haiku and of Bashō's poetry, which has been deeply influenced by the modern Japanese approaches to haiku, has been even more deeply colored by subjective/objective critical discourse, particularly as a result of the Imagists, who appeared in the 1910s, and the North American haiku movement, which emerged in the 1960s. The Imagists were a small group of English and American poets—Ezra Pound, Amy Lowell, D. H. Lawrence, William Carlos Williams, H.D., John Gould Fletcher, F. S. Flint, and others—who worked together in London in the early twentieth century, especially between 1912 and 1914, and whose poetry was to have a profound influence on the development of T. S. Eliot, Wallace Stevens, and other major twentieth-century poets. As René Taupin, in the first major study of the Imagist period, has noted, Imagism was not a doctrine or even a school so much as the "association of a few poets who were for a certain time . . . in agreement on a small number of principles."[23] In the March 1913 issue of *Poetry*, F. S. Flint defined those principles:

1. Direct treatment of the "thing" whether subjective or objective.

2. To use absolutely no word that does not contribute to the presentation.

3. As regarding rhythm: to compose in the sequence of the musical phrase, not in the sequence of the metronome.

In an accompanying essay, Ezra Pound provided a one-sentence definition of a fourth rule, which Flint referred to as "a certain Doctrine of the Image": "An 'Image' is that which presents an intellectual and emotional complex in an instant of time."[24] In the preface to one of the earliest Imagist anthologies, called *Some Imagist Poets* (1915, 1916, 1917), edited by Amy Lowell, the original three rules were expanded to six:

5. To produce poetry that is hard and clear, never blurred nor indefinite.

6. Finally, most of us believe that concentration is of the very essence of poetry.[25]

The Imagists stressed concentration, directness, precision, and freedom from metrical laws, and gravitated toward a single, usually visual, dominant image or a succession of related images. The Imagist poet wished to communicate emotion without articulating it directly. That goal could be achieved by presenting an "object," or what T. S. Eliot called an "objective correlative," which would arouse in the reader that particular emotion without the poet stating it.[26] Although the Imagists were unaware of it, the seasonal word (*kigo*) in haikai, which was anchored in the communal memory, functioned like an objective correlative in being able to arouse emotions in the reader through what appeared to be an objective description of nature or the external world.

Pound also stressed the notion of juxtaposition, especially sharp contrasts in texture and color, which often created vivid, compact metaphors—a notion that, we shall see, lay at the heart of the haikai imagination. In an article in *Fortnightly Review* (Sept. 1, 1914) entitled "Vorticism," Pound wrote:

A Chinaman said long ago that if a man can't say what he has to say in twelve lines he had better keep quiet. The Japanese have evolved the still shorter form of the *hokku*.

> "The fallen blossom flies back to its branch :
> A butterfly."

That is the substance of a very well-known *hokku*. . . .

The "one-image poem" is a form of super-position, that is to say it is one idea set on top of another. I found it useful in getting out of the impasse in which I had been left by my metro emotion. I wrote a thirty-line poem, and destroyed it because it was what we call work "of second intensity." Six months later I made a poem half that length; a year later I made the following *hokku*-like sentence:

> "The apparition of these faces in the crowd :
> Petals, on a wet, black bough."

I dare say it is meaningless unless one has drifted into a certain vein of thought. In a poem of this sort one is trying to record the precise instant when a thing outward and objective transforms itself, or darts into a thing inward and subjective.[27]

Pound's "super-position" implied the layering of one image over another; later he moved toward pure juxtaposition, or a temporal succession of images, which could never be reduced to a singularity. This aspect of Imagism, which was interested not so much in reproducing things as in setting them in motion (what Pound would later call Vorticism), is evident in the earliest printing in the April 1913 issue of *Poetry* magazine.

> The apparition   of these faces   in the crowd :
> Petals   on a wet, black bough.

Here Pound presented not just two lines but five intersecting perceptions, in which "a thing outward and objective transforms itself, or darts into a thing inward and subjective." High Modernist poetry and art, epitomized in part by the Imagists, stressed the notion of juxtaposition and attempted to undo the expectations elicited by representational art by replacing description with the notion of "realization" or with that of collage, which broke up the representational plane. Haikai did in fact stress the notion of juxtaposition, but it differed significantly from the modernist notion of non-representational collage in that it often required a double reading of the juxtaposed texts, both as paratactic collage and as representational fragments of a larger scene or narrative.

Haiku in English

During the 1950s, America suddenly took an avid interest in Japanese culture and religion, especially Zen Buddhism and haiku. Alan Watts, D. T. Suzuki, the San Francisco poets, the Beats (in New York)—especially Jack Kerouac's *Dharma Bums*, a best-selling novel centered on a protagonist (modeled on Gary Snyder) who composes haiku—and American scholar-translators such as Donald Keene contributed to the popular interest in haiku, but most of all it was R. H. Blyth, Kenneth Yasuda, and Harold Henderson and their books—the four-volume *Haiku* by Blyth (published between 1949 and 1952), Yasuda's *Japanese Haiku: Its Essential Nature, History, and Possibilities in English* (1957), and Henderson's *Introduction to Haiku: An Anthology of Poems and Poets from Bashō to Shiki* (1958)—that generated widespread fascination with haiku and set the stage for a North American English haiku movement, which flourished in the 1960s and continues to this day.[28]

Following Pound and the Imagists, Blyth focused on the "concrete thing" but without the "intellectual and emotional complex" that had interested Pound. For Blyth, haiku was the poetry of "meaningful touch, taste, sound, sight, and smell," "the poetry of sensation"[29]—as opposed to that of thought and emotion. Furthermore, Blyth, influenced by D. T. Suzuki's view of Zen, believed that reading and composing haiku was a spiritual experience in which poet and nature were united. Zen, which becomes indistinguishable from haiku in much of Blyth's writing, was "a state of mind in which we are not separated from other things, are indeed identical with them, and yet retain our own individuality."[30] "Haiku is the apprehension of a thing by a realization of our own original and essential unity with it."[31] In the last of the *Haiku* volumes, Blyth even went so far as to say that haiku is a "self-annihilative" means of grasping "the thing-in-itself": when the ultimate spiritual goal is attained, the haiku becomes disposable.[32] This view of haiku as a spiritual subject/object fusion had a profound impact on subsequent Western reception of haiku. In *The Way of Haiku* (1969), J. W. Hackett, an early leader of the American haiku movement, wrote: "I have written in the conviction that the best haiku are created from direct and immediate experience with nature, and that this intuitive experience can be expressed in any language. In essence, I regard haiku as fundamentally existential and experiential, rather than literary."[33] There are certain elements of Bashō's poetics—such as the notion of "self-and-object-as-one" (*butsuga ichinyo*) and "following the Creative" (*zōka zuijun*)—that bear external resemblances to these Zen-inspired interpretations, but they do not derive primarily from Zen Buddhism and have, as we shall see in Chapter 9, more to do with the poet's need both to transform and to be rooted in the cultural landscape than with the direct union of the poet with nature.

In *The Japanese Haiku*, Kenneth Yasuda, like Blyth before him, stressed the "haiku moment" when the poet reaches "an enlightened, Nirvana-like harmony" and the "poet's nature and environment are unified."[34] This "haiku moment," which finds its ultimate embodiment in Bashō's poetry, is marked by three elements ("where," "what," and "when"), as exemplified by the following poem. (The translation is Yasuda's.)

Where	On a withered bough
What	A crow alone is perching;
When	Autumn evening now[35]

The seasonal word, which represents the "when," "is an aesthetic symbol of the sense of seasons, arising from the oneness of man and nature, and its function is to symbolize this union." In Yasuda's view, the haiku poet also "eschews metaphor, simile, or personification." "Metaphor is always an interference for the haiku poet. His aim is to render the object so that it appears in its own unique self, without reference to something other than itself."[36] This attempt to negate the function of metaphor, which also occurs in Blyth's writings, is misleading in that haikai, like all poetry, is highly metaphorical: the essential difference, as we shall see, is that the metaphorical function is implicit rather than stated and often encoded in a polysemous phrase or word.

In discussing classical Chinese poetry, Pauline Yu has argued that Western metaphor tends to be based on a fundamental dualism, the assumption of a disjunction between two realms, usually concrete and abstract, or physical and metaphysical. In such a context, poetry tends to embody concretely or physically a more transcendental, often spiritual realm. Nature serves as a vehicle for understanding a more abstract, transcendental world, which is given priority.[37] This kind of metaphor, which actually represents only one limited type, rarely, if ever, occurs in Bashō's haikai. Nature exists as something concrete and living before the viewer's eyes, as immediate, and is respected as such. At the same time, however, nature can implicitly have a semi-metaphorical function, particularly as a projection of the poet's inner or outer state or as that of the addressee. The natural imagery functions on both the literal and the figurative levels, collapsing I. A. Richards's noted distinction between vehicle and tenor. As we shall see later, the image of a hokku generally functions both metonymically, as part of a larger scene, and semi-metaphorically, as a reflection or expression of another sphere that usually exists within the immediate world of the speaker or addressee.

Harold Henderson's *Introduction to Haiku*, which was an updated version of an earlier book called *The Bamboo Room* from the 1930s, provided a major stimulus to the North American haiku movement, as it emerged in the 1960s. In contrast to Blyth and Yasuda, Henderson did not regard haiku as a spiritual or aesthetic experience and downplayed the notion of Zen illumination. Instead, he drew attention to the "overtones," the highly suggestive quality of good haiku, the techniques of condensation and ellipsis, and stressed the importance of the reader, who works by the process of association. Unlike

Yasuda, who believed that the haiku should have only one focal point, Henderson drew attention to the role of the cutting word, which divided the haiku in half, creating two centers and often generating what he called the "principle of internal comparison," an implicit comparison, equation, or contrast between two separate elements—a dynamics that he saw as a major characteristic of Bashō's poetry and that overlaps with Pound's notion of "super-position."[38]

The Haiku Anthology (1974), edited by Cor van den Heuvel, the first major anthology of haiku in English, reveals the deep impact of Blyth, Yasuda, and Henderson.[39] Much of the haiku, which is usually in three lines, focuses on moments of intense perception, especially the sensory aspects of physically small objects, or on a particular instant in time, commonly referred to as the "haiku moment." As Geraldine Little, a contributor to *Haiku Anthology*, notes, "Haiku's appeal for me is its world in a grain of sand philosophy, the here and now of it."[40] Anita Virgil, another contributor, writes: "I saw the haiku as a logical extension of all I had known and preferred: drawing that is spare and essential, the particular and the whole implied by it, Nature in its broadest sense—the nature of all things in the world: their unique identity and yet their sameness, their evanescence and their eternal quality."[41] The majority of these haiku in English as well as haiku translations from Japanese are done in the style of the Imagists and modernists such as Stevens, Eliot, and Williams. These English haiku, which often omit capitalization and standard punctuation, have their own internal rhythm and are in what might be called a lean, spare style, which have influenced the translations of Bashō, including the ones in this study.

As this brief overview of Anglo-American reception suggests, haiku has largely been conceived as the poetry of the object (particularly small things), of "sensation," and of the moment. There has also been a strong tendency to treat the haiku in a spiritual context or in an autobiographical, personal mode, especially as "haiku experience." Haiku in English inherited the doctrines of the Imagists and the early twentieth-century High Modernist poets, but with important differences. T. S. Eliot's notion of "objective correlative," which embodied one of the goals of Imagism, was intended to be anti-Romantic, to stress impersonality, to emphasize craftsmanship and detach the poet from personal experience. In "Tradition and Individual Talent" (1919), Eliot wrote: "Poetry is not a turning loose of emotion, but an escape from emotion; it is not the expression of personality, but an escape from personality."[42] By stressing the unity of the poet and the object, writers such as Blyth and Yasuda transformed the "impersonality" that the Imagists had stressed into a highly subjective, personal moment, closely tied to the spiritual state of the poet. Indeed, Western scholars have tended to regard Bashō as an autobiographical, confessional poet, as a part of a larger literary and cultural tradition that gives priority to "truth," "fact," and "sincerity." One Western scholar, in a major study of the "I-novel" (*watakushi-shōsetsu*) writes: "In a culture that views 'reality' as only an immediate experience of the natural world, literature not surprisingly becomes a chronicling or transcribing of that experience rather than a imaginative reconstruction of it."[43] This view of Japanese literature as one that prizes "immediate experience" and devalues "imaginative reconstruction" is, like Shiki's notion of the "sketch" (*shasei*), a modern Japanese construction that emerged under heavy Western influence and runs counter to much of haikai poetics.[44]

The modern reception of Bashō's poetry has tended to stress either objectivity or subjectivity, usually at the expense of its perceived opposite, while ignoring what I call "haikai imagination." As we shall see, one of the remarkable aspects of Bashō's poetry is the seemingly paradoxical coexistence of different textual and perceptual planes—figurative and literal, monologic and dialogic, referential and parodic, objective and subjective, personal and impersonal, metaphorical and metonymical, representation and collage—which is made possible in large part by the fundamental haikai assumption that the meaning of the text is relative and dependent on its context, which is subject to constant change. For example, the seasonal word, the requirement of every hokku, often exists simultaneously on a number of axes or in different contexts: as a reference to an external scene, as an implicit metaphor or extension of the poet's inner state, as a complex literary and cultural sign, and as a greeting to the addressee. The first is highly objective and referential; the second tends to be highly subjective; the third is often highly fictional and intertextual, and the fourth is a performative utterance.

A typical hokku by Bashō presents a natural scene that can also be read as a reflection of the state of the poet or that of the addressee. This is true even when the poem appears to be completely objective, devoted exclusively to nature, such as the following.

> hiding in the water—
> the grebes of Lake Biwa
> at year's end

> kakurekeri | shiwasu | no | umi | no | kaitsuburi
> hidden | Twelfth-Month | 's | lake | 's | grebe[45]

The hokku, which Bashō composed late in the Twelfth Month of Genroku 3 (Jan. 1691), probably at Ōmi, describes the grebes (*kaitsuburi*), small birds that float on the surface of Lake Biwa and occasionally dive beneath the water, "hiding" (*kakurekeri*) before popping up in an unexpected location. The larger context suggested by "Twelfth Month" (*shiwasu*, literally, "teacher running")—a seasonal word for winter and for the end of the year, when everybody is rushing about cleaning up and settling their financial accounts—implies that the observer is a carefree, reclusive person, someone who has the leisure to observe the grebes at the busiest time of the year. This kind of haikai reading differs significantly from an Imagistic "objective correlative" or the American Zen reading that fuses the subject with the object. The reader must develop a metonymic and contextual imagination that fills out the scene based on impressionistic details and encoded words such as *shiwasu*. What is not said is as important as what is said. No mention is made of the viewer or speaker, and yet it is his or her implied presence that opens up the poem. At first glance, the hokku seems focused on a seemingly minor, if not insignificant, detail, but it gradually expands in the eye of the beholder, creating a tension between the smaller object and the implied landscape, or between the specific moment and the larger river of time.

As a text ready to be recontextualized, to be added to, expanded upon, and changed, the haikai text could serve a variety of functions simultaneously, as in the following hokku, which Bashō composed at the beginning of 1692 (Genroku 5), at the age of 49.

a spring no one sees—
plum blossoms
   on the back of a mirror

hito | mo | minu | haru | ya | kagami | no | ura | no | ume
person | also | not-see | spring | : | mirror | 's | back | 's | plum

The back of a mirror, normally ignored, is engraved with plum blossoms (*ume*), which are blooming out of people's sight. The hokku fulfills a socio-religious function as a *saitangin*, or New Year's poem, celebrating the arrival of the New Year by describing the fragrant plum blossoms that bloom in the First Month. At the same time, the larger biographical context—Bashō went into retreat at this time, closing himself off even from his disciples—also suggests a figurative, allegorical reading in which the plum blossoms hidden behind the mirror express Bashō's desire for solitude, to retreat from the world.

In its simplest form, poetry "says one thing and means another." As the modern critic Michael Riffaterre has argued, a poetic text is marked by indirections—displacement (such as metaphor, metonymy), distortion (ambiguity, hyperbole, contradiction), and the creation of textual space (symmetry, rhyme)—that threaten the first level of reading, that of the words as "literary representation of reality."[46] These incompatibilities cause the reader to move to the second level of reading, at which the reader makes various transcodings from the first level and reads the words as parts of other networks or systems of signs. The lack of obvious signs of indirection in the hokku combined with the Western notion of a "haiku moment" often causes modern readers of Bashō's haikai to stop at the first level, which is the most obvious and the most striking. In contrast to Danrin haikai, which delighted in the fantastic and the absurd, Genroku landscape (*keiki*) haikai, of which Bashō's mature haikai was a part, stressed verisimilitude, describing the external world "as it is." As a consequence, there has been a strong modern tendency to read Bashō's haikai only on the level of the scene. Bashō's haikai, however, require the reader not only to move to the second level but, contrary to Riffaterre's model, to maintain simultaneously the first level, creating a double vision that allows the reader to take pleasure in the disjunction or resonance between the two.

One of Bashō's innovations in the mid-1680s was the presentation of external landscape with subtle, emotional connotations. In the famous frog poem, for example, the sound of water rising from an old pond implies, as Shikō and other disciples argued, the eye and ear of a recluse attentive to the minute changes in nature and suggests a larger meditative loneliness, sometimes referred to as *sabi*: the sound of water paradoxically deepens the sense of surrounding quiet. For Shikō and other haikai readers, the invisible, undescribed world of the frog poem loomed as large, if not larger, than the visible detail, and it was the tension—the reader's mind floating between the detail and the possibilities of the larger scene—that gave the poem its greatest force. The haikai reader, in short, enjoyed the famous frog poem as an objective, "immediate" hokku about a frog jumping into an old pond, as a parodic, haikai-esque challenge to a classical topos, and as a subjective poem that explores the ambiance and nuances of reclusion and solitude. This range of readings emerged from the haikai imagination, which regarded the hokku as a text in constant motion, revealing various aspects of itself from different angles.

CHAPTER 3

Haikai Language, Haikai Spirit

Every concrete utterance of a speaking subject serves as a point where centrifugal as well as centripetal forces are brought to bear. The process of centralization and decentralization, of unification and disunification, intersect in the utterance.
—Mikhail Bakhtin, *The Dialogic Imagination*

A situation is always comic when it belongs at the same time to two series of events that are absolutely independent, and when it can be interpreted simultaneously in two quite different senses.
—Henri Bergson, "Laughter"

As the Russian critic Mikhail Bakhtin has acutely observed, language is not monolithic, neutral, and closed but pluralistic and socially and ideologically inscribed. Bakhtin sees language as a constant struggle among systems or groups, between a centripetal, unifying force deriving from those in power, which attempts to impose a unitary order on language, and centrifugal, stratifying forces created by various social groups, which fracture and divide language into many different, socially accented tongues—a phenomenon that he calls "heteroglossia."[1] In Bakhtin's view, every utterance serves as a point where these centripetal and centrifugal forces converge, often in tension or conflict. Commenting on European literature, Bakhtin contrasts poetry, particularly the lyric, which in his view attempts to maintain the unitary order of the established literary language, with what he calls the polyphonic novel, which reflects and encourages the dynamics of heteroglossia. A similar kind of sociolinguistic interaction between centripetal and centrifugal forces, occurred *within* the Japanese poetic tradition, particularly from the sixteenth century, an age of great social and political upheaval, through the seventeenth century, when commoners, both in the provinces and in the urban centers, emerged to create the base for a new cultural and social order.

Waka, the 31-syllable classical form, employed a unitary language; classical poets generally banned all forms of language not found in the highly circumscribed, aristocratic diction of what Fujiwara Teika (1162–1241) had designated the Heian classics, particularly *Kokinshū*, *The Tales of Ise* and *The Tale of Genji*. Subject matter, at least in the imperial waka anthologies, was likewise confined to a cluster of highly elegant topics, focused primarily on love and the four seasons. The same restrictions applied to renga, which carried the classical tradition into the late medieval period. By contrast, haikai, which drew freely on non-classical languages—and in this sense followed *imayō*, *saibara*, *kouta*, and other folk song genres found in the medieval period—challenged, inverted, and otherwise subverted the unitary language of classical poetry and exhibited the kind of scatological, bawdy, corporeal materialism found in Rabelais. *Dog Tsukuba Collection* (*Inu tsukuba shū*; 1532), one of the earliest anthologies of haikai, begins with:

> a robe of mist
> soaked at the hem
>
> kasumi | no | koromo | suso | wa | nurekeri
> mist | 's | robe | hem | as-for | soaked

The added verse (*tsukeku*) composed by Sōkan (d. ca. 1539–40), one of the pioneers of haikai and thought to be the editor of *Dog Tsukuba Collection*, is:

> Princess Saho
> with the coming of spring
> stands pissing
>
> Sahohime | no | haru | tachinagara | shito | o | shite
> princess-Saho | 's | spring | beginning/standing | piss | (acc.) | doing[2]

Part of a long scroll (8.9 x 203.5 in.) sketched in light black ink by Bashō and colored by a local artist at Ōgaki. Originally attached to two other scrolls, one by Ryūho (1595–1669) on a blind person and another by Kikaku (1661–1707) on a beggar. This picture scroll, which Bashō did in the spring or summer of 1694, at about the time as he was writing *Narrow Road to the Interior*, illustrates ten different scenes of travel in different seasons, beginning with this scene in early winter. The traveler, in priestly garb, with a rain hat (*kasa*) and cane (*tsue*), is blown by the winter showers (*shigure*)—a symbol of Bashō's poetics—which is highlighted by the pines in the back and the bright autumn leaves in the front. Bashō apparently planned to add calligraphy and his signature but departed on his last journey before completing the scroll. (Courtesy Kakimori Collection)

It was a convention of classical poetry that Sahohime, the beautiful goddess of spring, should stand in the midst of a spring mist, which became her robe. The added verse, which uses the vernacular phrase *shito o su* (to piss), parodies that classical convention by having the princess urinate while standing, as commoner women did in those days. The two sociocultural worlds occupy the same homonym *tatsu*, which means both "to stand" and "to begin" (as in the coming of spring).

Haikai differed from classical poetry and classical linked verse in the use of "haikai words" (*haigon*)—vernacular, Chinese, Buddhist terms, slang, common sayings, and other language banned from classical poetry—which tended to anchor haikai in popular, contemporary culture. Haikai has been traced by modern literary historians to the witty 31-syllable waka found in the *Kokinshū* under the special category of "haikai classical poetry" (*haikaika*)[3] and to "short linked verse" (*tanrenga*), which consisted of a seventeen-syllable (5/7/5) verse followed by a fourteen-syllable (7/7) verse or vice versa and which also emerged in the Heian period (794–1185). Both these poetic genres possessed what was later called "haikai spirit" (*haii*) in their emphasis on humor, wit, and wordplay, but neither of them was marked by the popular, commoner culture implicit in haikai words. By contrast, the haikai that emerged in the medieval period and that culminated in the *Dog Tsukuba Collection* combined haikai spirit with haikai words. The haikai collected there, which reflect the wider, late-medieval, sociocultural phenomenon of "the low transgressing the high" (*gekokujō*), employed popular language, parodied the literary classics, poked fun at social customs, satirized Shinto gods, Buddhas, and other figures of authority and power, displayed a profound interest in money, food, and sex—topics that had been taboo in classical poetry—and portrayed contemporary society, particularly the life of commoners and farmers, in all its sordid detail. As we shall see, the approach to these two central issues—those of haikai spirit and hakai language—changed significantly from group to group and from period to period.

Controlling Haikai Language

In contrast to renga, which raised itself to the level of classical po-
etry by purging itself of non-classical languages, haikai, at least that
which evolved from the late medieval period, depended on the use
of haikai words to distinguish itself from renga and the classical tra-
dition. Teitoku, founder of the Teimon school and leader of haikai
in the first half of the seventeenth century, offered an extremely
conservative and limited definition of haikai—linked verse embed-
ded with haikai words[4]—that appealed greatly to the new Tokugawa
popular audience, particularly those with little education. For the
educated elite, who had composed haikai as an amusing diversion,
haikai words in linked verse created a humorous linguistic and social
disjunction. For the new social classes, however, haikai words had
another significance—an opportunity to represent their own lives
and create their own literature.

The problem that faced Teitoku, a highly educated scholar and
poet of classical waka, was how to maintain and encourage haikai as
a popular art, one that would be accessible to a wide but not neces-
sarily highly educated audience, while making it a respectable form
and part of the larger poetic tradition. Teitoku's answer was to stress
haikai words, which gave haikai its popular character, while reject-
ing or tempering the kind of ribald, irreverent humor and language
found in *Dog Tsukuba Collection* and earlier haikai, which he criti-
cized as immoral and vulgar. Under Teitoku, the Teimon school
continued the lexical play and parody that had characterized six-
teenth-century haikai, but it restricted the nature of the haikai
words to Chinese words (*kango*) and acceptable vernacular Japanese,
excluding vulgar and highly colloquial phrases. In the *New Dog Tsu-
kuba Collection* (*Shinzō inu tsukuba shū*; 1643), a haikai anthology ed-
ited by Teitoku, Teitoku presented his response to the "robe of
mist" poem cited earlier.

a robe of mist
soaked at the hem

heavenly creatures
descending it seems—
   the sea of spring

tennin│ya│amakudaru│rashi│haru│no│umi
heavenly-creatures│descend│it-seems│spring│'s│sea[5]

Except for the haikai word *tennin* (heavenly creatures), a Chinese compound, which had no vulgar implications, the content is no different from that of an elegant verse in classical renga.

The Teimon school, to which Bashō belonged at the beginning of his career, while still in his home province of Iga, also alluded heavily to classical poetry (*honkadori*) and to classical narratives (*honzetsu*), both techniques drawn from classical poetry and classical renga. In order to demonstrate that haikai was not simply frivolous play, Teimon leaders such as Teitoku urged the composition of poems that revealed a knowledge of the Heian classics or of historical events. For the new commoner and samurai audience, many of whom became enamored of the notion of high culture, haikai in fact presented an opportunity to acquire a taste for classical literature, particularly a knowledge of its famous places (*meisho*) and elegant seasonal motifs. Teitoku, who was as much a classical educator and scholar as a haikai poet, came to regard haikai as a critical means of educating the populace and as a bridge to the composition of classical poetry.[6]

Since it was impossible for commoners with little educational background to read Heian poetry and prose, a number of Teimon scholars wrote extensive commentaries, which made widely accessible *The Tale of Genji*, *The Pillow Book*, *Essays in Idleness*, and other texts, which became part of a popular literary canon.[7] Indeed, Teitoku and his disciples regarded a knowledge of *The Tales of Ise*, *The Tale of Genji*, and *Kokinshū* as an absolute requirement for haikai. In *Haikai yōi fūtei* (Essential style for haikai; 1673), Kigin (1624–1705), the most outstanding of the Teimon scholars and one of Bashō's earliest teachers, wrote:

In haikai, words are used to describe the ways of the present world, but that style must also be one with the poetry of the *Kokinshū*. Since haikai is poetic art, the heart of the poet should enter into the way of classical poetry, admire the cherry blossoms, yearn for the moon, establish the way of father and son, ruler and subject. It should not forget love between men and women. . . . If one does not read books of poetry such as *The Tale of Genji* or *The Pillow Book*, if one does not soak one's spirit in the ancient style, if one does not use that language in various ways, how can one know true haikai?[8]

Although haikai has been widely characterized as the epitome of popular literature, which reflected the new world of commoners, it had another, equally important function: to provide a window onto the classical past and a convenient means of absorbing the cultural memory, especially that of high culture as it was embodied in classical poetry and the seasonal landscape. Even as haikai parodied the Japanese classics, wittily twisting classical associations, it was often framed by the traditional discourse. As Kigin's remarks suggest, the educated leaders of the Teimon school in fact incorporated the Neo-Confucian ideology of the Tokugawa rulers—establishing the way of the father/son, ruler/subject—suggesting that a classical framework or foundation could provide a means of controlling or rectifying the content and language of a commoner form that tended, from their perspective, to be vulgar, erotic, and subversive.

Swimming in the Waves of Cherry Blossoms

Danrin haikai, which became popular in the 1670s, especially in the Enpō era (1673–81), and dominated the haikai world after the decline of the Teimon school in the late 1660s, employed many of the techniques found in Teimon haikai: word association (*engo*), homophonic play (*kakekotoba*), parody, and visual comparisons (*mitate*). However, for Sōin, the founder of Danrin haikai, haikai was not an intermediary, learning stage, a means of entering the world of classical poetry and renga. Unlike the Teimon school, which was based in Kyoto, the center of aristocratic culture, and looked back to the classical tradition, Danrin haikai grew out of

Osaka, the new center of commerce, where a new society of increasingly wealthy and powerful urban commoners sought to create their own culture. If Teitoku had attempted to impose order on linked verse, Sōin, who came from Osaka, stressed spontaneity and freedom of form and movement, linking verses without excessive concern for rules or precedent. Indicative of the Danrin's iconoclastic character was the practice of excessive syllables (*jiamari*), exceeding the formal limit of seventeen syllables, particularly in the last five syllables of the hokku. Instead of placing constraints on haikai language or avoiding the vulgarity of the *Dog Tsukuba Collection*, Danrin poets, including Bashō, explored the myriad aspects of contemporary culture, including that of the pleasure quarters and the popular kabuki theater.

Like Teimon poets before them, Danrin poets also sought to parody classical poetry and narratives such as *The Tales of Ise*, as well as famous historical events, but they did this in a bolder and more dynamic fashion, not hesitating to place full weight on the popular or vulgar. Like Teimon haikai before it, Danrin haikai relied heavily on a knowledge of classical literature, which most commoners could not readily acquire. It was in this cultural milieu that Noh drama—which had become popular in the form of *utai*, as songs to be memorized and chanted—emerged as a new and more accessible "classic" for commoners, who could easily combine famous lines from Noh drama with haikai words to create their own contemporary allusive variations. For Danrin poets, who were far less educated than their Teimon predecessors, the notion of the classics in fact became extremely circumscribed, limited almost entirely to famous classical poems in the *Kokinshū* and *Shinkokinshū* (New collection of old and new poems; 1205), well-known passages from Noh plays, *The Tales of Ise*, *The Tale of Genji*, or selected Chinese poetry by Po Chü-i and others. Danrin poets used these classical fragments, along with *yoriai* (established lexical associations), to link verses, and it was the highly conventionalized state of these associations that enabled Saikaku to engage in rapid-fire solo sequences of immense length—the *yakazu haikai*, or "countless arrow" haikai.

Danrin poets deliberately sought to maximize the tension between haikai words and classical diction, believing that the greater the collision between disparate languages, the greater the haikai effect. *Indōshū* (Teachings collection; 1684), a Danrin haikai handbook edited by Saikoku (1647–1695), a merchant from Bungo (Kyūshū) and a disciple of Saikaku, uses the following verse as an example of the Danrin method.[9]

> making sea lions and whales
> swim in the cherry blossom waves
>   at the hill top

mine|no|hana|no|nami|ni|ashika|kujira|o|oyogase
hill-top|'s|flower|'s|waves|in|sea-lion|whale|(acc.)|make swim

The hokku links cherry blossoms, closely associated with waves and hill tops in classical poetry, with sea lions (*ashika*) and whales (*kujira*), two haikai words. The poem comically deconstructs a familiar classical convention—"waves of cherry blossoms"—by using this figurative cliché in its original, literal meaning, as the "waves of water" in which sea lions and whales swim. The resulting disjunction, in which two different socially inscribed languages inhabit the same word, produced not only haikai humor but absurd, unrealistic poetry, which Ichū (1639–1711), a Danrin spokesman, referred to as *gūgen haikai* (allegorical haikai).[10] Like Danrin haikai, Bashō's haikai in the 1680s often sought pleasure in the collision of languages, especially between classical and vernacular, but, as we shall see, it simultaneously sought out congruity in the incongruity, linking disparate subcultures and words in a regenerative fashion while working within the context of landscape poetry and exploring various dimensions of contemporary commoner life.

Parody and the Chinese Style

In the first half of the 1680s, during the Tenna era (1681–84), the haikai world was swept by the "Chinese style" (*kanshibun-chō*), which not only employed Chinese words and compounds, considered to be haikai words,[11] but also utilized Chinese-style syntax, following the *kundoku* tradition of reading Chinese in a semi-Japanese manner. Instead of humorously drawing phrases from classical poetry, Heian romances, and Noh drama, haikai poets now parodied noted passages from Chinese literature. In the late 1670s, Chinese poetry, which the intellectual elite had always considered the epitome of literary study, suddenly entered the popular domain, no doubt under the influence of Tokugawa Neo-Confucian educational policy and the rise of Chinese studies. Commoners and samurai took an interest in both reading and composing Chinese poetry, and a large number of introductory anthologies and handbooks—such as Sakakibara Kōshū's (d. 1706) *Teaching Beginners Chinese Poetry* (*Shihō juyōshō*; 1679) and Kaibara Ekiken's (1630–1714) *Chinese Poetry for Beginners* (*Shogaku shihō*; 1680)—were published in rapid succession. Haikai in the Chinese style, which rode on the back of this new interest in Chinese poetry, led to a series of haikai anthologies—such as *Musashi Style* (*Musashiburi*; 1682), *Empty Chestnuts* (*Minashiguri*; 1683), and *Sequel to Empty Chestnuts* (*Zoku minashiguri*; 1687)—that contained poems by Bashō and his circle.[12]

Chinese words (*kango*) had been banned from classical poetry and classical renga and thus were considered haikai words, and yet they differed from vernacular, contemporary Japanese in that they carried the connotations and authority of a revered tradition of poetry and prose. Bashō incorporated Chinese words, especially in the form of recluse poetry, into haikai in a fashion that had not been possible either in classical poetry or in renga. In the winter of 1680, during the period he was involved with the Chinese style, Bashō abandoned his haikai business in the middle of Edo, in the area of Nihonbashi, and moved to Fukagawa, on the western outskirts of Edo. There he began composing haikai that drew on his own life as a recluse, creating, probably for the first time in haikai history, what appeared to be a personal, confessional mode—a movement no doubt influenced by his readings of Chinese recluse poets such as Li Po and Tu Fu. At Fukagawa, Bashō wrote poems and *haibun* (haikai prose) such as "The Brushwood Door" ("Shiba no to," 1680).

After nine years, growing weary of living in the city, I moved my home to the bank of the Fukagawa River. "Ch'ang-an was, from long ago, a place of profit and fame, making it difficult for those who were empty-handed and penniless to survive." Is it because I found the person who said this to be so wise that I am now so poor?[13]

> against the brushwood door
> gathering tree leaves for my tea—
>   a storm

shiba|no|to|ni|cha|o|ko|no|ha|kaku|arashi|kana
brushwood|'s|door|in|tea|(acc.)|tree|'s|leave|gather|storm|!

(NKBZ 41: 407)

Bashō here emerges as a "poet of life" who implicitly asks us to read his poetry against his personal life. One consequence has been that generations of readers have imagined Bashō eking out a lonely and humble existence in a small grass hut, an image sustained and fostered by Edo artists and later poets such as Chōmu. At the same time, Bashō's Chinese-style poetry, like the earlier Teimon haikai that alluded to Heian classical literature, opened a window on to another world, on to the "past," as in the following *haibun*, which Bashō composed in the winter of 1681.

> In the window, the snow of a thousand autumns
>   on the Western Peak
> Stopping at the gate, the ships traveling
>   a thousand leagues to the Eastern Sea
>   —Owner of the Hall of Stopping Ships
>   Flower Tōsei

I know this poem, but I do not know his feelings. I can imagine his poverty, but I cannot know his pleasure. I am superior to the elder Tu Fu only in the sense that I have more ills. Hidden in the leaves of the plantain at the side of my simple thatched hut, I call myself "beggar old man."

> oar sounds hitting the waves
> guts freezing at night—
>   tears

rosei | nami | o | utte | harawata | kōru | yo | ya | namida
oar-sound | wave | (acc.) | hitting | freeze | night | ! | tears

    a kettle at Poor Temple
    whistling in the frost—
      a cold voice

hinzan | no | kama | shimo | ni | naru | koe | samushi
Poor-Temple | 's | kettle | frost | to | cry | voice | cold[14]

Buying water

    quenching its thirst
    with bitter ice—
      a sewer rat

kōri | nigaku | enso | ga | nodo | o | uruoseri
ice | bitterly | sewer-rat | (nom.) | throat | (acc.) | moisten

Year's End

    as the year ends
    echo of rice-cake pounding—
      a lonely bed

kurekurete | mochi | o | kodama | no | wabine | kana
year-ending | rice-cake | (acc.) | echo | 's | lonely-sleep | !
            (NKBZ 41: 410–411)

This haibun opens with the last two lines of a *chüeh-chü* (J. *zekku*), or quatrain, by Tu Fu, in which the Chinese poet looks out from his hermitage. The result is a double vision (*mitate*): the local view from Fukagawa becomes that from Tu Fu's hermitage, Mount Fuji turns into China's Western Peak, the boats on the Sumida River merge with the boats heading "a thousand leagues to the Eastern Sea," and Bashō's hut fuses with that of Tu Fu. As Ogata Tsutomu has noted, the speaker assumes the shadow of Tu Fu, transforming his physical poverty into poetic poverty and implicitly joining the company of noted Chinese recluse-poets. In contrast to earlier haikai, which tended to parody or debase the target text, Bashō popularizes or vernacularizes the Chinese motifs while transforming haikai into recluse poetry, a prestigious genre in the Chinese tradition.

The kind of humorous cultural or linguistic incongruity found in Danrin and earlier haikai also appears here, but with an added twist, as suggested by the following poem, which Bashō composed in 1681 and included in *Musashi Style*.

Thoughts in a Thatched Hut

> plantain in an autumn gale—
> a night listening to rain
> drip into a tub

basho | nowaki | shite | tarai | ni | ame | o | kiku | yo | kana
banana-plant | autumn-gale | blows | tub | in | rain | (acc.) | hear | night | !

According to legend, Rika (active 1688–1704), one of Bashō's disciples, sent his teacher the root of a *bashō*, or Japanese plantain, a familiar motif in Chinese poetry and painting, which was planted in front of Bashō's grass hut and from which Bashō subsequently took his pen-name. In contrast to the banana tree, which grows in the tropics and bears fruit, the *bashō* grows in moderate to cold climates and rarely bears fruit. The *bashō* plant, which can stand as high as four meters, grows vigorously in the summer, and its leaves stretch as far as two meters in length in a long oval shape. In the autumn these extended leaves are torn by the wind and rain, creating a pitiable appearance and as a result became, in both the Chinese and Japanese poetic tradition, a symbol of the impermanence of this world. Bashō's hokku seems to reflect the hardship and loneliness of the recluse—the *nowaki* (autumn gale) implicitly breaks the fragile leaves of the *bashō* plant and causes the rain to leak through the roof—but another headnote to the same hokku suggests far more.

> Tu Fu composed a poem on "A Thatched Hut Ravaged by the Wind." Su Tung-p'o, nostalgic for that suffering, composed a poem on a leaking hut. Hearing the rain of that evening in the leaves of the plantain, I slept alone in my grass hut.

By the late T'ang period, the idea of planting a plantain in one's garden and listening to the sound of the leaves breaking in the wind had become a popular motif not only in Chinese poetry but also in paintings and decorative illustrations as well.[15] As Bashō's references to Chinese recluse poetry suggest, the speaker in Bashō's hokku hears not just the rain outside but the evening rain found in the poetry of Tu Fu, Su Tung-p'o (1037–1101), and other noted Chinese poets. Instead of listening to the raindrops fall on the plantain leaves, however, the recluse, in a haikai twist, hears the sound of the rain falling into a "tub" (*tarai*), a vernacular word that brings the world of the Chinese recluse down to everyday, commoner life.[16]

In contrast to sixteenth-century haikai, which tended to reduce the refined to the vulgar, Bashō sought a different kind of haikai inversion, exploring the high in the low, the spiritual in the mundane, richness in poverty, often in the manner of *wabi* aesthetics. The term *wabi*, at least as it developed in connection with *wabicha* (*wabi* tea), meant to be externally poor—free of the desire for wealth, power, and reputation—and yet internally in possession of the highest spirit.[17] In the following hokku, which Bashō wrote in 1681 and which appears in *Musashi Style*, Tsukiwabisai (Moongazer), an elegant fictional name for a recluse, eats *naracha*, a simple meal of rice gruel, a symbol of a humble *wabi* (ascetic) life, while singing a *naracha uta*, a drinking song.

> I suffer as I gaze at the moon, suffer as I think of my lowly position, and suffer as I contemplate my lack of talent. If someone should ask how I am faring, I would tell them, as Yukihira did in his famous poem, but no one answers, causing me even more suffering:

> > live poor! be bright!
> > Moongazer sings
> > a song of Nara gruel

> wabite | sume | Tsukiwabisai | ga | naracha | uta
> poorly | live | Moongazer | 's | Nara-rice-gruel | song
> (NKBZ 41: 409)

In the preface, the speaker despairs at his misfortune, his lack of talent, and his isolation, alluding to Ariwara Yukihira's famous poem on exile, but the hokku urges the speaker himself not only to "live in poverty" (*wabite*) but to make that impoverished life "bright and pure" (*sume*)—*sumu* means both "to live" and "to be pure"—transforming *wabi* from a negative sense into a positive one. In a haikai twist, the hokku laments the poet's impoverished life even as it celebrates it, urging the poet to be even more *wabi*, more impoverished, and thus purer in spirit.

During periods of uncertainty and disillusionment the human mind often turns away from the surrounding world and looks, as many did at this time, to distant cultures or earlier periods for escape or alternatives to the present. In stark contrast to the 1670s, the Kanbun (1661–73) and Enpō (1673–81) eras, during which Danrin haikai flourished, the Tenna era (1681–84) was a dark age. The fourth shogun Ietsuna (1641–80) presided over a period of remarkable commercial and urban growth that gave the middle- and upper-level townspeople unprecedented economic power, which was reflected in the character and popularity of Danrin haikai. In 1680, however, Ietsuna died and was succeeded by the fifth shogun Tsunayoshi (1646–1709), whose fanatically repressive measures cast a dark shadow over the new *chōnin* culture and society. Tsunayoshi rigidified the four-class system, placed farmers under strict control, and severely restricted the lives of commoners. At the same time, a series of natural disasters—extensive drought, famine, floods, and repeated conflagrations—drove up the price of rice and caused widespread hardship and starvation. The city of Edo was engulfed in flames in 1680, 1682, and 1683, the last two described as "living hell."[18]

During this period, Bashō's retreat at Fukagawa became a kind of liberated zone for Bashō and his fellow poets—Kikaku, Sodō (1642–1716), Sanpū, Ransetsu, and others—providing a setting to wander freely in other worlds, carrying on a poetic dialogue across time and space. Each haikai group attempted to develop its own set of identifiable poetic images and motifs. For Bashō's circle, at least during the Tenna era, it became the themes of "poverty" (*hin*), "impoverished dwelling" (*hinkyo*), coldness, loneliness, social failure—topics found in the Taoist *Chuang-tzu* and in Chinese recluse poetry, particularly that of Tu Fu and Su Tung-p'o. The modern scholar Shiraishi Teizō has even gone so far as to say that Bashō's grass hut existed only in the "communal imagination" of the Bashō's circle.[19] Later audiences were to look back on Bashō as a cultural hero, as recluse and traveler who had freed himself of the bonds of Tokugawa feudal society, but it was a freedom attained primarily in the poetic imagination.[20]

The Renga Style and Poetic Madness

In the mid-1680s, the haikai world was dominated by what modern scholars now call the "renga style" (*renga-tai*), a gentle, elegant, neoclassical linked verse style that required no haikai words and that appears to have emerged in reaction to the excesses of the Danrin style, particularly the complex wordplay and the absurd poetry. In 1687, in a work called *Teibōshū*, Isshō (d. 1707), an Edo poet and Bashō acquaintance, criticized the new trend: "From last year and the year before, haikai poets have all become fond of the gentle style. As a consequence, everyone attempts to be as elegant as possible, and generally speaking, one out of every three sequences resembles one-armed renga or truncated classical poetry."[21] Ichū, a Danrin theoretician, even refused to recognize the new renga style as haikai. Popular genres such as haikai had emerged in an antithetical relationship to the traditional high genres, but as the seventeenth century drew to a close, these new popular genres came into their own in such a way that the participants were less conscious of their traditional counterparts. Indeed, writers and poets such as Bashō who had matured in the late 1680s and early 1690s did not have the classical training and knowledge that their haikai predecessors possessed. Teitoku, the founder of Teimon haikai, had learned classical renga and poetry from such notables as Jōha (1524?–1602) and Hosokawa Yūsai (1534–1610), and Sōin, the pioneer of Danrin haikai, had been a classical renga master, a profession he returned to late in life. By contrast, Bashō, like many of his Genroku contemporaries, almost never composed classical linked verse or waka, had little classical training, and mixed elements from the traditional and the new popular genres with few qualms.

What, then, defined the essence of haikai for Bashō at this time? As the following passage in *Sanzōshi* (Three booklets; 1702) suggests, Bashō reformulated the nature of haikai in at least three fundamental ways, through language (*kotoba*), construction (*sakui*), and spirit/attitude (*kokoro*),

> "A willow in spring rain" is entirely renga. "A crow that plucks a mud snail" is entirely haikai.
>
>   in the summer rains
> I'll go and see the floating nests
>   of the grebe!
>
> samidare | ni | nio | no | ukisu | o | mi | ni | yukan
> summer-rains | in | grebe | 's | floating-nest | (acc.) | see | to | will-go
> (Bashō)

This verse has no haikai in the diction. But the idea of going to see the floating nest belongs to haikai.

>   the Eleventh Month—
> storks listlessly
>   standing in a line
>
> shimotsuki | ya | kou | no | tsukutsuku | narabi | ite
> Eleventh-Month | = | stork | 's | listlessly | lined-up | standing
> (Kakei)

> This hokku is followed by a second verse:

> deeply moving!
> the morning sun in winter
>
> fuyu | no | asahi | no | aware | narikeri
> winter | 's | morning-sun | 's | deeply-moving | be!
>
> (Bashō)

The second verse has no haikai either in diction or in spirit. But the manner in which the second verse joins with the opening verse to function like a single waka is haikai. Haikai can be either in the diction or in the spirit. It can also be found in the construction [*sakui*]. Do not believe that haikai derives from any single element. (NBKZ 51: 524–25)

The first criterion, that of words, reiterates the position taken by Teitoku, who had defined haikai as linked verse with haikai words. "A willow in spring rain" (*harusame no yanagi*), an elegant phrase from classical poetry, represents classical renga; "A crows that plucks a mud snail" (*tanishi toru karasu*), a vernacular phrase, represents haikai. As an example of construction (*sakui*), Bashō cites the opening verses of the fifth sequence (*kasen*) in *Winter Days*, in which a hokku by Kakei ends with the continuative auxiliary verb *te*, a convention usually found in the third verse (*daisanku*) but never in an opening verse. The second verse by Bashō likewise violates the standard practice of ending with a nominal (*taigendome*) by ending with the copula predicate *narikeri*. Most important, the hokku and the second verse come together to form a single waka, contrary to the conventions of linked verse.

Bashō also asserts that haikai may lie in the spirit (*kokoro*) or attitude of the poetic persona, which, in Bashō's hokku cited above, is embodied in the seemingly eccentric desire of the speaker to travel to Lake Biwa during the wet season to see the grebe's floating nest, which was made of waterweed and floated up and down during the long summer rains. This notion of haikai spirit was embodied, at least for Bashō in the mid-1680s, in the notion of poetic madness (*fū-kyō*)—literally "madness" (*kyō*) in pursuit of "art" (*fū*)—which became a cornerstone of Bashō's poetics during his *Skeleton in the Fields* journey of 1684 to Nagoya.

> market shoppers!
> let me sell you this hat
> full of snow

> ichibito|yo|kono|kasa|urō|yuki|no|kasa
> market-buyers|!|this|hat|sell|snow|'s|hat[22]
> (NKBZ 41: 295)

In a comic style reminiscent of the speech of a *kyōgen* (comic drama) actor, the speaker offers to sell a hat piled with snow. Such a hat is priceless to the poet, who prizes snow, a major object of poetic beauty, but worthless to merchants dealing in material goods. In a haikai-esque inversion, the useless becomes valuable.

The mad (*fūkyō*) poet in Bashō's poetic world is inebriated not only, as he is here, by snow, moon, and cherry blossoms—the classical seasonal motifs—but also by darker images such as withering winds (*kogarashi*), winter showers (*shigure*), and objects that were "withered" (*kare*), "chilled" (*hie*), and "meager" (*yase*), a *wabi* aesthetic developed by medieval poets.[23] This aspect of Bashō's poetic madness is revealed most dramatically in Bashō's fondness for winter showers (*shigure*)—the thin, silver lines of early winter rain that disappear as quickly as they appear—on which Bashō composed at least nineteen verses.[24] Sōgi's (1421–1502) famous hokku in *New Tsukuba Collection* (*Shinsen tsukuba shū*; 1495), which puns on the word *furu* ("to fall" and "to pass one's life"), draws on the traditional association of winter showers with uncertainty and impermanence.[25]

> life in this world:
> just like a temporary shelter
> from a winter shower

yo | ni | furu | mo | sarani | shigure | no | yadori | kana
world | life | in | fall | spend | also | especially | winter-shower | 's | shelter | !

Sōgi alludes to a winter poem by Nijō-no-in no Sanuki (d. ca. 1217) in the *Shinkokinshū* (1205; Winter, no. 590).

Yo ni furu wa	Life in this world
kurushiki mono o	is so difficult,
maki no ya ni	and yet the first winter shower
yasuku mo suguru	passes over the black-pine house
hatsushigure kana	so easily!

Like Sanuki's poem, Sōgi's verse laments the difficulties of life—most specifically the Ōnin War (1467–77), which was devastating the country at the time—but in contrast to Sanuki, who finds comfort in the ease with which the first winter shower comes and goes, for Sōgi, the winter shower and the temporary shelter become metaphors for the darkness and transience of human life. In the following haibun called "Crafting a Hat" ("Kasa hari") Bashō parodies Sōgi's verse.

> When I grow weary of living alone in my grass hut and the autumn wind sounds lonely, I borrow Myōkan's sword and, imitating the Bamboo Cutter, cut pieces of bamboo, bend them, and call myself the Old Maker of Hats. Having little skill, I am unable to finish a hat even if I devote an entire day to it. Short on patience, I grow tired as the days pass. In the morning, I stretch paper over the bamboo; and in the evening I dry it and stretch on more paper. I dye the hat with persimmon dye, apply lacquer, and wait for it to harden. After twenty days, it is finally finished. The hat slopes down and turns inward and outward at the edges so that it resembles a half-opened lotus leaf. Its form is more interesting than a perfectly balanced hat. Is it the shabby hat that Saigyō wore? Or the hat that Su Tung-p'o put on his head? Shall I travel to see the dew on Miyagi field? Or shall I take my walking cane to see the snows of distant Wu? As my heart quickens at the thought of falling snow pellets and I wait impatiently for the winter showers, I find myself admiring the hat and finding special pleasure in it. In my excitement, I suddenly have a thought. Drenching myself once more in Sōgi's winter shower, I take up my brush and write on the inside of the hat.

> life in this world:
> just like a temporary shelter
>   of Sōgi's!

yo|ni|furu|mo|sarani|Sōgi|no|yadori|kana
world|in|rain/live|also|especially|Sōgi|'s|lodge|!²⁶
(NKBZ 41: 553–54)

The poetic madness emerges not only in the poet's child-like purity of spirit but also in the manner in which the poet treats material objects as poetic signs. The misshapen hat (*kasa*), which reminds Bashō of the hats worn by such poets as Su Tung-p'o, Saigyō, and Sōgi, becomes a medium—much like the grass hut and the Japanese plantain—through which the poet communes playfully with the "ancients." In a haikai twist, the winter showers, which traditionally deepen the feeling of sorrow and transience, enable Bashō to be like

Sōgi, a literary experience that brings him joy and pleasure. *Shigure*, in other words, becomes the medium through which the poet, in seemingly mad fashion, travels across time to join the "ancients."[27]

Perhaps the most famous and influential *shigure* poem is the following hokku by Bashō, which stands at the beginning of *Monkey's Straw Coat (Sarumino)* and after which Bashō's most important haikai anthology is named.

> first winter shower—
> the monkey too seems to desire
>   a small straw coat

hatsushigure | saru | mo | komino | o | hoshige | nari
first-winter-shower | monkey | too | small-straw-coat | (acc.) | seems-to-desire | is

In both the Japanese and the Chinese poetic traditions, the wrenching cries of the monkey echoed the sorrow and vicissitudes of the lonely traveler.[28] In *Gathered Gems (Renju gappeki shū)*, the renga handbook by Kaneyoshi, for example, the monkey is associated with "tree leaves," "screaming," "moistening the robe (with tears)," "mountain gorge," and "misery."[29] Bashō's famous hokku appears to follow these classical associations, but in a haikai twist, Bashō replaces the mournful voice with a human-like figure who seems to desire a "small straw coat" (*komino*), a miniature version of the traveler's *mino*, so as to be able to seek protection from and frolic in the first winter shower. The *hatsu* (first) in *hatsushigure* (first winter shower)—as in the *hatsu* in *hatsuhana* (first cherry blossoms)—here suggests the excitement and sense of anticipation felt by both the poet and the monkey. Like the *kasa* (hat), the straw coat (*mino*) protects the traveler from the rain and snow even as it serves as a means of poetic communion with the winter shower, which, while unpleasant and cold in the classical tradition, becomes an object of *fūkyō* desire. Bashō, in short, transforms the classical monkey into a haikai monkey, into a comic projection of the *fūkyō* poet himself, thereby creating a poem that is at once light and dark, humorous and sorrowful.

Both in origin and by definition, haikai was an oppositional poetics. In the mid-1680s Bashō reconceived that poetics in terms of a dramatic persona, the recluse or perpetual traveler. Haikai had been labeled "crazy verse" (*kyōku*), as opposed to classical linked verse (*ushin renga*). The names of a number of other Japanese literary gen- res—comic waka (*kyōka*), comic prose (*kyōbun*), comic Chinese po- etry (*kyōshi*) and comic drama (*kyōgen*)—also begin with the charac- ter for "madness" (*kyō*). Each of these literary forms emerged as a popular, comic, and deviant counterpart to an established, officially sanctioned, or aristocratic literary genre—*waka*, Chinese prose (*kan- bun*) and classical prose (*wabun*), Chinese poetry (*kanshi*), and Noh drama—which it parodied or worked against. Here that oppositional stance, which Bashō infused with *wabi* aesthetics and the Taoist phi- losophy and humor of *Chuang tzu*, is embodied in a poetic persona who stands outside society and its values or who madly pursues po- etic and spiritual goals.[30] The Bashō circle, which came to regard this attitude as an integral part of the haikai spirit, called such poets "mad recluses" (*kyōinja*), "masters of crazy verse" (*kyōka no saishi*), "mad guests" (*kyōkaku*), "mad people" (*kyōsha*), and "mad priests" (*kyōsō*).[31] Whether Bashō actually led the life of a recluse is question- able. He was successful, however, at creating a distinctive serio- comic persona who embodied the haikai spirit in his actions and thoughts.

Double Vision

Another characteristic of Bashō's poetry in the renga-style period is double vision (*mitate*), in which the speaker or poetic persona simultaneously sees, often in borrowed landscape (*shakkei*) form, two intersecting landscapes, usually one contemporary and another foreign or distant, usually as a result of an allusive variation (*hon- kadori*) on a classical poem. Fujiwara Teika (1162–1241), the great pioneer of allusive variation and its foremost practitioner, borrowed phrases from texts that he considered the Japanese classics—such as *Kokinshū*, *The Tales of Ise*, and *The Tale of Genji*—to generate a particular aesthetic, classical atmosphere as well as to create complex tonal and imagistic effects. For Teika, allusive variation offered a means of liberating himself from the world around him, entering into the elegant and often sensual world of Heian literature, and taking on the persona and lyric sensibility of imaginary figures in that world. By contrast, allusive variation enabled Bashō to juxtapose past and present, to bring together classical, Chinese, and contemporary landscapes. In the early 1680s, that other world was usually China, whereas in the mid-1680s, in the Jōkyō and Genroku eras, when Bashō began to travel to the Kamigata area and then to the Tōhoku region, it also became the imagined landscape of medieval Japan, as in the following poem on Yoshino, a noted poetic place (*utamakura*), which appears in *Skeleton in the Fields*, the travel diary that commemorates Bashō's journey in 1684.

> Alone, I traveled deep into the hills of Yoshino, where the mountains were high, the white clouds covered the peaks, and the smoky rain buried the valley. Here and there were the small houses of the woodcutters: the sound of a tree being cut in the west echoed in the east; the sound of the temple bells sunk deep into the heart. Many of those, who, from the distant past, have entered these hills, leaving the world behind, took refuge in Chinese and Japanese poetry. Indeed, it would be correct to call this Mount Lu in China.

> Lodging for a night at a temple inn.

> strike the fulling block
> let me hear it!
> temple mistress

> kinuta | uchite | ware | ni | kikase | yo | bō | ga | tsuma
> fulling block | strike | me | to | let-hear | ! | temple | 's | mistress
> (NKBZ 41: 292–93)

In the classical tradition, the fulling block, a stone or wooden plank on which cloth was pounded with a wooden mallet to soften and bring out the luster of the fabric, was associated with autumn evenings, loneliness, thoughts of a distant home, longing for the past, as in the following *Shinkokinshū* (1205; Autumn II, no. 483) poem by Fujiwara Masatsune to which Bashō alludes.

On striking the fulling block

miyoshino no	The autumn winds
yama no akikaze	in the hills of Yoshino
sayo fukete	growing late with the night:
furusato samuku	in the old capital
koromo utsu nari	the cold sound of pounded cloth.

In Bashō's hokku, the speaker, in seemingly mad fashion, asks the priest's wife to strike a fulling block, which was no longer used in the seventeenth century, to make him feel lonelier and thus closer to the poetic essence of Yoshino.

Bashō's haikai predecessors Teitoku and Sōin also relied heavily on allusive variation, but their approach differed significantly from Bashō's, as the following hokku (NKBZ 42: 83) by Sōin reveals.

gazing at
the cherry blossoms
   I hurt my neck bone

nagamu|to|te|hana|ni|mo|itashi|kubi|no|hone
gaze|so|thinking|flower|at|also|hurt|neck|'s|bone

Sōin alludes to the following poem by Saigyō in the *Shinkokinshū* (Spring II, no. 126).

nagamu to te	Thinking to gaze at them,
hana ni mo itaku	I grew extremely close
narenureba	to the cherry blossoms,
chiru wakare koso	making the scattered parting
kanashikarikere	ever so painful.

Sōin exploded the serious tone and content of the foundation poem: the classical word *itashi* (extremely) becomes the haikai word *itashi* (it hurts), and the sorrow of parting is replaced by neck pain from gazing up at the cherry blossoms too long. In contrast to Teika's allusive variations, in which the poet escapes from the harsh realities of Kamakura society into the imaginary world of Heian literature, or Sōin's hokku, which dismantles the classical waka and vulgarizes the foundation poem, Bashō's poem generates a hybrid vision in which the classical world of Yoshino and the contemporary world of the temple mistress (*bō ga tsuma*), a haikai phrase, occupy the same space, allowing the contemporary poet to enter into an implicit dialogue with the "ancients," the noted poets of the past. If, in Teimon and Danrin haikai, the link between the classical and the contemporary worlds was often homophonic, based on lexical associations, in Bashō's haikai from the mid-1680s that link becomes largely visionary.

Genroku Landscape Poetry

Haikai in the Genroku period was dominated by the landscape (*keiki*) style, which focused on the scenic presentation of the external world, especially nature and the countryside,[32] and which was part of the larger trend toward naturalistic depiction found in Genroku vernacular fiction. This landscape style represented a return to an orthodox style of classical poetry as well as to a style of classical linked verse. Early medieval waka treatises referred to this style as *keikyoku* or *miru yō* (things as they appear) style. In *Secrets of Renga* (*Renri hishō*; 1349), Nijō Yoshimoto (d. 1388), one of the founders of renga, included the *keiki* style as one of the established styles of classical renga.[33] The Genroku *keiki* style was also characterized by "links by landscape" (*keiki-zuke*), in which each verse was linked to the next by scenic extension, as opposed to verses closely tied by wordplay, homophones, or established poetic associations.

One characteristic of the landscape style, particularly in Bashō's haikai, was that it often infused the external landscape (*kei*) with human emotion or sentiment (*jō*)—a fusion influenced both by the medieval waka tradition and by the Chinese poetry that came into fashion in the 1680s. In *Chinese Poetry for Beginners*, Kaibara Ekiken noted: "In poetry, the scene [*kei*] is always in the emotion [*jō*], and the emotion is always in the scene." In *Haikai Ten Discussions* (*Haikai jūron*; 1719), Shikō, one of Bashō's late disciples, developed this notion into one of the central tenets of the Bashō style, using the famous frog poem, composed in 1686, as an example.

> an old pond ...
> a frog leaps in,
>   the sound of water

Truly, when it comes to what is called contemporary haikai, one sees the image [*sugata*] of the frog in the old pond. Although it appears that the poem possesses absolutely no emotion [*jō*], Bashō has managed to suggest the emotion [*fuzei*] of quiet loneliness [*sabishisa*]. This is what is called the overtones [*yosei*] of poetry. Isn't this what haikai is all about?"[34]

Sugata is an image that suggests emotion without stating it. Here the sound of water rising from an old pond implies a larger meditative, lonely silence as well as the attentive eye and ear of an observing recluse. In *Haikai Ten Discussions*, Shikō wrote, "In the poetry of the present, one sees the *sugata* with one's eyes and leaves the emotions outside the words [*gengo no soto*]."[35]

If Genroku landscape haikai embraced the contemporary world of commoners and samurai, the connotative sentiments, at least in Bashō's haikai from the late 1680s, were often drawn from classical or Chinese poetic tradition. It is no accident that the submerged emotion or sentiment in Bashō's landscape poetry sometimes takes the form of what is referred to as *sabi*, in which the landscape—such as that in the famous frog poem—is infused with the sentiment of quiet loneliness (*sabishisa*), a negative term that implicitly takes on positive value. Bashō did not define the term *sabi*, but his disciples, especially Kyorai, elaborated on the notion, albeit in garbled form.[36] In *Kyoraishō* (Kyorai's gleanings; 1704), Kyorai elaborated:

Yamei asked, "What is the meaning of the *sabi* of a verse?"

Kyorai answered, "*Sabi* is the complexion of the verse. It does not mean a quiet and lonely verse. For example, when an elderly man puts on helmet and armor and enters the battlefield, or when he wears a beautiful uniform and attends a banquet for nobles, he still has the form [*sugata*] of an old man. The same is true of *sabi*, which exists in both brilliant verses and in quiet verses. Let me give one example.

> cherry blossom guardians
> their white heads
>   bumping together

hanamori | ya | shiroki | kashira | o | tsukiawase[37]
cherry-guardians | ! | white | head | (acc.) | bumping-together

The Master said of this poem, "The complexion of *sabi* clearly manifests itself. That pleases me." (NKBZ 51: 512–13)[38]

Although the physical body of the old man who dresses in armor or wears a colorful uniform at a banquet may be completely hidden, the observer can still sense the figure of the old man. *Sabi* is suggested in the "complexion" of the verse, as opposed to the conception, diction, or subject matter.[39] In the hokku by Kyorai, cherry blossoms imply brilliance, fragrance, and splendor, but the image of the elderly guardians huddled together, their white heads bumping, suggests the loneliness of old age.

If *sabi* implied a sense of quiet, meditative loneliness, *shiori*, another emotional overtone, suggested a sensitivity toward a weak or delicate object, particularly a feeling of pathos (*aware*).[40] This sense of pathos, like that of *sabi*, is not expressed directly but instead emerges "outside the words," in the overtones (*yosei*). According to *Kyoraishō* (NKBZ 51: 514), Bashō praised the following hokku by Kyoriku for possessing *shiori*.

> even the Ten Dumplings
> have turned to crumbs—
>   autumn winds

tōdango | mo | kotsubu | ni | narinu | aki | no | kaze
ten-dumplings | also | crumb | to | turn | autumn | 's | wind[41]

The tea shops at Utsunoyama (Utsu Mountain), one of the difficult passes on the Tōkaidō (Eastern Highway) in Suruga (Shizuoka), were famous for their Ten Dumplings (*tōdango*, a haikai word), small dumplings sold in units of ten skewered on a stick or string.

The hokku suggests that the mountain villages, which made their living by selling special products to travelers, are now in straitened circumstances, causing even their famous dumplings to become smaller. The implied sense of pathos and disappointment is echoed by the "winds of autumn" (*aki no kaze*), a classical phrase associated with loneliness.

Shiori and *sabi* often appear as a pair and are sometimes referred to collectively as *sabi*. Together they represent an attitude of restraint and understatement, which has roots in the medieval poetic and aesthetic tradition, particularly *wabi* tea and "no-mind" (*mushin*) Noh drama as it evolved under Zeami (1363–1443). As Zeami noted, "If what you feel in the heart is ten, what appears should be seven."[42] The two terms, particularly *shiori*, also suggest the spiritual attitude of the poet, which was characteristic of medieval poetics but rarely, if ever, a consideration in earlier haikai. According to *Kyoraishō* (NKBZ 51: 464), *shiori* must be cultivated by the poet and allowed to emerge naturally in the verse. *Sanzōshi* states, "If one attempts to create *shiori*, one will not have *shiori*."

Bashō's ability to discover and draw out such poetic overtones—particularly loneliness, pathos, and emotional uncertainty—from seventeenth-century provincial culture and languages is most evident in the haikai in *Monkey's Straw Coat*. The following (verses 25–26) appears in the *kasen In the Town* (*Ichinaka wa*).

> quietly making
> straw sandals beneath
> the moonlight
> —Bonchō

kosokoso-to | waraji | o | tsukuru | tsukiyo | sashi
quietly | straw-sandals | (acc.) | make | moonlight | shines

> rising to shake off
> the fleas in early autumn
> —Bashō

nomi | o | furui | ni | okishi | hatsu-aki
flea | (acc.) | shake-off | to | rise-up | early-autumn

In the previous verse, someone, probably a farmer, is quietly making straw sandals beneath the moon. In the added verse, someone (probably a woman), perhaps bitten by fleas while asleep, gets up to shake out her nightgown on an early autumn night. *Hatsu-aki* (early autumn), a classical word traditionally associated with loneliness and tranquillity, endows the sequence, which describes life at the bottom rung of Tokugawa society, with an atmosphere of loneliness, pathos, and meditative depth.

In *Sanzōshi*, Bashō noted: "The value of haikai lies in rectifying everyday words" ("Haikai no eki wa zokugo o tadasu nari"), that is, haikai poets should transform vernacular, popular words into proper language. The word "rectify" (*tadasu*), which has Neo-Confucian connotations, suggests both self-justification, the legitimation of haikai, as well as the appropriation and control of popular language by the dominant sociocultural order. Hokushi's *Dialogue at Yamanaka* (*Yamanaka mondō*), which records Bashō's teachings during his journey to the Interior, explains how this "rectification" is carried out.

> In composing poetry and prose, one must not forget what is called *fūga*, the art of poetry. *Sabi*, *shiori*, *hosomi*, and elegance are *fūga*. Without this understanding, vernacular poetry will become a collection of commonplace words, it will become rude, or vulgar, or it will be trapped by logic, losing the original spirit of haikai. For those pursuing the way of haikai, this is of utmost importance.[43]

Although representing a return to the landscape poetry of medieval waka and of Chinese poetry, the Genroku landscape style drew on a wide range of languages, both classical and vernacular. In Bashō's last years, particularly after his return to Edo in 1691, when he advocated lightness, Bashō in fact deliberately employed vernacular and sometimes colloquial words. The poetics of *sabi* and *shiori* transformed this contemporary language, which was always in danger of becoming vulgar or crude, into *fūga*, or poetry of the highest order; that is, it imbued the new words and topics of haikai with the kind of overtones and sentiments—such as quiet loneliness—hitherto found only in waka or Chinese poetry. Instead of deriving its energy and humor from the collision of classical and vernacular languages or from a comic rupturing of convention or established hierarchy, this kind of haikai sought to bring these disparate languages and topics together in a regenerative fashion, following the poetics of "awakening to the high, returning to the low" (*kōgo kizoku*) in which a heightened spiritual and poetic awareness transfigured contemporary words and topics, thereby offering new life to a greatly expanded poetic tradition.

CHAPTER 4

The Art of Juxtaposition

Cutting and Joining

> Here I lay a spot of red paint down on my canvas. Next I choose a green
> which I dot near it. The red is immediately changed, and so is the green.
> In contrast to the green the red has taken fire, and the green now glows
> inwardly like an emerald. The reaction is mutual.
>
> —Ernest Fenollosa, "The Logic of Art" (1906)

In "The Chinese Written Character as a Medium for Poetry," an
essay edited and published by Ezra Pound in 1919, which some have
called the *Ars poetica* of the twentieth century, Ernest Fenollosa (d.
1908) wrote mistakenly that Chinese characters are, to a greater or
lesser degree, images or visual representations of things they signify.
Ezra Pound transformed this notion of the pictogram into a poetic
method and principle in which the poet juxtaposes different im-
ages—"one idea set on top of another"—so as to create a new matrix
of meaning. This method has been referred to as "asyndetic compo-
sition," in which connectives or conjunctions are omitted, or as a
"paratactic method."[1] In Pound's view, the ideogram method also
imitates perception itself: the poet juxtaposes separate items so that
the reader can reintegrate them in the way that objects and events
are integrated in the normal perception of the external world. The
emphasis is shifted from a static description or representation of ob-
jects to a more presentational or performative form that emphasizes
relations, motion, energy, and action. An example from Pound's
Lustra is:

Swiftly the years beyond recall.
Solemn the stillness of this spring morning.

William Empson, who analyzed this poem at length, noted: "My feelings of transience are held in tension with my desire to linger amid present pleasures, as the flight of time is in tension with the loveliness of this spring morning."[2] What Pound called "super-position" was not simply a contrast or incongruity, or to use Pound's own words, "any decayed cabbage cast upon any pale satin sofa." Instead, as Hugh Kenner has argued, these juxtapositions in-volved an Aristotelian *peripeteia*, an unexpected change in trajec-tory, a process that, as we shall see, is of relevance to understanding the *toriawase*, the hokku that combines different topics.

Haikai imagination, however, differs from the notion of non-representational collage in that it requires a double reading of the text both as a paratactic collage *and* as representational fragments of a larger scene or narrative. Although haiku is often thought to be a snapshot—or a sketch (*shasei*), to use Masaoka Shiki's term—of an existing scene, either real or imagined, the brevity of the hokku pre-cludes the kind of detail or coherence normally associated with de-scriptive representation. The hokku or the successive verses in linked verse can provide only fragments of the represented scene, with the words functioning like dots or broad strokes on a blank canvas. Like the cadenza in pre-Romantic music in which the com-poser leaves part of the music sheet blank for the performer to fill in, the cutting word (*kireji*) in the hokku summons the reader to be an active performer and interpreter, to create and complete the work. In *ikebana*, the art of flower arrangement, the artist, instead of attempting to imitate nature, "cuts" the flower, opening up space that the audience can enter into with his or her imagination. The "cutting word" in the hokku similarly opens up a space that the haikai reader occupies metonymically or synecdochically, by mov-ing from the detail or part to an imagined whole, filling out the scene or the narrative, *and* in montage, collage fashion, by exploring

Painting by Kyoriku; calligraphy and poem—*horohoro to/yamabuki chiru ka/taki no oto* (petal by petal the yellow mountain roses scatter—sound of the rapids)—by Bashō. 12.6 x 20.7 in. The hokku, which was first composed by Bashō in 1688, during his journey to Yoshino, and which was published in *Desolate Fields* (1689), appears in *Backpack Notes* with the headnote, "West River" (Nijikō), a swift section of the upper reaches of the Yoshino River. Kyoriku met Bashō in the fall of 1692, while in Edo on samurai duty, and returned nine months later, in 1693. This painting was done during this short but extremely fruitful period. Signed "Bashō Tōsei." (Courtesy Tenri University Library)

the reverberations and interactions among the different parts. This exploration, as we shall see, was not simply left to the individual imagination but guided by an elaborate system of poetic associations and reading conventions.

From Word Links to Scent Links

The nature of haikai juxtaposition is best understood by examining what Bashō and his disciples described as the three fundamental types of links in haikai: the "word link" (*kotoba-zuke*), "content link" (*kokoro-zuke*), and "scent link" (*nioi-zuke*). *Kyoraishō* notes:

> The Master said, "The hokku has changed repeatedly since the distant past, but there have been only three changes in the nature of the haikai link. In the distant past, poets valued word links. In the more recent past, poets have stressed content links. Today, it is best to link by transference [*utsuri*], reverberation [*hibiki*], scent [*nioi*], or status [*kurai*]." (NKBZ 51: 503)[3]

Bashō associated three historical periods with three types of links: the "distant past" (Teimon haikai) with word links, the "recent past" (Danrin haikai) with "content links," and the present (Bashō school), with transference, reverberation, scent, and status—all of which fall under the broad rubric of "scent link."

"Word links," or "object links" (*mono-zuke*) as they are called in haikai, rely on lexical associations, which range from *yoriai*, established lexical associations based on classical precedent, to *engo*, a freer form of word association (e.g., *ito*, "thread," and *yoru*, "to twist together") that included haikai words or non-classical diction, to homophonic linkage such as *ura*, "bay," and *urami*, "resentment." An example of *yoriai*, the basis of much linking in classical renga, is iris (*kakitsubata*) and Eight Bridges (*Yatsuhashi*), which appear together in a famous episode in *The Tales of Ise*, or "long time ago" (*mukashi*) and "orange blossoms" (*tachibana*), regarded as the flower of memory in classical poetry.

A typical word link in haikai is the opening to *Song, Which One?*

(*Uta izure*)—a solo hundred-verse sequence by Teitoku (NKBZ 32: 469).

> which song is better—
> that of the Komachi Dance?
> the Ise Dance?

uta | izure | Komachi-odori | ya | Ise-odori
song | which | Komachi-dance | Ise-dance

> which Festival of the Dead
> will Tsurayuki return to?

doko | no | bon | ni | ka | oriyaru | Tsurayuki
which | 's | Festival-of-Dead | to | ? | return | Tsurayuki

In the hokku, the speaker cannot decide which of the two popular folk dances—implicitly as equally matched as Ono no Komachi and Lady Ise, two noted Heian women poets—is superior. In the second verse, the speaker wonders which place the spirit of Ki no Tsurayuki (868?–945?), the most noted Heian poet, who can act as a judge, will visit during Bon, the Festival of the Dead. Tsurayuki, Ono no Komachi, and Lady Ise, like Bon and dancing (*odori*), are haikai words linked by *engo* (as opposed to *yoriai*).

The two parts of a hokku could also be linked in similar fashion, as in the following hokku by Teitoku, which appears in *Puppy Collection* (*Enokoshū*; 1633).[4]

> even the spring mist
> rises in spots and patches—
> Year of the Tiger

kasumi | sae | madara | ni | tatsu | ya | tora | no | toshi
spring-mist | even | spots-patches | with | rises | ! | tiger | 's | year
(KHT 1: 67)

Teitoku links spring mist (*kasumi*), a classical word, to tiger (*tora*), a haikai word, via two homonyms: *madara ni* (in spots and patches), associated with both mist and tiger, and *tatsu* (to stand, rise, begin), a verb for the tiger "getting up," the mist "rising," and the New Year (the seasonal topic) "beginning."[5] In typical haikai fashion, the gap between the classical image (spring mist) and the contemporary vernacular is humorously bridged through puns and lexical associations.

In a "content link," the added verse is joined to the previous verse by cause and effect, narrative development, scenic extension, temporal progression, or any other logical connection based on "content" (*kokoro*).[6] By contrast, the "scent link" relies neither on classical lexical associations nor on narrative connections. Instead, the added verse is joined to the previous verse by shared connotations, carrying the atmosphere of its predecessor much as the fragrance of a flower is carried by the wind. The difference is revealed in two different responses to a hokku composed by Bashō in April 1690 (3.10.Genroku 3).

> beneath the trees
> in the soup, salad, everywhere
> cherry blossoms!
> —Bashō

ko | no | moto | ni | shiru | mo | namasu | mo | sakura | kana
tree | 's | base | at | soup | also | pickled-fish | also | cherry | !

> a spring that brings regrets
> to tomorrow's visitor
> —Fūbaku

asu | kuru | hito | wa | kuyashigaru | haru
tomorrow | come | person | as-for | regret | spring

Apparently dissatisfied with this sequence, which was composed at the residence of Fūbaku in Iga, his home province, Bashō presented the same hokku later that same month in a haikai sequence with two other disciples, Chinseki and Kyokusui (1660–1717), at Zeze, on the south shore of Lake Biwa, and placed the completed 36-verse sequence at the beginning of *Gourd*.

> beneath the trees
> in the soup, salad, everywhere
> cherry blossoms!
> —Bashō

a western sun gently
bringing good weather
        —Chinseki

nishibi | nodoka | ni | yoki | tenki | nari
western-sun | gent | ly | good | weather | is

In the first sequence, the second verse directly expands on the content of the opening verse, establishing a causal relationship between the two, implying that since the cherry blossoms have already fallen, tomorrow's visitors will be disappointed. By contrast, the added verse in the second example is linked to the previous verse primarily through overlapping connotations: both verses share the mood of a balmy spring day. As Shikō, one of Bashō's later disciples, noted in *Explanation of Ten Discussions* (*Jūron'i benshō*; published 1725): "What is called an overtone [*yosei*] in classical poetry is called scent and reverberation in haikai."[7] The poetics of scent, which can be traced to classical poetics, worked with new commoner topics and language, enabling Bashō and his disciples to absorb various elements of classical and medieval poetics—such as the aesthetics of quiet, meditative loneliness (*sabi*)—into popular linked verse even as it broadened and gave new life to the larger poetic tradition.

Combination and Equivalence

The modern linguist Roman Jakobson has argued that in ordinary language words are linked by syntactic constructions, by combination, whereas in poetry there is an added dimension: non-contiguous elements are joined by phonetic equivalences (rhyme, alliteration, etc.), grammatical equivalences, and other types of connotative parallels and contrasts.[8] These two fundamental types of connections—combination and equivalence—correspond roughly to the "content link" and the "scent link." Bashō's haikai are generally a mixture of both types, of narrative or scenic connections *and* non-contiguous parallels and antitheses, as in the opening to the two-poet (*ryōgin*) sequence that Bashō composed with Yaba in Edo

in early 1694 (spring of Genroku 7) and subsequently published in
Charcoal Sack.

>   in the scent of the plum blossoms
> suddenly, the sun comes up—
>   a mountain path
>
> >   —Bashō
>
> ume | ga | ka | ni | notto | hi | no | deru | yamaji | kana
> plum | 's | scent | in | suddenly | sun | 's | appear | mountain-path | !

>   here there pheasants
> crying as they fly away
>
> >   —Yaba
>
> tokorodokoro | ni | kiji | no | nakitatsu
> here-there | at | pheasant | 's | cry-fly-away

In the second verse, the pheasants along the mountain path fly out
from the grass, crying as they flee, apparently surprised at the sound
of the footsteps. The primary function of the second verse (*wakiku*)
was to expand the content of the hokku, the opening verse, main-
taining the same season and filling out and extending the setting. At
the same time, Jakobson's principle of equivalence, like that of a
scent link, is at work. The sharp cries of the pheasants as they scat-
ter and fly out of the grass connotatively echo the startling, bracing
feeling of the sun as it suddenly appears in the early morning amid
the scent of the plum blossoms.

The dynamic of the scent link also appears within the frame of a
single hokku, especially the combination poem. Bashō composed
the following hokku in October 1694, on Chrysanthemum Festival
Day (Chōyō), which fell on the Ninth of the Ninth Month, while
stopping in Nara on the way to Osaka, on his last journey.

>   chrysanthemum scent—
> in Nara ancient statues
>   of the Buddha
>
> kiku | no | ka | ya | Nara | ni | wa | furuki | hotoke | tachi
> chrysanthemum | 's | scent | ! | Nara | in | as-for | ancient | buddha | s

Nara, the capital of Japan in the eighth century when Buddhism flourished as a state religion, was known for its many temples and statues of the Buddha. The hokku can be read as a single scene in which the "many ancient Buddhas" (*furuki hotoketachi*), a haikai phrase, are surrounded by chrysanthemum flowers (*kiku*), a seasonal word for autumn. But the poem is better read as a combination poem in which the two parts are joined by scent or connotative equivalences. The chrysanthemum, considered the aristocrat of flowers in classical poetry, possessed a strong but refined fragrance. The many Buddhas in the ancient capital of Nara evoke a similar sense of dignity, solemnity, and refinement as well as a nostalgia for a bygone era.

Many modern readers, perhaps influenced by mimetic notions of poetry, tend to read Bashō's hokku as the depiction or sketch of a single scene, but as the following passage in *Kyoraishō* suggests, the hokku often started out as part of a combination poem with the poet seeking to find the corresponding or matching part.

> Southern Kyoto—
> on a blanket of snow
>   the evening rain
>   —Bonchō

Shimogyō|ya|yuki|tsumu|ue|no|yoru|no|ame
Southern-Kyoto|:|snow|pile-up|top|'s|evening|'s|rain[9]

> Initially, the opening phrase was missing. Everyone, beginning with the late Master, tried his hand at capping the verse, before the late Master decided on this version. Although Bonchō acquiesced, he did not appear convinced. In response, the late Master said, "Bonchō, cap this verse and reveal your talent! If you can find a better alternative, I will never discuss haikai again." (NKBZ 51: 434–35)

The passage, which shows the dynamics of communal poetry operating even in the composition of a single hokku and Bashō's confidence in the art of linking, reveals that the poet did not begin with the place—Shimogyō, the southern part of Kyoto, from Third Avenue (Sanjō) south—and attempt to describe it. Instead, he started

with an image of rain quietly falling on a blanket of snow and at-
tempted to match its connotations. In contrast to the aristocratic
northern half of Kyoto, southern Kyoto was a bustling, energetic
area filled with merchants and craftsmen, which echoes the warm
feeling of the accumulated snow.

The following hokku, which Bashō composed during his late Dan-
rin and Chinese-style period, in the spring of 1681 (Third Month of
Enpō 9), also appears to present a single scene, though it can simul-
taneously be read as a combination poem on a seasonal topic.

> on a leafless branch
> a crow comes to rest—
>   autumn nightfall

kareeda | ni | karasu | no | tomarikeri | aki | no | kure[10]
leafless-branch | on | crow | 's | stopping | autumn | 's | dusk

Aki no kure—which can be read as either "end of autumn" or "au-
tumn nightfall"—forms the temporal setting for the crow(s) that
have come to rest on a withered branch. In *Eastern Diary (Azuma
nikki*; 1681), a haikai collection edited by Gonsui (1650–1722), the
hokku is preceded by the title "On Evening in Autumn" ("Aki no
kure to wa"), indicating that the poem was initially written on a sea-
sonal topic embodied in the last phrase and closely associated with
Fujiwara Shunzei (d. 1204) and his medieval aesthetics of quiet,
meditative loneliness. Crows perched on a withered branch, on the
other hand, was a popular subject in Chinese ink-painting (*sui-
bokuga*). Bashō's hokku, in short, juxtaposes a medieval waka topic
with a Chinese painting motif, causing the two to resonate in mon-
tage fashion.

The notion of the scent link also informs the relationship be-
tween Bashō's haibun, or haikai prose, and the accompanying
hokku. The following passage comes at the end of *Record of an Un-
real Dwelling (Genjūan no ki*; 1690), considered to be Bashō's model
haibun.

> This is not to say that I sought to escape into the mountains and fields
> out of a love for quiet and loneliness. I am simply like someone who,

growing ill, finds it tiresome to be with people and turns his back on
the world. When I look back over the years, I am painfully reminded of
my shortcomings. I once coveted public office with property. At an-
other time, I decided that I should enter the priesthood. But desiring to
capture the beauty of the birds and beasts, I was swept away by the
floating clouds and drifting winds. For a while that alone was my life.
Now at the end, I cling, without talent or ability, to this one thread: the
art of poetry. Po Chü-i, it is said, exhausted his five organs composing
poetry, and Tu Fu grew lean doing the same. Needless to say, I have
none of their wisdom or poetic talent. But is there anyone who does not
live in an illusory dwelling? With those thoughts, I lie down.

> for now I will turn
> to the large pasania tree—
>   a summer grove

> mazu | tanomu | shii | no | ki | mo | ari | natsu | kodachi |
> first | rely | pasania | 's | tree | also | is | summer | grove
> (NKBZ 41: 504)

The pasania tree, a tall evergreen, stands inside a summer grove
(*natsu kodachi*), which, in the classical tradition, implied a thick,
lush, overgrown cluster of trees. Bashō's hokku alludes to the fol-
lowing classical poem by Saigyō (*Sankashū*, no. 1401), which sug-
gests that the speaker is a bird coming to rest on a pasania.

narabi ite	Always side by side,
tomo to hanarenu	never parting from its mate,
kogarame no	the small sparrows seek
negura ni tanomu	out a nest in the lower
shii no shitaeda	branches of the pasania.

In the fashion of a scent link, the mood of weariness expressed by
Bashō in the prose is echoed in the image of the bird, a symbol of
the perpetual traveler, coming to rest in a grove of thick lush trees.
(The haibun is also a greeting to Kyokusui, represented by the large
tree, thanking him for lending Bashō a relaxing dwelling that has al-
lowed him to recover from his long journey through the Interior.)
The prose does not, as in Heian poem-tales (*uta-monogatari*) or
other prose fiction, elaborate on the circumstances of composition.

Nor does it explain the meaning or significance of the poem. Instead, the prose and the hokku are juxtaposed in montage fashion, forcing the reader to leap from the prose to the poetry and back.

The dynamic of the scent link can be found in a variety of traditional Japanese arts, from architecture to flower arrangement, and forms part of the larger aesthetics of overtones. In the *gasan* (literally, praise of a painting), or more specifically, the *haigasan* (praise of a haikai painting), the practice of adding haikai poetry or prose to an open area in a painting, usually to complement it—a practice inherited from medieval ink paintings (*suibokuga*)—the haikai painting (*haiga*) could illustrate the poem or present a scenic or narrative extension of it, as in a content link, or vice versa. At other times, however, the relationship between the painting and the poem was more distant, like a "scent link," in which the two different forms were joined only by shared connotations. Buson, one of the great masters of haiga, believed that the distant, scent link between painting and poem should be the ideal of haikai painting.[11]

Transference, Reverberation, and Status Links

Bashō and his disciples divided the scent link into various subcategories: transference (*utsuri*), reverberation (*hibiki*), status (*kurai*), and scent (*nioi*) in the narrow sense. The last meant quiet, meditative, and usually lonely, overtones, as in the following sequence in *In the Town* (*Ichi naka wa*), a 36-verse sequence in *Monkey's Straw Coat.*

> a priest growing cold
> as he returns to a temple?
> > —Bonchō
>
> sō | yaya | samuku | tera | ni | kaeru | ka
> priest | gradually | cold | temple | to | return | ?
>
> > monkey trainer
> > spending his life with a monkey—
> > > autumn moon
> > > > —Bashō

saruhiki|no|saru|to|yo|o|furu|aki|no|tsuki
monkey-trainer|'s|monkey|with|life|(acc.)|pass|autumn|'s|moon

The priest is not necessarily walking on the same road as the monkey trainer. Instead the two verses are linked primarily by the quiet solitude and sadness of those—a priest and a monkey trainer—who stand outside the warm embrace of society. A reverberation link, by contrast, implies an excited, dramatic mood, an emotional intensity and tension. *Kyoraishō* explains:

> A reverberation link is like hitting an object so that it reverberates. For example,
>
> on a veranda
> smashing to bits
>   a silver-glazed bowl
>
> kure'en|ni|gin-kawarake|o|uchikudaki
> veranda|on|silver-glazed-bowl|(acc.)|smash
>
> look at the arch
> in the slender sabre!
>
> mihosoki|tachi|no|soru|koto|o|miyo
> slender|sabre|'s|arch|it|(acc.)|look!
>
> The Master gave this link as an example, his right hand pretending to smash a bowl and his left hand pretending to draw a sabre. (NKBZ 51: 504)

In the first verse someone smashes a decorative, silver-glazed bowl on a mansion veranda, suggesting a dispute in an upper-class setting. This dramatic tension reverberates in the added verse, in which a slender sabre, the type worn by aristocrats, is drawn, presumably in preparation for a violent confrontation. A hokku example of a reverberation would be the following, which Bashō composed in September 1688 (Eighth Month of Jōkyō 5), during the journey to Obasuteyama (Abandoned-Old-Women Mountain) in present-day Nagano Prefecture, on the way back to Edo. The poem is recorded at the end of *Journey to Sarashina*.

sinking into the body
bitterness of the white radish—
    winds of autumn

mi | ni | shimite | daikon | karashi | aki | no | kaze
body | in | pierce | radish | bitter | autumn | 's | wind

The bitterness of the large white radish (*daikon*), which "sinks into the body," reverberates with "winds of autumn," which similarly cut into the body of the speaker. The whiteness, the semi-translucence of the *daikon*, also resonates with "winds of autumn," traditionally referred to as "colorless wind" (*iro naki kaze*). In a haikai twist, the white radish, a vernacular word, injects new life into the fatigued metaphor of "winds of autumn," a classical topic that in turn transforms the lowly *daikon* into a poetic image.

Utsuri, sometimes written with the graph for "transference" 移り and sometimes with that for "reflection" 映り, is another subcategory of the "scent link." When written with the graph for "transference," it implies a link in which the mood moves in one direction, from the previous verse to the added verse, as *Sanzōshi* observes:

    "Look at the moon!"
    the embarrassment
        of being awakened

tsuki | miyo | to | hikiokosarete | hazukashiki
moon | look | saying | pulled-and-woken-up | embarrassing

    having her hair fanned,
    dew on a silk robe

kami | aogasuru | usumono | no | tsuyu[12]
hair | have-fanned | thin-silk-robe | 's | dew

The appearance of the person in the previous verse is transferred to the second verse, which depicts a lady-in-waiting. (NKBZ 51: 585)

In the first verse, which evokes a scene from a Heian romance (*monogatari*), someone is shaken from sleep—probably a woman asked by a lover to enjoy the beautiful moon—and feels embarrassed. This soft, erotic mood is "transferred" to the second verse, where a court lady, wearing only a thin silk robe, is having her attendants fan her hair dry. When written with the graph for "reflection," *utsuri* suggests that the connotations of the previous verse and the added verse "reflect" upon each other, thereby deepening the connotations of both.[13]

Another variation on the poetics of scent is the status link in which the two verses are joined by socioeconomic connotations, usually based on clothing, possessions, or other material signs. *Kyoraishō* notes:

> Bonen asked, "What is a status link?"
>
> Kyorai answered, "When one grasps the social status found in the previous verse and adds an appropriate verse. Even if the added verse is superb, if it does not match the social status found in the previous verse, the result will be disharmony. Allow me to explain, using a love verse by the Master.[14]

> even while chopping
> the dried vegetables
>   her heart was aflutter

> uwaoki | no | hoshina | kizamu | mo | uwa | no | sora
> topping | 's | dried-vegetable | chop | also | above | 's | sky[15]

> when the horse stays in
> the groom makes love at home

> uma | ni | denu | hi | wa | uchi | de | koisuru
> horse | on | not-leave | day | as-for | inside | at | make-love

> In the first verse, the woman is neither a proper wife nor a female attendant in the house of a samurai or townsman. She is a maid working at a post station or a warehouse. (NKBZ 51: 504–5)

Dried vegetables (*hoshina*)—probably dried radish leaves—were placed on top of a bowl of rice to make an inexpensive dinner. Realizing from the nature of the food that the character in the preceding verse was a woman of extremely low station, perhaps a maid working in a warehouse, Bashō matched her with a groom, a man of equally low social stature. An example from the *In the Town* (*Ichi naka wa*) sequence in *Monkey's Straw Coat* is:

suffering the winters
at Nanao in Noto
—Bonchō

Noto|no|Nanao|no|fuyu|wa|sumiuki
Noto|'s|Nanao|'s|winter|as-for|living-difficult

  growing old
sucking the bones
  of a fish
    —Bashō

uo|no|hone|shiwaburu|made|no|oi|o|mite
fish|'s|bone|suck|until|'s|old-age|(acc.)|meeting

The figure of the old man, who has lost his teeth and can only suck on fishbones, echoes the implied social circumstances, provincial and impoverished, of the people of Noto, where the local inhabitants have difficulty surviving the harsh winters.

The terms used by Bashō's disciples can be confusing and are frequently indistinguishable. Sometimes the term "scent link" is used to refer to the general poetics of scent, including reverberation and other Bashō-style links, and sometimes it refers to scent in the narrow sense, implying a link based on a sense of loneliness or quietude. *Utsuri* can refer to either the general principle of reflection, or more specifically the notion of transferring a mood or emotion from one verse to the next. Furthermore, a scent link, reverberation, and transference may simultaneously be status links. The silver-painted bowl on the mansion veranda, for example, echoes the socioeconomic implications of the slender sword, which were worn only by aristocrats. In all instances, however, the successive verses were linked, not by close word associations or narrative extension, but by intersecting connotations that emerged from the juxtaposed imagery and that were drawn from a combination of classical and vernacular words.

Modern film terminology, particularly the notion of the montage, can be helpful in analyzing the dynamics of linking. Each verse in a linked verse sequence may be compared to a "shot" (a single un-interrupted action of a camera, the smallest functional unit of film-making), and the combination of previous verse (*maeku*) and added verse (*tsukeku*) to what is called the "scene," a series of shots that the viewer perceives as taken at the same location. Like shots in film, verses may be classified into an extreme long shot, a long shot, a medium shot, a close-up, or an extreme close-up. In a typical content link an extreme long shot of the hills and mist may be followed by an extreme close-up of the dew on the grass; or a medium shot of a samurai on a horse could be followed by a close-up of the clothing or the sword. The scent link and its various subcategories, by contrast, resemble what S. M. Eisenstein, who was in fact influenced by the dynamics of Japanese haiku, called "montage by association," the reinforcement of the meaning of one image by another image that is not necessarily part of the same episode. The filmic equivalent of a reverberation would be a juxtaposition of a shot of an explosion rocking a brick building and a shot of sleepy-faced lion suddenly roaring. A cinematic transference would be a shot of a couple kissing followed by a shot of an avocado being peeled: the second shot is "colored" by the first, given a definite sexual resonance. A status link would be the juxtaposition of a shot of a garbage pail and that of a beggar in a park, or a shot of a lady in a fur coat followed by one of a Rolls-Royce.

The first part of the hokku often establishes a broad temporal or spatial frame (long shot), which is followed by a close-up or extreme close-up in the second part, moving from the general to the specific, or from large to small, as in the following hokku, which Bashō composed in December 1684 (11th Month of Jōkyō 1), while visiting the Ise area with Bokuin (1646–1725) during the *Skeleton in the Fields* journey to Nagoya and the Kansai area.

> early dawn—
> whitefish, an inch
> of whiteness

akebono | ya | shirauo | shiroki | koto | issun
dawn | ! | whitefish | white | ness | one-inch

Drawing on the phonic overtones of *shirauo* (literally "white fish"), a seasonal word for spring but here winter because of the "inch," Bashō establishes a connotative correspondence between the semi-translucent, pale "whiteness" (*shiroki koto*) of the tiny fish and the faint light of early dawn (*akebono*). The first draft of this hokku was:

> thin snow—
> whitefish, an inch
>   of whiteness

> yuki | usushi | shirauo | shiroki | koto | issun
> snow | thin | whitefish | white | ness | one-inch

The correspondence between the implied whiteness of the thin snow and the implied whiteness of the *shirauo* fish was probably too obvious or too close. In the revised version, which also beongs to the spring season, the dim light (a kind of whiteness) resonates more subtly, as in a scent link, with the pale color of the fish. The revised version also has a more striking melody, resulting from the repeated "o" vowel (akebono ya/shirauo shiroki/koto issun) mixing with the consonantal "s."

Sometimes the relationship between the two parts of the hokku resembles a metaphorical montage, as when Eisenstein juxtaposes a shot of workers being gunned down with one of oxen being slaughtered or a shot of a Russian prime minister with that of a peacock. The following hokku, which Bashō composed in May 1688 (4.11.Jō-kyō 5), appears in *Backpack Notes*.

> On the road:

> exhausted,
> time to find a lodging—
>   hanging wisteria

> kutabirete | yado | karu | koro | ya | fuji | no | hana
> exhausted | inn | lodge | time | : | wisteria | 's | flower

The exhaustion of a traveler at the end of the day is reflected in the wisteria (*fuji no hana*), with its long drooping flowers. The relationship between the parts differs, however, from the standard metaphor, of B as a vehicle for understanding the tenor A, in that A and B are metonymically linked, as in a content link, by scenic extension even as they stand in a metaphorical relationship to each other. The wisteria is blooming outside the lodge even as it echoes the traveler's heart.

Cutting and Joining

The cutting word (*kireji*), a requirement of the hokku, often gave the hokku the dynamics of two linked verses within the confines of a seventeen-syllable hokku. As Bashō observed in *Sanzōshi*: "A verse without a cutting word does not have the form of a hokku, or opening verse. Instead, it takes the shape of an added verse. Even if a cutting word is added to the hokku, it may still take the form of an added verse. These are verses that have not been truly cut" (NKBZ 51: 531).

Classical renga developed a tradition of eighteen cutting words, which became the standard for haikai:

> Kana, mogana, zo, ka, yo, ya, keri, ran, tsu, nu, zu (su), ji, se, re, he, ke, ikani, shi.

Kana, mogana, zo, ka, yo, and *ya* are sentence-ending particles or adverbial particles; *keri, ran, tsu, nu, zu (su),* and *ji* are auxiliary verbs; and *se, re, he,* and *ke* imperative verb endings. *Ikani* (how) is a speculative adverb, and *shi* an adjectival ending. Tokugawa haikai handbooks such as Kigin's *Haikai Buried Tree* (*Haikai umoregi*; 1656, published 1673) added more cutting words, but the hokku in Edo haikai collections rarely stray from the eighteen *kireji* found in renga.

The cutting word usually came at the end of the first phrase (first five syllables), at the end of the second phrase (middle seven syllables), or at the end of the third phrase (last five syllables). The cutting word at the end of the hokku, such as the familiar emphatic *kana*, brings the reader back to the beginning, initiating a circular pattern.[16] In English haiku, or translations into English, where the visual line remains an indispensable unit of the English poetic tradition, the visual spacing, usually units of two or three lines, carries out the cutting function that the *kireji* often performs in Japanese.

The Japanese hokku was normally written or printed in one line, or more precisely, without lines, with the calligraphic version often broken out into arbitrary units, but the poet remained keenly aware of the three phrases (5/7/5), which gave the hokku a rhythm and a slight accent at the beginning of each phrase, particularly in conjunction with the cutting word, which added a pause or silent syllable at the point of the cut. This 5/7/5 rhythm could work with or against the grammatical structure and the semantic flow of the hokku, producing the kind of enjambment found in the following poem by Bashō, where the grammatical structure of 5/9/3 syllables moves against the 5/7/5 rhythm, resulting in an accent on both the word *koto* (white-*ness*) and the last 3 syllables (*issun*, "one inch").

5 syllables	7 syllables		5 syllables	
akebono ya	shirauo	shiroki	koto	issun
early dawn!	whitefish	white	ness	one-inch
5 syllables	9 syllables			3 syllables

The cutting-word had the paradoxical function of both cutting and joining, of allowing for both Jakobson's combination and his equivalence. In Teimon haikai, for example, the cutting word frequently functioned as a "judgment" (*handan*) in which the grammatical subject was set off by the particle *wa* and was followed by a predicate and an exclamatory cutting word *kana* at the end, thereby equating the two parts, as in the following hokku from *Puppy Collection*.[17]

> falling snow—
> hairs of the willow
> turned white
> —Shigeyori

furu | yuki | wa | yanagi | no | kami | no | shiraga | kana
falling | snow | as-for | willow | 's | hair | 's | white-hair | !

The cutting word not only separates the hokku into two parts, it establishes a visual correspondence (*mitate*) between the two images, implying that the latter represents the haikai essence of the former, a classical topic.

In the following hokku, which Bashō composed in August 1694 (6.24.Genroku 7) during his stay at Kyorai's Rakushisha in Saga, in the west of Kyoto, the cutting word functions as a marker of equivalence. The exclamatory particle *ya* that follows "Sixth Month" (*rokugatsu*) transforms the first phrase into an independent subject/predicate sentence, something like "It is the Sixth Month" or "It must be the Sixth Month!" At the same time, the cutting word implies that the second part embodies the poetic essence of the seasonal topic in the first part.

> the Sixth Month—
> high clouds sit on the peak
>   of Arashi Mountain

Rokugatsu | ya | mine | ni | kumo | oku | Arashiyama
Sixth-Month | : | peak | at | cloud | lies | Arashi-mountain

In the classical tradition, the "poetic essence" (*hon'i*) of the Sixth Month was unbearable summer heat. (*Minazuki*, or Sixth Month, is given the Sino-Japanese reading of *rokugatsu*, the heavy, round accented syllables suggesting the sense of motionless heat.) The white clouds "sit on" (*oku*) the peak of Arashi Mountain (literally, storm mountain), inverting the usual expression "clouds stand" (*kumo tatsu*) and suggesting a suffocating pressure or movement, which captures the traditional seasonal association in a new, haikai fashion. The word *mine* (peak)—which implies the phrase *kumo no mine* (tall, nimbus clouds)—also creates a sense of oppressive, motionless heat, which stifles the implied wind of "storm mountain."

The cutting word can also emphasize contrast, another aspect of Jakobson's poetics of equivalence. The following hokku, which Bashō composed at Gichūji Temple (Kiso Yoshinaka's grave) near Lake Biwa on the 15th of the Eighth Month of Genroku 3 (September 1690) and which appears in *First Cicada* (*Hatsusemi*; 1696), is on the topic of harvest moon (*meigetsu*), which the classical poet praised for its refulgent aura.

bright harvest moon—
on the viewing stand
    not one beautiful face

meigetsu | ya | za | ni | utsukushiki | kao | mo | nashi
harvest-moon | : | stand | at | beautiful | face | even | none

The speaker looks up at the harvest moon (*meigetsu*), which implicitly dazzles him, but when he looks down, he is disappointed by the undistinguished faces of the moon-viewers on the viewing stand. The cutting word *ya*, which emphasizes the contrast between two worlds, also suggests a correspondence that is implied by its very absence—a beautiful face that would resonate with the beautiful moon.

an old pond ...
a frog leaps in,
    the sound of water

furuike | ya | kawazu | tobikomu | mizu | no | oto
old-pond | : | frog | jumps-in | water | 's | sound

In the famous frog poem, the cutting word *ya* similarly establishes an implicit contrast between the old pond, with its connotations of winter hibernation and stillness, versus the "frog," a seasonal word for spring, which implies a warm, slow-moving spring day marked by the sound of new life. The hokku is simultaneously a narrative, temporal sequence—in which the frog leaps into an old pond followed by the sound of water—and a contrastive montage.

Unlike earlier renga and haikai handbooks, which address the question of which particular words or syllables can be used as cutting words, Bashō discusses *kireji* in terms of function and effect. In *Kyoraishō*, Bashō noted:

> First, the cutting word is inserted in order to cut the verse. If the verse is already cut, it is not necessary to employ a word to cut it. For those poets who cannot distinguish between a cut and not-cut poem, earlier poets established cutting words. If one uses one of these words in a hokku, seven or eight times out of ten the hokku will be cut. The remaining two or three times, however, the hokku will not be cut even though it

includes a cutting word. On the other hand, there are hokku that are
cut even though they include no cutting words. (NKBZ 51: 478–79)

For Bashō, it was the cutting effect rather than the cutting word it-
self that ultimately mattered. A hokku could be cut without a *kireji*,
and the use of a cutting word did not necessarily ensure that a
hokku had been cut. The following hokku, which Bashō composed
in July 1689 (5.16.Genroku 2) during his journey to the Interior, is
split into three parts without a cutting word.

> fleas, lice
> a horse passing water
> by my pillow

nomi | shirami | uma | no | shitosuru | makura | moto
fleas | lice | horse | 's | pass-water | pillow | side

The original *kaishi* (poetry sheet) of the following hokku, which
Bashō composed while visiting Kyoto in the Twelfth Month of
Genroku 3 (Dec. 1690–Jan. 1691) and which he later included in
Monkey's Straw Coat, opens with a headnote.

> While sleeping in a lodge in the capital and hearing each night the sor-
> rowful chanting of the Kūya pilgrims.

> dried salmon
> the leanness of a Kūya pilgrim
> in the cold season

karazake | mo | Kūya | no | yase | mo | kan | no | uchi
dried-salmon | also | Kūya | 's | leanness | also | cold-season | 's | during

Kūya were lay monks or pilgrims who commemorated the an-
niversary of the death of Priest Kūya by begging and chanting
Buddhist songs in the streets of Kyoto for 48 days beginning from
the Thirteenth of the Eleventh Month. *Kan* (cold season) or *kan no
uchi* (during the cold season) was a roughly 30-day period at the end
of the lunar year, the coldest part of the year. The two "cuts," after
the first and the second phrases, which are achieved without the use
of a cutting word, also form "joints" among the three parts—dried
salmon (*karazake*), the gauntness of the Kūya pilgrim (*Kūya no*

yase), and the cold season (*kan no uchi*)—each of which is accent-
uated by a hard beginning "k" consonant and by the repeated *mo*
(also). Bashō's headnote implies that the images are a metaphor for
the loneliness of a traveler on a distant journey.[18] The end result is
to suggest three different dimensions—material, human, and season-
al—of the feeling of stark loneliness.

Combining Seasonal Words

Kyoriku believed that the combination poem, the hokku that
combined two or more different topics, was the central technique of
the Bashō style.[19] Furthermore, he argued that the "combination
poem" should join topics unassociated in classical poetry, leaping
beyond the poetic essence and established associations of a given
topic. As Kyoriku explained in *Haikai Dialogue* (*Haikai mondō*;
1697–98):

> The Master: "In composing a hokku, my students begin by searching
> within the topic. This will not yield anything. But if they begin by
> searching outside the topic, they will find a plethora of material."
>
> I said, "I discovered this while reading *Desolate Fields* and *Monkey's
> Straw Coat*. My approach can be compared to placing the topic in a box,
> climbing on top of that box, and viewing heaven and earth from that
> perspective."
>
> The Master: "That is absolutely correct. That is why you were able
> to come up with verses such as:

> next to even
> the winter chrysanthemums—
> live radishes

> kangiku | no | tonari | mo | ari | ya | ikedaikon[20]
> winter-chrysanthemum | 's | neighbor | even | is | ! | live-radish

> I then realized that if I search within the boundary of the topic, there
> will be nothing new. Even if, by some remote chance, something is left,
> if a neighbor decides to compose on the same topic on the same day, the
> neighbor will undoubtedly find it. Since the neighbor is following the
> same route, he or she is bound to come across it. This would be even

more true if someone from a distant province or village were looking in a place that I was not familiar with. What would I find? On the other hand, if I leap beyond the boundary, it will be like a child who thinks differently from its parents, or parents who conceive differently from their child."

The Master: "Ultimately, you should think of the hokku as something that combines. Those who are good at combining or bringing together two topics are superior poets." (KHT 10: 147)[21]

Using the metaphor of the box, Kyoriku argued that the poet must look beyond the "boundary" (*kuruwa*, originally meaning "castle wall"), that is, beyond the established associations of the topic.[22] In classical renga, the added verse was typically linked to the previous verse by *yoriai*, by established lexical associations, which were conveniently listed in renga handbooks. In the example that Bashō praises, Kyoriku goes beyond the "boundary" of "winter chrysanthemums" (*kangiku*), a classical seasonal topic, by combining it with a haikai word, *ikedaikon*, the large white radishes that farmers pulled out of the field and buried "alive" (*ike*) in the dirt, where they were stored until spring. Winter chrysanthemums (*kangiku*) was a flower (usually yellow, sometimes white) that bloomed in the winter after the other flowers had died and that was admired in classical poetry for its ability to endure the frost. The juxtaposed images, which at first glance seem antithetical, are unexpectedly joined by their implicit ability to endure the winter cold "alive." (The hokku can also be read as a greeting from the guest, Kyoriku, who implicitly compares himself to the lowly radish lying at the feet of the elegant chrysanthemum, the master and host Bashō.)

Kyoriku states that the combination poem should not only go beyond the boundary, the natural essence of the classical topic, but also combine hitherto unrelated seasonal words (such as winter chrysanthemums and live radishes). In *Correspondence Between Kyoriku and Yaba* (*Kyoya shōsoku*), he wrote:

The two bush warbler poems that the Master composed are, first of all, seasonal combinations in which he brings together those aspects that communicate with each other. The coarse and natural aspect—"droppings left on the rice cakes"—of one poem was especially outstanding. Generally speaking, when it comes to the master's hokku, seven to eight out of ten are hokku that combine seasonal words. (KHT 10:326)[23]

The "coarse" bush warbler poem that Kyoriku refers to is the following hokku, composed by Bashō in Edo in a two-poet sequence with Shikō at the end of the First Month of Genroku 5 (mid-March 1692).

> bush warbler—
> leaves droppings on the rice cakes
>   at the veranda edge
>
> uguisu | ya | mochi | ni | funsuru | en | no | saki
> bush-warbler | : | rice-cake | on | defecate | veranda | 's | edge

The bush warbler leaves droppings on the rice cakes, which were made for the New Year's celebration, at the beginning of spring (First Month), and which were left to dry out on the veranda. The seasonal association of the bush warbler with the arrival of the New Year and with early spring is recaptured from a new, commoner, slightly vulgar angle, through the rice cakes (*mochi*) and droppings (*fun*), both haikai words, avoiding the traditional association of the bush warbler with singing and plum blossoms.

In *Sanzōshi*, Dohō, Bashō's most talented and faithful disciple in Iga, argued that the hokku should have the "spirit of going and returning," a movement similar to that found between a previous verse and an added verse in a linked verse sequence.

> The hokku involves a spirit of the mind that moves in a specific direction and then returns. An example is:
>
> > in the mountain village
> > the New Year dancers are late—
> >   plum blossoms
> >
> > yamazato | wa | manzai | ososhi | ume | no | hana
> > mountain-village | as-for | dancers | late | plum | 's | flowers[24]

The poet first states that in the mountain village the Manzai, the New Year dancers, are late and then comes back to reveal that the plum trees are already in bloom. This spirit of going and returning lies at the heart of the hokku. If the poem were simply

> in the mountain village
> the New Year dancers are late

it would have no more force than a single verse in a linked verse sequence. (NKBZ 51: 592)

To borrow Dohō's metaphor, the reader first "goes" to part A, explores its connotations, and then "returns" by another route to part B, seeking to find a common path between A and B. The emotional or atmospheric flow moves first in one direction and then returns in a different direction, resulting in a mixing of the two currents.

As these examples suggest, Bashō's notion of the combination poem did not simply mean the juxtaposition or collision of disparate elements—Pound's "any decayed cabbage cast upon any pale satin sofa"—it also implied finding resonance in dissonance, congruity in incongruity, especially between different languages and subcultures, a process that was accomplished through "the spirit of going and returning" and that was often regenerative and humorous. As Sigmund Freud noted in *Jokes and Their Relationship to the Unconscious*, humor often derives from the discovery of "similarity between dissimilar things": "Jean Paul has expressed this thought itself in joking form: 'Joking is the disguised priest who weds every couple.' Vischer carries this further: 'He likes best to wed couples whose union their relatives frown upon.'"[25] A good example of such a wedding is the following hokku, which Bashō composed during the winter of 1690–91 while residing in the Kyoto area.

> withering winds—
> the face of one suffering
> from swollen cheeks

kogarashi | ya | hohobare | itamu | hito | no | kao
withering-wind | ! | cheek-swell | hurt | person | 's | face

The two parts of the hokku—separated by the cutting word *ya*—can be read together, as one continuous scene, or separately, as two parts reverberating against each other. In the former, a person suffering from mumps (*hohobare*, literally "swollen cheeks") stands outside, his face contorted by the *kogarashi*, the strong winds that blow the leaves off the trees in the winter. In the latter, the face of a man inflamed by and suffering from mumps echoes the cold, stinging wind. The expectations generated by withering winds, a classical topic associated with cold winter landscapes, are humorously undercut by the haikai phrase "pained by swollen cheeks," which then leads to a double reversal: after the initial collision, the reader discovers a connotative fusion between the withering winds and the painfully swollen cheeks.

Intermediaries

To bridge the gap the two parts of the combination poem, Kyoriku urged the use of an "intermediary word" (*torihayashi kotoba*), which brought together the incongruous elements, especially traditional seasonal topics and haikai words. In *Haikai Dialogue* (*Haikai mondō*; 1697) Kyoriku noted that the "newness" (*atarashimi*) in *Charcoal Sack* and *Separate Parlor* (*Betsuzashiki*; 1694), two late Bashō-circle anthologies, lay entirely in the use of these intermediary words.

> Recently, I thought that "scent of plum blossoms" would make a good combination with "blue lacquer bowl" and tried various middle phrases, but none of them felt right.

> scent of plum blossoms—
> pickled vegetables and
>   a blue lacquer bowl

> ume | ga | ka | ya | shōjin-namasu | ni | asagiwan
> plum | 's | scent | ! | pickled-vegetable | with | blue-bowl

> scent of plum blossoms—
> arranged in a row
>   blue lacquer bowls

ume|ga|ka|ya|sue-narabetaru|asagiwan
plum|'s|scent|!|arranged-in-row|blue-bowl

> scent of plum blossoms
> from somewhere or other
>   a blue lacquer bowl

ume|ga|ka|no|dokotomonashi|ni|asagiwan
plum|'s|scent|'s|somewhere-or-other|-ly|blue-bowl

I tried these various possibilities but none of them were successful. When the subject matter and the combination are excellent but a good hokku does not materialize, it means that the necessary intermediary has yet to be found. After more searching, I came up with the following.

> scent of plum blossoms—
> beneath the guest's nose
>   a blue lacquer bowl

ume|ga|ka|ya|kyaku|no|hana|ni|wa|asagiwan
plum|'s|scent|:|guest|'s|nose|at|as-for|lacquer-bowl
(KHT 10:147–48)[26]

Kyoriku attempted to cross the gap between the scent of plum blossoms, a classical phrase and topic, and the haikai word *asagiwan*, a pale-blue or aqua lacquer bowl painted with birds and flowers. Kyoriku tried various intermediaries until he settled on "beneath the guest's nose," an intermediary that brings plum blossom scent and the aqua bowl together to suggest a larger banquet scene: the guest, smelling the fragrance of plum blossoms, raises the elegant bowl to his mouth. In contrast to Teimon haikai, which relied on homophonic intermediaries or established lexical associations, the Bashō school stressed links by both scene and "scent." Here, in the fashion of a status link, the fragrance of the plum blossoms resonates with the atmosphere of the exquisitely painted bowl.

In *Correspondence Between Kyoriku and Yaba*, Kyoriku praised the following combination poem for its unique intermediary: "Drooping in the mud—" (KHT 10: 329). Bashō composed the hokku in

March 1694 (3.3.Genroku 7), during low tide, and later included it in *Charcoal Sack.*

> green willow branches
> droop into the mud—
> the tide gone out

aoyagi|no|doro|ni|shidaruru|shiohi|kana[27]
green-willow|'s|mud|in|droop|low-tide|!

According to Kyoriku, the combination poem is superior because of the superb intermediary "drooping in the mud," which humorously brings together green willow and low tide, two hitherto unrelated classical topics. The lithe, gracefully drooping branches of the green willow were usually found trailing in a river, but here, with the tide out, those same branches are unexpectedly hanging on the muddy bottom.[28]

The Single Object Poem

In response to Kyoriku's emphasis on the "combination poem" and his claim that combining separate topics was the central technique of the Bashō style, Kyorai argued that, although combining was certainly important, it did not take precedence over other techniques and that Bashō also composed "single-object" (*ichibutsu shitate*) poems, which focused on a single topic and in which the hokku flowed smoothly from start to finish, without the leap or gap found in the combination poem. In *Kyoraishō*, he noted:

> The Master said: "A hokku that moves smoothly from the opening five syllables to the end is a superb verse."
> Shadō remarked: "The master once told me, 'The hokku is not, as you believe, something that brings together two or three different things. Compose the hokku so that it flows like gold being hit and flattened by a hammer.'" . . .
> Kyorai: "If a poet composes by combining separate things, he can compose many verses and compose them quickly. Beginning poets should know this. But when one becomes an accomplished poet, it is no longer a question of combining or not combining." (NKBZ 51: 498)[29]

In *Travel Lodging Discussion* (*Tabineron*; 1699), Kyorai even went so far as to say that all hokku are single-object poems.

> Generally speaking, all hokku focus on a single object. Allow me to ex-
> plain and give some examples. First of all, the following verse is on a
> single object.

> warmly wrapped
> in its feathered robe—
>   feet of the wild duck
>   —the late Master

> kegoromo | ni | tsutsumite | nukushi | kamo | no | ashi[30]
> feathered-robe | in | wrap | warm | wild-duck | 's | feet

They say that the Master took delight in this poem and told Shikō,
"This hokku was deliberately composed on a single object." Other ex-
amples include:

> well, then,
> let's go snow-viewing
>   until we tumble over!
>   —the late Master

> iza | saraba | yukimi | ni | korobu | tokoro | made
> well | then | snow-viewing | for | tumble | place | until

>   scratching
> its beautiful face—
>   the pheasant's spurs
>   —Kikaku

> utsukushiki | kao | kaku | kiji | no | kezume | kana
> beautiful | face | scratch | pheasant | 's | spurs | !

· · · · · · · ·

Someone might say that the "feet of the wild duck" and "the feathered
robe" form a combination or that the poet combines "the pheasant's
spurs" with "face," but what could they say "snow-viewing" was com-
bined with? When the late Master spoke about combining objects, he
appeared to make a distinction between those that worked within the
boundary and those that worked outside it. Kyoriku, it seems, defined
the combination poem as something that went outside the boundary.

But there are poems that combine within the boundary just as there are those that combine without.

   spring
gradually takes shape—
     moon and plum blossoms
       —the late Master

haru | mo | yaya | keshiki | totonou | tsuki | to | ume[31]
spring | also | gradually | form | takes | moon | and | plum

. . . .

These poems all combine within the boundary. (KHT 10: 206–7)[32]

Kyorai was arguing that since the combination poem can be composed quickly and relatively easily, it is suited for beginners, but that the more accomplished poet will not be limited to this particular technique. Furthermore, a number of good combination poems, especially impromptu ones, remain within the "boundary" or circle of established poetic associations. In *Kyoraishō* (NKBZ 51: 498), Kyorai suggested that beginners should compose distant combinations: as Kyoriku pointed out, going outside the established boundary makes it easier to find new material and avoid plagiarism. The rule, however, does not apply to accomplished poets who, as Bashō's examples suggest, can either discover new connections within the boundary of established associations or approach the traditional associations in new, haikai-esque ways. For example, "spring," "moon," and "plum blossoms," which appear together in Bashō's hokku, were closely associated in classical poetry, especially as a result of *The Tale of Genji*, where the scent of the plum blossoms in the light of the misty evening moon represented one of the beauties of spring. The haikai character of Bashō's hokku lay not in the combination, which was purely classical, but in the manner of the expression, especially in the rhythm. The middle phrase—which comes to a slow stop, ending on three, drawn out, successive "o" sounds, the last sliding into the vowel "u"—suggests the gradual vernal movement that brings together the moon and the plum blossoms.

In contrast to the combination poem, which combined different topics, a single-object poem focused on a single topic, but on closer examination even single-object poems can usually be broken down into two parts, consisting of a traditional seasonal topic, which established a horizon of expectations, and the description or presentation, which often worked against those expectations. A good example is the "wild duck" hokku cited above, which Bashō composed in Edo in the winter of Genroku 6 (1693–94) and which Kyorai considered a single-object poem. In the classical tradition, the wild duck (*kamo*) was often found floating on a winter pond or ocean, and its figure and voice were associated with loneliness, longing for home, uncertainty, and, most of all, with coldness. In a haikai reversal, this wild duck appears "warm" (*nukushi*), its feet tucked beneath its "feathered robe" (*kegoromo*). The circular movement, the "going and returning," in such a single-object poem occurs not between the two parts of the hokku so much as between the implied topic (wild duck) and the unusual, haikai-esque approach, between the text and the horizon of expectations raised by the seasonal topic.

Both the combination and the single-object approach had a profound influence on the course of modern haiku. Both Masaoka Shiki (1867–1902) and his successor Takahama Kyoshi (1874–1959) pressed for mimetic poetry, which tended to focus on a single object that could be depicted directly, through the senses. On the other hand, the notion of the combination poem found new life with other modern poets. In the Taishō period (1912–26), for example, Ōsuga Otsuji (1881–1920) stressed the importance of placing the cutting word or the break in the middle of the haiku, thereby causing the part with the seasonal word to interact with the other half.[33] In the Shōwa period Yamaguchi Seishi (1910–94), harking back to Bashō and spurred on by the notion of Eisenstein's montage (reimported to Japan), believed that haiku should focus on the interrelationship between different objects of nature, a relationship that must "leap beyond" the predictable.[34] The Pursuit of Humanity (Ningen Tankyū) group, which was active at the same time as Seishi and also looked back to Bashō, attempted to explore more subconscious or symbolic connections, as in the following haiku written by its leader Nakamura Kusatao (1901–83) in 1933.[35]

> a toad—
> the eldest son with no reason
> to leave the house

hikigaeru | chōshi | ie | saru | yoshi | mo | nashi
toad | eldest-child | house | leave | reason | even | have-not

The startling gap between the two images causes the reader to explore the symbolic and psychological connotations of the large, slow-moving, somewhat comic toad, a seasonal word for summer, which usually lives under the floorboards or in the grass, and its relationship to the eldest son (the poet), who seems somehow fated to take on the responsibilities of the house or family.

Bashō's haikai similarly cause the reader to explore the gap between disparate parts but differ significantly from Nakamura Kusatao's highly symbolic and psychologically charged haiku in that, even as they describe the external landscape, Bashō's haikai, belonging to an earlier stream of parodic literature or culture, work against the classical tradition, leaping beyond the established associations or combining classical topics with vernacular language. The same could be said of the links in Bashō's haikai, which avoided the established lexical associations on which classical renga had depended. At the same time, Bashō and his disciples attempted to harmonize or fuse these disparate elements through various means, the spirit of "going and returning," new seasonal correspondences, unique intermediaries, and the poetics of scent and reverberation, which, while drawing on the classical poetics of overtones (*yosei*), sought out emotional and aesthetic connotations in the new commoner languages and subject matter, thereby poeticizing the vernacular, internalizing the new landscape, and enabling Bashō and other contemporary poets to expand the foundations of Japanese poetry.

CHAPTER 5

Linking and Communal Poetry

—the fragment is like the musical idea of a song cycle . . . each piece is
self-sufficient, and yet it is never anything but the interstice of its
neighbors.
                                                                —Roland Barthes

Haikai was the poetry of perpetual recontextualization in which
the ownership of a text was playfully seized and passed from one in-
dividual or subculture to another. This movement lay both at the
heart of haikai parody, which recontextualized classical texts and
transformed them into popular, contemporary images, and at the
center of linked verse, which constantly shifted the perspective of
the preceding two verses. Like classical linked verse, haikai depen-
ded on two simultaneous movements: the meeting (*tsukeai*), the link
to the previous verse (*maeku*), and the parting (*yukiyō*), the separa-
tion from the verse prior to the previous verse (the *uchikoshi*). Each
added verse (*tsukeku*) joined the previous verse to form a new poetic
world, while standing in a negative relationship to the penultimate
verse, from which it pushed off, thus ensuring constant change.[1] If
the added verse resembled the penultimate verse in content, mood,
or imagery, it was called a *kannonbiraki* (literally, "opening the
doors of Buddhist altar," in which the left and right doors are iden-
tical) and was forbidden. As Bashō stated in *Sanzōshi* (51: 535), "The
kasen consists of 36 steps. One cannot go back even one step."

Linking and Shifting

In *Dialogue at Yamanaka*, Hokushi, a Bashō disciple from Ka-
nazawa in Kaga, systematically categorized the techniques of link-

ing, dividing verses into two fundamental types: "emotion" or "person" (*ninjō*) verses, which focus on the action, thought, emotions, or situation of people, and "non-emotion" or "non-person" (*ninjō-nashi*) verses, now sometimes referred to as "place" verses (*ba no ku*), in which no people appear.[2] The person verses are further divided into "self" (*ji*) verses, which view the world from a first-person perspective, "other" (*ta*) verses, which view people from a third-person, external perspective, and "self and other" verses (*ji-ta-han*), which combine both perspectives, as in:

> a priest growing colder
> as he returns to a temple?
>
> sō | yaya | samuku | tera | ni | kaeru | ka
> priest | gradually | cold | temple | to | return | ?

This verse describes the priest from a third-person perspective, but the questioning stance, indicated by the interrogative particle *ka*, also makes it implicitly a subjective, first-person, self verse. Hokushi believed that change in haikai could be ensured by never repeating the same type of verse in three successive verses. Thus a sequence may move from a person/self verse to a non-person verse to a person/other verse, but it should not come back to a person/self within three successive verses. In actual practice, the Bashō school did not follow this principle strictly. It is not unusual, for example, to find three or four non-person verses in succession. But Hokushi's rules reveal the kind of shifting and change that Bashō encouraged between the natural and human worlds, and external and internal points of view. The lack of stated subjects and tense in Japanese make it relatively easy to shift perspective, subject, gender, time, and number: women are transformed into men, aristocrats into warriors, children into adults, single figures into multiple figures, domestic landscape into foreign. Linked verse thrived on the seemingly limitless ways in which words and phrases could be reinterpreted through even the slightest shift in context.

Prior to Bashō's time, the standard length for both renga and haikai was the 100-verse sequence (*hyakuin*). From around 1678, how-

Poem, calligraphy, and ink painting by Bashō, probably done in the spring of 1691. 16.9 x 10.6 in. Shows a branch of *yamabuki* (yellow mountain rose), one of Bashō's favorite topics, with leaves and fourteen flowers. The poem—*yamabuki ya Uji no hoiro no niou toki* (yellow mountain roses—when the aroma drifts from the tea ovens of Uji)—appears in *Monkey's Straw Coat* (published summer 1691) with the headnote, "Accompanying a painting" (*gasan*), which was probably this one. Uji, south of Kyoto, was known both for its tea production—the harvesting and drying of tea leaves—and for its *yamabuki*, which combine here in an unexpected fashion. Signed "Painting by Bashō himself" (*Bashō jiga*). (Courtesy Kakimori Collection)

ever, when Bashō began to develop his own style, he turned to the much shorter 36-verse sequence (*kasen*), which had rarely been used in classical renga. By 1682, almost all Bashō's haikai, as well as those of his contemporaries, appeared in this shorter form.[3] The shift to the *kasen* resulted, at least in part, from the new socioeconomic circumstances of the participants. In the early seventeenth century, haikai was primarily a leisure activity of the upper class, but by the latter half of that century, haikai had spread to a wide range of social groups—merchants, artisans, rich farmers, samurai of various levels—who did not have the time and leisure of their more aristocratic predecessors. Unlike the 100-verse sequence, which normally took around eight to ten hours—a *hyakuin* at the residence of Nijō Yoshimoto (1320–88), one of the founders of classical renga, customarily began in the morning and ended late in the evening—a *kasen* could be composed in about three-and-a-half hours. For Bashō, the *kasen* also offered more control, allowing him to give greater attention to each verse and link. From the mid-1680s even the *kasen* sometimes proved too long, and Bashō occasionally turned to the *han-kasen*, or eighteen-verse "half-*kasen*."

The 36 verses of the *kasen* were recorded on two rectangular sheets of paper (*kaishi*), about 6 by 9 inches, referred to as the "first sheet" (*sho ori*) and the "second sheet" (*nagori no ori*, literally, "remaining sheet"), each of which had a "front" (*omote*) and "back" (*ura*).

first sheet (*sho ori*)		second sheet (*nagori no ori*)	
front	back	front	back
(*omote*)	(*ura*)	(*omote*)	(*ura*)
6 verses	12 verses	12 verses	6 verses

The *kasen*, which required two sheets, had four parts: six verses on the front of the first sheet, twelve on the back of the first sheet, twelve on the front of the second sheet, and six on the back of the second sheet. The sequence as a whole assumed the *jo/ha/kyū* (overture/intensification/finale) structure found in traditional Japanese music (*gagaku*) and Noh drama. The front of the first sheet, or the first six verses, formed the overture (*jo*), which was quiet in tone and slow in tempo, avoiding such heavy topics as love (*koi*), confession (*jukkai*), and impermanence (*mujō*) and allowing the participants to become comfortable with each other. The back of the first sheet, the next twelve verses, and the front of the second sheet, another twelve verses, constituted the intensification (*ha*, literally, "break"), which was full of twists and turns, enabling the participants to display their talents. The back of the second sheet, or the last six verses, was the finale (*kyū*, literally "presto"), which was light and smooth, aimed at bringing the sequence to a close.[4]

Haikai linked verse fused two seemingly incompatible movements, unceasing change and a larger sense of continuity, a contradiction made possible in large part by a set of elaborate and complex rules (*shikimoku*): the prohibitions (*sashiai*), which restricted the use of identical or similar syllables, words, or seasons, and the rules for seriation or duration (*kukazu*) and for intermission or intervals (*sarikirai*). The rules for duration, for example, dictated that the spring and autumn verses, once initiated, had to have a minimum of three verses and a maximum of five.[5] The topic of love (*koi*), the most important of the *ninjō* verses, had to appear at least once and, once introduced, had to have at least two verses (in later years, one verse was enough for Bashō) but could extend for no more than five verses. Summer and winter verses should continue for between one and three verses. The rules for intervals stipulated that a certain number of verses on other subjects had to be composed before the same item could appear again. Five verses, for example, had to separate the appearance of the same season. Three verses must separate sequences of love verses. The moon (*tsuki*) and the cherry blossoms (*hana*), representing autumn and spring, the two most important seasons, respectively, were required to appear at specific points (with some flexibility): a moon verse had to appear three times[6] and the cherry blossom verse had to appear once toward the end of each sheet.[7] These complex rules, which were inherited from classical linked verse and reached back to the poetry of the *Kokinshū*, preserved the broader cultural memory, which was now absorbed in vernacular form by commoners and samurai, ensuring that the new

Tokugawa audience carried on the classical poetic tradition, with its emphasis on love and the seasons, particularly spring and autumn, and that the seasonal landscape became the fabric out of which the sequence was woven.

Conducting *"Withering Gusts"*

The participants presented each additional verse to the scribe (*shuhitsu*), who made sure that it followed the rules before handing it to the haikai master (*sōshō*), who would offer comments, sometimes making corrections or improvements, before returning it to the scribe, who read it aloud and recorded it on the *kaishi*, or poetry sheet.[8] Generally speaking, the order or rotation of the participants was determined in advance—called *hizaokuri* (literally, "passed along the knees")—or it moved more freely and competitively—in a fashion now referred to as *degachi* (winning by submission)—with the haikai master choosing the next verse from among those submitted by the participants.[9] The haikai master, who combined the functions of poet, scholar, teacher, literary judge, conductor, and team coach, moved the sequence along at an appropriate pace, helped participants when they were stumped, provided a bridge to the poetic tradition, maintained the mood or atmosphere of the gathering, and ensured the proper degree of variety and change. The success of the sequence depended on the talent and interaction of the participants, but the presence of the haikai master, who "conducted" (*sabaku*) the session, was felt in almost every verse, much like the leader of a jazz group.

Bashō, who was first and foremost a *haikai sōshō*, avoided the solo format (*dokugin*) that was a favorite among both classical renga and haikai poets.[10] Contrary to his popular image, Bashō was not a social recluse. Instead, he constantly cultivated a community of disciples and poets with whom he engaged in poetic dialogue.[11] The *kasen* called *Withering Gusts* (*Kogarashi*), which is often thought to mark the beginning of the Bashō style, reveals the socio-literary dynamics of Bashō's communal art. In the early fall of 1684, at the age of 41, Bashō left his home on the outskirts of Edo and began a journey

that was later commemorated in *Skeleton in the Fields*. In December
he arrived in Nagoya, one of the major urban centers at the time,
where he was invited to compose with a group of local poets—
Tokoku, Yasui, Jūgo, Shōhei, and Kakei—with whom he eventually
produced five *kasen*, including *Withering Gusts*, all of which were
published in *Winter Days* (*Fuyu no hi*), the first major haikai anthol-
ogy of the Bashō school.[12] With the exception of Kakei (1648–1716),
a doctor of samurai origin and the local haikai leader (38 years old),
all the participants in *Withering Gusts* were young, well-educated,
wealthy, urban merchants, who had the leisure and training to de-
vote themselves to traditional arts such as *chanoyu* (tea ceremony).
Yasui (1658–1743) was an affluent dry-goods merchant and an expert
in the tea ceremony; Jūgo (1654–1717) was a well-to-do lumber
dealer; and Tokoku (d. 1690) was a successful rice merchant. The
Nagoya group, which was not rooted in the Danrin haikai that
dominated Edo at the time, provided Bashō with an unique oppor-
tunity to experiment with his new haikai. The Nagoya group, in
turn, rose to the occasion, making this one of the most memorable
and historically significant haikai sessions in Bashō's career.

The following diagram shows how the participants were proba-
bly seated.[13]

alcove (*toko*)
scroll (*kakemono*) with divine image

Kakei	Shōhei (scribe)	Bashō (main guest)
(3rd verse)	writing table (*bundai*)	(1st verse)
Tokoku		Jūgo
(5th verse)		(4th verse)
Yasui (host)		
(2nd verse)		

As the honored guest and visiting haikai master, Bashō composed
the hokku, the opening verse. Yasui, the host, wrote the second
verse (*wakiku*), and Kakei, the local haikai master, added the third
verse (*daisanku*). Jūgo and Tokoku, composing the fourth and fifth
verses, were followed by Shōhei, the scribe, who closed out the first

round (*ichijun*). The order of the participants was fixed in advance: except for the second round, in which the second (Yasui) and fourth (Jūgo) participants composed after four-verse intervals, all the participants alternated between six- and two-verse intervals.[14]

The Front of the First Sheet
(Overture)[15]

The rains of the long journey have torn my hat, and my coat has crumpled in the daily storms. Accustomed as I am to extreme poverty, I feel sorry for myself. Suddenly remembering that master of mad verse who traveled long ago to this province, I wrote:

> mad verse:
> in the withering gusts
> a wanderer—how much like Chikusai
> I have become!
> —Bashō

kyōku | kogarashi | no | mi | wa | Chikusai | ni | nitaru | kana
comic-verse | withering-gust | 's | self | as-for | Chikusai | to | resemble | !
[no. 1 of sequence, no. 1 of front. Winter: withering gust][16]

Bashō, the main guest, greets his Nagoya hosts in self-deprecatory fashion, comparing himself to Chikusai, the eponymous anti-hero of a popular seventeenth-century comic novel (*kana-zōshi*) in which the protagonist, a poor, eccentric, quack doctor from Kyoto, embarks for Edo, composing comic waka (*kyōka*) along the way, and finally arrives in Nagoya, his clothes in tatters.[17] Bashō has similarly arrived in Nagoya, composing haikai, blown about by the withering gusts, a seasonal word for winter and an implicit metaphor for the hardship of his journey and his lowly position. Through the word *kyōku* (mad verse),[18] which implies that Bashō's haikai, like Chikusai's *kyōka*, is the object of seemingly mad, "burning" devotion— *kogarashi* homophonically implies *mi o kogasu*, "to burn one's body"[19]—Bashō invites his hosts to join him in the new poetics of *fūkyō*, or poetic madness, in which the poet's pursuit of poetic beauty, especially dark, cold, and impoverished images like "withering gusts," is so extreme as to appear mad to the world. In a haikai twist, the withering gusts, which were normally considered unpleasant, become, like the winter showers (*shigure*), an object of poetic desire.

mad verse:
in the withering gusts
a wanderer—how much like Chikusai
I have become!

who's that? sasanqua
spraying over a rain hat

—Yasui

taso|ya|tobashiru|kasa|no|sazanka
who|?|spray|rain-hat|'s|sasanqua
[no. 2, no. 2 of front. Winter: sasanqua]

In the words of Kyoriku's *Uda Priest,* the second verse "must take up what is left unstated by the hokku," maintain the same season as the hokku, and end with a nominal. The white or crimson flowers of the sasanqua, a seasonal word for winter, scatter over or "spray" from the *kasa,* the large traveler's hat, perhaps as a result of the withering gusts.[20] In contrast to the first-person, "self" perspective of the hokku, Yasui responds with a third-person, "other" verse, or rather "self and other" verse, that expresses amazement at the unusual appearance of the visitor. Yasui, the host of the session, implies that although his guest may claim to be an impoverished, windblown traveler, his appearance is in fact bright and colorful, thereby tacitly accepting Bashō's invitation to poetic madness.[21]

who's that? sasanqua
spraying over a rain hat

making
the Master of Early Dawn
construct a brewery

—Kakei

ariake|no|mondo|ni|sakaya|tsukurasete
early-dawn|'s|master|at|brewery|causing-to-build
[no. 3, no. 3 of front. Autumn: early dawn. Moon verse]

Kakei, the local haikai master, shifts directly from winter to autumn without the usual "non-seasonal" (*zō*) transitional verse.[22] The autumnal moon verse, which was required to appear in the fifth verse on the front of the first sheet, emerges here two verses earlier in the word *ariake*, early dawn, and by implication, early dawn moon. *Mondo*, a haikai word translated here as "Master," was a bureaucratic position (Director of Water Management) in the imperial palace. The elegant nickname Master of Early Dawn suggests a colorful, elegant dandy, thus pushing off from the dark figure in the penultimate verse. The Master of Early Dawn, whose hat is decorated with sasanqua flowers, has been ordered to oversee construction of a brewery (*sakaya*).[23] The verse can also be read as a face-to-face link in which the Master of Early Dawn is opening up a wine bar for the visitor with the sasanqua hat, which would make this verse a greeting from Kakei, the local haikai master, to the guest Bashō, who is invited to relax at the bar. In contrast to the second verse, which was required to close with a nominal, thereby coupling it closely with the hokku, the third-verse ends, as it does here, with the continuative verb ending *te*, leaving the verse open ended and launching the sequence in a new direction.

> making
> the Master of Early Dawn
> construct a brewery
>
> a red-haired horse
> shaking dew off its mane
> —Jūgo

kashira | no | tsuyu | o | furuu | akauma
mane | 's | dew | (acc.) | shake | red-horse
[no. 4, no. 4 of front. Autumn: dew]

The red-haired horse (*akauma*, a haikai word), which appears to be tied up in front of a brewery or a wine bar, is a pack horse—as opposed to an elegant thoroughbred or riding horse, which was usually black or white—and may be carrying a barrel of wine. In the fashion of a status link, the socioeconomic connotations of the red-haired horse, which belongs to the world of merchants and farmers, directly echo that of the wine bar or brewery. The horse, having come to a stop in front of the brewery or wine bar, is shaking dew—associated with autumn and with early morning and freshness—off its mane.

a red-haired horse
shaking dew off its mane

    Korean grass
the long thin blades
    colorless

                    —Tokoku

chōsen | no | hosori-susuki | no | nioinaki
Korea | 's | narrow-grass | 's | colorless
[no. 5, no. 5 of front. Autumn: narrow grass]

The red-haired horse, which had been tethered to the front of the wine shop or brewery, now stands in a large field of narrow-bladed grass in Korea, perhaps amid a group of wild horses. *Chōsen*, or Korea, a haikai word, was thought at the time to be a kind of wild frontier, with vast plains. The adjective "colorless" suggests a desolate field of dried, brown grass, turning the setting into late autumn. The successive verses are linked, as they are elsewhere, both by scenic or narrative extension, and by semi-metaphorical and seasonal resonances: here the colorless grass shares with the red-haired work horse a sense of impoverishment and coldness.

    Korean grass
the long thin blades
    colorless

in the scattered light
harvesting rice plants in the fields
                    —Shōhei

hi | no | chirichiri | ni | no | ni | kome | o | karu
sunlight | 's | scattering | -ly | field | in | rice | (acc.) | harvest
            [no. 6, no. 6 of front. Autumn: harvest rice][24]

Shōhei's verse, the sixth and last verse on the front of the first sheet, marks the end of the overture (*jo*). Shōhei, who was the scribe and whose participation was limited to this one verse, moves from a close shot to a distant shot, establishes the time (sunset) of the previous verse, and adds a human element: a farmer or farmers harvesting rice in a field—probably poor farmers working a small plot on the edge of a wild field of Korean grass. The approaching darkness and the scattered light of the fading sun echoes the sense of desolation in the previous verse.

The Back of the First Sheet
(Intensification)

in the scattered light
harvesting rice plants in the fields

    my grass hut—
where I offer the heron
    a lodging
                —Yasui

waga | io | wa | sagi | ni | yado | kasu | atari | nite
my | hut | as-for | heron | to | lend | place | at
[no. 7, no. 1 of back. No season][25]

After the two winter and four autumnal verses (one more than the minimal requirement) of the overture, the sequence moves to a miscellaneous or non-seasonal verse. Yasui's verse, which marks the beginning of the intensification (*ha*) and the back of the first sheet, transforms a third-person landscape verse into a first-person, subjective verse: we look through the eyes of a recluse onto the field where the farmers are harvesting rice. "My hut" (*waga io*), a familiar phrase from classical recluse poetry, and the action of "lending a lodge to the heron," a bird known to avoid humans, suggest a nature-loving recluse—all of which resonate with the implied loneliness of the autumn evening in the previous verse. The verse can also be read allegorically: Yasui, as the gracious host of the session, implicitly offers his humble residence ("my hut") to the visiting haikai master (the heron).

my grass hut—
where I offer the heron
    a lodging

having to hide
while the hair grows back
            —Bashō

kami|hayasu|ma|o|shinobu|mi|no|hodo
hair|grow|while|(acc.)|hide|self|'s|position
[no. 8, no. 2 of back. No season. Love: to hide][26]

Bashō, seizing his first opportunity to demonstrate his own style, boldly transforms the person in the grass hut into someone taking refuge[27] and growing back his hair while in hiding—perhaps a monk who has taken the tonsure but is impatient to return to the secular world. The added verse, which elevates the tempo to the intensification (*ha*) level, raises such intriguing questions as: Why did the person take vows? What has caused the person to want to return to secular life? Is it related to a failed love affair? This narrative dimension, which the Nagoya participants were quick to adopt, is one of the salient features of *Winter Days*. The word *shinobu* ("to hide," but also meaning "to long for") makes this a love verse, or more accurately, a "summoning love verse" (*koi no yobidashi*), laying the ground for a full-blown "love verse" (*koi no ku*).[28]

having to hide
while the hair grows back

    "the pain of deception"
she thought
    squeezing dry her breasts
            —Jūgo

itsuwari|no|tsurashi|to|chichi|o|shiborisute
illusion|'s|painful|saying|breast|(acc.)|squeezing-dry
[no. 9, no. 3 of back. No season. Love: illusion, painful]

Jūgo, who composes the important love verse, transforms the secluded male figure into a woman who has recently given birth and is now nursing a child. As with many of the links, various interpretations are possible. A woman seems to have been betrayed or deceived by someone (her husband or lover?) who has taken her child away, causing her pain and resentment. Whatever the reason, the love affair has caused the woman to escape to a place, perhaps a temple, where she is waiting for her hair to grow back, and in the process she has left behind a suckling infant, forcing her to "squeeze dry her [swollen] breasts" (*chichi o shiborisute*), a startling haikai phrase.[29]

> "the pain of deception"
> she thought
> squeezing dry her breasts
>
> by an unfading stupa
> sobbing with heavy heart
> —Kakei
>
> kienu | sotoba | ni | sugosugo | to | naku
> not-fade | stupa | at | heavy-heart | -edly | weep
> [no. 10, no. 4 of back. No season][30]

Kakei transforms the previous "love" verse into a Buddhist verse (*shakkyō*) on the topic of impermanence (*mujō*): the "pain" is no longer caused by betrayal or deception (*itsuwari*) but by death, by the "illusory" (*itsuwari*) nature of life. The woman squeezing milk out of her swollen breasts has become a mother whose child has just died and who weeps next to a newly marked grave, which stands as an "unfading" reminder of the illusory nature of all things.

> by an unfading stupa
> sobbing with heavy heart
>
> a silhouette
> in the early dawn cold
> lighting a fire
> —Bashō
>
> kagebō | no | akatsuki | samuku | hi | o | takite[31]
> silhouette | 's | early-dawn | cold | fire | (acc.) | lighting
> [no. 11, no. 5 of back. Winter: cold]

Bashō turns the mother weeping in front of the stupa into some-
one who has spent the night at a wake: during the Edo period rela-
tives of the deceased customarily remained in a mourning hut
(*moya*) all night and read sutras. Now, in the early dawn twilight, it
is so cold that someone, perhaps the sobbing woman herself, has lit
a fire, which casts a shadow or silhouette (*kagebō*). The "coldness" of
early morning echoes the "heavy-hearted weeping" (*sugosugo to
naku*) of the previous verse. After four non-seasonal verses, the se-
quence returns to winter, indicated by the word "cold."

> a silhouette
> in the early dawn cold
>   lighting a fire

> an empty house
> the owners disappeared of poverty
> —Tokoku

aruji | wa | hin | ni | taeshi | karaie
owners | as-for | poverty | from | disappeared | empty-house
[no. 12, no. 6 of back. No season][32]

Tokoku transforms the person lighting the small fire into a va-
grant or beggar living in an abandoned house whose family has left
or disappeared as a result of poverty. The implied desolation of the
empty house and the poverty resonate with the hollow feeling of
the silhouette in the previous verse. To some readers, the silhouette
may even suggest the ghost of the dead owner.

> an empty house
> the owners disappeared of poverty

> in a rice field
> the Koman willow
>   dropping its leaves
> —Kakei

tanaka | naru | Koman | ga | yanagi | otsuru | koro
rice-field | be | Koman | 's | willow | drop | time
[no. 13, no. 7 of back. Autumn: willow drop]

After five consecutive people verses, Kakei shifts to a landscape verse and a new locale. Koman, a popular name for provincial prostitutes, suggests that the empty house is part of an abandoned post town, where prostitutes used to sell their favors to travelers. Or perhaps it was the presence of the prostitutes that caused the house to be abandoned. In either event, a willow named after a legendary prostitute now stands "in a rice field."[33] The phrase "willow (leaves) fall" (*yanagi otsuru*) transforms the previous non-seasonal verse into autumn.[34] The sense of autumnal fading, including the implied death of a once-famous prostitute, reflects the mood of decay and emptiness in the abandoned house.

> in a rice field
> the Koman willow
>   dropping its leaves
>
> a man pulling the boat
> in the mist—is he lame?
>   —Yasui
>
> kiri | ni | fune | hiku | hito | wa | chinba | ka
> mist | in | boat | pull | man | as-for | lame | ?
> [no. 14, no. 8 of back. Autumn: mist]

Yasui's verse, which continues the autumn season with the image of mist, places the willow tree next to a riverbank where a man is pulling a boat upstream. The boat-puller appears to be lame, pulling in uneven, jerky movements. Yasui composes another first-person, "self" verse, attempting to inject some humor or lightness into a sequence that has been, for a number of verses, extremely dark. "Lame" (*chinba*), a haikai word, echoes the haikai word *Koman* in the previous verse.

> a man pulling the boat
> in the mist—is he lame?
>
>   at dusk
> gazing sideways at
>   the thin moon
>   —Tokoku

tasogare|o|yoko|ni|nagamuru|tsuki|hososhi
dusk|(acc.)|sideways|at|gaze|moon|thin
[no. 15, no. 9 of back. Autumn: moon. Moon verse]

The seventh verse—and in later years the eighth verse—of the back of the first sheet was designated for the important moon verse, which appears here two verses late. "Gazing sideways" implies that the "thin moon" still lies low on the horizon. The person wondering about the boat-puller now becomes a passenger in the boat, probably lying in bed, looking out sideways. (Or the boat-puller, bent over as he pulls the boat, may be gazing sideways.) Like a scent link, the awkwardness of the boat passenger, who must lean sideways to look at the moon, echoes the awkwardness of the lame man pulling the boat unevenly. A connotative parallel also emerges between the implied insufficiency of the thin dawn moon and the lameness of the boat-puller.

at dusk
gazing sideways at
     the thin moon

retiring from court
to a street of gossipy neighbors
                    —Jūgo

tonari|sakashiki|machi|ni|oriiru
neighbor|gossipy|street|to|retire
[no. 16, no. 10 of back. No season]

Jūgo transforms the person gazing sideways at the moon into someone (a lady-in-waiting?) who has retreated from the imperial palace to a city block with gossipy neighbors. In contrast to a direct allusion link (*jika-zuke*), characteristic of both classical renga and earlier haikai, in which the reader must recognize the base text, the Bashō school used the shadow link (*omokage-zuke*), which suggested a figure or event from classical literature or history without mentioning the name or the event itself, leaving only its "shadow."[35] Here the classical verb *oriiru* (to retire or retreat from court service) generates a Heian, classical atmosphere, suggesting a fictional character, perhaps Evening Faces (Yūgao) in *The Tale of Genji*, whom the highborn hero discovers in a dusty corner of the capital. The word *nagamuru* (to gaze with melancholy thoughts), which in the previous link suggested the boredom of a slow boat ride, here implies the boredom of an aristocratic lady, now living amid talkative commoners. The sense of discomfort and dislocation also resonates with the uneasiness or awkwardness of gazing sideways at the moon. After three autumn verses, the sequence shifts to a non-seasonal verse, which makes for an easier transition to the important cherry blossom verse (spring), which was expected to appear next, in the eleventh verse on the back of the first sheet.

> retiring from court
> to a street of gossipy neighbors

>   asking the Second Nun
> about the cherry trees in full bloom
>   at the imperial palace
>   —Yasui

ni | no | ama | ni | konoe | no | hana | no | sakari | kiku
Second | 's | Nun | to | palace | 's | cherry | 's | peak | ask
[no. 17, no. 11 of back. Spring: cherry blossom]

As the Noh play *Saigyō's Cherry Blossoms* (*Saigyō-zakura*) suggests, the imperial palace, particularly its guard quarters (*konoe*), was known for its cherry blossoms. In composing the cherry blossom (*hana*) verse, Yasui deepens the Heian aristocratic atmosphere of the previous verse and transforms the person who retired to a city street into a Second Nun (*ni no ama*, a haikai word), a high-ranking female imperial attendant who took the tonsure upon the death of an emperor. Yasui's verse, which shifts the sequence from non-season to spring, has been interpreted in at least two substantially different ways. A woman or child from the local neighborhood is asking the Second Nun, who has recently retired from the palace, about a distant, imperial world. Or in the fashion of a face-to-face link (*mukai-zuke*), in which a character in the added verse faces another person in the previous verse, another nun, presumably the First

Nun, who has retired from the palace to a gossipy street, is asking the Second Nun about the cherry blossoms at the palace.

> asking the Second Nun
> about the cherry trees in full bloom
>   at the imperial palace

> "butterflies in the thick weeds"
> she wept blowing her nose
>   —Bashō

chō | wa | mugura | ni | to | bakari | hana | kamu
butterfly | as-for | weed | in | saying | only | nose | blow
[no. 18, no. 12 of back. Spring: butterfly]

Taking up the traditional association of butterflies with cherry blossoms, Bashō continues the spring narrative. In this face-to-face link, the Second Nun, responding to questions by the speaker in the previous verse, stops in mid-sentence, "butterflies in the thick weeds" and breaks down in tears. The phrase "to blow one's nose" (*hana kamu*), which means "to weep," and "thick weeds" are both drawn from *The Tale of Genji* and suggest Suetsumuhana's (Safflower) once-grand residence, neglected and overrun by weeds. The Second Nun implicitly compares her previous high position at court, when the cherry blossoms were at their peak, with her present fallen position, symbolized by "thick weeds." The butterflies, associated with her former "high" life, now fly forlornly amid the weeds. Bashō's added verse, which brings the back of the first sheet to an end, deepens the Heian aristocratic mood of the previous verse even as it moves in a new direction.

The Front of the Second Sheet

> "butterflies in the thick weeds"
> she wept blowing her nose

> a palanquin:
> behind a bamboo blind
>   faintly a face
>   —Jūgo

norimono | ni | sudare | suku | kao | oboro | naru
palanquin | in | blind | appear-through | face | faint | is
[no. 19, no. 1 of front of 2d sheet. Spring: faint]

Pursuing the implications of social or political tragedy in Bashō's verse, Jūgo places the weeping person in a palanquin, making her face faintly visible through the "bamboo blinds." The word *oboro* (faint), which often suggests the misty air of spring evenings, here gives an erotic, mysterious quality to the female figure in the palanquin, who is viewed from outside.[36] In the manner of a status link, the social circumstances of the Heian lady who has fallen on hard times is echoed in the palanquin (*norimono*),[37] an elegant vehicle used by high-ranking ladies that suggests exile.

> a palanquin:
> behind the bamboo blind
>   faintly a face

> "now's the time!"
> releasing an arrow of resentment
>   —Kakei

ima | zo | urami | no | ya | o | hanatsu | koe
now | ! | resentment | 's | arrow | (acc.) | release | voice
[no. 20, no. 2 of front of 2d sheet. No season]

Kakei, the local haikai master, no doubt wanting to show his ability to make the bold turn, dramatically transforms the waka-esque, feminine, aristocratic world of the Heian romance into the rough-and-tumble world of the medieval warfare. The man who "shouts as he releases the arrow" is either in the palanquin or outside, shooting at the obscured face in the palanquin, which now appears to be that of a man.

> "now's the time!"
> releasing an arrow of resentment

>   a pine in memory
> of a bandit bends
>   broken by the wind
>   —Bashō

nusubito | no | katami | no | matsu | no | fukiorete
bandit | 's | memento | 's | pine | 's | break-in-wind
[no. 21, no. 3 of front of 2d sheet. No season]

Throughout the development (*ha*), Bashō, the main guest and vis-
iting haikai master, and Kakei, the local haikai master, test each
other out. Here Bashō responds to Kakei's brilliant verse with an
equally strong verse. The early commentaries note that the "pine in
memory of a bandit" was associated with Kumasaka Chōhan of
Mino Province (Gifu), a noted bandit said to have killed Tokiwa
Gozen, Yoshitsune's mother, before being killed by Yoshitsune
himself. In the fashion of a reverberation (*hibiki*) link, the cry of the
warrior releasing the assassin's arrow "reverberates" with the sharp
crack of a tree breaking in the wind.

> a pine in memory
> of a bandit bends
> broken by the wind

> for a while it lasted
> a stream named for Sōgi
> —Tokoku

shibashi | Sōgi | no | na | o | tsukeshi | mizu
awhile | Sōgi | 's | name | (acc.) | called | water
[no. 22, no. 4 of front of 2d sheet. No season]

"A stream named for Sōgi" refers to a famous spring known as
"Sōgi's Stream" (*Sōgi no shimizu* or *Hakuunsui*) in Mino, the same
province where the noted Kumasaka Chōhan pine stood. Legend
has it that after Sōgi, the noted renga master, received the secret
transmission of the *Kokinshū*, the first imperial anthology of classi-
cal Japanese poetry, from the local warrior chieftain Tō no Tsune-
yori (d. 1494?), they parted at this stream. As a narrative extension
of the previous verse, Tokoku's verse suggests a traveler who, per-
haps disappointed at finding the famous pine broken, visits the
spring named after Sōgi, a haikai word. At the same time, the image
of the stream echoes that of the pine: both are memorials that have

succumbed to the Buddhist law of impermanence, that have lasted only "for a while." In striking contrast to Bashō's previous verse, however, with its violent connotations, Tokoku's added verse possesses elegant, poetic associations, recalling Sōgi's famous journeys through the provinces.

> for a while it lasted
> a stream named for Sōgi

> > doffing a rain hat
> to soak deliberately
> > in the northern showers
> > —Kakei

kasa | nugite | muri | ni | mo | nururu | kitashigure
rain-hat | removing | forceful | ly | also | soak-in | northern-showers
[no. 23, no. 5 of front of 2d sheet. Winter: northern showers]

After three spring verses and three non-seasonal verses, the sequence returns to winter, the season that opened the series. Drawing on the association of Sōgi with poetry, travel, and poetic places, Kakei transforms the traveler into a *fūkyō* poet who, despite the cold winter rain from the north, takes off his rain hat to soak "deliberately" in the passing showers that Sōgi had written about earlier. As noted earlier, for Sōgi and other medieval poets, the winter showers (*shigure*), which disappeared as quickly as they came, symbolized the impermanence of this world and its hardships. For Bashō, however, the winter showers, like the withering gusts, became an object of seemingly mad poetic desire, a medium through which the *fūkyō* traveler could share in the world of the ancients, especially that of Sōgi. Kakei, who had hitherto resisted the visitor's new poetics, here pays his guest tribute, suggesting a readiness to become a *fūkyō* poet himself. It is even possible that Kakei is "taking his hat off" to Bashō.

> doffing a rain hat
> to soak deliberately
> in the northern showers

parting the withered winter grass
a single green endive
                              —Yasui

fuyugare | wakete | hitori | tōchisa
withered-winter-grass | parting | single | endive
[no. 24, no. 6 of front of 2d sheet. Winter: withered winter grass]

The traveler comes across a single Chinese endive (*tōchisa*, a *haigon*), known for its perennial green leaves, in a field of withered grass and trees. Or the endive may be alone, parting the winter grass. Yasui's added verse can be read as a scenic extension of the previous scene *and* as a scent link. The traveler who has deliberately soaked his head in the winter showers comes across a single endive in a withered field. Or, in a spatial juxtaposition, the sensibility of the traveler who soaks his head in winter showers resonates with the appearance of a green endive in the winter field. In either case, poetic beauty appears amid the cold and physically impoverished.

parting the withered winter grass
a single green endive

    shattered white shards
someone's bones
    or what?
                              —Tokoku

shirajira | to | kudakeshi | wa | hito | no | hone | ka | nani
white | -ly | pounded | as-for | person | 's | bone | ? | what
[no. 25, no. 7 of front of 2d sheet. No season]

The person who is making his way through the withered winter fields comes across something white and shattered and wonders if it might be human bones. As Ogata Tsutomu has noted, in the Edo period, there were two kinds of cemeteries: a *mairibaka* (visiting cemetery), which was close enough for the family to visit easily, and an *umebaka* (burial cemetery), where the cremated remains were buried in more distant hills and fields. In the latter, the bones were often exposed by the wind and rain, as they appear to be here.[38]

Tokoku creates a striking contrast between colors (green and white) as well as between life (green endive) and death (white bones).

> shattered white shards
> someone's bones
>   or what?

> squid shells
> divination in a barbarian country
>   —Jūgo

ika | wa | ebisu | no | kuni | no | urakata
squid | as-for | barbarian | 's | country | 's | divination
[no. 26, no. 8 of front of 2d sheet. No season]

Jūgo answers the question posed by Tokoku's verse: what appeared to be white human bones are in fact squid shells used for divination by the Ebisu (barbarians), a non-Chinese tribe on the border of China.[39] Injecting some comic relief into an emotionally dark sequence, Jūgo fantasizes that the Ebisu have done with squid shells what the ancient Chinese did with tortoise shells, burned them for divination.

> squid shells
> divination in a barbarian country

>   I can't solve
> sorrow's mystery
>   a cuckoo
>   —Yasui

awaresa | no | nazo | ni | mo | tokeji | hototogisu[40]
sorrow | 's | mystery | of | also | can-not-solve | cuckoo
[no. 27, no. 9 of front of 2d sheet. Summer: cuckoo]

After two winter and two non-seasonal verses, the sequence shifts to summer. The person examining the squid shells becomes a diviner who cannot solve the mystery (*nazo*, a haikai word) surrounding the sorrowful fate (*awaresa*) of someone exiled to the land of the barbarians. Most commentators believe that the speaker is the famous Emperor of Shu (J. Shoku), or Szechwan, who, according to legend, died longing for home and whose spirit turned into a cuckoo (*hototogisu*). Others believe that the verse alludes to Wang Chao-chün (J. Ōshōkun), the beautiful consort who, having failed to bribe a court painter, was painted as an ugly woman and sent off by an unknowing emperor to marry the ruler of the barbarians. In the latter, the *hototogisu*, a bird associated with sorrow, symbolizes the consort's sad fate. In either interpretation, a diviner, using squid shells, cannot solve the mystery behind the exile's sorrow.

> I can't solve
> sorrow's mystery
>   a cuckoo

> a long night consuming
> an urn of autumn water
>   —Bashō

shūsui | itto | moritsukusu | yo | zo
autumn-water | one-urn | seep-out | night | !
[no. 28, no. 10 of front of 2d sheet. Autumn: autumn water]

The tendency of the Nagoya group to exercise their scholarly knowledge in a witty and pedantic fashion, presenting intellectual puzzles, as in the last several links, has slowed down the sequence and flattened the atmospheric resonance. Rising once more to the occasion, Bashō re-ignites the session, moving the sequence back to Japan and transforming the *hototogisu* into a poetic topic, which a poet has struggled with all night. A whole urn of autumn water[41] in the water clock has been consumed, or "dripped dry," in the process, implying the arrival of dawn. The transition from one season to another is usually accomplished through the intermediary of a non-seasonal verse, but here Bashō manages to move directly from summer to autumn in anticipation of the required moon verse, which must be autumn.

> a long night consuming
> an urn of autumn water

at the temple lodging
of Japan's Li Po—
   moon-gazing

                          —Jūgo

Jittō|no|Rihaku|ga|bō|ni|tsuki|o|mite
Japan|'s|Li-Po|'s|'s|temple-lodging|at|moon|(acc.)|gazing
[no. 29, no. 11 of front of 2d sheet. Autumn: moon. Moon verse]

The urn of water that dripped through the waterclock becomes
an urn of "autumn water," the name of a new liquor, that has been
consumed by the guests at the temple lodging of the Li Po of Japan
(*Jittō no Rihaku*, a haigon phrase). According to a poem by Tu Fu,
Li Po composed 100 verses while drinking an urn of wine. Some
commentators believe Jittō no Rihaku refers to Ishikawa Jōzan
(1583–1672), the noted Japanese poet of Chinese verse who built the
Shisendō in Kyoto, a famous residence for viewing the moon. The
Chinese atmosphere of the Jūgo's verse, especially the shadow of Li
Po, builds on the Chinese syntax and vocabulary of the previous
verse. This is the last of the three autumn moon verses, appearing
exactly where it was required, in the eleventh verse of the front of
the second sheet.

at the temple lodging
of Japan's Li Po—
   moon-gazing

a lute player sticking
rose of sharon in his hood
                          —Kakei

kin|ni|mukuge|o|hasamu|biwauchi
hood|in|rose-of-sharon|(acc.)|stick|lute-player
[no. 30, no. 12 of front of 2d sheet. Autumn: rose-of-sharon]

The moon viewer of the previous verse becomes an eccentric lute
player who decorates his hood with rose of sharon, flowers that fade
the same day that they bloom and that were considered in the Chi-
nese tradition a symbol of the impermanence of glory.[42] By using

the Chinese word *kin* (instead of the standard Japanese *zukin*), Kakei suggests a Chinese-style *biwa* (lute) player who bears the shadow of the noted Chinese musician who danced for the T'ang Emperor Hsuan-tsung (J. *Gensō kōtei*) with a sprig of *mukuge* balanced on her head. Kakei also uses the word *biwauchi*, which was no longer used by the mid-1680s, instead of the standard term *biwahiki* (biwa player), thus giving the verse an anachronistic mood. The added verse may also be taken as part of a face-to-face link in which a lute player visits the moon viewer in the previous verse. In either reading, the two figures are linked together by their Chinese associations and by their *fūkyō* character, their eccentric, seemingly mad devotion to poetic or aesthetic life.

The Back of the Second Sheet
(Finale)

a lute player sticking
rose of sharon in his hood

    an offering
to the traces of a dead ox
    grass at dusk
            —Bashō

ushi | no | ato | tomurau | kusa | no | yūgure | ni
ox | 's | trace | pray-for | grass | 's | dusk | in
[no. 31, no. 1 on back of 2d Sheet. No season]

Composing the opening verse on the back of the second sheet, Bashō shifts to a non-seasonal verse after three successive autumn verses. Bashō transforms the Chinese-style lute player into a wandering lute player or minstrel (*biwa-hōshi*) who prays to the traces of a dead ox, perhaps at the request of pilgrims at Sekidera Temple (in Ōmi Province) where a pagoda was built in honor of an ox. The "grass" is both part of the evening scene and an offering, the ox's favorite food. The connotations of impermanence echo that of the rose of sharon, a symbol of transience. At the same time, the sequence shifts dramatically from the elegant, refined world of the poet of Chinese verse to a commoner, provincial setting.

an offering
to the traces of a dead ox
   grass at dusk

carrying on the head
a basket of shad
         —Tokoku

mi | ni | konoshiro | no | uo | o | itadaki
basket | in | shad | 's | fish | (acc.) | carry-on-head
[no. 32, no. 2 on back of 2d sheet. No season]

A woman (or a group of women) is carrying on her head a win-
nowing basket (*mi*) filled with shad (*konoshiro*), a small low-grade
fish that smelled bad when burned and that were used as offerings to
deities.[43] The woman seems to be bringing the shad as an offering to
a burial mound for oxen, animals cherished by farmers. The interest
of the haikai does not lie in the content of the verses themselves so
much as in what they suggest between them: the atmosphere of a
poor farming village along the sea.

carrying on the head
a basket of shad

   my prayers to
an early dawn star
   to be pregnant
            —Kakei

waga | inori | akegata | no | hoshi | haramubeku
my | prayer | early-dawn | 's | star | to-be-pregnant
[no. 33, no. 3 on back of 2d sheet. No season. Love: to be pregnant][44]

Kakei, shifting from a third-person ("other") perspective to a
first-person ("self") perspective, composes a love verse, required of
each sequence. The woman carrying the basket of *konoshiro* on her
head prays to Venus, an early morning star, asking "to be made
pregnant."[45] Making a homophonic link between *konoshiro* (shad)
and *ko no shiro* (substitute for child), Kakei draws on the popular be-
lief that a childless woman could become pregnant if she made an
offering of shad to an early morning star.

                    my prayers to
              an early dawn star
                    to be pregnant

today going to the eyebrow ceremony
for the younger sister
                                        —Yasui

kyō|wa|imoto|no|mayukaki|ni|yuki
today|as-for|younger-sister|'s|eyebrow-ceremony|to|going
[no. 34, no. 4 on back of 2d sheet. No season. Love: eyebrow ceremony]

Yasui shifts the context from commoner life in the provinces to that of the Heian nobility. The elder sister, who had been praying for a child, is going to an eyebrow ceremony (*mayukaki*), in which her younger sister's eyebrows will be shaved or painted. *Mayukaki*, a Heian court ritual, implies that the younger sister is a lady of high rank, perhaps even an imperial consort.[46] The soft, *hiragana* style of the added verse contributes to the atmosphere of a Heian court romance. Each linked verse sequence was required to take up the topic of love (*koi*), which normally continued for at least two verses. In contrast to the earlier love verses—on "growing back the hair" and "the pain of deception!"—these two love verses are bright, setting up the proper mood for the ending, which was expected to be auspicious.

today going to the eyebrow ceremony
for the younger sister

              for the court bath
filtering out the Shiga blossoms
              with silk gauze
                                        —Tokoku

aya|hitoe|oriyu|ni|Shiga|no|hana|koshite
silk|one-layer|bath|in|Shiga|'s|blossom|filtering
[no. 35, no. 5 on back of 2d sheet. Spring: cherry blossom][47]

Each *kasen* required two cherry blossom verses, one at the eleventh verse of the back of the first sheet ("cherry blossoms in full bloom at the imperial palace") and one here, on the fifth verse on the back of the second sheet, called the "flower of fragrance" (*nioi no hana*), the crowning piece of the sequence. Tokoku deepens the Heian aristocratic mood of the previous verse, moving from cosmetics to the lady's bath. The dark, wintry mood that dominated most of the sequence has given way to a warm, bright mood befitting the "finale" (*kyū*). Shiga, a province associated in classical poetry with cherry blossoms, *aya hitoe* (single-layer silk), and *oriyu* (court bath) all evoke the elegance and splendor of Heian court culture, building on the romantic mood of the eyebrow ceremony. In contrast to the normal custom of bathing in water heated from beneath the bathtub (*sueburo*), *oriyu* meant bathing in hot water that had been boiled elsewhere and transferred to the bathtub, a luxury only court aristocrats could enjoy. The attendants, considering even the cherry blossoms in the water brought especially from Shiga to be dirty, "filter them out" with a silk gauze. In the fashion of a status link, the elegant bath is befitting of a lady honored with an eyebrow-painting ceremony.

> for the court bath
> filtering out the Shiga flowers
>   with silk gauze
>
> the walkway reflecting
> the shadows of the wisteria
>   —Jūgo

rōka | wa | fuji | no | kage | tsutau | nari
walkway | as-for | wisteria | 's | shadow | reflects | be
[no. 36, no. 6 of back of 2d sheet. Spring: wisteria]

The closing verse (*ageku*), which was supposed to be light and auspicious, augments the aristocratic splendor of the previous verse. The shadow of the wisteria blossoms, which suggests the end of a day, falls across the *rōka*, a haikai word, a long hallway leading to the bathhouse. The wisteria, an elegant late spring flower that usually follows the scattering of the cherry blossoms, joins with the image of the court bath to generate a felicitous spring atmosphere.[48] In scent-link fashion, the word "shadow" resonates with the filtered-out cherry blossoms in the previous verse: both flowers appear indirectly, as if through a veil.

Since a linked verse sequence must also be read as a single continuous text, for the larger flow, the text is presented here without notes and commentary.

> mad verse:
> in the withering gusts
> a wanderer—how much like Chikusai
> I have become!
> > —Bashō

> who's that?
> sasanqua spraying over a rain hat
> > —Yasui

> making
> the Master of Early Dawn
> construct a brewery
> > —Kakei

> a red-haired horse
> shaking dew off its mane
> > —Jūgo

> Korean grass
> the long thin blades
> colorless
> > —Tokoku

> in the scattered light
> harvesting rice plants in the fields
> > —Shōhei

> my grass hut—
> where I offer the heron
> a lodging
> > —Yasui

> having to hide
> while the hair grows back
> > —Bashō

"the pain of deception"
she thought
   squeezing dry her breasts
             —Jūgo

by an unfading stupa
sobbing with heavy heart
             —Kakei

   a silhouette
in the early dawn cold
   lighting a fire
             —Bashō

an empty house
the owners disappeared of poverty
             —Tokoku

   in a rice field
the Koman willow
   dropping its leaves
             —Kakei

a man pulling the boat
in the mist—is he lame?
             —Yasui

   at dusk
gazing sideways at
   the thin moon
             —Tokoku

retiring from court
to a street of gossipy neighbors
             —Jūgo

   asking the Second Nun
about the cherry trees in full bloom
   at the imperial palace
             —Yasui

"butterflies in the thick weeds"
she wept blowing her nose
             —Bashō

a palanquin:
behind a bamboo blind
   faintly a face
                —Jūgo

"now's the time!"
releasing an arrow of resentment
                —Kakei

  a pine in memory
of a bandit bends
   broken by the wind
                —Bashō

for a while it lasted
a stream named for Sōgi
              —Tokoku

  doffing a rain hat
to soak deliberately
   in the northern showers
                —Kakei

parting the withered winter grass
a single green endive
              —Yasui

  shattered white shards
someone's bones
   or what?
              —Tokoku

squid shells
divination in a barbarian country
                —Jūgo

  I can't solve
sorrow's mystery
   a cuckoo
              —Yasui

a long night consuming
an urn of autumn water
              —Bashō

at the temple lodging
of Japan's Li Po—
   moon-gazing

             —Jūgo

a lute player sticking
rose of sharon in his hood

             —Kakei

   an offering
to the traces of a dead ox
   grass at dusk

             —Bashō

carrying on the head
a basket of shad

             —Tokoku

   my prayers to
an early dawn star
   to be pregnant

             —Kakei

today going to the eyebrow ceremony
for the younger sister

             —Yasui

   for the court bath
filtering out the Shiga flowers
   with silk gauze

             —Tokoku

the walkway reflecting
the shadows of the wisteria

             —Jūgo

As we can see here, each verse (*ku*) must be appreciated in various contexts simultaneously (1) in isolation, (2) in relationship to the previous verse, (3) as a shift away from or recontextualization of the penultimate verse, and (4) as part of the flow and mood of the larger sequence. As with a combination poem, successive verses are read separately, as independent collage fragments, *and* together, as a single scene. The most important dynamic, however, is the unexpected shifts in both the literal meaning of the words and the significance of the scene as the existing text is decontextualized and recontextualized—a process that lies at the heart of the haikai imagination.

Of the three basic types of links outlined by Bashō's disciples, word links, content links, and scent links, the latter two types dominate. A number of links have embedded in them established word associations, such as "dew"/"grass," "mist"/"moon," "willow"/"bank," and "cherry blossoms"/"butterflies," which can be found in classical renga handbooks such as *Gathered Gems* (*Renju gappeki shū*; 1476) or in Teimon haikai handbooks such as the *Accompanying Boat* (*Ruisenshū*; 1676). Given that Kakei was originally a Teimon haikai master and the Nagoya group had followed the Teimon style, which relied heavily on word links, it comes as no surprise that lexical associations appear in the sequence, but in almost no case—the obvious exception being the *konoshiro* (shad) and *ko no shiro* (substitute for child) link—do they rely, as earlier haikai did, on word associations and homophonic play for wit or humor or as the primary means of linking. Almost all the links, including those with word associations, are either content links and/or scent links, in which the verses are joined by narrative extension as well as by intersecting overtones or atmospheric associations.

The sequence closely follows the principle of shifting (*yukiyō*) or movement across three verses (*sanku no watari*), which had been stressed in classical linked verse since the time of Sōgi. On occasion, as in the "carrying on the head / a basket of shad" (*mi ni konoshiro no uo o itadaki*), "my prayers to / an early morning star / to be pregnant" (*waga inori akegata no hoshi haramubeku*), and "today going to the eyebrow ceremony / for the younger sister" (*kyō wa imoto no mayukaki ni yuki*) sequence, the same topic—pregnancy—seems to persist over three verses, but even here the sequence shifts from a poor, provincial woman (bearing the shad) to a court lady, and the verse on the eyebrow ceremony need not be read in relationship to pregnancy. Almost all the verses push off the penultimate verse while transforming the meaning of the previous verse. (The same principle applies to reading linked verse: when in doubt, it is best to take the interpretation that moves away from the penultimate verse.) The result is an ever-changing, palimpsestic vision, of a new image and an after-image. The participants journey from one social world to the next, passing through all four seasons, moving between nature and the human world, country and city, Japan and China, past and present, from tragedy to comedy. Kabuki, which emerged in the major urban centers in the seventeenth century alongside haikai and was followed by a similar audience, was one of the many Tokugawa popular forms influenced by this haikai process of change and recontextualization. The late Tokugawa kabuki dramatist and writer Nishizawa Ippōken (1801–52) made the following observation in *Denki sakusho* (Record of unusual happenings; 1851), a treatise on popular drama, "A haikai sequence is marked by ceaseless change—a character that appears to be a noble turns out to be a beggar, a scene of love becomes one of death and transience, the mansion of an aristocrat is transformed into a dirt-floor hovel. Truly, *kabuki* performance should be like the changes of haikai."[49]

Much of the interest of *Withering Gusts*, as with haikai in general, derives from the interactions among different literary voices drawn from a variety of sources. Jūgo evidently had a love for "foreign" or "Chinese" topics, which is evident in "squid shells / divination in a barbarian land" (*ika wa ebisu no kuni no urakata*) and "at the temple lodging / of Japan's Li Po—/ moon-gazing" (*Jittō no Rihaku ga bō ni tsuki o mite*), which frame a sequence of five China-related verses, one of the highlights of *Withering Gusts*. Yasui, on the other hand, had a great fondness for the aristocratic world of the Heian romance (*monogatari*), as revealed in "asking the Second Nun / about the cherry trees in full bloom / at the imperial palace" (*ni no ama ni konoe no hana no sakari kiku*) and "today going to the eyebrow ceremony / for the younger sister" (*kyō wa imoto no mayukaki ni yuki*). Yasui was also interested in different aspects of nature, as evident in his verses on sasanqua, the heron, cherry blossoms, and Chinese endive (*tōchisa*).

As a communal practice, haikai not only joined different indi-

viduals in an intimate way but also "linked" the participants to liter-
ary and historical worlds, to a common cultural past, which in-
cluded China. Haikai, which did not require the extensive knowl-
edge necessary for renga, quickly became a means for newly edu-
cated commoners and samurai to acquire a taste for and explore a
cultural tradition as it was shaped by haikai masters, who served as
bridges to the past. In the medieval period, renga provided, both in
the farm villages and in the cities, an opportunity for its participants
to escape together, if only for a while, from the surrounding warfare
and chaos, into the elegant world of Heian court culture via the
words and associations of classical poetry. Seventeenth-century hai-
kai likewise allowed its participants to share in a communal vision
that was often at odds with surrounding reality. In contrast to med-
ieval renga or the haikai composed at Bashō's retreat at Fukagawa
during the early 1680's, however, the haikai of *Withering Gusts* was
practiced in a time of peace and relative stability, especially for the
well-to-do participants at Nagoya. One consequence is a haikai that
provides a window both onto an imagined past, one more wide-
ranging than that found in medieval renga, and onto various aspects
of seventeenth-century life. As we can see here, *Withering Gusts*
moves back and forth between contemporary worlds of the brew-
ery, breast-feeding, lameness, fishing villages, and pregnancy, *and*
the more distant worlds of the Heian court, of medieval warrior so-
ciety, and of China. As the heavy mixture of haikai words and clas-
sical diction reveals, Bashō and his disciples joined these disjunctive
languages and subcultures through the poetics of "scent," of inter-
secting overtones, which gave new life to worn classical images
while transforming contemporary material life into poetry, much of
it for the first time.

One social function of linked verse was to create harmony, to
bring the participants, who could be of diverse backgrounds,
together by composing verses that had to be shared and drawn out
of the verses of others. Part of the interest of *Withering Gusts* also
derives from the intense interaction, which borders on rivalry,
particularly in the first half, between Kakei, the local master, and

Bashō, the distinguished guest. When one of Kakei's outstanding verses—*ima zo urami no ya o hanatsu koe* ("Now's the time!"/ releasing an arrow of resentment)—transformed the world of Heian romance into a medieval scene of revenge, it immediately stimulated two equally strong verses—Bashō's *nusubito no katami no matsu no fukiorete* ("A pine in memory/of a bandit bends/snapping in the wind") and Tokoku's *shibashi Sōgi no na o tsukeshi mizu* ("for a while it lasted/a stream named after Sōgi")—which replaced the world of medieval warfare with that of Muromachi high culture. This tension between Bashō, the outsider, and Kakei, the insider, which produced some of the more exciting exchanges in the intensification section, gradually dissolved into harmony as the Nagoya poets became comfortable with Bashō and joined him in the poetics of *fū-kyō*, which Bashō introduced in the opening verse on Chikusai and which they gradually took up in the course of the session. The eccentric figure madly devoted to poetic beauty, particularly to dark, cold phenomenon such as "withering gusts," was echoed by the Nagoya poets and emerged in the form of such characters as the Chinese-style moon-gazer and the eccentric biwa player.

Haikai, like the tea ceremony, was a performance art, a one-time happening. The group dynamics, the dialogic exchange, and the mood, which lay at the heart of haikai, all disappeared when the session was over. In *Sanzōshi* (NKBZ 51: 549), Bashō stated, "Once the *kaishi* [poetry record] is taken down from the writing stand, it is no more than trash." For Bashō, however, there was another kind of community of poets who wrote for each other and who responded to printed texts. Haikai in this broader sense meant linking across time and space, responding to texts and poetry outside the immediate linked verse session. Kakei, the Nagoya haikai master, published *Winter Days*, including *Withering Gusts*, within two months of the haikai sessions, allowing the haikai to circulate among a larger circle of interested poets. Bashō, who exploited the new literary market created by print capitalism, was intensely concerned that haikai could be appreciated outside its original context. Haikai linked sequences, like their classical predecessors, were generally difficult to read because of the gap between the one-time performance and the written record. Consequently, renga and haikai masters (such as Teitoku and Sōin) provided self-commentary (*jichū*). As a haikai master and an editor, Bashō reworked the original sequence in such a way that it could be appreciated independently of its original context, frequently rewriting and rearranging the verses and sometimes even switching the names of the participants in order to create a more dramatic, interesting, and readable sequence. Bashō-school *kasen* consequently did not require the kind of self-commentary or footnotes that earlier haikai demanded, making them popular for subsequent readers and haikai poets. Even today, the overwhelming majority of those who practice *renku*, modern linked verse, look back to the Bashō style for their literary model and follow the rules designed by Hokushi, Shikō, and other prominent Bashō disciples.

Point-Garnering

Bashō's career as a haikai master and his ideal of communal art should be understood in the larger context of "verse-capping" (*maeku-zuke*) and "point-garnering haikai" (*tentori haikai*), which dominated the haikai world and became the mainstream in the Genroku period. One of the central occupations of the haikai master in Bashō's day was grading or marking haikai submitted by students, so much so that the term "marker" (*tenja*) or "judge" (*hanja*) became interchangeable with "haikai master." Like the classical renga masters before them, the haikai masters gave "marks" or "points" (*ten*) to indicate the level of merit of a particular verse. A diagonal line, or *heiten* (average point), indicated "one point," and a double line, or *chōten*, meant "two points." As the number of points gradually increased with time, point-giving, which had begun as a means of instructing beginners, lost its pedagogical function and became a new form of entertainment, called *tentori haikai* (point-garnering haikai), in which the participants competed with each other to see who could garner the most points from the marker or judge. Instead of instructing their students on the finer points of haikai composition, the markers or judges began catering to their "students" as customers to be entertained and flattered. Although haikai teachers also earned income from activities such as secret transmissions (*hidensho*) and calligraphy, their primary source of income became *tenryō*, the charge for giving "points."[50]

Equally important, point-garnering became a key component of verse-capping. At the beginning of the Tokugawa period, haikai was generally practiced in two forms: verse-capping, or *maeku-zuke* (literally, "linking to the previous verse"), consisting of only two verses, and the extended form, usually the *hyakuin* (100-verse sequence) or *kasen*. In verse-capping, a seventeen-syllable or fourteen-syllable verse was set out as a "topic" (*dai*) to be capped by either a fourteen- or seventeen-syllable verse, resulting in a 31-syllable linked verse. Both classical renga and early haikai masters composed *maeku-zuke*, or *maeku* as it was usually called, but little of it, except in the extant haikai anthologies, was recorded since it was considered light entertainment or intermediate training for the longer form. *Hobby Horse Mad Composition Collection* (*Chikuba kyōgin shū*; 1499) and *Dog Tsukuba Collection* (1532), the first major collections of Muromachi haikai, and the *Puppy Collection* (1633), the first major haikai anthology of the Tokugawa period, are all collections of *maeku-zuke*. In the late seventeenth century, this practice of *maeku-zuke* had particular appeal for provincial poets who found it difficult to travel to large cities to receive direct instruction from urban-based haikai teachers but were able to have them send "topics," or the opening verses, on which they would compose a *maeku-zuke*, to be evaluated by the judge or marker. This practice, which blossomed from the Manji era (1658–61) onward, became a national pastime that involved competition and prizes for the best *maeku-zuke*. Haikai masters charged fees for establishing the topics (*dai*) and for selecting, marking, ranking, and publishing the best verse-cappings.[51] *Haikai mizukuki no oka* (1692), edited by Wakyū (d. 1692), a Kyoto poet, records the activities of a judge who, at one competition alone, collected over 3,000 verses, concentrating on the Ōmi, Wakasa, and Echizen provinces, and selected 30 to 50 winners, listing them with names and addresses, beginning with the verse that had earned the highest points. This kind of *maeku-zuke*, with its publicity and high stakes, became a form of betting or lottery, and on a number of occasions, the Tokugawa bakufu even intervened to prohibit this type of gambling.[52]

In the mid–seventeenth century, haikai masters, perhaps because of their limited number and the difficulty of becoming a publicly recognized master, led a comfortable life and enjoyed considerable prestige. By the Genroku period, however, there was an overabundance of instructors, and their prestige and ability fell dramatically. In the mid–seventeenth century, a poet had to undergo a period of training before gaining the qualifications necessary to judge and give "points."[53] By the Genroku era, however, haikai poets became judges after only minimal training. According to *Kyōto Silk* (*Kyōhabutae*; 1691), Kyoto had as many as 68 judges.[54] The following passage, which describes the degraded state of haikai, appears in Tesshi's (d. 1707) *Flower-Viewing Carriage* (*Hanami-guruma*; 1702).

> Today's haikai is completely different from the haikai of the past. Long ago, if the participants wanted to hold a session, they would compose a round of verse ten days in advance; and on the day of the session, no matter how busy they were at the time, they would gather together, hang a portrait in the alcove, and burn incense. Each time the participant contributed a verse, he or she would give a bow and express deep appreciation. No chatting would occur during the session, and when the last verse was read, the participants would sit in formal fashion and act politely. After the session, some wine would be offered, and when the master rose to leave, one would send him off and properly express respect. On the next day, the participants would put on a formal dress, pay a visit to the master's house, reveal their gratitude for yesterday's efforts, and hand over the wrapped remuneration on a wooden board. Nowadays, it is completely different. The judge is the one who devotes himself to arranging the session and offers one dish after another. Even before the first round is over, the cups of wine have been passed around, and when it is not their turn to compose, the participants talk to each other in a loud voice about what they think of certain kabuki actors. . . . On the day after, the judge goes about politely thanking the participants, "Yesterday was such a wonderful treat. You gave me a

truly fine verse, which I shall treasure." . . . In the past, masters were owners who could charge rent and could easily go on pilgrimages in their old age, but today's masters, even when they host sessions, do not receive enough fees and have to fawn on the participants. That's how far their status has fallen. (pp. 381–83)

According to *Flower-Viewing Carriage* (p. 391), "Prostitutes make a living selling their bodies; haikai masters make a living selling their names."

Bashō initially went to Edo in order to become a haikai master, a marker who could charge fees for grading haikai, and he fulfilled his ambitions around 1677. But only three years later, in the winter of 1680, he suddenly moved to Fukagawa, on the outskirts of Edo, abandoning his career as a marker, thereby turning his back on the most lucrative aspect of haikai. Even as a marker in Edo, Bashō apparently was reluctant to charge fees, which may have contributed to his apparent financial difficulties. Most of his disciples also avoided the profession of marker.[55] In a letter to Kyorai, dated the seventh day of the Fifth Month of 1692 (Genroku 5), Bashō lamented a decision by Tōrin (1649–1719), a disciple, to become a marker, which, in Bashō's opinion, "dropped him in the mud."[56]

Bashō's abhorrence for point-garnering haikai, particularly of the *maeku-zuke* variety, is evident in a letter—sometimes referred to as "The Three Grades of Poetry" ("Fūga santō no bun")—that he wrote while in Edo to his disciple Kyokusui in Ōmi Province on the eighteenth day of the Second Month of 1692 (Genroku 5).[57]

Generally speaking, people involved in haikai can be divided into three grades. First are those who spend their days and nights garnering points; constantly competing and oblivious to the true way, they run from one session to the next. One could call them the lost children of poetry, and yet they fill the bellies of the marker's wife and children and bring a profit to the landlord, and as a consequence, they are probably better than those who commit serious crimes.

Next are those who have wealth and high status and who are afraid of the kind of pleasure-seeking that draws attention and want to avoid being the object of rumors. These people would prefer to spend their days and nights garnering points at two or three sessions of haikai, take no pride in winning, and do not grow angry when they lose. "Well, let's have another round," they think, do what they can while the five-minute incense stick burns, and take pleasure in the scoring immediately afterward. For them, haikai is no different from a children's card game. But when you consider that they prepare meals, provide endless drinks, help the poor, and fatten the markers, you could probably say that they too are part of the haikai profession.

Third are those who take satisfaction in their unswerving devotion to poetry, who are not easily distracted by the opinions of others, and who see this way as a means to attain the true Buddhist path. These poets seek the distant bones of Fujiwara Teika, follow the sinews of Saigyō, cleanse the intestines of Po Chü-i, and leap into the breast of Tu Fu. In all the cities and provinces, the number of such individuals is fewer than the fingers on my hands. You are one of these ten. Be extremely careful and continue your training.[58]

Bashō divides haikai poets into three types, of which the lowest are addicted to point-garnering haikai; less evil are those who engage in haikai simply for diversion.[59] Bashō's ideal, which was highly unorthodox for the time, is the third type, those who are devoted to the spirit of poetry rather than to the material benefits and who seek the poetic tradition of Teika and Tu Fu.[60] While Bashō did not charge fees for points, and never engaged in verse-capping, he had to depend on contributions from his students and patrons, who looked after his every need, providing clothing, food, furniture, and shelter. The first "grass hut" at Fukagawa was given by Sanpū (1647–1732), a wealthy Edo fish merchant who sold to the bakufu government and various daimyō mansions in Edo, and the second "grass hut" was built with funds raised by Bashō's friend and fellow poet Sodō. Without the aid of such patron/disciples, Bashō would not have been able either to travel or to survive as a haikai master.

Bashō also condemned verse-capping, which had become indistinguishable from point-garnering, as antithetical to his ideal of poetry as a dialogic, communal process. Point-garnering *maeku-zuke* produced a genre in which the participant, competing for attention against numerous other submissions on the same topic (or *maeku*), sought shock value, usually through an unexpected, humorous twist on the topic or through unusual vocabulary. The *karumi* (lightness) style that Bashō advocated at this time, from the early 1690s, attempted to focus on everyday commoner life, on things as they were, leaving a broad space for interpretation or for the next verse. Verse-capping, by contrast, tended to be fantastical, with a tendency to personify animals and plants, or to be conceptual (what Bashō referred to as "heaviness," *omomi*). It also fostered exaggerated expressions, used startling vocabulary, and brought the previous verse to a sudden close, leaving little or nothing to the imagination.[61]

CHAPTER 6

The Poet as Guest

The word is a two-sided act. It is determined equally by whose word it
is and for whom it is meant.

—V. N. Volosinov

Modern readers have tended to read Bashō's poems monologi-
cally, in isolation, either in an expressive, lyrical mode, as an expres-
sion of the speaker's subjective state, or in a descriptive, mimetic
mode, as a reflection of the external world as perceived by the
speaker. This tendency overlooks the crucial fact that much of
Bashō's prose and poetry, like those of his contemporaries, func-
tioned dialogically, in a communal context, fulfilling socio-religious
functions such as complimenting a host, expressing gratitude, bid-
ding farewell, making an offering to the land, or consoling the spirit
of a dead person. Despite the eremitic image that he cultivated,
Bashō was constantly meeting with people to compose linked
verse—encounters that usually resulted in greetings or expressions of
gratitude. Almost half of the roughly 250 hokku in Bashō's three
most famous travel accounts—*Skeleton in the Fields, Backpack Notes,*
and *Narrow Road to the Interior*—originally functioned as social ad-
dresses or replies of this sort.[1] In contrast to the apostrophic mode,
in which the speaker of an English Romantic poem addresses a dead
or absent person ("O thou with dewy locks") or speaks to an ab-
stract notion or object as if it were alive ("O Rose, thou art sick!"),
these poems appear to be lyrical or descriptive statements without a
specific addressee even as they function dialogically.

Poetic Greetings

Poetry has enjoyed a long history as extemporaneous dialogue in Japan. The "dialogue poems" (*mondōka*) in the *Kojiki* (Record of ancient matters; 712), the "love poems" (*sōmonka*) in the *Man'yōshū* (Collection of ten thousand leaves; 759), and the "exchanged waka" (*zōtōka*) popular in the Heian period were all written in a quasi-epistolary form, with the expectation of a poetic reply. As *Instructions for Beginners* (*Shogaku yōshashō*; ca. 1473), a renga handbook attributed to Sōgi, suggests, linked verse inherited this long tradition of poetic dialogue.

> First, composing linked verse is like having a conversation in which individuals speak to each other about various aspects of life. If someone says, "The wind yesterday was fierce, wasn't it!" one must answer with a phrase such as: "Yes, the cherry blossoms have been scattered completely, leaving nothing."[2]

Typically, the main guest would be invited to compose a hokku, the opening verse of a linked verse sequence, and the host would reply with the second verse (*wakiku*).[3] The following hokku, which Bashō composed in the summer of 1689 and later placed in *Narrow Road to the Interior*, is a greeting to Bashō's friend and host Tōkyū (1638–1715), a station master at Sukagawa, at the entrance to Michinoku, in present-day Fukushima.

> beginnings of poetry—
> the rice-planting songs
> of the Interior

> fūryū | no | hajime | ya | oku | no | taueuta
> poetry | 's | beginning | : | Interior | 's | rice-planting-song

Hearing the rice-planting songs in the fields (probably owned by Tōkyū), Bashō composed a poem that complimented the host on the elegance of his home and region—which he associated with the historical "beginnings" (*hajime*) of *fūryū*, or poetic art—while suggesting his joy and gratitude at being able to compose linked verse or "po-

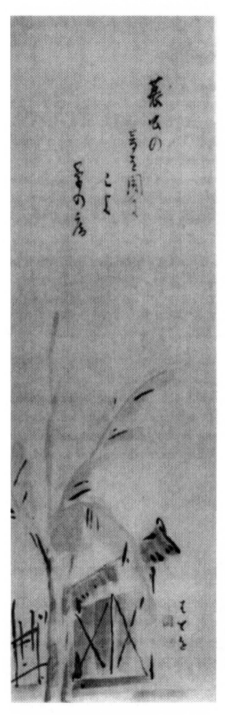

The poem, the calligraphy, and the
painting by Bashō, probably done
after he began taking lessons from
Kyoriku, in the latter half of 1692
or later. 36.7 x 11.7 in. The paint-
ing, which suggests the Bashō Hut
at Fukagawa, shows a tall Japanese
plantain (*bashō*), after which the
poet took his most famous pen-
name, in front of a bamboo fence
and a roofed brushwood gate
(*saimon*). The poem—*minomushi
no / ne o kiki ni / koyo / kusa no io*
(come listen to the sound of the
bagworm!—a grass hut)—was
composed in 1687 and appears in
Sequel to Empty Chestnuts with the
headnote, "Listening to the Quiet."
Because of a passage in *The Pillow
Book*, the bagworm (*minomushi*), a
seasonal word for autumn, was
considered a creature that plain-
tively and faintly cries, "Father!
father!" (*chichi yo chichi yo*), with
the arrival of the autumn winds. In
this poem Bashō invites a friend to
come join him at his hermitage, to
enjoy the sad quiet of the autumn
wind—quiet enough to hear the
sound of the *minomushi*, which is
normally never heard. (Courtesy
Idemitsu Art Museum)

etry" (*furyū*) for the "first time" (*hajime*) in the Interior (Oku). Tō-kyū answers with a second verse, which is also a greeting (KBZ 4: 107).

> gathering wild strawberries
> my humble treat
>
> ichigo | o | otte | waga | mōkegusa
> strawberry | (acc.) | gathering | my | grass-treat

In response to the hokku, which flatters the host, the second verse is self-effacing and humble, implying that, being in the country, the rustic host has nothing appropriate to offer his cultured guest: the most that he can do is collect some strawberries, not considered a delicacy. Following poetic protocol, the second verse maintains the same season as the hokku: both "strawberries" (*ichigo*) and "rice-planting songs" (*taueuta*) are seasonal words for summer.

In principle, any one of the 36 verses in a *kasen* could function as a salutation. The *ageku*, or closing verse, of the "rice-planting" sequence, for example, is another greeting to the host Tōkyū from Sora, Bashō's travel companion.

> at the silkgrower's house
> piles of silk robes
> —Sora
>
> kogaisuru | ya | ni | kosode | kasanaru
> silkgrowing | house | in | robe | pile-up

The closing verse, coming at the end of the haikai session, had to be felicitous, generating an atmosphere of peace and warmth. Sora's verse describes an abundance of *kosode*, wadded robes of fine silk, suggesting the opulence of Tōkyū's residence and praising the host, who was a successful silk producer.

Most of Bashō's poetic greetings appear at first glance to be purely lyrical or descriptive, but there are usually one or two words that implicitly represent the object or person to be greeted, causing the reader to interpret the poem both mimetically and dialogically. In *Sanzōshi*, Dohō commented on the technique.

polished anew
the holy mirror too is clear—
blossoms of snow

togi-naosu | kagami | mo | kiyoshi | yuki | no | hana
re-polish | mirror | also | clear | snow | 's | flower

longing for the plum blossoms
I pray to the white deutzia—
tears in my eyes

ume | koite | unohana | ogamu | namida | kana[4]
plum | longing | white-deutzia | pray | tears | !

The poem on snow was composed on the occasion of the reconstruction of the Atsuta Shrine. The first five syllables "polish anew" directly express the spirit of rebuilding and reveal the stature of the shrine.

The poem on plum blossoms was composed on the death of Bishop Daiten of Engakuji Temple. The speaker pays tribute to the deceased by comparing him to plum blossoms and then bowing before the white deutzia in bloom at the time. The feelings of the speaker are revealed not directly but through an object that captures the character and status of the person in question. (NKBZ 51: 559)

Dohō selected two representative poems by Bashō, a celebration and a lament, in which the speaker's respect is expressed through "an object" (*mono*) that reflects the "status" (*kurai*) of the addressee. In the first example, from *Backpack Notes*, the "clearness" (*kiyoshi*) of the newly polished mirror, which resonates with the whiteness of the snowflakes, symbolizes the purity of the newly reconstructed shrine. In the second hokku, from *Skeleton in the Fields*, the elegant plum blossoms reflect the refinement and high status of the bishop, who died in the First Month (February), when the plum tree is in bloom. Bashō did not hear of the bishop's death until the summer, the Fourth Month (May), the season of the *unohana* (deutzia), an ornamental shrub with white flower clusters, which reminded the poet of the whitish plum blossoms.

Another common technique in the poetic address was the incorporation of homonyms (*kakekotoba*) or word associations (*engo*), which allowed for extreme semantic condensation. The following hokku, composed by Bashō in the Second Month of Genroku 1 (March 1688), is a greeting to Sonome, Bashō's most outstanding female disciple, the wife of a doctor (*Ichiu*), who lived in Ise Yamada (Mie Prefecture) and is here symbolized by the "plum blossoms to the north" (*kita no ume*), a seasonal phrase for spring.

> beyond the curtain
> a quiet depth—
> northern plum blossoms

> nōren | no | oku | monofukashi | kita | no | ume
> curtain | 's | interior | deep-quiet | north | 's | plum

Between the southern guest room and the northern "inner room" (*okunoma*) hangs a *nōren* (hanging curtain; modern Japanese, *noren*), beyond which the speaker can glimpse a plum tree in bloom. The word *oku* (inner, within), which suggests "depth," refers not only to the inner room but to *oku niwa* (inner garden) as well as to *okusan* ("wife" or "person within"). *Kita* (north) similarly implies *kita no kata* (literally, "lady of the northern quarters"), a classical word for principal wife. The description of the setting thus becomes a tribute to the quite refinement and "depth" (*monofukashi*) of the lady of the house, represented by the plum blossoms.

Sometimes the poem may be overtly symbolic or semi-allegorical, with nature personified, as in the following hokku, which appears in *Skeleton in the Fields* (NKBZ 41: 298) and which Bashō composed when he left the house of Tōyō (1653–1712), a friend in Atsuta (Nagoya), in May 1685 (Fourth Month, Jōkyō 2).

> Having stayed once more at the residence of Master Tōyō, I was about to leave for the Eastern Provinces.

> from deep within
> the peony pistils—withdrawing
> regretfully the bee

> botan | shibe | fukaku | wakeizuru | hachi | no | nagori | kana
> peony | pistil | deep | withdraw | bee | 's | regret | !

The bee (Bashō) has rested peacefully within the peony (*botan*), an elegant summer flower that symbolizes Tōyō's residence, joyfully imbibing the rich pollen of the pistils (*shibe*), but now, with much reluctance, it must leave. The hokku is an expression of gratitude and a farewell not only to Tōyō but to all the Nagoya area poets who have hosted him on this journey.

Sometimes the insertion of a single word was sufficient to make the poem a greeting. In an age without air conditioners, the word "cool" (*suzushisa*), a seasonal word for summer, was the ultimate compliment that could be paid to the host of a summer's lodging. Bashō composed as many as 25 hokku with the word "coolness" (*suzushisa* or *suzushimi*), many of them in 1689 and 1694, when he traveled during the summer. Bashō composed the following in the summer of 1689, during the *Narrow Road to the Interior* journey, at the home of Seifū of Obanazawa in Dewa (Yamagata).

> I visited a person named Seifū at Obanazawa. Although wealthy, he had the spirit of a recluse. Having traveled repeatedly to the capital, he understood the tribulations of travel and gave me shelter for a number of days. In a variety of ways, he eased the pain of the long journey.

> taking coolness
> for my lodging
>   I stretch out

> suzushisa | o | waga | yado | ni | shite | nemaru | nari
> coolness | (acc.) | my | lodging | as | making | stretch-out | indeed
>   (NKBZ 41: 367)

Bashō, exhausted from a difficult journey, finds Seifū's residence and hospitality to be "coolness" itself and "relaxes" (*nemaru*)—a word deliberately taken from the local dialect—as if he were at home.

Many of Bashō's poetic greetings present an external scene, usually one taken from nature, which functions on several levels at the same time, lyrical, descriptive, and dialogic, as in the following hokku, which Bashō composed in the winter of 1686 and which appears in Bashō's collection *Gathered Verses* (*Atsumeku*; edited 1687).

Offered in return for a container of wine from Priest Genki

> cold in the water
> unable to sleep—
>   a seagull

mizu | samuku | neirikanetaru | kamome | kana
water | cold | fall-sleep-can-not | seagull | !⁵

The seagull (*kamome*) is floating on water so cold that it has trouble falling asleep ("cold," *samusa*, is a seasonal word for winter). On a more figurative, lyrical level, the seagull becomes a symbol of the poet, who is having difficulty sleeping on the journey. The head-note, "Offered in return for a container of wine from Priest Genki," indicates that the hokku also operates on the dialogic, performative level as an expression of the poet's gratitude for the priest's generous gift of wine on this cold night: in an inversion of the first two levels, the third level implies that the hitherto frozen traveler, now filled with the wine and thoughts of the considerate priest, will sleep warmly tonight.

Sometimes the admiration or respect is shown through the creation of a specific mood or atmosphere, as in the following hokku, which Bashō composed when he visited the hermitage of Roboku (1628–1706), a haikai master in Ise, during the *Skeleton in the Fields* journey in 1684.

Upon visiting the thatched hut of a recluse

> vines planted
> four or five bamboo trees
>   stirring in a storm

tsuta | uete | take | shi | go | hon | no | arashi | kana
vine | planting | bamboo | four | five | tree | 's | storm | !
(NKBZ 41: 291)⁶

Bamboo and vines, along with thatched huts, frequently appear in Chinese recluse poetry. The bright leaves of the vine (*tsuta*), a seasonal word for autumn associated in medieval Japanese poetry with reclusion, and the strong wind stirring the leaves of only four or five bamboo trees suggest a spare, lonely, quiet residence, thereby expressing Bashō's admiration for the reclusive lifestyle of the host.

The poetic compliment was composed for a specific person, who was expected to reply in kind. As a consequence, a poem could fail if it were not composed quickly and spontaneously, as Tokugen (1559–1647) notes in *Instructions for Haikai Beginners* (*Haikai sho-gaku shō*; 1641).

> No matter how good a poet is, there are times when he cannot produce a poem on the spot. But even on these occasions, it is best to compose spontaneously, on the cherry blossoms or autumn leaves in the garden, or on something unusual in the setting. Impromptu composition is far more desirable than a verse prepared in advance. Is there anything better than a salutation?[7]

Similar advice appears in *Kyoraishō*, which records an episode in which Kyorai, the honored guest, had difficulty responding to a host's request for a hokku.

> The Master said, "We went to Masahide's residence for the first time to-day. As the honored guest, you must be ready to present the opening verse. When asked to compose, you cannot spend time pondering the merits or demerits of the verse. You must present as quickly as possible. Today, you did neither. There is only so much time in an evening. Had you continued to consume time, the session would have been spoiled and the atmosphere destroyed. That is why I presented a hokku in your place." (NKBZ 51: 446)

In Bashō's opinion, it was far better to present a poem immediately, even if it meant offering an inferior verse. Like the art of tea, haikai was a performance art, a one-time spontaneous meeting of its participants, who had to interact closely and pay their respects to each other. To fail to observe this social dimension was to fail in the art. The poetic greeting was consequently judged by and valued for its appropriateness to the immediate situation. In June 1694 (5.23.Genroku 7), while on his last journey, Bashō, hearing that his Nagoya disciple Yasui was building a hermitage, composed these two hokku.

a blueprint for coolness
it appears—
this dwelling

suzushisa | no | sashizu | ni | miyuru | sumai | kana
coolness | 's | blueprint | in | appear | dwelling | !
(NKBT 45: 78)

for coolness
the craftsman of Hida
has a blueprint

suzushisa | o | Hida | no | takumi | ga | sashizu | kana
coolness | (acc.) | Hida | 's | craftsman | 's | blueprint | !
(NKBT 45: 77)

Suzushisa (coolness), in addition to being a complimentary word, suggests the refreshing, ideal nature of the planned residence as well as the spirit of its architect and future inhabitant. The first hokku, which implied that the design or blueprint (*sashizu*) alone presages an excellent dwelling, is a poetic prayer for the rapid completion of the building. The second hokku playfully suggests that the legendary carpenter of Hida Province has been reincarnated in the form of Yasui, who is about to create another ideal dwelling. Bashō chose the first of the two hokku and sent it to Yasui, but in a June 1694 letter to Sanpū, his Edo disciple and patron (KBZ 8: 233), Bashō noted that the second hokku was superior as a poem. Bashō, in short, chose the poem best suited for the occasion, the more effective greeting.

Despite the overwhelming number of poetic greetings in Bashō's oeuvre, relatively few appear in the modern Japanese canon of Bashō's famous poems (*meiku*). Of the two basic types of hokku—the *tateku*, the opening hokku, which started a linked verse sequence, and the *jibokku*, the autonomous hokku—the *tateku* usually served as a greeting to the host of the linked verse session except in instances where the participants were already very close to the host and had no need to observe such etiquette. (Such is the case with a *kasen* such as *In the Town* in *Monkey's Straw Coat*, which was composed by Bashō, Kyorai, and Bonchō, who had been working together for some time and did not exchange greetings.) Since a large number of the over 900 hokku that Bashō composed were *tateku*, or opening verses to linked verse sequences, many of them were also greetings. After Bashō retreated to Fukagawa in 1680, his poetry and prose appeared to become highly confessional, an unprecedented phenomenon in haikai. Modern poets and writers have tended to favor these seemingly autobiographical, lyrical hokku, which, when gathered together, especially in the form of a travel account, appear to take the form of a spiritual record of a solitary individual. This tendency was encouraged by Masaoka Shiki, the pioneer of modern haiku, who stressed the notion of haiku as "autonomous art" and severed the hokku from linked verse, which he regarded as a trivial game, thereby encouraging a monologic view of the hokku. The frequent use of symbolism (e.g., plum blossoms to represent a hostess) in the poetic greeting was also incompatible with Masaoka Shiki's notion of *shasei*, or "sketch from life." The situation has been further complicated by the passage of time, which has made it difficult to recover the original context, which is vital to understanding or appreciating such poetry.

The existence of numerous variants reveals that Bashō constantly rewrote his poems—which are limited in number for a haikai master of his time—long after they had served their initial social purpose and that he often recontextualized them so they took on a different meaning and a new life. If a haikai session occurred in the summer, the hokku had to avoid the word "hot" (*atsushi*), and if the poet was invited by a patron during the winter, he could not use the word "cold" (*samushi*). Bashō, who was not constrained by such circumstances in revising his poems, routinely changed or eliminated the original prefaces. During his *Narrow Road to the Interior* journey, Bashō composed at least seventeen hokku (*tateku*) for linked verse sessions. Of the twelve that Bashō chose for inclusion in the travel account, seven were revised and most were recontextualized. The following hokku on the Mogami River, which flowed from the mountains of Dewa (Yamagata) to the Japan Sea, at the port city of Sakata, was composed in July 1689 (6.14.Genroku 2), as part of a *kasen* at the residence of Terajima Hikosuke, a wealthy merchant at Sakata.

> coolness—
> pouring into the sea
>   Mogami River

suzushisa | ya | umi | ni | iretaru | Mogamigawa
coolness | : | sea | into | pour-in | Mogami-River[8]

The hokku praises the view from Hikosuke's house, which over-looks the Mogami River at the point where the giant river flows into the Japan Sea. A number of years later Bashō revised the poem for inclusion in *Narrow Road to the Interior*.

> pouring the hot day
> into the sea—
>   Mogami River

atsuki | hi | o | umi | ni | iretari | Mogamigawa
hot | day | (acc.) | sea | into | pour | Mogami-River
(NKBZ 41: 371)

Instead of the river pouring into the sea, the Mogami River pours the *atsuki hi*, which can be read either as "hot sun" or "hot day," suggesting both a setting sun washed by the waves at sea and a hot summer's day coming to a dramatic close in the sea. Bashō drops the word "coolness" (*suzushisa*) and the constraints of the poetic greeting to create a more dramatic image, one that suggests coolness without using the word.

A similar kind of transformation occurs in another poem on the Mogami River that Bashō composed on the same journey, at the residence of Takano Ichiei, a wealthy shipping agent who owned a boathouse on the Mogami River.

> gathering the rains
> of the wet season—cool
>   the Mogami River
>   —Bashō

samidare | o | atsumete | suzushi | Mogamigawa
summer-rains | (acc.) | gathering | cool | Mogami-River

a wharf post tying
a firefly to the bank
            —Ichiei

kishi | ni | hotaru | o | tsunagu | funagui
bank | to | firefly | (acc.) | tie | wharf-post[9]

Bashō's hokku praised the view of the river from Ichiei's residence
by commenting on the "cool" sight of the huge Mogami River gath-
ering in *samidare* (Fifth-Month rains), the steady rains of the wet
season. In the second verse, Ichiei compared himself to the wharf
posts that restrain the beautiful firefly (Bashō), thereby thanking his
distinguished guest for the opportunity to entertain him. When
Bashō wrote *Narrow Road to the Interior* three or four years later, he
transformed the hokku.

> The Mogami River originates in the Interior, with its upper reaches in
> Yamagata. As one descends, one encounters frightening rapids with
> names like Scattered-Go-Stones or Flying Eagle. The river skirts the
> north side of Mount Itajiki and then finally pours into the sea at Sakata.
> As I descended, passing through the dense foliage, I felt as if the moun-
> tains were covering the river on both sides. When filled with rice, these
> boats are apparently called "rice boats." Through the green leaves, I
> could see the falling waters of White-Thread Cascade. Sennindō, Hall of
> the Wizard, stood on the banks, directly facing the water. The river was
> swollen with rain, making the boat journey perilous.

    gathering the rains
of the wet season—swift
    the Mogami River

samidare | o | atsumete | hayashi | Mogamigawa
summer-rains | (acc.) | gathering | swift | Mogami-River
                (NKBZ 41: 369)

The revised version, which drops the word "cool" (*suzushi*), is no
longer a greeting to a host, although it can still be interpreted as a sa-
lute to the spirit of the river. The Mogami River, the largest river in
the province, the main artery for all the other tributaries and
streams, is "gathering" (*atsumete*) or has been gathering over time—

one interpretation is that the wet season (*samidare*) is already over—the rains of the entire province, resulting in a massively swollen river, the force of which is captured and condensed in the quick sound and meaning of the word *hayashi* (swift). In the process, Bashō gave a new poetic essence (*hon'i*), based on personal experience, to the Mogami River, an *utamakura* (poetic place) associated from the time of the *Kokinshū* (Azuma-uta, no. 1092) with rice-grain boats (*inabune*), which were thought to ply the river.

Prose Greetings

Most of Bashō's haibun, or haikai prose, were also dialogic, serving as greetings or expressions of gratitude or praise to a host.

> come listen
> to the sound of the bagworm!
> a grass hut

minomushi | no | ne | o | kiki | ni | koyo | kusa | no | io
bagworm | 's | sound | (acc.) | listen | to | come | grass | 's | hut

In response to this hokku by Bashō, Yamaguchi Sodō (1642–1716), a scholar of Chinese literature and a *kanshi* poet, wrote the haibun essay "Comment on the Bagworm" ("Minomushi no setsu"), which in turn caused Bashō to compose "Postscript to 'Comment on the Bagworm,'" in which he praised the beauty of Sodō's poetic prose. The result is an extended prose dialogue, like that of linked verse, in which Bashō and Sodō alternately meditate on the nature of reclusion. Some of Bashō's haibun, such as "Mourning for Matsukura Ranran" ("Matsukura Ranran o itamu"), are laments. Others such as "On Parting from Kyoriku" ("Kyoriku ni ribetsu no kotoba") are the prose equivalents of parting poems. "Record of an Unreal Dwelling" ("Genjūan no ki"), which Bashō considered his model haibun, was originally written as an expression of gratitude to Kyokusui (d. 1717), a disciple who offered him a cool summer dwelling at Ishiyama in Ōmi (Shiga), where Bashō stayed for almost four months in the summer of 1690 (Genroku 3), after his journey through the Interior.

A typical haibun was written in gratitude to a host on a journey with the praise often expressed in Chinese allusions and forms, which were often the prototypes for Bashō's haikai prose. The well-known "Tower of Eighteen" ("Jūhachirō no ki"; 1688), for example, was written when Bashō was invited to the house of Kashima in Mino (Gifu), on his way back from the *Backpack Notes* journey.

> A stately tower stands on the banks of the Nagara River in Mino Province. Mr. Kashima is the owner's name. Inaba Mountain rises in the rear, and mountains, which are high and low, neither too near nor too far, stand to the west. A cedar grove hides a temple in the middle of the rice fields, and the dwellings along the shore are wrapped in the deep green of bamboo. Water-bleached cloth has been stretched out to dry here and there, and to the right a ferryboat floats on the water. The villagers walk back and forth ceaselessly; the houses of the fisherfolk stand side by side; fishermen pull in their nets and cast out their lines, each one working as if to enhance the setting of the stately mansion. The vista is enough to make one forget the heat of the lingering summer sun. The moon at last replaces the rays of the setting sun, and the light of the flares reflected in the waves gradually comes closer as the residents begin cormorant fishing at the base of the mansion—a startling sight! In the cool breeze, I find the famous Eight Views of Hsiao-hsiang and the Ten Sights of West Lake. If one were to give this tower a name, Eighteen Sights would be appropriate.

> from this spot
> all that meets the eye
> 　　is coolness

> kono | atari | me | ni | miyuru | mono | wa | mina | suzushi
> this | spot | eye | in | appear | thing | as-for | all | cool
> 　　　　　　(NKBZ 41: 456–57)

The haibun, which is written in prose couplets with contrastive and parallel images, is an elegant homage to Bashō's host, climaxing with a comparison of the dwelling to the famous sights of China—the views of Hsiao-hsiang and West Lake—and the image of "coolness" in the hokku. The compact parallel structure, the terse Chinese style, and the gentle poetic overtones quickly turned it into an exemplary haibun that was widely admired and repeatedly anthologized.[10]

Bashō gathered a number of these haibun, prose in haikai spirit, and wove them into commemorative travel accounts, which he sometimes sent to the primary host of the journey. *Skeleton in the Fields*, Bashō's first travel account, is based on at least five such appreciatory haibun. Almost all the haibun Bashō composed during his visit to the northern region—at least thirteen notable works survive—were later incorporated into *Narrow Road to the Interior*. The same applies to *Backpack Notes*. After passing the Shirakawa Barrier, the symbolic entrance to Michinoku, Bashō gave Tōkyū, the station master at Sukagawa, the following haibun, which contains the hokku examined earlier.

> Looking forward to the various famous places in the Interior, I traveled north, where I was drawn, first of all, to the ruins of the Shirakawa Barrier. I followed the ancient road to that former checkpoint, crossing along the way the present barrier at Shirakawa. I soon arrived at Iwase County and knocked on the fragrant gate of the gentleman Satansai Tōkyū. Fortunately, I was able, in the words of Wang Wei, "to cross the Yang Barrier and meet an old friend."

>   beginnings of poetry—
> the rice-planting songs
>   of the Interior

> fūryū | no | hajime | ya | oku | no | taueuta
> poetry | 's | beginning | : | Interior | 's | rice-planting-song
>   (NKBZ 41: 474)

Compared with the corresponding passage in *Narrow Road to the Interior*, this haibun is far more flattering, comparing the host to a figure in a Chinese poem by Wang Wei and making no mention, as *Narrow Road to the Interior* does, of the visitor's laborious trek across the Shirakawa Barrier. After accumulating a sufficient number of such haibun, Bashō rewrote and recontextualized them to fit into a larger travel narrative.

The composition of haibun, like that of hokku, was inseparable from the practice of calligraphy and painting or sketching. Poems and haikai prose by haikai masters were prized as much, if not more, for their calligraphy as for their literary content, and the material forms of haikai became significant sources of income for Bashō and other haikai masters. Initially, Bashō's situation resembled that of a promising painter who pays his rent by giving signed sketches or paintings to his landlord. As Bashō's reputation grew, the material form—calligraphy, painting, the signed poem, the sheet of haibun—took on greater exchange value. A single hokku was sufficient to fill a *tanjaku* (*tanzaku*), a small, narrow (36.4 × 6.1 cm) sheet for displaying poetry in the poet's own hand; a *kaishi*,[11] a slightly larger, rectangular paper, usually required something more. Sometimes Bashō would copy a passage from a Noh libretto next to the hokku, but the best solution was usually a *haiga* (haikai sketch or painting) or a haibun. Often the painting and the poetry/calligraphy were composed in a dialogic exchange. In the *haigasan* (praise of a haikai painting), the practice of adding haikai poetry or prose to an open area in a painting, the poem was often added to someone else's painting, thereby "praising" or "greeting" it; or the poetry could be composed first, with the painting added later, to complement and "reply" to the poem.

Bashō sometimes even illustrated his own travel accounts, presenting the entire work in a picture scroll (*emaki*) format that could, like his *tanjaku* and *kaishi*, serve as a memento for a patron or host of the journey.[12] The most notable example is a revised version of *Skeleton in the Fields* now referred to as *Kasshi ginkō emaki* (Picture scroll of the journey of 1684), a long, multi-panel scroll with delicate color illustrations by Bashō with the accompanying text in Bashō's own hand.[13] As his correspondence two years prior to the journey reveals, Bashō initially planned the trip in response to an invitation from disciples in Ōgaki, in Mino (Gifu), particularly Bokuin (1646–1725), a shipping agent, who encouraged him to embark on his first provincial tour as a haikai master and to whom the illustrated scroll, which contains 26 separate painting/sketches interwoven with prose and poetry, was probably sent.[14] *Skeleton in the Fields* reaches a climax with the following passage:

> When I stopped for the night at Ōgaki, I became a guest at Bokuin's residence. Since I had begun this journey from Musashi Plain with thoughts of a weather-beaten skeleton, I wrote:

> end of the journey
> and still alive!
> the last of autumn

> shini | mo | senu | tabine | no | hate | yo | aki | no | kure
> dying | even | do-not | travel-sleep | 's | end | ! | autumn | 's | end
> (NKBZ 41: 294)

Bashō's poem, which echoes the opening poem on the "skeleton in the field" (*nozarashi*), is an expression of gratitude to Bokuin, thanking him for his warm hospitality, which has saved Bashō's frail body from the vicissitudes of the road.[15]

Respecting the Land

Bashō wrote poetic greetings not only to people but also to the spirit of the land as well as to rocks, trees, mountains, and other natural objects. The "beginnings of poetry" (*fūryū no hajime ya*) hokku examined earlier is a salutation to Bashō's host Tōkyū as well as a greeting to the Interior (Oku), to the region of Michinoku, complimenting the land for its fertility (rice harvest) and culture (song). *Sanzōshi* comments on this type of greeting.

> fragrance of early rice—
> pushing through the fields, on the right
> Rocky Coast Sea

> wase | no | ka | ya | wakeiru | migi | wa | Arisoumi
> young-rice | 's | scent | : | wading | right | as-for | Ariso-Sea

> one of the ridges
> clouded with winter showers?
> snow-covered Fuji

> hito | one | wa | shigururu | kumo | ka | yuki | no | Fuji[16]
> one | ridge | as-for | winter-showering | cloud | ? | snow | 's | Fuji

With regard to these verses, the Master said, "When you enter a large province and compose a poem on it, you must understand that province. Once a famous person from the capital went to Kaga Province and composed a poem about treading on small fish at a river called the Kunze. Even if this were a superb poem, it does not reflect the dignity and status of that province and thus is inappropriate." The Arisoumi, or Rocky Coast Sea, poem was composed with these considerations in mind. The same is true of the verse on Mount Fuji. Unless the mountain is presented on this scale, Mount Fuji becomes just another mountain. (NKBZ 51: 556–57)

The poem must reflect the character and size of the province. If the poet enters a large province such as Kaga (Ishikawa) and composes on an obscure place like the Kunze River or on a lowly subject such as "treading on *gori*," a type of small fish, the poem will be an insult to the province. In the first example, which appears in the second half of *Narrow Road to the Interior*, the fragrance of the ripening rice plants implies a rich, bumper crop. Arisoumi (Rocky Coast Sea), which the traveler views from a distance, is a famous *utamakura* (poetic toponym) from the *Man'yōshū*. Together, the two expansive and felicitous images—the waves of ripening rice plants and the waves of Arisoumi—suggest the grandeur and richness of Kaga Province. In the second poem, also by Bashō, a cloud of winter showers on one of the many ridges, indicating that atmospheric conditions differ from one part of the mountain to the next, reveals the awesome size of Mount Fuji, covered with dazzling snow. The result is a laudatory address to the large province of Suruga (Shizuoka).

A greeting to the land may focus on the local products. The following poem, probably written for Bashō's host Joshū (1641–1724), a disciple from Suruga, in early June 1694 (5.17.Genroku 7), during his last journey, and then later anthologized in *Charcoal Sack*, can be read as a greeting to Suruga Province.

On entering Suruga Province

Suruga road—
even the orange blossoms have
the aroma of tea leaves

Surugaji | ya | hanatachibana | mo | cha | no | nioi
Suruga-road | : | orange-blossoms | also | tea | 's | aroma

The poem praises the province by making reference to two of its famous local products, blossoming orange trees (*hanatachibana*) and tea (*cha*), both seasonal words for summer. The scent of the orange blossoms is overwhelmed by the fragrance of the fresh-roasted tea leaves—all of which suggests the aromatic pleasures of Suruga.

Greetings to the spirit of the land often employed complex wordplay, homophones, and associative words, which interwove the place-name into the physical description, as in the following poem on Haguro Mountain, one of the three holy mountains of Dewa, which Bashō composed in July 1689 (6.9.Genroku 2) and which forms one of the climactic moments in *Narrow Road to the Interior*.

coolness—
faintly a crescent moon over
  Feather Black Mountain

suzushisa | ya | hono | mikazuki | no | Haguroyama
coolness | : | faint | third-day-moon | 's | Haguro-Mountain
(NKBZ 41: 371)

In this hokku the prefix *hono* ("faintly" or "barely") and *mikazuki* (third-day moon) create an implicit visual contrast between the thin light of the crescent moon and the blackness of the night, implied in the name Haguroyama, Feather Black Mountain. The silver hook of the moon, which casts a thin ray of light through the darkness, brings, amid the summer heat, a sense of "coolness" (*suzushisa*), suggesting both the hospitality and the spiritual purity of the sacred mountain.

Pacifying the Dead

Bashō's poetry and prose often functioned as an offering to the spirit of the dead, a ritual derived from a long Japanese tradition of spirit pacification (*chinkon*). *Backpack Notes* may have, as Ogata Tsutomu has argued, served as a literary prayer to the spirit of Tokoku (d. 1690), the wealthy rice merchant from Nagoya and Bashō's disciple and close friend.[17] In the journey described in *Backpack Notes*, Bashō traveled to Mikawa Province (Aichi), where Tokoku was in exile (serving a sentence for illegal trading).

> Honeyama is a place where they capture hawks. It is on the southern peninsula, facing the sea. They say that it is the place where the migrating hawks first cross. When I remembered that the Irago hawks appeared in classical poetry, I was even more deeply moved and wrote:

> one hawk
> the joy of finding it
> 　at Irago Point

> taka | hitotsu | mitsukete | ureshi | Iragosaki
> hawk | single | finding | happy | Irago-Point
> 　　　　　　(NKBZ 41: 316)

On one level, the poem expresses the traveler's joy at finding a hawk at a place long associated in Japanese poetry with this bird. At the same time, the hokku reveals the poet's joy at meeting Tokoku, who had been exiled to Irago Point and who is, like the solitary hawk, living a lonely existence on this isolated peninsula.[18] *Backpack Notes*, which commemorates a journey that Bashō took in 1687–88, was not written until much later, after the journey to Michinoku (Interior), around 1690–91, shortly after the death of Tokoku in the Third Month of 1690—circumstances that strongly suggest that *Backpack Notes* served, at least in part, as a memorial to his beloved disciple.[19]

One of the most notable examples of a poetic prayer to the spirit of the dead is the following hokku in *Narrow Road to the Interior*, which Bashō composed when he visited Tada Shrine at Komatsu in Kaga (Ishikawa), on the Japan Sea coast.

> We visited Tada Shrine where Sanemori's helmet and a piece of his brocade robe are stored. They say that, long ago, when Sanemori belonged to the Minamoto clan, Lord Yoshitomo offered him the helmet. Indeed, it was not the gear of a common soldier. A chrysanthemum and vine carved design inlaid with gold extended from the visor to the earflaps, and a two-horn frontpiece was attached to the dragon head. Kiso Yoshi-

naka offered the helmet and a prayer sheet to this shrine after Sanemori
had died in battle, and Higuchi Jirō acted as his messenger—such details
in the shrine history made the past appear before my eyes.

"How piteous!"
under the warrior's helmet
   the cry of a cricket

muzan | ya | na | kabuto | no | shita | no | kirigirisu
piteous | ! | ! | warrior-helmet | 's | beneath | 's | cricket
                                 (NKBZ 41: 378)

In one of the more famous scenes in *The Tale of Heike*, Saitō
Sanemori (Saitō Bettō), not wanting the other soldiers to realize his
advanced age, dyes his white hair black and fights valiantly before
being slain by the retainers of Kiso Yoshinaka (1154–84). According
to legend, Yoshinaka, who had been saved by Sanemori as a child,
wept at seeing the washed head of the slain warrior and subse-
quently made an offering of the helmet and brocade to Tada Shrine.
In *Sanemori*, a warrior Noh play by Zeami, a wandering priest trav-
els to Shinohara Village in Kaga, where he encounters an old man
who turns out to be the spirit of Sanemori and who narrates the
story of his death in battle at that site. In a passage narrated by the
ghost, Higuchi Jirō (d. 1184), one of Yoshinaka's retainers, is sum-
moned to identify the washed, white-haired head of the slain war-
rior and exclaims, "Oh, how piteous! / It's Saitō Bettō!" ("muzan ya
na. Saitō bettō nite sōraikeru zo ya").[20] In Bashō's hokku, the trav-
eler, presumably reminded by Sanemori's helmet of the washed
head of the slain warrior, utters Higuchi Jirō's words; and then,
awakening from these thoughts of the distant past, he hears a cricket
(*kirigirisu*) beneath the warrior's helmet. The following poem by
Saigyō in the *Shinkokinshū* (1205; Autumn II, no. 472) reveals the
classical associations of the cricket, a seasonal word for autumn.

kirigirisu	The cricket,
yosamu ni aki no	as the autumn nights
naru mama ni	grow cold,
yowaru ka koe no	seems to weaken, its voice
tōzakari yuku	fading into the distance.

The voice of the cricket in the cold, frosty autumn night embodies the pathos and loneliness of steady, inevitable decline, of fading life. In Bashō's poem, these associations of the *kirigirisu*, particularly the pathos of old age, resonate, as in a combination poem, with the image of the severed head of the white-haired warrior.[21] As Sora's diary reveals, Bashō originally composed the hokku as a religious offering (*hōnō*) to the Tada Shrine, near Shinohara, the old battlefield where the head of Sanemori had been washed.

Narrow Road to the Interior often takes on the framework and mood of a Noh play in which a traveling priest addresses the spirit of the dead as if in a dream. In *Miscellaneous Talk Collection* (*Zōtanshū*; published 1691), Kikaku, one of Bashō's earliest Edo disciples, noted that "*Utai* is *The Tale of Genji* of haikai,"[22] that is, Noh was as vital to the composition of haikai as *The Tale of Genji* was to the writing of classical poetry. Noh texts, familiar to urban commoners in the form of *utai*, the singing of Noh librettos, formed a substantial body of subtexts for seventeenth-century haikai, but unlike Danrin haikai, which comically inverted or parodied famous lines from the Noh, Bashō drew on the dramatic structure, particularly the two-part "dream play" (*mugen nō*), in which the *shite* (protagonist) encounters the spirits of the dead, listens to their stories of grief, and offers a prayer in a ritual of spirit pacification.[23] In this context, the cries of the cricket in Bashō's hokku can be taken as those of Sanemori's anguished soul, which the traveler, like the wandering priest in the Noh play, pacifies with a poetic prayer.

Dialogue with the Ancients

Perhaps the most intriguing and original greetings in Bashō's literature are those addressed to an "ancient" (*kojin*), a major poet of the past whom Bashō admired, particularly Nōin, Saigyō, and Sōgi, or an ancient spiritual figure such as Gyōki (668–749).[24] Indeed, the entire text of *Narrow Road to the Interior*, which traces Bashō's journey of 1689, can be interpreted as an offering or tribute to the spirit of Saigyō (1118-90) on the five-hundredth anniversary of his death. As the ultimate host of Bashō's journey, Saigyō becomes the object of various poems of gratitude, tribute, or remembrance, particularly at the *utamakura*, the poetic places in which the poet's spirit resides. The following passage in *Narrow Road to the Interior* takes place at Ashino Village (in Nasu) in Shimotsuke (Tochigi), shortly before the traveler's arrival at the Shirakawa Barrier.

> The willow that was the subject of Saigyō's poem, "Where a crystal stream flows," still stood in Ashino Village, on a footpath in a rice field. The district officer, a man named Kohō, had repeatedly offered to show this willow to me, and I had wondered where it was. Today I was able to stand in the shade of that very willow.

> a whole field of
> rice seedlings planted—I part
>   from the willow

> ta | ichimai | uete | tachisaru | yanagi | kana
> rice-field | one | planting | leave | yanagi |!
>   (NKBZ 41: 350)

The entire passage is an allusive variation on *The Wandering Priest and the Willow* (*Yugyō yanagi*), a Noh play based on the following poem in the *Shinkokinshū* (Summer, no. 262) by Saigyō.

michi no be ni	I thought to pause
shimizu nagaruru	on the roadside
yanagi kage	where a crystal stream flows
shibashi tote koso	beneath a willow
tachidomaritsure	and stood rooted to the spot.

In the Noh play an itinerant priest (the *waki*), retracing the steps of Saigyō through the Interior (Michinoku), meets an old man (the *shite*) who shows him the withered willow that is the subject of Saigyō's famous poem and who later turns out to be the spirit of that willow. At the end of the drama the priest offers prayers to the spirit of the willow, thereby enabling it to achieve salvation.[25] When the district officer offers to introduce Saigyō's willow to the traveler, the passage takes on the atmosphere of a Noh dream play in which the poet, bearing the aura of a traveling priest, encounters the spirit of Saigyō, embodied in the willow.

In contrast to Saigyō's classical poem, in which time passes as the traveler rests near a beautiful stream, in Bashō's hokku time passes as the traveler journeys to meet Saigyō's spirit. Most modern commentators, finding it hard to believe that Bashō would plant rice seedlings himself, interpret the hokku as having two subjects: farm girls, who are planting the seedlings in the rice paddy in the summer, and Bashō, who stands under the willow. In a meditative state, filled with thoughts of Saigyō, who had stood by the same tree and composed the famous poem on the "crystal stream" and whose spirit is embodied in the tree, the poet loses track of time, and before he knows it, the farm girls have planted an entire field of rice. The context of the Noh play and the grammar of the poem, however, also suggest that Bashō, imagining himself an itinerant monk, helps plant rice seedlings in the field as an offering to the spirit of Saigyō, his poetic host and patron.

In *The Anxiety of Influence*, Harold Bloom sees all major English Romantic poets as participating in an intertextual dialogue with their poetic predecessors, engaged in an Oedipal struggle to overcome and "slay" the poetic father, to carve out a poetic space for themselves. In contrast to Bloom's antagonistic struggle, Bashō's writings and poetry take the form of a dialogue, especially as communal or familial greetings, signs of reverence and intimacy, through which the poet attempts to establish ties to his poetic predecessors, to draw on the authority of the ancients while creating his own poetic genealogy, one that would ultimately transform the classical legacy into a vernacular, commoner tradition.

CHAPTER 7

Seasonal Associations and Cultural Landscape

"Shelley speculated that poets of all ages contributed to one Great Poem perpetually in progress."
—Harold Bloom, *The Anxiety of Influence*

"Newness is the flower of haikai."
—*Sanzōshi*

For Bashō and other haikai poets, the poetic canon was conceived not so much as a body of texts but as a highly encoded body of poetic topics (*dai*) and their poetic essences, which the haikai poet inherited, worked against, and transformed. Over the centuries, the Japanese used a wide range of words to describe various aspects of the four seasons. Rain, for example, took on a different name according to the season and the type. *Harusame* (spring rain) referred to the soft, steady drizzle of spring; *samidare* (literally, rains of the Fifth Month) meant the wet season or the extended rains of summer; and *shigure* signified the brief, intermittent showers of early winter. In the poetic tradition, these became seasonal topics (*kidai*) with specific poetic associations, referred to as the "poetic essence" (*hon'i*). These associations were derived from classical precedent and commonly recognized as the most appropriate for and essential to that particular topic, and the classical poet was expected to compose on them. Spring rain, for example, became associated with soft, dreamy thoughts; the wet season, particularly that of the Fifth Month (June), implied a sense of unending depression; and the in-

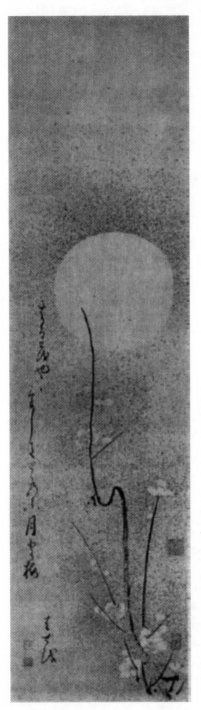

Painting by Kyoriku, poem and calligraphy by Bashō. 43.9 x 12.4 in. Bashō composed the hokku—*haru mo yaya/keshiki totonou tsuki to ume* (spring gradually takes shape—moon and plum blossoms)—in the First Month of Genroku 6 (1693). In the *fukie* (sprinkled painting) style, paper cutouts of the full moon and the plum blossoms were placed on blank paper, sprinkled with black ink (sumi), and then removed. The painter then filled in the plum tree and added the colors of the blossoms. (Courtesy Yamadera Bashō Memorial Center)

termittent showers of winter connoted impermanence and uncertainty. These seasonal topics and their associations, which formed the heart of the cultural landscape, provided the horizon of expectations against which haikai established its newness or implied difference.

Seeking the Poetic Essence

In the medieval period, Heian classical texts such as the *Kokinshū*, *The Tales of Ise*, and *The Tale of Genji* became the canon largely because they were the fountainhead for these poetic associations, knowledge of which was considered indispensable for the cultivation of poetic sensibility and for poetic composition. The same was even more true of classical renga poets, who depended on a knowledge of these poetic associations to link verses and who systematically categorized them, compiling lists of lexical associations (*yoriai*) in such *renga* handbooks as *Gathered Gems* (*Renju gappeki shū*; 1476), edited by Kaneyoshi (1402-81). The entry for "frog" (*kawazu*) in *Gathered Gems*, for example, lists: "Ide, globeflower [*yamabuki*], lodging together [*aiyadori*], beneath a hut [*kaiya ga shita*], water bed for rice seedlings [*nawashiro mizu*], living in water [*mizu ni sumu*], and song [*uta*]"—all associations based on classical precedent.[1] In the Edo period, these poetic associations were expanded into the form of haikai seasonal almanacs (*kiyose*) such as Kigin's *Mountain Well* (*Yama no i*; 1647),[2] which provided short explanations of the poetic associations, or took the form of haikai handbooks such as Baisei's (1619-1702) *Accompanying Boat* (*Ruisenshū*; 1676), which provided extensive lists of associated words for haikai linking.[3] The tradition continues today in the form of *kiyose* and *saijiki* (literally, record of seasons), seasonal almanacs that provide seasonal words and topics, along with examples and explanations, which modern haiku poets continue to use for the composition and the appreciation of haiku.[4]

A major criterion in the judgments at *utaawase*, or classical poetry contests, which became increasingly popular from the mid-Heian period onward, was whether a particular poem was in accord with the poetic essence of a given topic. As the practice of composing poetry on fixed topics (*daiei*) became widespread, each topic acquired a complex core of associations. The end result was the conceptualization of a wide range of natural objects and seasonal phenomena, which was further refined and systematized by classical renga poets. In *Renga Treasures* (*Renga shihōshō*; 1586), Jōha (1525–1602), the last of the great renga poets, reveals the authority of the poetic essence of a topic.

> Renga has what is called *hon'i*, or poetic essence. For example, even though a strong wind or a thundershower may occur in spring, the wind and the rain must be quiet. That is the poetic essence of spring.

And on the poetic essence of summer night:

> The poetic essence of the summer night is brevity. In a poem, when night arrives, it immediately becomes dawn.[5]

The classical renga poet in the medieval period looked, not to nature, but to classical precedent, to understand the poetic essences that lay at the heart of renga composition.

The hokku required a seasonal word (*kigo*), and in linked verse the classical renga poet had to know to which season a word belonged and to be aware, for example, that "light snow" (*awayuki*) meant winter, that "chill" (*hiyayaka*) indicated autumn, and that "lingering snow" (*zansetsu*) signified spring. Classical renga poets depended on these poetic associations to join one verse to the next and to follow the rules for seasonal duration and intermission. Haikai handbooks in the early Edo period both preserved and expanded these poetic and seasonal associations. In *Mountain Well*, considered the archetype for subsequent seasonal handbooks (*saijiki*), Kigin, the Teimon poet thought to be one of Bashō's early teachers, observed, in keeping with the classical tradition, that "the poetic essence of the cherry blossoms is a feeling of admiration and yearning."[6]

Haikai poets inherited this highly encoded seasonal landscape, but they approached the poetic essence in a fundamentally different manner, as the object of parody and humor, especially as double vision (*mitate*), and frequently transformed classical associations into commoner or vulgar form. The following hokku, which appears in

Puppy Collection (1633), the first major Teimon collection, is typical of early seventeenth-century haikai.[7]

> spring rain—
> oil from the hair
> of the willow!
> —Kyūho

> harusame | wa | yanagi | no | kami | no | abura | kana
> spring-rain | as-for | willow | 's | hair | 's | oil | !

Gathered Gems gives the following lexical associations for the willow (*yanagi*), a favorite classical spring topic:

> Thread [*ito*], smoke [*keburi*], eyebrow [*mayu*], jewel [*tama*], river [*kawa*], riverbank [*kishi*], to bend or sway [*nabiku*], hair [*kami*], warbler [*uguisu*], and green [*midori*].[8]

The haikai poet comically transforms these classical associations, in particular the elegant association of the slender, drooping willow branches with the long trailing hair of a woman, into a vulgar, everyday image.

As we shall see in the next chapter, *utamakura*, poetic toponyms or places associated with classical poetry, were the spatial or topographical equivalent of seasonal topics (*kidai*) in that they functioned both as referential markers, indicating a specific geographical location or object, and as a matrix of poetic associations based on classical precedent, usually a specific "foundation poem" (*honka*). As Fujiwara Tameaki's *Bamboo Garden Collection* (*Chikuenshō*; 1285), a medieval waka treatise, suggests, in classical poetry the poetic essence took precedent.

> In composing poetry on Naniwa Bay, one should write about the reeds even if one cannot see them. When it comes to Akashi and Sarashina, one should compose so that the moon shines brightly even if it is a cloudy evening. As for Yoshino and Shiga, one composes as if the cherry trees are in full bloom even if they are already scattered.[9]

Shōtetsu (d. 1459), a late medieval waka poet, writes in *Shōtetsu monogatari* (Conversations with Shōtetsu; 1448):

If someone were to ask me what province Mount Yoshino is in, I would answer that when it comes to cherry blossoms I think of Mount Yoshino, when it comes to bright autumn leaves, I think of Mount Tatsuta. I would write my poems accordingly, not caring whether these places are in Iga or Hyūga Provinces. It is of no practical value to remember which provinces these places are in. Though I do not attempt to memorize such things, I have come to know that Yoshino is in Yamato Province.[10]

As these remarks suggest, the medieval waka poet was concerned not with the actual physical appearance or location of the *utamakura* but rather with its poetic essence. Thus, Yoshino and Shiga were associated with cherry blossoms, Tatsuta Mountain with bright autumn leaves, Ōyodo River and Sumiyoshi with pines, the Bay of Naniwa with reeds, Akashi and Sarashina with the autumn moon. Indeed, for classical Heian poets, who rarely, if ever, left their homes in the capital, *utamakura* were often a means of enjoying the pleasures of travel without traveling.

A tradition gradually developed, especially in the medieval period—centered on such traveler-poets as Nōin, Saigyō, and Sōgi—of traveling to the *utamakura* and composing on these poetic sites, a tradition that Bashō would eventually join, but the poetic essence of these places remained largely unchanged, and the poet traveled to the *utamakura* to be inspired by their poetic associations. As with seasonal topics, the poetic associations of the *utamakura* and the foundation poems from which they derived were catalogued and made readily available to renga poets and then to haikai poets in such collections as *Classified Collection of Japanese Poetry on Famous Places* (*Ruiji meisho waka shū*; 1617) and *Pine Needle Collection of Japanese Poetry* (*Matsuba meisho waka shū*; 1660), both of which Bashō used. In preparation for Bashō's journey to the Interior in 1689, Sora, his travel companion, took extensive notes from the *Classified Collection of Japanese Poetry on Famous Places*, which listed waka on famous places from the imperial anthologies according to place.

Haikai poets approached these *utamakura*, as they did seasonal topics, from a fundamentally different perspective from that of their classical predecessors, as the object of parody, ironic inversion, or humorous double vision. The following example appears in *Haikai Pillow* (*Haimakura*;1680), a haikai collection edited by Yūzan (d. 1702).

> Mount Fuji for a hand fan
> Clear View Barrier for
> my sweat!
> —Yamaguchi Sodō[11]
>
> Fuji | wa | ōgi | ase | wa | Kiyomi | ga | seki | nare | ya
> Fuji | as-for | hand-fan | sweat | as-for | Clear-View | 's | barrier | is | !

One of the classical associations of Mount Fuji, a former volcano, was "fire" (*hi*) and "suppressed desire" (*omoihi*), which smoldered beneath the surface. In a haikai inversion, which replaced the poetic essence of Mount Fuji with an image of coolness, it becomes an inverted, v-shaped hand fan, used for cooling off in the summer, and Clear View Barrier (Kiyomi-ga-seki), located nearby, provides a refreshing view, taking care of the sweat (*ase*), a haikai word.

Observing the Time and the Place

In contrast to their haikai predecessors, who tended to debase or parody the traditional associations of the *utamakura*, Bashō and other Genroku haikai poets who followed the landscape (*keiki*) style stressed the need both to describe nature and places as they were in the external world *and* to be haikai-esque, to work against the established associations and seek out new perspectives. As the following example from *Commentary on the First Poetry of the New Year* (*Hatsukaishi hyōchū*; 1686), Bashō's only detailed commentary on a haikai linked verse sequence, suggests, Bashō made a deliberate attempt to go beyond the established associations.

> the night moon clouding over:
> hail on an umbrella
> —Bunrin
>
> arare | tsukiyo | no | kumoru | karakasa
> hail | moonlit-night | 's | to-cloud | umbrella

The verse describes the deep cold of a winter night. The sound of the hail falling on an umbrella is very interesting. The clearness of the moon is also extremely refreshing. It would have been bad to link closely to "fox trap."[12]

> a stone gutter—
> at a priest's quarters on Kurama
>   living in poverty
>   —Kyohaku

ishi | no | toi | Kurama | no | bō | ni | sumi | wabite
stone | 's | gutter | Kurama | 's | priest-quarter | in | live | suffer

Since hail gives a more eerie, colder, windier feeling than that of frost or snow, the poet thought of the place called Kurama. In the past, the use of a poetic place was based on a classical poem, which provided a precedent: Suma Bay, Tōchi Village, Yoshino Village, and Tamagawa were associated with the fulling block; the bamboo fields of Nasu with hail, Mount Fuji and Sarashina with snow. But today, the poet thinks of poetic places in response to the atmosphere of the previous verse. It is important to understand this. (KBZ 7: 412–13).

Instead of automatically composing a verse on Nasu, a poetic place (*utamakura*) associated in classical poetry with hail (*arare*), Kyohaku presented a verse on Kurama, a mountainous, barren area in northern Kyoto, the home of Kurama Temple, thereby binding the two successive verses through a sense of coldness. Rather than depending on the established associations of an *utamakura*, Bashō stressed the need to focus on the specific scene of the previous verse, to imagine how things actually are in such circumstances.[13]

As the following passage in *Kyoraishō* suggests, for Bashō a poetic place existed both as a physical entity, to be personally viewed and closely observed, and as a medium for communing with the ancients, a means of exploring cultural memory.

> spring going—
> with the people of Ōmi
>   I lament its departure

yuku | haru | o | Ōmi | no | hito | to | oshimikeri
go | spring | (acc.) | Ōmi | 's | person | with | regret

The Master said, "Shōhaku criticized this verse, saying that 'Ōmi' should be replaced by 'Tanba' or that 'spring going' (*yuku haru*) should be replaced by 'year going' (*yuku toshi*). What do you think?"

Kyorai answered, "Shōhaku's criticism is not appropriate. The reason for 'Ōmi' is that the surface of Lake Biwa is misty, making one regret the passage of spring. Most of all, it is based on what you experienced at that time."

The Master: "Exactly. The people of long ago regretted the passing of spring in this province with the same intensity as those in the capital." (NKBZ 51: 422–23)

Shōhaku, the oldest of the Ōmi disciples, suggested that Bashō should have changed either the place or the season, replacing "Ōmi" with "Tanba" or *yuku haru* (spring going) with *yuku toshi* (year going). Kyorai disagreed, arguing that altering the setting or season would violate Bashō's personal experience at Ōmi. At the same time, Bashō stressed the experience of the poets of the past who wrote on Ōmi, especially on Lake Biwa and the beauties of its spring, mist, and cherry blossoms. In Bashō's hokku, "the people of Ōmi" are both Bashō's present hosts at Ōmi—the poem is an expression of gratitude for his wonderful experience there—and the many ancient poets who composed on this same sight. The suggestion here is that poetry must emerge from the interaction between the immediate experience based on direct observation, which provided new perspectives and approaches but which alone was insufficient to create lasting poetry, and the broader experience embodied in the *utamakura*, in the associations of the poetic place, which bore the collective memory. As we shall see, these two fundamental experiences, one rooted in the present and the other in the past, interacted in haikai fashion in Bashō's poetry and prose, defamiliarizing and refamiliarizing the cultural landscape.

The Seasonal Pyramid

Bashō, at least from the mid-1680s, distinguished those hokku that used seasonal words but did not capture the seasonal atmosphere from those that, though not possessing a seasonal word (*kigo*), provided a sense of the season.[14] The same can be said of "love words" (*koi no kotoba*), which indicated a "love verse" (*koi no ku*), traditionally considered the most important of the "person/emotion" (*ninjō*) verses in linked verse. If a poet inserted one of the designated words for love—Jōha's *Renga Treasures* lists such words as *chigiri* (vow), *kinuginu* (separation the morning after), *sasamegoto* (whispers), and *mutsugoto* (intimate conversation)—it became a love verse. For Bashō, by contrast, the atmosphere or depiction of love was more important than the use of a designated word. As *Sanzōshi* (NKBZ 51: 525) states, "The truth of haikai occurs when the poet sees and listens to all things, when the feelings of the poet becomes a verse." Danrin poets had used words such as *matsu* (pine) to evoke the Noh plays *Takasago* (on the theme of twin pines) or *Matsukaze* (Wind in the Pines). Bashō moved away from this type of automatic, lexical association, which enabled Saikaku to compose solo sequences at phenomenal speeds, toward a poetry that pushed off from the traditional poetic associations while approaching nature as a phenomenon to be observed closely.

In Bashō's time, the seasonal words in haikai formed a vast pyramid, capped at the top by the most familiar seasonal topics—cherry blossoms (*hana*), cuckoo (*hototogisu*), moon (*tsuki*), bright leaves (*momiji*), and snow (*yuki*)—which represented spring, summer, autumn, and winter, respectively. Spreading out from this narrow peak were other topics from classical poetry—spring rain, returning geese (autumn), orange blossoms (summer), warbler (spring), willow (spring), and the like—and then, further down, those added by classical renga—for example, paulownia flower, a seasonal word for summer. Occupying the base and the widest area were the haikai words added by haikai poets, which numbered in the thousands by the mid-seventeenth century. In contrast to the elegant, refined images at the top of the pyramid, the seasonal words at the bottom—such as the spring words dandelion (*tanpopo*), garlic (*ninniku*), horseradish (*wasabi*), and cat's love (*neko no koi*)—were taken from everyday commoner life. The pyramid, in short, embodied the hybrid character of haikai, its roots in classical poetry and its unbounded, sociocultural horizons.

In the Meiji period, the four seasons—spring, summer, autumn, winter—were expanded, at least in terms of seasonal almanacs and haikai collections, to include a fifth season, New Year (Shinnen), which possessed a rich cluster of seasonal topics and words (for example, Manzai, the New Year's dancers), many of which were seasonal words at the bottom of the pyramid. The seasonal calendar in Bashō's day was based on the lunar calendar, with spring extending from the First through the Third Month (roughly February to April in the solar calendar). In the lunar calendar, the New Year came at the beginning of spring, at the beginning of the First Month, and was thus an important phase of the spring season, which began with snow and cold. But with the shift to the solar, Gregorian calendar in the Meiji period, New Year no longer coincided with the arrival of spring, which came much later, and became an independent seasonal category.

With the emergence of haikai in the seventeenth century, the number of seasonal words literally exploded. Shigeyori's (1602–80) *Hanahi Grass* (*Hanahigusa*; 1636), one of the earliest haikai handbooks, contains over 590 seasonal words divided by months, and his *Fur-blown Grass* (*Kefukigusa*; 1645) contains 950 seasonal words for haikai and 550 for orthodox renga, listed separately.[15] Tokugen's *Instructions for Haikai Beginners* (*Haikai shogaku shō*; 1641) lists over 770 seasonal words; and Kigin's *Mountain Well* (1648), the earliest handbook devoted entirely to seasonal words, has over 1,300 seasonal words; and Baisei's *Timely Boat* (*Binsenshū*; 1669), which was later revised and expanded into *Accompanying Boat* (*Ruisenshū*; 1676), includes as many as 2,000 seasonal words. But while the number of seasonal words grew at an astounding pace, the number of seasonal topics remained limited.

Haikai poets made a distinction between seasonal words (called *kigo* in the modern period), which indicated a specific season and which included haikai words, and seasonal topics (later called *kidai*), which had specific poetic associations, usually centered on a poetic essence, and which became topics for poetic composition. Most seasonal words in classical poetry—such as "cherry blossoms"—were simultaneously seasonal topics, whereas others—such as *momo*, or peach, a seasonal word for autumn—indicated a particular season but lacked a core of poetic associations that would have made it a seasonal topic. In the two volumes of hokku in *Kefukigusa*, which contains 950 seasonal words for haikai and 550 for renga, there are only 166 seasonal topics, which are basically those found in the imperial anthologies of classical poetry. The spring section of *Puppy Collection*, the Teimon haikai collection, consists almost entirely of established topics such as New Year's Day (*ganjitsu*), plum blossom (*ume*, spring), remaining snow (*zansetsu*, spring), tree bud (*ko no me*), spring grass (*shunsō*), and spring moon (*haru no tsuki*). Over time, however, some new seasonal words, which developed a core of poetic associations and which became familiar topics for haikai composition, turned into seasonal topics. The *Cherry River* (*Sakuragawa*; 1674) collection, for example, contains hokku composed on such seasonal topics as soup with rice cakes (*zōni*, New Year), herring roe (*kazu no ko*, New Year), whitebait (*shirauo*, spring), baby octopus (*iidako*, spring), cat's love (*neko no koi*, spring), and other commoner topics that had appeared earlier only as seasonal words.

The slow but perceptible growth of haikai topics at the bottom of the seasonal pyramid represents a significant expansion of the cultural landscape, the development of a commoner poetics. A good example is "cat's love for a mate" (*neko no tsumagoi*)—later simply called "cat's love" (*neko no koi*), a haikai seasonal topic that became popular in the Edo period. Bashō composed the following hokku in 1691 (Genroku 4) and included it in *Monkey's Straw Coat*.

At a farmhouse

a cat's mate—
grown thin from
love and barley?

mugimeshi | ni | yatsururu | koi | ka | neko | no | tsuma[16]
barley-meal | by | emaciated | love | ? | cat | 's | mate

Bashō humorously depicts a female cat that has grown emaciated not only from being fed barley—a situation that reflects a poor farmhouse—but from intense love-making. The following hokku, composed by Bashō in 1692 (Genroku 5), juxtaposes the loud cater-wauling with the subsequent quiet of the misty moonlight (*oborozuki*), a traditional spring seasonal word, causing the two erotic moods to interfuse.

> cats making love—
> when it's over, misty
> moonlight in the bedroom

neko | no | koi | yamu | toki | neya | no | oborozuki
cat | 's | love | stop | time | bedroom | 's | misty-moonlight

If the deer's longing for its mate (*tsuma kou shika*)—expressed by its mournful, lonely cries—was the archetypal seasonal topic on love in classical poetry, then cat's love—with the baby-like crying of the male as it chased the female—embodied the down-to-earth, humorous character of the haikai seasonal topic.

In *Uda Priest* (*Uda no hōshi*; 1702), Kyoriku, one of Bashō's samurai disciples from Ōmi (Hikone), divided poetic topics into "vertical topics" (*tate no dai*), the "province of classical poets," and "horizontal topics" (*yoko no dai*), the "province of haikai poets" (KBZ 7: 274). In the following passage in *Travel Lodging Discussion*, Kyorai, one of Bashō's Kyōto disciples and the editor of *Monkey's Straw Coat*, takes exception to Kyoriku's position, arguing that haikai traverses both the "province" of haikai and that of classical poetry.

> Someone asked, "Kyoriku has argued that the province of classical poetry and that of haikai, that is to say, the topics of classical poetry and the topics of haikai, are separate. If so, when a haikai poet composes on a classical topic, it is as if he or she is invading the province of classical poetry. What do you think?"
>
> Kyorai answered, "You have good reason to doubt. From the distant past, people have spoken of poetic places in classical poetry and of those in haikai as if they were separate. But the actual situation is different. Classical poetry has many regulations, which place limits on the topics and on poetic places. These rules cannot be violated. Consequently, po-

etic places and topics in classical poetry are fixed, but those in haikai are unbound. Any thing can be a haikai topic; any place can be a poetic place in haikai; there is no word that haikai cannot use. The difference between classical poetry and haikai lies in their perception and their atmosphere. For example, one could call cherry blossoms a topic of classical poetry and rapeseed a topic of haikai, but it would be a mistake to say that cherry blossoms is not a haikai topic. One could call Yoshino a poetic place in classical poetry and Nyoi a poetic place in haikai, but it would be a mistake to say that Yoshino is not a famous place in haikai. Thus, to compose haikai on cherry blossoms or on Yoshino does not mean invading the province of classical poetry. Cherry blossoms and Yoshino also belong to the territory of haikai. (KHT 10: 199–200)[17]

In Kyoriku's opinion, cherry blossoms, a traditional seasonal topic, and Yoshino, an *utamakura* or noted poetic place in classical poetry, belonged to the "province of waka," but rapeseed (*natane*), a haikai topic, and Nyoi, an obscure mountain north of Kyoto, were the "province of haikai." Kyorai, by contrast, believed that haikai had no borders: it could take up topics and places found in classical poetry as well as those outside it. Unlike classical poets, who could not leave their own province, haikai poets were free to enter either province. The difference lay in language and approach, particularly to the poetic essence, which were generally fixed for classical poets but unrestricted for haikai poet.

Haikai poets freely explored topics in both provinces, that of classical poetry and that of haikai; but of the two regions, they ultimately spent more time in what Kyoriku called the "province of waka." Haikai poets took pleasure in traversing the "province of haikai," composing on places and topics that had never appeared in classical poetry. Bashō himself was to discover a number of haikai places, or *haimakura*, during his journey to the Interior. At the same time, however, haikai poets, including Bashō, tended to gravitate toward the "province of waka," toward *utamakura* or classical toponyms—such as Yoshino, Suma, Akashi, Matsushima—which had a rich cluster of associations. For Bashō in particular, the *utamakura* provided a critical means of communing with ancient poets, a function that *haimakura*, or new haikai places, could not easily provide.

Haikai poets also gravitated toward the classical topics at the top of the seasonal pyramid such as the moon, snow, cherry blossoms, and the cuckoo, which offered a poetic matrix around which the poet could build the entire hokku and which were no doubt easier to parody and deconstruct than those at the bottom of the pyramid. Developed through hundreds of years of waka history, the traditional seasonal topic contained a rich fictional world communally shared by composer and audience that could not easily be duplicated by new seasonal words or topics. Indeed, during the renga-style period, in the mid-1680s, Bashō, like a number of other haikai poets, concentrated on classical or Chinese topics. In 1687, for example, Bashō compiled *Gathered Verses* (*Atsumeku*), an anthology of 34 of his hokku, including the famous frog poem, which focused almost exclusively on classical waka topics or on topics taken from Chinese poetry.

At the same time Bashō did not ignore the vernacular seasonal words at the base of the seasonal pyramid. *Kyoraishō* in fact suggests that Bashō encouraged the discovery and use of new seasonal words.

> Rochō asked, "Has bamboo-planting day been regarded as a seasonal word from the distant past?"
>
> Kyorai answered, "I don't know. I saw it for the first time in the Master's verse. Even if a word has not traditionally been used as a seasonal word, if it is appropriate for the season, one should use it. The Master told us that if you discover even one new seasonal word, it will be a present for future generations." (NKBZ 51: 488)

Bashō's hokku on Bamboo-Planting Day (*take uuru hi*) appears in *Backpack Diary*.[18]

On bamboo, at Bokuin's residence

    though no rain falls
on Bamboo-Planting Day
    raincoats and hats

furazu|tomo|take|uuru|hi|wa|mino|to|kasa
not falling|but|bamboo|planting|day|as-for|rain-coat|and|hat

It was believed that if one planted or transplanted bamboo on Bamboo-Planting Day, an annual rite adapted from China probably in the seventeenth century, the bamboo would thrive or grow thick. The idea of wearing a *mino* and *kasa*, both rain gear, even when it is not raining, humorously captures the seasonal atmosphere of Bamboo-Planting Day—which occurred on the thirteenth of the Fifth Month (June), in the middle of the wet season when the summer rains (*samidare*) seem to fall incessantly—a day when it was necessary to be outdoors, in the fields or in the grove, digging bamboo. The preceding passage suggests that the Bamboo-Planting Day had yet to be widely recognized as a seasonal word, but it would later become part of the canon as a result of Bashō's verse.

It was not until his last years, when Bashō began advocating lightness (*karumi*) and emphasizing haikai words (*haigon*), that he wrote a modest number of hokku using new seasonal words. A famous example is the following, composed by Bashō in December 1693 (11.8.Genroku 6), at the age of 50, and included in *Charcoal Sack*, an anthology with a *haigon* title.

On harvesting radishes:

in the saddle seat
a little boy—
radish harvest

kuratsubo | ni | kobōzu | noru | ya | daikonhiki
saddle-seat | on | small-boy | ride | : | radish-harvest

The hokku provides a pictorial view of a commoner activity previously never considered in Japanese poetry: "pulling up radishes" (*daikonhiki*), a winter farm ritual in which the entire family went out into the field to harvest large white radishes, which were usually deposited in a basket on a horse. In this hokku, the little boy has been placed in the saddle seat, probably to prevent him from disturbing the rest of the family. Bashō probably supplied the headnote "On harvesting radishes" since *daikonhiki* was still not easily recognized as a seasonal topic.[19] Although Bashō used more new seasonal words in his last years, he did not actively create new seasonal words except for a few such as Bamboo-Planting Day. In this regard, the passage in *Kyoraishō* that encourages the discovery of new seasonal words may be better interpreted to mean not just finding new seasonal words, but finding new life in existing seasonal topics, which, as they were repeatedly used, gradually ossified and needed to be renewed and re-envisioned.

Bashō and other haikai poets gravitated toward the top of the seasonal pyramid, dwelling in the province of waka, but they approached these seasonal topics, as they did *utamakura*, from a haikai angle, often using haikai words. Bashō composed the following hokku, which appears in *Skeleton in the Fields*, late in the Ninth Month (October–November) of 1684.

At Fuwa Barrier

autumn wind—
nothing but thickets and farm fields
    at Fuwa Barrier

akikaze | ya | yabu | mo | hatake | mo | Fuwa | no | seki
autumn-wind | : | thicket | also | farm-field | also | Fuwa | 's | barrier

Fuwa Barrier, near Sekigahara in Mino Province (Gifu), originally one of the three central checkpoints of Japan, was abandoned in the late eighth century but continued to exist as an *utamakura*, or poetic place, immortalized in a poem by Fujiwara Yoshitsune (1169–1206) in the *Shinkokinshū* (Misc. II, no. 1599).

hito sumanu	Since the eaves
fuwa no sekiya no	of the abandoned
itabisashi	guardhouse at Fuwa
arenishi nochi wa	have collapsed—
tada aki no kaze	only autumn wind.

The traveler in Bashō's hokku finds that even the decayed guardhouse (*sekiya*) has disappeared: nothing visually remains from before. Bashō's hokku follows the traditional poetic associations of Fuwa Barrier, the desolation and pathos of decay, an atmosphere deepened by "autumn wind" (*aki no kaze*), a seasonal word associated with loneliness, but Bashō expresses the poetic essence of the *utamakura* in a new manner, with the haikai words: *yabu mo hatake mo* (nothing but thickets and farm fields). The result is a striking double vision, of the present and of the past, which seems to linger in the autumn wind.

Bashō, like many of his contemporaries, gravitated toward traditional poetic topics, which were sometimes implied rather than stated, using language and subject matter that was new and haikaiesque. In the following hokku, which Bashō composed in Kyoto in the Seventh Month of 1691 (Genroku 4), the seasonal word, "autumn breeze" (*aki no kaze*), differs from the implied seasonal topic, which is lingering summer heat (*zansho*).

> in a cowshed
> mosquito voices weakening—
> an autumn breeze

ushibeya | ni | ka | no | koe | yowashi | aki | no | kaze
cowshed | in | mosquito | 's | voice | weak | autumn | 's | breeze

The poetic essence of lingering summer heat, which did not become a poetic topic until the late Heian period, was the contrast between the desire for the coolness that normally accompanies the arrival of autumn and the unbearable reality of the lingering summer heat. Here Bashō approaches that classical topic from a farmer's point of view. The weakened buzz of the mosquitoes (*ka no koe yowashi*), a haikai phrase, suggests both the lasting heat and the arrival of early autumn. (The implied topic indicates that "autumn breeze" is a faint early autumn breeze which brings some relief but not enough—as opposed to the lonely, piercing wind of late autumn.) According to *Sanzōshi* (NKBZ 51: 566–67), Bashō later revised the hokku to make the seasonal topic explicit.

> in a cowshed
> mosquitoes buzzing darkly—
> lingering summer heat

ushibeya | ni | ka | no | koe | kuraki | zansho | kana
cowshed | in | mosquito | 's | voice | dark | lingering-summer-heat | !

Bashō replaced "autumn breeze" with "lingering summer heat" (*zan-sho*) and "weak" with "dark," thereby intensifying the sense of hot, stifling air and suggesting the buzz of the mosquitoes through four alliterative "k" consonants. A similar approach is taken in the following hokku, which Bashō composed at Fukugawa in 1693 (Genroku 6) and which appears in *Backpack Diary*.[20]

> a fishy smell!
> minnow guts lying
>   on the water weeds

namagusashi | konagi | ga | ue | no | hae | no | wata
fishy-smell | waterweed | 's | top | 's | dace | 's | entrails

The entrails of a dace (*hae*)—here translated as "minnow"—a small, commercially useless fish, have been left on top of the *konagi*—a haikai seasonal word for autumn—water weed that grows in swamps and rice paddies and that blooms in late summer and early autumn. Bashō captures the sense of the lingering summer heat (*zansho*) in earthy fashion: through the strong, fishy smell (*namagusashi*), a startling haikai word, of a fish rotting in the sun at the water's edge. The following hokku, which appears in *Backpack Diary* and which Bashō composed in 1694 at the residence of Mokusetsu in Ōtsu (near Lake Biwa),[21] uses *hiyahiya* (cool) as a seasonal word for autumn, but it too is representative of the lingering summer heat topos.

> taking a midday nap
> feet placed
>   on a cool wall

hiyahiya | to | kabe | o | fumaete | hirune | kana
cool | ly | wall | (acc.) | placing-feet | midday-nap | !

The speaker, cooling the bottoms of his bare feet on the wall, has fallen asleep on a hot afternoon. The transition from summer to autumn implied in the lingering summer heat topos is captured from a haikai, humorous angle, in the feet, through which the speaker feels the arrival of autumn.

The traditional seasonal topic, like the associations of the *utama-kura*, provided a frame against which the haikai poem could establish its newness, its implied difference. The following hokku, which Bashō composed in 1694 (Genroku 7) and included in *Charcoal Sack*, is implicitly on the seasonal topic of lingering winter cold (*yokan*),[22] the spring counterpart of the lingering summer heat topos.

> in the scent of plum blossoms
> suddenly, the sun comes up—
> a mountain path

ume|ga|ka|ni|notto|hi|no|deru|yamaji|kana
plum|'s|scent|in|suddenly|sun|'s|appear|mountain-path|!

In Bashō's hokku, the speaker is walking along a mountain path, smelling the fragrance of the plum blossoms (*ume ga ka*), a seasonal phrase for early spring, when, perhaps turning a corner, the sun comes up "suddenly" (*notto*), a haikai word. The seasonal frame implies that although spring has arrived, it remains cold, particularly on an early morning mountain path, into which the sun suddenly brings brightness—a movement embodied in *notto*, a haikai adverb with a roundish, warm sound. As these poems on lingering summer heat (*zansho*) and lingering winter cold (*yokan*) suggest, the seasonal topic, which was sometimes only implied, provided a broader context for the haikai poem, which in turn gave new life to that topic through contemporary language and new perspectives.

The Question of Newness

Bashō approached the topics at the top of the seasonal pyramid by adding new poetic associations to the established core *or* by approaching the established associations from a new, haikai-esque perspective, often with haikai words. In the following episode in *Kyoraishō*, Kyorai strongly urged the latter.

> the sound of the bells at dusk
> gives me strength—
> a temple in autumn
> —Fūkoku

yūgure | wa | kane | o | chikara | ya | tera | no | aki[23]
dusk | as-for | temple-bell | (acc.) | strength | : | temple | 's | autumn

In the original version the sound of the evening temple bells was not lonely. I have forgotten the exact wording.

Fūkoku: "When I heard the evening bells of the mountain temple, they did not make me feel lonely at all, and as a consequence, I wrote that verse."

Kyorai responded, "That was an insipid scene. Whether it was a mountain temple, an autumn evening, or evening temple bells, each is the ultimate embodiment of loneliness. To say that you did not feel lonely since you happened to hear the temple bells in the midst of autumn festivities is to be extremely self-centered."

Fūkoku: "But what should I do if I had those feelings on that particular occasion? Am I forbidden to write such poetry if I had those feelings?"

"If you had those emotions, you could have tried to compose like this," Kyorai replied, revising the verse to its present wording. Though the revised poem cannot be described as outstanding, at least the poetic essence has not been lost. (NKBZ 51: 460–61)

In the classical tradition, the poetic essence of a temple (*tera*), of an autumn evening (*aki no kure*), or of temple bells (*kane*) was in each case loneliness. Fūkoku, however, heard the evening temple bells during a raucous celebration of bright autumn leaves (*momiji*) and felt no such loneliness. For Kyorai, this poetic essence represented the accumulated experience of hundreds of poets over many centuries. To ignore or go against it, as Fūkoku did, was a self-centered, willful act. But not wanting to ignore Fūkoku's actual feelings at the time of composition, Kyorai rewrote the poem to accommodate both the traditional seasonal associations and the poet's personal experience.[24] For Kyorai, the haikai poet must preserve the poetic essence—here, the feeling of loneliness—but approach or express it in new, haikai-esque ways.

In *Hentsuki* (1698) Kyoriku, who debated Kyorai on a number of key issues, took the opposite position, arguing that the haikai poet must go outside the established essence and seek new poetic associations.

On the bush warbler and the cuckoo

> bush warbler
> hanging upside down—
>   first song of the year!
>   —Kikaku

uguisu | no | mi | o | sakasama | ni | hatsune | kana
bush-warbler | 's | body | (acc.) | upside-down | -ly | first-song | !

The bush warbler is usually a difficult topic to compose on. Kikaku's discovery of a "bush warbler hanging upside down," reveals insight. Surely, it is one of the best poems on the warbler in recent years. Since the Master composed "droppings on the rice cakes," nothing this new has appeared. There may be a number of poems superior to this one, but without newness they cannot be called haikai. The Master once said, "It is possible to compose an appropriate verse on the cuckoo, but doing the same with the bush warbler is quite difficult." (KHT 10: 174)[25]

The poetic essence of the bush warbler (*uguisu*), one of the most popular seasonal topics in classical poetry, was its singing and its bright, cheery voice, which marked the arrival of spring and the New Year. The bush warbler, sometimes referred to as *haru-tsuge-dori* (harbinger-of-spring bird), was often joined with the plum blossoms to create an elegant combination poem. Kyoriku is overjoyed to find that Kikaku has found a new poetic essence for this familiar and difficult topic: the physical movement of the bush warbler, which, in a seemingly mad motion, hangs upside down from the branch as it sings for the first time (*hatsune*) in the New Year.[26] Kikaku's poem was, in Kyoriku's view, the best example of "newness" since Bashō's "bush warbler—/ leaves droppings on the rice cakes / at the veranda edge" (*uguisu ya mochi ni funsuru en no saki*) hokku in 1692. Discovering a new angle on the bush warbler, with its thick accumulation of classical associations, was, as Bashō noted, extremely difficult, and Bashō himself composed only two poems on this topic.

In contrast to Kyorai, who stressed the traditional essence and emphasized new ways to strengthen the communal memory, Kyo-riku urged the discovery of new seasonal associations and combinations that went beyond the boundary of the traditional topic and expanded the cultural landscape. An examination of Bashō's poems on the *hototogisu* (Japanese cuckoo), on which he composed 22 hokku, reveals how he explored both approaches, often mixing the two. The *hototogisu*, a gray-headed Asian cuckoo (*Cuculus poliocephalus*) whose song is a series of notes rather than the two notes (cuc-koo) associated with the cuckoo, appears in the Fourth Month (May), at the beginning of summer, after migrating from the south. According to Jōha's *Renga Treasures*, "Even if the *hototogisu* sings noisily, one must compose in such a way that one hears it only on occasion, so that it sings rarely, and so that one waits impatiently to hear its voice."[27] As a consequence, *hototogisu* is often translated as "the cuckoo's song" or "voice of the cuckoo." Bashō composed the following hokku in the summer of 1687, at the age of 44, and included it in *Gathered Verses*.[28]

> the cuckoo
> singing, flying, singing,
>   ever busy

hototogisu | nakunaku | tobu | zo | isogawashi
cuckoo | crying-crying | flying | ! | busy

Here Bashō, following Kyoriku's approach, deviates from the traditional natural essence—of waiting for the rarely heard, beautiful voice of the *hototogisu*—by focusing on the way the bird actually behaved. Unlike most birds, which rest on trees while they sing, the *hototogisu* sings or cries even as it flies, leading a "busy" (*isogawashi*) existence.

Bashō, reflecting Kyoriku's principle of seeking out new poetic essences and new combinations, pursued another aspect of the *hototogisu*, based on close observation of its physical motion: the arrow-like flight of the bird, the sharp cry heard only once before it disappears from view. In the following poem, which Bashō wrote in 1688, during his *Backpack Notes* journey, the speaker implicitly hears the *hototogisu*, but by the time he looks up in the "direction" (*kata*) of the *hototogisu*, it has disappeared, replaced by a single island, presumably Awajishima, the small island across the bay from Suma and Akashi, where the speaker stands.

> a cuckoo—
> where it disappears
>   a single island

hototogisu | kieyuku | kata | ya | shima | hitotsu
cuckoo | disappear-go | direction | : | island | one

"Where it disappears" (*kieyuku kata*), which may refer either to the voice or the body of the *hototogisu*, is replaced on the horizon by "an island, one" (*shima hitotsu*). In haikai fashion, the hokku is also parodic, playing off a well-known classical poem in the *Senzaishū* (1188; Summer, no. 161).[29]

hototogisu	When I gaze
nakitsuru kata o	in the direction of
nagamureba	the crying cuckoo,
tada ariake no	only the moon
tsuki zo nokoreru	lingers in the dawn.

The flight or sound of the *hototogisu* leads the eye of the reader not just to one island but, in a haikai twist, to the classical past.

Another parodic turn occurs in the following poem, which Bashō composed in 1689 (Genroku 2) and included in *Monkey's Straw Coat* and *Narrow Road to the Interior*.

> across the field:
> "Turn the horse's head!"
>   a cuckoo's cry

no | o | yoko | ni | uma | hikimuke | yo | hototogisu
field | (acc.) | sideways | to | horse | pull | ! | cuckoo

In Bashō's hokku, which again focuses on the rapid, arrow-like flight of the bird, the *hototogisu* flies perpendicular to the direction of the horse, which is walking across (*yoko ni*) the field. The traveler on the horse gives the groom a military command: "Sideways, turn the horse's head" (*yoko ni uma hikimuke yo*), but in a haikai shift, the objective is not to go into battle, but to turn the horse's head so that the traveler can, in *fūkyō* manner, follow the flight of the poetic object.

The following poem, which Bashō composed in May 1691 (4.20.Genroku 4), while staying at the Rakushisha in Saga, and which appears in *Saga Diary* (*Saga nikki*; 1691), depends for its full effect on understanding both the traditional seasonal association— waiting impatiently to hear the rare cry of the *hototogisu*—and the new, haikai poetic essence, its rapid flight.

> a cuckoo's cry—
> moonlight seeping through
> a large bamboo grove

> hototogisu | ōtakeyabu | o | moru | tsukiyo
> cuckoo | large-bamboo-grove | (acc.) | seep-through | moonlight

Flying over a large bamboo grove, the *hototogisu* leaves a horizontal trail of sound, which cuts through the implicit silence of the night. The moonlight, by contrast, descends vertically or "seeps down" (*moru*) through the leaves of the tall bamboo trees, creating an intersection of sound and light.

One of the traditional essences of the *hototogisu* was its association with death and nostalgia for a lost past, particularly as a result of a *Kokinshū* (905; Summer, no. 146) poem, "When I hear the singing of the cuckoo, I long for even the old village where we once parted" (*hototogisu naku koe kikeba wakarenishi furusato sae zo koishikarikeru*). According to a letter addressed to Keikō (d. 1712), a disciple from Mino (Gifu), Bashō wrote the following hokku in June 1693 (4.29.Genroku 6), after being urged by his disciples Sanpū and Sora to compose on the topic of "Cuckoos on the water's edge."

> a cuckoo—
> the voice lies stretched
> over the water

> hototogisu | koe | ya | yokotau | mizu | no | ue
> cuckoo | voice | : | lies-sideways | water | 's | top

As the *hototogisu* flies overhead, it makes a sharp penetrating cry, which "lies sideways" (*yokotau*),[30] hanging over the quiet surface of the water, probably at dusk or night, when the *hototogisu* traditionally sings. The *hototogisu* quickly disappears, but the sound lingers, like an overtone. In the letter to Keikō, Bashō notes that the poem was written shortly after the death of his young nephew and that he drew on Su Tung-p'o's couplet "The gleaming water extends to heaven, / and the white mist lies stretched across the water," which strongly suggests that the lingering sound of the *hototogisu* echoes the vanishing spirit of the dead youth.[31] In other words, the Chinese poem provided the medium for transforming the poetic essence into a new, striking form.

The humor of the following hokku, which follows Kyorai's dictum to preserve the communal memory at the heart of the topic, comes from the humorous juxtaposition of the traditional poetic essence, the longing to hear the rare cry of the *hototogisu*, with a haikai-esque glimpse of commoner life, in an urban marketplace.

> the squid seller's call
> so confusing—
> the cry of a cuckoo

> ikauri|no|koe|magirawashi|hototogisu
> squid-seller|'s|voice|confusing|cuckoo

The speaker is implicitly waiting, straining to hear the cry of the *hototogisu* when a squid merchant (*ikauri*), hawking his produce in a high-pitched voice—unexpectedly like that of the elegant *hototogisu*—causes the speaker to confuse the two. Reflecting Kyoriku's earlier observation on the importance of seasonal correspondence between the disparate parts of a combination poem, Bashō also finds a seasonal correspondence between the *hototogisu*, which arrives in early summer, and the squid, a haikai word, which were harvested in abundance in early summer.

Bashō's hokku are often read as poems that either focus on the immediate object or that fuse the poet with nature, but as we can see here, whatever referential or expressive function the text may have, each poem, via the seasonal word and implied seasonal topic, is firmly anchored in a larger cultural landscape, the Great Seasonal Poem, that is refracted, re-visioned, or expanded in extremely subtle ways. To the informed haikai reader, the seasonal topic, like the poetic place, created a specific horizon of expectations, which, to use E. H. Gombrich's words, registered "deviation and modification with exaggerated sensitivity."[32] Haikai spirit (*haii*) originally referred, as the word *haikai* itself did, to the comic or humorous element (*kokkei*) in popular linked verse, but it also came to imply, as it did in the renga-style period, in the mid-1680s, the discovery of new worlds or perspectives, especially those that went against convention and tradition and that manifested themselves in the constant search for new associations or new approaches to the seasonal topic.

CHAPTER 8

Remapping the Past: Narrow Road to the Interior

> The uniqueness of a work of art is inseparable from its being imbedded in the fabric of tradition. This tradition itself is thoroughly alive and extremely changeable.
> —Walter Benjamin, "The Work of Art in the Age of Mechanical Reproduction"

> Poetic influence—when it involves two strong, authentic poets—proceeds by a misreading of the prior poet, an act of creative correction that is actually and necessarily a misinterpretation.
> —Harold Bloom, *The Anxiety of Influence*

Bashō remapped the cultural landscape of the Interior, or the northern region of Japan, through *haibun*, or haikai prose, a new genre that combined, in unprecedented fashion, Chinese prose genres, Japanese classical prototypes, and vernacular language and subject matter, thereby bringing together at least three major cultural axes. Bashō wrote haikai prose throughout his literary career, but it was not until around 1690, shortly after his journey to Michinoku or Oku[1]—the area now occupied by Fukushima, Miyagi, Iwate, and Aomori prefectures—that he consciously strove to develop haibun, or prose with a haikai spirit, as a new literary genre and that he began to use the word *haibun*, which first appeared in a letter to Kyorai probably written in the summer of 1690. It was not until the end of his life, in 1694, that he wrote *Oku no hosomichi* (Narrow road to the interior), which may best be understood as an attempt to reveal the different possibilities of haibun in the form of travel literature.

The resulting fusion of vernacular Japanese, classical Japanese, and classical Chinese had a profound impact on the development of Japanese prose, one comparable in importance to the emergence in the Kamakura period (1185–1333) of the "mixed Chinese-Japanese style" (*wakan konkō bun*), which combined classical Japanese and Chinese.

Haikai Prose

The Japanese literary travel journal, which can be traced to a long tradition of arranging travel poems (*kiryo*) and their headnotes in chronological order, effectively began in the Heian period—Ki no Tsurayuki's (868?–945?) *Tosa Nikki* (Tosa diary; 935?) being the earliest extant example in the *kana* syllabary—and bloomed in the Kamakura period, when the political center shifted to the Eastern Provinces, resulting in heavy travel between Kyoto and Kamakura, in such exemplary texts as *Travels on the Seaboard* (*Kaidōki*; 1223), *Journey to the East* (*Tōkan kikō*; 1242?), and Nun Abutsu's *Diary of the Sixteenth Night Moon* (*Izayoi nikki*; 1279–80)—which were written by waka poets either in *wabun* (classical Japanese prose) or the mixed Chinese-Japanese style, both of which had a profound influence on Bashō's travel writings.[2] The genre continued to flourish in the Muromachi period (1336–1573), when classical renga masters, who traveled from one patron to another in the war-torn provinces, began writing travel diaries, the most important of which, for understanding *Narrow Road to the Interior*, were probably Sōgi's *Journey to the Shirakawa Barrier* (*Shirakawa kikō*; 1468) and *Journey to Kyūshū* (*Tsukushi michi no ki*; 1480).

Haibun in the broad sense existed before Bashō in the form of prefaces, headnotes to hokku, and short essays written by haikai masters. Prominent early examples include Kigin's *Mountain Well* (1648), a haikai seasonal almanac, and Genrin's (1631–72) *Treasure Storehouse* (*Takaragura*; 1671), a haibun anthology, but the prose style of these works often resembles that of classical prose. Bashō's new notion of haibun, by contrast, was characterized by the prominent inclusion of haikai words (*haigon*), particularly a combination

Painting of Bashō, followed presumably by Sora, both dressed in priestly attire, on the journey to the Interior, by Kyoriku. 34.4 x 11 in. Of the surviving portraits, this is considered the most reliable since it was done while Bashō was alive, in 1693, by Kyoriku, the best painter among Bashō's disciples, and most closely fits the extant descriptions of Bashō's physical appearance: longish face, high cheeks, extended eyebrows, small mouth, eyes slightly apart, large ears, medium height. (Courtesy Tenri University Library)

of vernacular Japanese (*zokugo*) and Chinese words (*kango*). In the preface to *Prose Mirror of Japan* (*Honchō bunkan*; 1717), an anthology of haibun edited by Shikō, one of Bashō's late disciples, the editor explains the significance of such prose.

> From long ago, there have been four poetic genres: Chinese poetry, classical poetry, renga, and haikai. If Chinese poetry and classical poetry have prose, so too should renga and haikai. . . . But an appropriate style for renga has yet to be established. Instead, renga has been consumed by the house of classical poetry, and its prose is marked by the slipperiness of *The Tale of Genji* or *The Tale of Sagoromo*. Renga has yet to create a graceful prose style. Thanks to Bashō's brush, however, the principles of haikai prose have been created for the first time.[3]

In contrast to waka and *kanshi* (Chinese poetry), which have established their own prose counterparts, *wabun* (classical prose) and *kanbun* (Chinese prose), respectively, classical linked verse (renga) had, in Shikō's opinion, failed to create a prose style distinguishable from classical prose, thus remaining within the sphere of waka. By creating a distinctive haikai prose style, Bashō gave haikai an autonomy and stature that classical renga never attained. A similar argument is put forward in Kyoriku's preface to *Prose Collection of Japan* (*Honchō monzen*; published 1706, later named *Fūzoku monzen*), the first anthology of the new haibun.

> The works of literature written in Japanese since the distant past are so great in number that they would leave storehouses and carriages overflowing. But much of the literature that circulates in the world has been written by court women. Works such as *The Tale of Genji* and *The Tale of Sagoromo*, which give detailed descriptions of the affairs between men and women, should be called handbooks for composing classical poetry. Both these texts follow the principles of classical poetry and classical linked verse. There is not a single word that offers a model for haikai prose. Bashō, my late teacher, was the first to create such a model and breathe elegance and life into it. In using vernacular Japanese or Chinese words, one should think enviously of the cherry blossoms at Yoshino and of the autumn leaves at Tatsuta, desire to gaze at the beauty of Wakanoura, and follow the narrow reeds at Naniwazu.[4]

In Kyoriku's view, haibun was closely affiliated with both vernacular prose (*zokubun*) and Chinese prose, in contrast to classical Japanese prose, which was associated with aristocratic women and the composition of classical poetry, but the writer of haibun, even as he or she uses vernacular or Chinese words, should "think enviously of cherry blossoms at Yoshino," that is, absorb the sensibility and cultural refinement of classical Japanese poetry, which could, as the following statement in the *Kyoraishō* implies, transform both the vernacular and the Chinese into elegant poetic prose.

> The Master said, "When I look at the haikai prose that is being composed today, I find, in some cases, that the Chinese prose has been softened by adding *kana* syllabary, and in other instances that Chinese phrases have been inserted into prose written in the style of classical poetry. In both cases, the diction is coarse and the expression vulgar. Even when it comes to depicting human emotions, the focus is on the clever minds of today. The result is Saikaku's degenerate style. By contrast, the prose composed by our school begins with a clear objective: if we borrow Chinese phrases, we use them in a smooth, soft fashion, and if the subject matter is vulgar, we express it in a gentle manner." (NKBZ 51: 486)[5]

In contrast to Saikaku's haibun, which combined classical prose and vernacular Japanese but which Bashō considered coarse or vulgar in both content and expression, Bashō's new haikai prose was, at least in Kyorai's opinion, graceful and gentle in expression; it had the flow of classical prose even as it incorporated the words and rhythms of vernacular Japanese and Chinese. Both Saikaku and Bashō began as haikai masters and took up haikai prose in mid-career, but unlike Saikaku, who sped up the pace of linked verse and minimized the shifting and change until it turned into prose fiction, or *ukiyo-zōshi* (tales of the floating world), Bashō moved in the opposite direction, reworking and condensing the prose into poetry. *Narrow Road to the Interior* is in fact best considered a long prose poem, which gives vernacular and Chinese phrases the cadence and tonality of poetry.

Most readers regard the medieval travel diaries or Bashō's early travel journals—*Skeleton in the Fields, Backpack Notes,* and *Journey to Sarashina (Sarashina kikō;* 1688–89?)—as the immediate predecessors to *Narrow Road to the Interior,* but the most important prose predecessor was probably *Record of an Unreal Dwelling,*[6] which Bashō rewrote a number of times in 1690 and which he considered the first example of haibun literature. In contrast to earlier haibun, which tended to be extremely short and to function primarily as salutations, *Record of an Unreal Dwelling,* which was closely modeled on Kamo Chōmei's prose essay *Ten-Foot Square Hut (Hōjōki;* 1212), was an extended prose poem in a highly elliptical, hybrid style of vernacular and classical Japanese and classical Chinese. While planning the publication of *Monkey's Straw Coat* in 1690, Bashō apparently conceived of a plan to add a companion volume of haibun centered around *Record of an Unreal Dwelling* called *Monkey's Straw Coat Prose Collection (Sarumino bunshū).* For reasons that are unknown—perhaps due to a dearth of appropriate prose texts—Bashō abandoned the plan for a haibun volume and included only *Record of an Unreal Dwelling* in *Monkey's Straw Coat.*

With the successful completion of *Record of an Unreal Dwelling,* which was published in 1691, Bashō probably gained the confidence to write an extended haibun that adapted the haibun prose of *Record of an Unreal Dwelling* to the travel genre. Like *Record of an Unreal Dwelling, Narrow Road to the Interior,* which was probably written in 1694, is characterized by a highly elliptical, rhythmic, Chinese style of parallel words (*tsuigo*) and parallel phrases (*tsuiku*).[7] In *Sanzōshi,* Bashō is quoted as saying:

> Alternating five and seven syllables is the rule for *chōka,* the long classical Japanese poem. Descriptive prose [*ji no bun*] is likewise often written with the odd count of three, five, or seven syllables. But when words can be paired, they should be paired. If a word refers to an ancient matter, the matching word should also refer to an ancient matter. The same is true of mountains and fields, of water, of living things. (NKBZ 51:532)[8]

In contrast to classical poetry or classical prose, which was based on an alternating 5/7 syllabic rhythm, haibun should have, in accordance with the Chinese model, an even or balanced rhythm (such as 4/4, 6/6), stressing paired words and parallel syntax,[9] as in the following passage on the Tsubo Stone Inscription (Tsubo no ishibumi) in *Narrow Road to the Interior.*

yama kuzure, kawa nagarete	Mountains disappear, rivers flow,
michi aratamari;	roads change;
ishi wa uzumorete, tsuchi ni kakure	rocks are buried, hidden in dirt,
ki wa oite, wakagi ni kawareba;	trees age, saplings replace them;
. . . .	. . . .
angya no ittoku	the virtues of travel
zonmei no yorokobi	the joys of existence
kiryo no rō o wasurete	forgetting the labors of travel
namida mo otsuru bakari nari	I shed only tears
	(NKBZ 41: 358)

Parallel syntax is combined with contrastive or corresponding words—mountain and river, rocks and trees, old age and youth, travel and life—to generate a folksong type of rhythm and a Chinese poetic pattern.[10]

As Japanese scholars have pointed out, various climactic scenes in the two halves of *Narrow Road to the Interior*, the Michinoku (Pacific Ocean) side and the Hokuriku (Japan Sea) side, also correspond like a gigantic Chinese couplet. For example, in contrast to Matsushima, on the front, which appears on a bright, clear day and is compared to "a beautiful woman who powders an already beautiful face," Kisagata, facing the back, is surrounded by mist and rain and similarly resembles a woman with a dark, brooding personality. A parallel also occurs between the two major sacred places: Nikkō, on the front, and the Three Dewa Mountains, on the back. Each section begins with the history or origins of the sacred mountain, pays poetic homage, and ends in respectful silence. But in contrast to Nikkō (literally, light of the sun), which is surrounded by bright light and colors, the three sacred mountains of Dewa are cold and dark. The topic of love (*koi*) in the front—the young, innocent girl Kasane at Nasu Field—is likewise echoed in the back by the dark story of the prostitutes at Ichiburi.[11] The effect of these and other correspondences—which create a contrast between the warm, bright, cheerful Michinoku side and the lonely, somber, mist-en-shrouded Hokuriku area—is to give the larger narrative the kind of complementary coupling, the yoking of similarity and difference, that is frequently found in the language of the text.

Bashō's Chinese prose models for *Narrow Road to the Interior* were probably taken from *The True Treasury of the Ancient Style* (*Ku-wen chen-pao*, J. *Kobun shinpō*), a Yuan-Ming period anthology treasured by Gozan monks during the Muromachi period and used by the Japanese as a textbook for learning Chinese poetry and liter-ary prose. During the Tokugawa period, numerous editions and commentaries were printed, and the anthology was read more wide-ly in Japan than in its country of origin, becoming a standard part of Japanese education and culture. The latter half of this anthology contains different expository genres—among them, rhapsody (*fu*), preface (*hsu*, J. *jo*), eulogy (*sung*, J. *shō*), record (*chi*, J. *ki*), biography (*chuan*, J. *den*), essay (*wen*, J. *bun*), treatise (*lun*, J. *ron*), inscription (*pei*, J. *ishibumi*), encomium (*tsan*, J. *san*), admonitions (*chen*, J. *shin*), lamentation (*tiao-wen*, J. *chōbun*)—which became models for many of Bashō's haibun, including his travel diaries. For example, the section on Hiraizumi in *Narrow Road to the Interior* closely re-sembles one of the Chinese "essays" (*wen*, J. *bun*) found in *The True Treasury of the Ancient Style*: "Essay on Mourning for the Dead at an Ancient Battlefield" ("Ku chan-chang tiao-wen," J. *Ko senjō o tomu-rau bun*) by Li Hua (J. Rika) in which the narrator stands on a height, looks down on a former battlefield, imagines the terrible carnage, and laments the fate of the dead soldiers. *Prose Collection of Japan* (*Honchō monzen*), the haibun anthology edited by Kyoriku, includes four such haibun—"Essay on Mourning for the Dead at an Ancient Battlefield" ("Kosenjō o chōsuru bun"), "Rhapsody on Ma-tsushima" ("Matsushima no fu"), "Tsubo Stone Inscription" ("Tsubo no ishibumi"), and "Preface to the Milky Way" ("Ginga no jo")—taken from different parts of *Narrow Road to the Interior*. As these haibun titles suggest, Bashō combined the conventions of the tradi-tional Japanese travel diary with Chinese prose models, thereby creating a new vernacular-based prose genre that he hoped could rival both the Chinese and Japanese classical models in literary quality.

For Tokugawa readers, the interest of the Matsushima section probably lay in the haikai approach to a Chinese *fu* (rhapsody), a prose-poem characterized by long (six-or-seven-word) lines, the use of the caesura, complex rhyme patterns, and balanced parallel phrases. Matsushima, one of Bashō's original destinations and one of the most famous *utamakura* in Michinoku, was second only to Shinobu and Sue no matsuyama in the number of classical poems composed on it: 59 poems on Matsushima are recorded in *Classified Collection of Japanese Poetry on Famous Places (Ruiji meisho waka shū).*[12]

> Well, it has been said many times, but Matsushima is the most beautiful place in all of Japan. First of all, it can hold its head up to Tung-t'ing Lake or West Lake. Letting in the sea from the southeast, it fills the bay, three leagues wide, with the tide of Che-chiang.[13] Matsushima has gathered countless islands: the high islands point their fingers to heaven, those lying down crawl over the waves. Some are piled two deep, some three deep. To the left, the islands are separated from each other, but to the right they are linked. Some islands seem to be carrying islands on their backs, others to be embracing them, like someone caressing a child. The green of the pine is dark and dense, the branches and leaves bent by the salty sea breeze—it seems as if the branches have been deliberately twisted. The landscape creates a tranquil, soft feeling, like a beautiful lady powdering her face. Did the god of the mountain create this long ago, in the age of the gods? Is this the work of the Creator? What words could a human being use to describe this?

As is revealed in *Classified Collection of Japanese Poetry on Famous Places*—which was widely used in the seventeenth century by haikai and renga poets for linking and word associations and from which Sora, Bashō's travel companion, took careful notes before departing on the journey to the Interior—Matsushima was associated in the classical tradition with the hovels (*tomaya*), beach shelters (*hamabisashi*), and boats (*tsuribune*) of fisherfolk (*ama*), and with plovers, the moon, and Ojima Island, some of which appear briefly at the end of the prose passage. Bashō, however, fundamentally refigures

Matsushima through Chinese poetic structure and allusions. The parallel, contrastive phrases—such as "the high islands point their fingers to heaven, those lying down crawl over the waves" and "some are piled two deep, some three deep"—echo the couplet structure of the Chinese *fu* while possessing haikai humor. At the same time, the allusions to Chinese landscape transform Matsushima into the Japanese equivalent of Tung-t'ing Lake or West Lake (Hsi hu), two lakes famous for their beauty in China, thereby creating a *mitate*, or double vision.

If the Shirakawa passage, which we will examine below, is a stylistic exemplar of a *michiyuki* (poetic journey) in the classical Japanese style and the Matsushima section a stunning haikai experiment in the Chinese *fu*, the Kisagata section is a notable example of a Chinese-Japanese hybrid style, interweaving Chinese, *fu*-esque motifs with classical Japanese prose.

> Having seen all the beautiful landscapes—rivers, mountains, seas, and coasts—I now prepared my heart for Kisagata. Moving from the port at Sakata toward the northeast, we crossed over a mountain, followed the rocky shore, and walked over sand—all for a distance of ten miles. The sun was on the verge of setting when we arrived. The sea wind blew sand into the air, and the rain turned everything to mist, hiding Chōkai Mountain. I groped in the darkness. Having heard that the landscape was exceptional in the rain, I decided that it must be worth seeing and squeezed into a fisherman's thatched hut to wait for the end of the rain.
>
> The next morning, when the skies had cleared and the morning sun was shining brightly, we took a boat to Kisagata. Our first stop was Nōin Island, where we visited the place where Nōin had secluded himself for three years. We docked our boat on the far shore and visited the old cherry tree, on which Saigyō had written the poem about "rowing over the flowers." On the shore of the river was an imperial mausoleum, the gravestone of Empress Jingū. The temple was called Kanmanju Temple. I wondered why I had yet to hear of an imperial procession to this place.
>
> We sat down in the front room of the temple and raised the blinds, taking in the entire landscape at one glance. To the south, Chōkai

Mountain was holding up the heavens, its shadow reflected on the bay of Kisagata; to the west, the road came to an end at the Muyamuya Barrier; and to the east, there was a dike. The road to Akita stretched into the distance. To the north was the sea, and the waves pounded into the bay at Shiogoshi, the shallows. The face of the bay, about two and a half miles in width and length, resembled Matsushima, but it was different. If Matsushima was like someone laughing, Kisagata resembled a resentful person. A feeling of sorrow was added to that of loneliness. The land was as if in a state of anguish.

> Kisagata—
> Hsi Shih asleep in the rain
> flowers of the silk tree

Kisagata | ya | ame | ni | Seishi | ga | nebu | no | hana
Kisagata | : | rain | in | Hsi-Shih | 's | silk-tree | 's | flower

> the shallows—
> cranes wetting their legs
> coolness of the sea

shiogoshi | ya | tsuru | hagi | nurete | umi | suzushi[14]
shallow | : | crane | shin | being-wet | sea | cool
(NKBZ 41:372–74)

Kisagata, an island-filled bay on the northern coast of Dewa Province (Akita) and a climactic point in *Narrow Road to the Interior*, was an *utamakura* associated, particularly as a result of a famous poem by Nōin, with wandering (*sasurau*), thatched huts of fisherfolk, lodging on a journey (*tabine*), and a rocky shore (*iso*)—all of which appear in the passage.[15] The traveler is also reminded of the following poem, which he attributes to Saigyō.[16]

> Kisagata no   The cherry blossoms
> sakura wa nami ni   of Kisagata are buried
> uzumorete   in the waves—
> hana no ue kogu   a fisherman's boat
> ama no tsuribune   rowing over the flowers.

The traveler relives the classical associations of the place, but in a haikai twist, Bashō draws on Su Tung-p'o's poem "West Lake" ("Hsi

Hu," J. Seiko), which compares the noted lake to Hsi Shih (J. Sei-shi), a legendary Chinese beauty employed during the Chou dynasty to debauch an enemy king and cause his defeat and who was thought to have a constant frown, her eyes half closed, as a result of her tragic fate. Echoing the Sino-Japanese mixed prose, the climactic hokku juxtaposes a Chinese figure with a Japanese seasonal image, Hsi Shih with the delicate flowers of the silk tree (*nebu* or *nemu*) whose slender hair-like stamen close up at night, suggesting that Hsi Shih is "sleeping" (*nemu*) or that her eyes are half-closed. Dampened and shriveled by the rain, the silk tree flower echoes the resentful Chinese consort: both in turn became a metaphor for the rain-shrouded, emotionally dark bay. With the hokku on the cranes, Bashō closed a series of contrasts: between Matsushima and Kisagata, lightness and darkness, laughter and resentment, the dark brooding atmosphere of Kisagata during the rains and the cool, light atmosphere that follows.

Narrow Road to the Interior is marked by a great variety of prose styles, which range from a heavily Chinese style to the soft classical style to vernacular prose to a mixture or fusion of all three. In some sections, the style is extremely dense and terse, falling into strict couplets, and in others it resembles the mellifluous, lengthy flow of *The Tale of Genji*. The passage on the Shirakawa Barrier, for example, draws heavily on classical diction and waka. The Matsushima and Kisagata sections, by contrast, are extremely Chinese in style and content. Bashō gathered a number of texts originally written for different purposes, rewrote them, and wove them together like a quilt, placing the Chinese-style passages at climactic points. The end result is that the reader journeys from one type of language and prose genre to another, exploring the diverse possibilities of hai-bun.[17]

The Spiritual Journey

In the spring of 1689 (Genroku 2), on the 27th day of the Third Month, Bashō and his companion Sora departed for Michinoku or Oku, the area north of the Shirakawa Barrier. Bashō traveled north

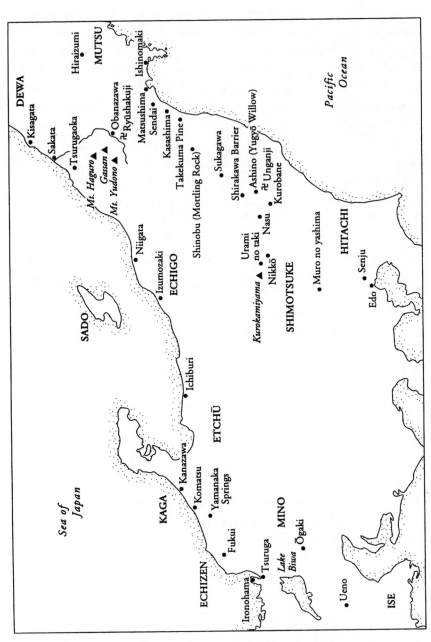

Places on *The Narrow Road to the Interior*

to present-day Sendai, crossed west into Dewa—now occupied by Akita and Yamagata prefectures—moved south along the Japan Sea coast through Kanazawa, and arrived at Ōgaki in Mino Province (Gifu) around the 21st of the Eighth Month. This five-month journey through the Tōhoku and Hokuriku areas should not be mistaken for that found in *Narrow Road to the Interior* the text, which was written as late as 1694 (Genroku 7), at the end of Bashō's life, over four years after the journey.[18] Sora kept careful notes, which reveal that the majority of the 50 hokku in *Narrow Road to the Interior* were either written after the journey, probably in 1693–94, or were revisions of earlier poems.[19] Although often praised as a work of confessional literature or regarded as part of the long tradition of travel accounts, *Narrow Road to the Interior* is best seen as a kind of fiction, loosely based on the actual journey, leaving out most of what actually happened. Key individuals are not mentioned or appear under fictitious or altered names. Bashō added incidents and characters for dramatic effect, and often rearranged or reconstructed those events that did occur. Bashō depicted an ideal poetic world in which practical matters—such as food, finances, business relations—have no place. The "I," the first-person narrator, who remains unnamed and who is never identified as Bashō, lives a life devoted to *fūga*, to poetic life, in a manner that Bashō himself probably aspired to but found impossible in the busy world of the Tokugawa haikai master.[20]

Like a linked verse sequence, to which it has often been compared, *Narrow Road to the Interior* has no absolute center, no single, overarching perspective. Instead, a focal point emerges, climaxes, and then is replaced by a new focal point. Bashō does, however, interweave the narrative with a series of interrelated journeys: a search for *utamakura*, or poetic places, especially traces of the ancients such as Saigyō; a journey to historical places such as the old battlefield at Hiraizumi; a spiritual pilgrimage to sacred places; and encounters with interesting individuals and poetic partners. The text moves from one main topos—an *utamakura*, a historical site, a sacred place, or an interesting individual—to another, shifting in such a way that the same topic rarely occurs twice in succession.

The spiritual journey is foreshadowed by a sequence of scenes toward the beginning of *Narrow Road to the Interior*, at Kurokami-yama (Black Hair Mountain), Urami no taki (Back View Falls), and Kurobane. The passage on Kurokamiyama (near Nikkō) describes Sora's decision, on the eve of the journey, to shave his head, change into the black robe of a priest, and take on a Buddhist name.

> I shave my head
> at Black Hair Mountain—
> time for summer clothes
> —Sora
>
> sorisutete | Kurokamiyama | ni | koromogae
> head-shaving | Black-Hair-Mountain | at | changing-to-summer-clothes
> (NKBZ 41: 345–46)

Embarking on a journey becomes synonymous with entering the Buddhist path: both imply a firm resolve and a new life, here symbolized by the seasonal word *koromogae* (change of clothes at the beginning of summer). The next hokku in the same passage (NKBZ 41: 346), at Urami no taki (also near Nikkō), depends on a similar homophonic twist: *ge no hajime* refers both to the beginning (*hajime*) of summer (*ge* is the Sino-Japanese reading for *natsu*) and to summer austerities (*ge* or *gegomori*) in which Buddhist practitioners remained indoors from the sixteenth of the Fourth Month to the sixteenth of the Seventh Month, fasting, reciting sutras, and carrying out ascetic and purification practices such as standing under a waterfall.

> secluded for a while
> in a waterfall—
> start of summer
>
> shibaraku | wa | taki | ni | komoru | ya | ge | no | hajime
> awhile | as-for | waterfall | in | seclude | : | summer | 's | beginning

The traveler stands behind the waterfall, which gives him, at least for a moment, the cool, pure feeling of being cleansed of the dirt of the world, as in a *gegomori*. Both the Black Hair Mountain and the Back View Falls verses were probably written long after the journey to stress the ascetic nature of the journey. The "I" also composes the following hokku at the Gyōjadō Hall in Kurobane (NKBZ 41: 348).

> summer mountains—
> praying to the tall clogs
> at journey's start

natsuyama | ni | ashida | o | ogamu | kadode | kana
summer-mountain | in | tall-clog | (acc.) | pray | journey's-start | !

Natsuyama (summer mountains), a classical seasonal word for the thick, verdant mountains of summer, refers to both the mountains surrounding the temple and the many mountain peaks that lie before the traveler. At the beginning of the journey, the traveler "bows before the high clogs," a prayer for the foot strength of En no Gyōja, the founder of a mountain priest sect (*shugendō*), a "man of austerities" (*gyōja*) believed to have acquired superhuman power from rigorous mountain training. The title *Oku no hosomichi* thus implies not only the narrow and difficult roads (*hosomichi*) of Michinoku (Oku), the relatively unsettled area of northeastern Honshū, but the difficulty of the spiritual journey "within" (*oku*).

Pilgrimages to sacred places, to temples and shrines, were popular as early as the Heian period and formed an integral part of the travel account tradition, particularly those written by hermit priests. Sōgi's *Journey to Kyūshū* (*Tsukushi michi no ki*), for example, movingly describes his visits to shrines and temples in northern Kyūshū, especially the Tenmangū Shrine in Dazaifu (dedicated to the spirit of Sugawara no Michizane) and the Sumiyoshi Shrine. Bashō, who may have been influenced by *Journey to Kyūshū*, includes far more sections—almost one-fourth of the text—on this topic than are usually found in medieval travel diaries.[21] A typical passage begins with a description of the landscape, the history of the shrine or temple, usually giving some detail about the founder or the name. The climactic hokku, which may be a greeting to the divine spirit or to the head of the temple/shrine, usually conveys a sense of the sacred quality or efficacy of the place. In the passage on the Ryūshaku Temple, or Mountain Temple (Yamadera), in Dewa (Yamagata), that quality is embodied in the word "stillness" (*shizukasa*), which later became the poetic essence (*hon'i*) of this new poetic place.

> In the Yamagata domain there is a mountain temple called Ryūshakuji. It was founded by the High Priest Jikaku and is an especially pure and tranquil place. Since we had been urged to see this place at least once, we backtracked from Obanazawa and traveled for about seven leagues. When we arrived, there was still light outside. We borrowed a room at a temple at the foot of the mountain and then climbed to the Buddha Hall at the top. Boulders were piled on boulders, creating a mountain; the pines and cypress trees had grown old; the soil and rocks were aged, covered with smooth moss. The doors to the temple buildings atop the boulders were closed and not a sound could be heard. We followed the edge of the cliff, crawled over boulders, and then prayed at the Buddha hall. As the beautiful surroundings settled into silence, I felt my heart growing pure.

> stillness—
> sinking deep into the rocks
>   cries of the cicada

> shizukasa | ya | iwa | ni | shimiiru | semi | no | koe
> stillness | : | rock | in | penetrate | cicada | 's | voice

In classical poetry, the cicada was associated primarily with impermanence, as a result of its short life and thin shell (*utsusemi*), but here Bashō focuses on its raucous sound. In a paradoxical twist, the sharp, high-pitched cries of the cicada deepen the stillness by penetrating the rocks on top of the mountain. The first version appears to have been "Mountain temple—sticking to the rocks, cries of the cicada" (*yamadera ya ishi ni shimitsuku semi no koe*), and the second version "Loneliness—seeping into the rocks, cries of the cicada" (*sabishisa ya iwa ni shimikomu semi no koe*).[22] In contrast to the verbs *shimitsuku* (to stick to) and *shimikomu* (to seep into), *shimiiru* (to penetrate, pass deep into) in the last version implies the non-physicality of the voice, which passes, as if untouched, deep into the rocks and by implication becomes stillness. As the last sentence of the prose passage suggests, the stillness (*shizukasa*) also passes deep into the poet, making his "heart grow pure" (*kokoro sumiyuku*).

Another climactic point in the spiritual journey is the difficult climb over Hagurosan, Gassan, and Yudono—the three holy mountains of Dewa Province. The following two hokku by Bashō are on Gassan (Moon Mountain) and Yudono (Bathhouse Mountain).

> cloud peaks
> crumbling one after another—
>   moon mountain
>
> kumo | no | mine | ikutsu | kuzurete | tsuki | no | yama
> cloud | 's | peak | how-many | crumbling | moon | 's | mountain
>
>   forbidden to speak—
> wetting my sleeves
>   at Bathhouse Mountain!
>
> katararenu | yudono | ni | nurasu | tamoto | kana
> cannot-speak-of | bathhouse | in | wetting | sleeve | !

Kumo no mine (literally, cloud peak), which takes the shape of a mountain peak, is a high, cumulonimbus cloud that results from intense moisture and heat. The mountain-shaped clouds, which have gathered during midday at the peak of Gassan (literally, moon mountain), crumble or collapse one after another until they are finally gone, leaving the moon shining over the mountain (*tsuki no yama*), a Japanese reading for Gassan.[23] The word *ikutsu* (how many?) is an interrogative implying "a good many" clouds crumbling. The preceding passage, which states that "the moon of Tendai insight was clear" (*Tendai shikan no tsuki akiraka ni*), also suggests a state of mind that is no longer "clouded." Movement, in short, occurs from midday, when the clouds block the view, to night, when the mountain stands unobscured; from the heat of midday to the cool of evening; from the ephemerality of the clouds, which disappear one after another, to the sacred mountain, which stands firm and awesome; and from mental obscurity to enlightenment.

In contrast to the first two mountains, Hagurosan and Gassan, which had never appeared in classical poetry, Yudono (literally, Bathhouse) was an *utamakura*, referred to in classical poetry as Koi no yama, Mountain of Love.[24] The body of the Yudono deity was a huge red rock that spouted hot water and was said to resemble sexual organs. "Forbidden to speak" (*katararenu*) refers to the rule, described in *Narrow Road to the Interior*, that all visitors to Yudono, the holiest of the Three Dewa Mountains, were forbidden to talk about the appearance of the mountain to others. The wetting of the sleeves, while echoing the erotic association with love and bathing, also suggests the speaker's tears of awe at the holiness of the mountain. The tempering of the sword and the late-blooming flower in the mountain snow in the preceding passage also suggest spiritual purification. As Hirai Shōbin has argued, the journey over the Three Dewa Mountains, in which the traveler almost dies from exhaustion and cold before coming to Yudono, a place of sexuality and fertility, represents a rite of passage, a kind of death and rebirth.[25]

Landscape Re-visioned

The traveler in *Narrow Road to the Interior* is a wanderer, or *hyō-hakusha*, one who floats on water or moves without direction, who leaves his "body to the wind." In the opening to *Backpack Notes*, Bashō called himself *fūrabō*, a thin garment or fabric easily torn by the wind; and elsewhere he named himself after the *bashō*, or plantain, of which he wrote: "I love the way its leaves are easily torn by the wind and rain" ("Bashō o utsusu kotoba"). *Narrow Road to the Interior* similarly opens with: "From which year was it? I was summoned by the winds of the scattered clouds, with no end to thoughts of wandering." This wanderer is paradoxically fated to seek out the traces of the "ancients," the spiritual and poetic figures of the past, who implicitly become the deities of the road (*dōsojin*) and summon the poet to embark on a journey through time.

The text of *Narrow Road to the Interior* mentions the year Genroku 2 (1689), but the narrator uses bureaucratic titles that were no longer used in the Edo period and rarely gives times or dates except those related to annual, seasonal events such as Koromogae or Tanabata (Weaver's Festival).[26] Unlike Sora's travel diary, which records the journey in terms of distances, place-names, weather, time, and day, the traveler in *Narrow Road to the Interior* journeys across time and space. Toward the beginning, which notes that the traveler "sheds tears of parting at the imaginary crossroads" ("maboroshi no chimata ni ribetsu no namida o sosogu"), the "I" seems to pass from this world into a liminal zone, often taking on the persona of the traveling priest who encounters the spirits of the past in a Noh play. At the end of this long journey, the "I" is welcomed at Ōgaki by his friends and disciples "like someone who had returned from the dead" ("yosei no mono ni au ga gotoku").

The traveler's journey into the past becomes an opportunity to revision and remap the cultural landscape, a movement foreshadowed by the passage on Muro no yashima, a shrine in Shimotsuke (Tochigi), at the beginning of *Narrow Road to the Interior*. The following love poem in the *Shikashū* (1144; Love I, no. 188) by Fujiwara Sanekata, which draws on the homophonic association of fire (*hi*) with longing (*omohi*) and love (*kohi*) and uses smoke (*keburi*) as a metaphor for suppressed desire, is typical of the many classical poems on Muro no yashima (Eight Islands of the Sealed Room).

Topic Unknown

ikade ka wa	How could
omohi ari to mo	I let you know
shirasubeki	of my longing
Muro no yashima no	were it not for the smoke
keburi narade wa	of Muro no yashima?

Classical poets believed that the vapors arising from a stream in Muro no yashima looked like smoke or that the smoke came from an oven (*kamado*), an association suggested by the word *muro* (sealed room). However, Sora, who came from a family of Shintō priests, presented a different explanation based on a close reading of the *Nihon shoki* (Chronicles of Japan) and other early texts.

We paid our respects to the shrine at Muro no yashima. My travel companion Sora said, "This deity is called the Goddess of the Blooming

Cherry Tree and is the same as that worshipped at Mount Fuji. Since the goddess entered a sealed hut and burned herself, thereby giving birth to Hohodemi, the God of Emitting Fire, and thus proving her vow, they call the place Muro no yashima, Eight Islands of the Sealed Room. The custom of including smoke on poems on Yashima also derives from this story." It is forbidden to consume a fish called *konoshiro*, or shad, which is thought to smell like burnt flesh. The essence of this shrine history is already known to the world.

Bashō here suggested that *Narrow Road to the Interior*, with the help of a learned companion (Sora), will take a revisionary approach to *utamakura*; it will not simply follow the established poetic associations but explore both the physical place and its historical roots in an effort to renew and recast the cultural landscape.

The interest of travel literature, at least in the Anglo-European tradition, generally lies in the unknown, in new worlds, new knowledge, new perspectives, new experiences. But for medieval waka and renga poets, the object of travel was to confirm what already existed, to reinforce the roots of cultural memory. The classical models of travel literature—such as the *Tosa Diary* (*Tosa nikki*) and *The Tales of Ise*—were written by aristocrats raised in the capital for whom the provinces were a foreign sphere. Medieval travel journals likewise tended to assume the superiority of the capital (*miyako*), which embodied high culture, and associated the provinces or the country (*hina*) with suffering and uncertainty. The journey into the dark Other, however, was modulated and guided by the visits to *utamakura*, which represented cultural nodes in the poetic tradition.[27] By visiting *utamakura*, the medieval poet-traveler hoped to relive the experience of his or her literary predecessors and to be moved to compose poetry on the same landscape, thereby joining his or her cultural forebears. The travel diary itself became a link in a chain of poetic and literary transmission.

As the following passage on the Shirakawa Barrier, one of the major *utamakura* in Michinoku, reveals, *Narrow Road to the Interior* both follows and twists this medieval paradigm of travel.

The days of uncertainty piled one on the other, and when we came upon Shirakawa Barrier, I finally felt as if I had settled into the journey. I can understand why that poet had written, "Had I a messenger I would send a missive to the capital!" One of the Three Barriers, Shirakawa has captured the hearts of poets. With the sound of the autumn wind in my ears and the image of the autumn leaves in my mind, I was moved all the more by the tops of the green-leafed trees. The flowering of the wild rose amid the white deutzia clusters made me feel as if I were crossing over snow. . . .

At the post station at Sukagawa, I visited a man named Tōkyū, who insisted that we stay for four or five days. To the question "How did you find the crossing at the Shirakawa Barrier?" I replied, "My body and spirit were tired from the pain of the long journey. My heart was overwhelmed by the landscape. The thoughts of the distant past tore through me, and I was unable to think clearly. But, not wanting to cross the barrier without producing a single verse, I wrote:

> beginnings of poetry—
> rice-planting songs
> of the Interior

fūryū | no | hajime | ya | oku | no | taueuta
poetry | 's | beginning | : | Interior | 's | rice-planting-song

This opening verse was followed by a second verse, and then a third verse, and before we knew it we had composed three linked verse sequences.

The Shirakawa Barrier here exists almost entirely in the traveler's imagination, as a circle of poetic associations. Taira Kanemori (d. 990), referred to as "that poet," was the first in a long line of classical waka poets to compose on it.

tayori araba	Had I a messenger
ikade miyako e	I would send
tsugeyaramu	a missive to the capital:
kyō Shirakawa no	"Today, I've crossed
seki wa koenu to	Shirakawa Barrier!"

Shūishū (1005; Parting, No. 339)

The following poem in *Goshūishū* (1086; Travel, no. 518) by Priest Nōin, who first traveled to Michinoku in 1025, associated Shirakawa Barrier with autumn wind (*akikaze*).

miyako oba	Though I left the
kasumi to tomo ni	capital together with
tachishikado	the spring mists,
akikaze zo fuku	autumn winds are blowing
Shirakawa no seki	at Shirakawa Barrier.

At a poetry contest in 1170, Minamoto Yorimasa (1104–80) composed an allusive variation on Nōin's poem that subsequently linked Shirakawa Barrier with bright autumn leaves (*momiji*).

miyako ni wa	In the capital
mada aoba nite	the leaves were still green
mishikadomo	when I saw them,
momiji chirishiku	but bright autumn leaves now scatter
Shirakawa no seki	at Shirakawa Barrier[28]

Senzaishū (1183; Autumn II, No. 365)

In a seemingly endless poetic transmission, Bashō, like many of his medieval predecessors, follows the traces of Saigyō, Yorimasa, and others, who had earlier sought the traces of Nōin, who in turn had followed the traces of Kanemori. Significantly, however, the passage ends with the hokku on the "beginnings of poetry" (*fūryū no hajime*)[29] in which Bashō leaves behind the web of classical associations—the white deutzia (*unohana*), autumn leaves, autumn wind, longing for the capital—to find *fūryū*, or poetic refinement, in the rice-planting songs (*taueuta*) sung by the laborers in the fields, an ancient practice that had died out in the Kyoto and Kantō areas by the early Edo period. In a haikai twist, Michinoku, or the Interior, rather than the capital (*miyako*), becomes the beginnings of poetic and artistic sensibility. Shirakawa Barrier, which stood at the entrance to Michinoku, marks not a turning back toward the capital, as the earlier classical poems on Shirakawa had, but an entry into the provinces as a poetic wellspring. In the subsequent passages, the traveler is drawn to local customs and culture such as *oku jōruri* (recitations by minstrels), silkworm growing (reminiscent of the seventh-century *Man'yōshū*), and straw sandals with blue thongs (at Miyagi Field). As the modern scholar Shiraishi Teizō has argued, Tsuta no hosomichi (Narrow Road of the Vine), at Utsu no yama, one of the major *utamakura* on the eastern seaboard, represented, as the Shirakawa Barrier did, the classical poetic essence of travel, that is, the traveler's longing for the capital. *Oku no hosomichi*, by contrast, which takes its title from an obscure *utamakura* called Hosomichi, or Narrow Road, near Miyagi Field (Sendai), represents a haikai-esque counterpart to the classical "narrow road."[30]

For Heian court poets, who had no need to visit the physical *utamakura*, there was only the *utamakura* of the poetic tradition: composing on *utamakura* meant travel without traveling. Bashō, by contrast, followed in the shoes of poet travelers such as Saigyō and Sōgi, who had visited the physical *utamakura*. Unlike Sōgi, however, who ultimately identified with the classical poetic essence of the *utamakura*, becoming one with the poetic world of the ancients, as he did at the climax of *Journey to Shirakawa*, the Bashō traveler encounters a disappointing gap between the physical *utamakura* and its classical associations. The traveler attempts to "look into the heart of the ancients" but is disappointed to find that the site has been destroyed or ravaged by time. As the traveler notes at the Tsubo Stone Inscription (near Sendai), "Although many of the places that have been composed on from the distant past continue to exist, mountains crumble, rivers change direction, roads are altered, rocks are buried in dirt, and old trees are replaced by new ones. As time passes and generations change, the traces of the poetic places become uncertain" (NKBZ 41: 358). At the Takekuma Pine, a major *utamakura*, the traveler finds the twin-trunked pine that Priest Nōin had written about and that preserved for the traveler "the shape of a thousand years"; and at Shiogama Shrine, the lantern "given by Izumi Saburō, Bunji 3 [1187]" sends him back five hundred years. These rare moments fill the traveler with great joy and emotion, but significantly they do not lead to new poetry. Instead, it is those moments of loss and disappointment—when the past has been ob-

scured and can be glimpsed only through the fleeting traces—that in-
spire poetry, as in the following passage on Shinobu (in present-day
Fukushima), the most famous *utamakura* in Michinoku.[31]

> The next day we went to Shinobu Village and visited Shinobu Mottling
> Rock. The rock was in a small village, half-buried, deep in the shade of
> the mountain. A child from the village came and told us, "In the distant
> past, the rock was on top of this mountain, but the villagers, angered by
> the visitors who had been tearing up the barley grass to test the rock,
> shoved it down into the valley, where it lies face down." Perhaps that
> was the way it was meant to be.
>
>   planting rice seedlings
> the hands—in the distant past pressing
>   the grass of longing
>
> sanae | toru | temoto | ya | mukashi | shinobuzuri
> rice-seedling | plant | hand | : | distant-past | longing-mottling

Shinobu mojizuri (Shinobu mottling), the technique of rubbing the
fronds of *shinobugusa* (hare's foot fern, literally, "longing grass")
onto woven cloth so as to create a wild pattern or design, became as-
sociated with uncontrolled longing (*shinobu*), due to the following
love poem in the *Kokinshū* (Love IV, no. 724) by Minamoto Tōru
(822–895), one of many classical poems that helped to transform
Michinoku from an area associated with barbarians (*ezo*) into a land-
scape for Heian courtly love.

> michinoku no   I am not one
> shinobu mojizuri   to long uncontrollably
> dare yue ni   like the wild
> midaremu to omou   Shinobu mottling
> warenaranakuni   of the Interior.

The traveler in *Narrow Road to the Interior* is disappointed to dis-
cover that an *utamakura* that had given birth to countless poems has
been neglected and abused. The damaged *utamakura*, however, in-
spires the traveler, who sees in the hands of the nearby farm girls
transplanting rice seedlings a glimpse of the hands of the young
women who used to press "longing grass" onto the Shinobu Mot-

tling Rock. Time has obscured the literary *utamakura*, but the powerful memory of that poetic place enables the poet to find new poetry in the mundane, in the everyday commoner life of the provinces. In a haikai movement, the refined and the mundane, the classical and the contemporary, merge momentarily in the hands of the farm girls.

A poem on an *utamakura* was implicitly a greeting to the spirit of the ancient entombed in the *utamakura*, enabling the poet to join the company of those who had written memorable poems on the same toponym. At the same time, the poet, hearing the voices of the past, could be overwhelmed and silenced by his poetic predecessors. In the following scene in *Backpack Notes*, Bashō visits the cherry blossoms at Yoshino, perhaps the most famous *utamakura* in Japan.

> We stayed for three days at Yoshino, while the cherry trees were in full bloom, and saw Yoshino both at dawn and at dusk. The beauty of the early morning moon sent my heart racing, filling me with emotion. I was swept away by thoughts of that famous poem on Yoshino by Fujiwara Yoshitsune, was left directionless at Saigyō's signpost, and recalled the poem that Teishitsu had tossed off—"What a scene! What a scene!" Unable to compose even a single poem, I regretfully closed my mouth. I had come charged with enthusiasm, only to see it all disappear. (NKBZ 41: 323)[32]

Reminded of one poem after another on Yoshino, including haikai by Teishitsu (1610–73), a Teimon poet, the traveler is paralyzed, unable to compose poetry. At other times, however, Bashō became what Harold Bloom calls a "strong" poet, overcoming and sometimes even erasing the traces of his poetic predecessors. Bashō in fact helped to transform the classical landscape of Michinoku—associated with distant exile, salt-burning, fishermen, thatched huts, autumn winds, frustrated love, and longing for home—into a more medieval landscape of warriors and hermits, as in the Hiraizumi section, one of the climactic passages of *Narrow Road to the Interior*.

> The glory of three generations of Fujiwara vanished in the space of a dream; the remains of the Great Gate stood two miles in the distance. Hidehira's headquarters had turned into rice paddies and wild fields.

Only Kinkeizan, Golden Fowl Hill, remained as it was. First, we climbed Takadachi, Castle-on-the-Heights, from where we could see the Kitakami, a broad river that flowed from the south. The Koromo River rounded Izumi Castle and, at a point beneath Castle-on-the-Heights, it dropped into the broad river. The ancient ruins of Yasuhira and others, lying behind Koromo Barrier, appear to close off the southern entrance and guard against the Ainu barbarians. Selecting his loyal retainers, Yoshitsune fortified himself in the castle, but his glory quickly turned to grass. "The state is destroyed, / rivers and hills remain. / The city walls turn to spring, / grasses and trees are green." With these lines from Tu Fu in my head, I lay down my bamboo hat, letting the time and tears flow.

> summer grasses—
> traces of dreams
> of ancient warriors

natsukusa | ya | tsuwamonodomo | ga | yume | no | ato
summer-grass | : | warriors | ' | dream | 's | trace

> in the deutzia
> Kanefusa appears
> white-haired
>   —Sora

unohana | ni | Kanefusa | miyuru | shiraga | kana
deutzia | in | Kanefusa | appears | white-hair | !

The four successive heavy "o" syllables in *tsuwamonodomo* (plural for warriors) suggest the ponderous march of warriors or the thunder of battle. As with most of Bashō's noted poems, this hokku depends on polysemous key words: *ato*, which can mean "site," "aftermath," "trace," or "track," and *yume*, which can mean "dream," "ambition," or "glory." The summer grasses are the "site" (*ato* as a spatial marker) of a former battlefield and of the dreams of glory of the many noted warriors who fought here in the distant past. *Ato* (literally "after") also refers to the passage of time: the summer grasses are the "aftermath" of the dreams of glory. All that is left of the once great ambitions are the "traces" or "tracks" (*ato*), the barely visible physical marks of the past. The "dreams of the many warriors" (*tsuwamonodomo ga yume*) are the dreams of the three generations of Fujiwara who valiantly conquered the Ainu tribesmen and built a glorious civilization only to see it disappear and of Yoshitsune's brave retainers, who died for their master. The ephemerality, the dream-like nature of such "ambitions" (*yume*), is foreshadowed in the opening phrase of the prose passage ("in the space of a dream," *issui no yume*), a reference to the Noh play *Kantan*, about a man (Rosei) who napped and dreamed a lifetime of glory and defeat while waiting for dinner. These dreams of glory have turned to grass (*kusamura*), leaving only the site or traces of the dreams.

The traveler here takes on the aura of the *waki* (traveling priest) in a Noh warrior play (*shuramono*) who visits the site of a former battlefield and then, as if in a dream, watches the ghost of the slain warrior re-enact his most tragic moments on the battlefield. A similar process occurs in the Chinese archetype in *The True Treasury of the Ancient Style*: "Essay on Mourning for the Dead at an Ancient Battlefield" by Li Hua, in which the poet gazes down at an old battlefield, imagines the terrible carnage, listens to the voices of the dead, before returning to the present to ponder the meaning of the past. The "dreams" in Bashō's hokku, in short, are also the dreams of the visitors, who have had a fleeting glimpse of the past, of the dreams of others.

Natsukusa (summer grasses), a classical seasonal word for summer, meant thick, deep grass, resulting from the continuous summer rains (*samidare*), and was associated in the classical poetry with *shigeru* (to grow thick), *musubu* (to tie blades, bond), *chigiru* (to tie, make a vow of love). Through the reference to Tu Fu's noted Chinese poem on the impermanence of civilization—"The state is destroyed, / rivers and hills remain / The city walls turn to spring, / grasses and trees are green"—Bashō transformed these classical associations of eroticism and fertility into those of battle and the larger topos of the ephemerality of human ambitions. *Natsukusa*, in short, is both the rich, thick, replenished grass of the present *and* the blood-stained grass of the past, an image both of nature's constancy and of the impermanence of all things.

Sora's poem, which was probably written by Bashō himself, continues the Noh-esque vision. The two hokku can in fact be read as linked verses: the white flowers of the *unohana* (deutzia), a kind of brier, appears in the midst of a field of summer grass, from which the figure of Kanefusa rises like a ghost, his white hair waving in the air. According to the *Gikeiki* (Record of Yoshitsune), Kanefusa, Yoshitsune's loyal retainer, helped Yoshitsune's wife and children commit suicide, saw his master to his end, set fire to the fort at Takadachi, felled Nagasaki Tarō, an enemy captain, grabbed Nagasaki's younger brother under his arm, and then leaped into the flames—a sense of frenzy captured in the image of the white hair.

Hiraizumi had been known for two prominent *utamakura*: Koromo no seki (Robe Barrier) and Koromogawa (Robe River), both of which were associated with robe (*koromo*) and sewing (*tatsu*) imagery and the vicissitudes of love. One of the earliest examples is this anonymous poem in the *Gosenshū* (951; Misc. II, no. 1160) in which Robe Barrier becomes a symbolic guard against an overly aggressive man.[33]

tadachitomo	I wish you would not
tanomazaranamu	count on me so quickly:
mi ni chikaki	something called
Koromo no seki mo	Robe Barrier lies
ari to iu nari	close to my body.

Bashō was obviously aware of the significance of Koromo no seki and Koromogawa, but he deliberately ignored their poetic associations and, drawing on the authority and precedence of the poetry of Tu Fu, one of China's most noted poets, transfigured Hiraizumi into a warrior landscape, which other haikai poets such as Tōrin and Gikū (1663–1733) followed.

> the power of armies
> no longer visible—
>   fireflies in the air
>   —Tōrin

gunsen | no | chikara | mo | miezu | tobu | hotaru
army | 's | power | also | not-visible | flying | firefly
(KHT 7: 246)

> leave behind
> the traces of the heroes!
> planting rice seedlings at dusk
> —Gikū[34]

eiyū | no | ato | uenokose | yūsanae
hero | 's | trace | plant-leave | evening-rice-planting

Expanding the Canon

Major *utamakura* such as Shirakawa Barrier and Matsushima, which appear in the first three imperial waka anthologies—*Kokinshū, Gosenshū, Shūishū*—should be distinguished from minor *utamakura*, which emerged later, particularly after the Heian period, and which had less of a hold on the imagination of subsequent poets.[35] *Classified Collection of Japanese Poetry on Famous Places*, for example, lists 94 different waka on Shinobu but only two poems on Kisagata. A critical contrast occurs between those *utamakura* in Michinoku, in the northeast of Japan, in the first half of *Narrow Road to the Interior*, which tend to be major *utamakura*—Shirakawa Barrier, Matsushima, Sue no matsuyama, Shinobu—and bear the weight of the classical tradition, and those found along the Hokuriku or Japan Sea side, in the second half of the narrative (such as Kisagata), which tend to be lesser *utamakura* or unknown in the classical tradition. In contrast to the *Backpack Notes* journey, which traversed an area densely packed with well-known toponyms and in which, at Yoshino, the ultimate *utamakura*, the narrator's voice is overwhelmed by the voices of the ancients, the area on the Japan Sea side was light in classical topography, enabling Bashō to break away from the grasp of the ancients whom he admired so greatly. Furthermore, many of the sacred places in *Narrow Road to the Interior* on which Bashō composed—Nikkō, Unganji Temple (site of Priest Butchō's hermitage), Sukagawa (home of the holy man Kashin), Chūsonji Temple (at Hiraizumi), Ryūshakuji Temple (Yamadera), Kurobane, Mount Haguro, Gassan, Natadera Temple (near Yamanaka Springs), Zenshōji Temple (at Kaga), Eiheiji Temple (founded by Dōgen), and the Kehi Shrine (in Tsuruga)—were *haimakura*, places that do not appear in classical poetry and yet became established topics in haikai, that is, new carriers of cultural memory.

Perhaps the best example of a *haimakura*, or haikai place, that Bashō explored is Sado Island, which is on the Japan Sea side.

> After we had crossed Nezu no seki, or the Mouse Barrier, we hurried toward the soil of Echigo and came to Ichiburi, in the province of Etchū. During this period of nine days, I suffered from the extreme heat, fell ill, and did not record anything.

> the Seventh Month—
> the sixth day too is different
> from the usual night

Fumizuki | ya | muika | mo | tsune | no | yo | ni | wa | nizu
Seventh-Month | : | sixth | also | norm | 's | night | to | as-for | not-resemble

> a wild sea—
> stretching to Sado Isle
> the Milky Way

araumi | ya | Sado | ni | yokotau | amanogawa
wild-sea | : | Sado | to | lay | River-of-Heaven

One of the difficulties of a new poetic place and the reason they were often avoided by haikai poets was that, like new seasonal words, they usually came with few, if any, poetic associations. By drawing on Sado's historical associations, however, Bashō was able to infuse the landscape (*kei*) with a particular emotion or sentiment (*jō*), to view the landscape through the eyes of the past, as he did at *utamakura* and ancient battlefields. Sado, an island across the water from Izumozaki (Izumo Point), was known for its long history of political exiles: Emperor Juntoku, Nichiren, Mongaku, Zeami, the mother of Zushiō, and others. As a consequence, the island, surrounded here by "wild seas" (*araumi*) and standing under the vast Amanogawa (literally, River of Heaven), or Milky Way, comes to embody the feeling of loneliness, both of the exiles at Sado and of the traveler himself. The poem has a majestic, slow-moving rhythm, especially the drawn-out "o" sounds in the middle line (*Sado ni yoko-tau*), which suggests the vastness and scale of the landscape. Bashō arrived at Izumo Point on the fourth day of the Seventh Month, but when he wrote *Narrow Road to the Interior* many years later, he added this hokku on the sixth day of the Seventh Month, thereby associating the Milky Way with Tanabata (the seventh day of the Seventh Month), when the legendary constellations, the Herdsboy and Weaver Girl, the separated lovers, cross over the Milky Way for their annual meeting. In this larger context, the island surrounded by "wild seas" also embodies the longing of the exiles (and implicitly that of the poet) for their distant loved ones. In the "wild seas" poem, Bashō replaces what grammatically should be an intransitive (*yodan*) verb *yokotawaru* (to lie sideways) with a transitive (*shimo nidan*) verb *yokotau* (to lay sideways), implying that the Creator (*zō-ka*) lays the Milky Way down so that it reaches Sado. The effect, which is characteristic of landscape description in *Oku no hosomichi*, is to personify and animate nature. As Andō Tsuguo argues, the Milky Way, laid down by the *zōka*, becomes like a boat or a bridge reaching out across the dark waters to the waiting exiles at Sado, that is to say, reaching out to the lonely soul of the poet.[36]

In his preface to *Sequel to Empty Chestnuts* (1687), Sodō, one of Bashō's close poetic acquaintances, using an example from Tu Fu, stressed that haikai must achieve the Chinese poetic ideal of "land-scape in human emotion, and human emotion in landscape," a notion that Bashō pursued during his *Narrow Road to the Interior* journey. Significantly, Bashō achieved that new poetic ideal with minor *utamakura* such as Kisagata and with *haimakura* such as Sado. Another example is Iro no hama, Color Beach, an obscure location in Tsuruga Province (Fukui), which the traveler visits toward the end of *Narrow Road to the Interior*.

Deeply moved by the loneliness of the evening

loneliness—
judged superior to Suma
a beach in autumn

sabishisa|ya|Suma|ni|kachitaru|hama|no|aki
loneliness|:|Suma|to|judged-superior|beach|'s|autumn

> between the waves
> mixed with small shells
> petals of bush clover

nami|no|ma|ya|kogai|ni|majiru|hagi|no|chiri
wave|'s|gap|:|small-shell|in|mix|bush-clover|'s|remains

Bashō is initially drawn to the beach at Tsuruga as a result of Saigyō's poem (*Sankashū*, no. 1194) on Iro no hama.

shio somuru	Is it because
masuho no kogai	they gather crimson shells
hirou tote	which dye the ocean tides
Iro no hama to wa	that they call this
iu ni ya aruran	Color Beach?

According to *Fubokushō* (1310?), a private waka anthology, Saigyō composed this poem at a shell contest at the imperial palace. In contrast to Saigyō, who was interested in Iro no hama, Color Beach, primarily for its lexical association with the word "color" (*iro*) and whose poem reflects Heian, aristocratic sensibility, Bashō saw the place as a toponym for quiet autumnal loneliness (*sabishisa*), a medieval aesthetic that Bashō assimilated into haikai. Suma, an *utamakura* closely associated with the poetry of Ariwara Yukihira (d. 893), who was exiled there, and with the banishment of the eponymous hero of *The Tale of Genji*, was considered to be the embodiment of loneliness in the classical tradition. As Ogata Tsutomu has pointed out, the phrase "the loneliness of evening" (*yūgure no sabishisa*) in the headnote also echoes the famous "three autumn evening poems" (*sanseki*, nos. 361–63) in the *Shinkokinshū*, which include Priest Jakuren's "Loneliness is not any particular color—a mountain of black pines on an autumn evening" (*Sabishisa wa sono iro to shimo nakarikeri maki tatsu yama no aki no yūgure*).[37] In contrast to the "front" of Japan, which appears bright, warm, and joyous in *Oku no hosomichi*, the "back" of Japan, extending from Kisagata in the north to Iro no hama to the south, is imbued with a monochromatic, mist-filled, white-ish, moonlit, lonely atmosphere. In a haikai twist, the quiet loneliness of Iro no hama, an obscure beach on the back side of Japan, is "judged superior" (*kachitaru*)—a phrase reminiscent of the judgments in traditional poetry contests—to that of Suma as well as to the famed loneliness of the *Shinkokinshū*. Instead of reaffirming the classical culture of the capital (*miyako*), the provinces have become a wellspring of poetic sensibility, a new carrier of cultural memory, that could match, if not supersede, that of the classical and medieval past, just as *Narrow Road to the Interior* itself as a haibun could equal, if not surpass, the best of the traditional travel diaries.

Time Going

Narrow Road to the Interior works against the traditional poetic essence of travel: to long for the capital. As Jōha's *Renga Treasures* notes, "When it comes to the poetic essence [*hon'i*] of travel, one's heart is that of a person of the capital even if one is in the country composing classical linked verse."[38] As exemplified by Ariwara Narihira's wandering in the Eastern Provinces in *The Tales of Ise*, the locus classicus for travel, the journey in classical poetry was an abnormal, transient, alien state, as opposed to life in the capital, which represented stability, comfort, and a permanent home. In a haikai twist, *Narrow Road to the Interior* makes the road home and establishes a new view for travel: one that has no center and no return.

> The months and days are travelers of a hundred ages;
> the years that come and go are voyagers too.
> For those who float away their lives on boats,
> for those who grow old leading a horse by the bit,
> each day is a journey and travel is their home.
> Many too are the ancients who perished on the road.
>
> (NKBZ 41:341)

As the opening lines suggest, to travel is to be at one with the ever-changing aspects of nature, as well as with the "ancients," who also died on the road. The first hokku suggests that dwellings, normally associated with a sense of home, are only temporary lodgings in life's journey.

> time even for the grass hut
> to change owners—
> house of dolls

kusa | no | to | mo | sumi | kawaru | yo | zo | hina | no | ie[39]
grass | 's | door | also | dwell | change | time | ! | doll | 's | house

Hina (dolls), a new seasonal word for late spring, referred to *Hinamatsuri*, the Girl's Festival on the third of the Third Month, when families with daughters displayed dolls in their houses. The time has come for even the hut of the recluse—symbolized by the "grass door"—to become a domestic, secular dwelling, a "house of dolls," occupied by a new owner with a wife and daughter(s).[40] At Miyagi Field (near Sendai), the traveler composes a poem on *Tango no sekku* (Boy's Festival, or Iris Festival), which echoes the hokku on the Girl's Festival. When Kae'mon, the eccentric painter and the traveler's host, gives the parting visitor a pair of straw sandals (*waraji*) with dark blue thongs (*o*), which echo the color of the iris (*ayame* or *ayamegusa*), the traveler responds with:

> I shall tie
> irises to my feet—
> sandal thongs

ayamegusa | ashi | ni | musuban | waraji | no | o
iris | feet | to | will-tie | sandal | 's | thong

During the Iris Festival, *ayame*, a seasonal word for summer, were placed on the eaves of each house to ward off illness and evil. In a *fukyō*-esque twist, the poet ties the irises to his feet, as a prayer for safety on the road. The journey, in short, becomes his dwelling (*tabi o sumika to su*).

The seasons also become travelers in *Narrow Road to the Interior*. *Yuku*, a key word in *Narrow Road to the Interior*, means both "to go" and "to pass time," thereby fusing temporal and spatial passage. The first travel poem in *Narrow Road to the Interior* is:

> spring going—
> birds crying and tears
> in the eyes of the fish

yuku | haru | ya | tori | naki | uo | no | me | wa | namida
go | spring | : | bird | crying | fish | 's | eye | as-for | tear[41]

Uo (fish) and *tori* (birds), which "cry out" (*naku*) and/or "weep" (*naku*), mourn the passing of spring and by implication the departure of the traveler. Some commentators see the fish as the disciples left behind and the birds as the departing travelers (Bashō and Sora); others interpret the departing spring as the traveler. In contrast to such conventional phrases as *haru no kure* (end of spring), which statically mark the end of spring, *yuku haru* (passing spring) personifies time, which "goes" (*yuku*), which must move on, thereby becoming a metaphor for life and for the journey. *Narrow Road to the Interior* ends with a similar poem.

> autumn going—
> parting for Futami
> a clam pried from its shell

hamaguri | no | Futami | ni | wakare | yuku | aki | zo
clam | 's | shell-body | into | parting | passing | autumn | !

Bashō's hokku turns on a series of homophones: *wakaru* means both "to depart for" and "to tear from," and Futami refers to a noted place on the coast of Ise Province (the traveler's next destination and a place known for clams) as well as the shell (*futa*) and body (*mi*) of the clam (*hamaguri*). The passing of the season becomes an implicit metaphor not only for the sorrow of parting, which lies at the heart of travel, but also for the ceaseless passage of time, the traveler's constant companion.

The sense of time passing and time past, of the journey in time and across time, is perhaps nowhere more dramatically expressed than in the passages on Hiraizumi and the Hall of Light (Hikaridō) at the Chūsonji Temple, near Hiraizumi.

> The two halls of which we had heard such wondrous things were open. The Sutra Hall held the statues of the three chieftains; the Hall of Light contained the coffins of three generations, preserving three sacred images. The seven precious substances were scattered and lost; the doors of jewels torn by the wind, the pillars of gold rotted in the snow. The hall should have turned into a mound of empty, abandoned grass, but the four sides were enclosed, covering the roof with shingles, surviving the snow and rain. For a while, it became a memorial to a thousand years.

> have the summer rains
> come and gone, sparing
> the Hall of Light?

samidare | no | furi | nokoshite | ya | hikaridō
summer-rain | 's | falling | sparing | ? | Hall-of-light

Commentators are divided on whether the *samidare*, the long summer rains, are falling now, before the speaker's eyes, or whether *samidare* refers to past summer rains, which have spared the Hikaridō over the centuries. The latter interpretation is borne out by the earlier version.

> summer rains—
> falling year after year
> five hundred times

samidare | ya | toshidoshi | furu | mo | gohyaku | tabi
summer-rain | : | year-after-year | fall | also | five-hundred | times

The power of the final version, like much of *Narrow Road*, lies in the coexistence of landscapes: the *samidare* falling immediately before the poet's eyes *and* the years and centuries of *samidare*, or monsoon seasons, which cause buildings and other human artifacts to decay but which the Hikaridō has miraculously endured. The two visions are linked by the verb *furu*, which means both for the rain "to fall" and for time "to pass." In contrast to the earlier version, which highlights this pun, the revised version discretely submerges the homonym, thus emphasizing both the corrosive effects of time and the divine brightness of the Hikaridō, the Buddhist Hall of Light, which implicitly glows amid the somber, dark rains of summer.

Returning to Communal Poetry

Just as Bashō alternated "person" verses with "place" verses in his linked verse sequences, he interwove sections on places—*utamakura*, historical sites, and sacred places—with those on people, especially obscure but interesting individuals, such as Hotoke Gozaemon near Nikkō or Kasane at Nasu Field. The most famous passages in *Narrow Road to the Interior*, like those in medieval travel diaries, tend to be on *utamakura* or noted historical sites, but *Narrow Road to the Interior* dwells as much on unknown commoners, who possess haikai-esque, often humorous, characteristics. This is particularly true in the second half of the text, where the poet encounters a variety of people from different walks of provincial life: the prostitutes at Echigo (Niigata), the child owner at Yamanaka hot springs, the priest at Zenshō Temple, local poets such as Tōsai at Fukui. These mini-portraits, which provide a change of pace or comic relief from the high-toned passages on *utamakura* and sacred places, function like the *ji* (background, plain) verses, which alternate with the *mon* (foreground, prominent) verses in classical linked verse. As Bashō noted on the passage on travel in *Backpack Notes*,

> If one meets someone who has even the slightest understanding of poetry, one's joy is endless. Even a person whom one usually despises and avoids as old-fashioned and hardheaded becomes a source of pleasure and conversation on a distant journey. When one discovers a person who understands poetry in a hut overrun with weeds, it is like finding a jewel amid a pile of rocks, gold amid the mud, and one feels the need to write down and relate that experience. This is one of the pleasures of the road. (NKBZ 41: 324–25)

If, in the first half of *Narrow Road*, the traveler engages in a dialogue with the spirits of the ancients, in the second half, he returns to the poetic community, to contemporary poetic dialogue.

In the actual journey that Bashō took in the spring of 1689, he had extremely limited success in finding new disciples in Michinoku. After journeying north from Edo, Bashō stayed at Nasu (Tochigi) with the samurai Kanokobata, referred to as Tōsui in *Narrow Road to the Interior*, and then visited Tōkyū, an established poet and an old friend, at Sukagawa, near the Shirakawa Barrier. Bashō moved on to Sendai in the Fifth Month, hoping to meet Michikaze (1639–1707), a prominent haikai master who had developed a considerable following in the area, but Michikaze was absent, leaving only Kae'mon (d. 1746), one of Michikaze's disciples, who appears in *Narrow Road to the Interior* as the eccentric painter. Bashō had no more connections until he traveled west across the mountains to Obanazawa (Yamagata), where he stayed for ten days with Seifū (1651–1721), a safflower (*benihana*) merchant, who helped him navigate the Mogami River and introduced him to haikai groups further west. Seifū, an established haikai master well known in the three major cities, had met Bashō during his visits to Edo.[42] Bashō, in short, made no significant new contacts in the northeast, the original destination of the journey, and his style and school did not take root in this area.

By contrast, Dewa and the area facing the Japan Sea, particularly the Shōnai region (northwest Yamagata, centered on Tsurugaoka and Sakata) and the Hokuriku area—Echigo (Niigata), Etchū (Toyama), Kaga (Ishikawa), and Echizen (Fukui)—proved to be a haikai goldmine. Although Bashō had almost no connections in the Shōnai region, he encountered a number of young and talented poets: Rogan, Kōu, Jūkō, Fugyoku,[43] and others. Rogan (d. 1693), a dyer from Haguro who appears in *Narrow Road to the Interior* under the name of Zushisakichi, guided Bashō over the Three Dewa Mountains and introduced him to Jūkō, a samurai who appears in the Sakata passage in *Narrow Road to the Interior*, and to his retainer Kōu (1649–1719), a samurai from Tsurugaoka.[44] The Shōnai poets, who had hitherto been under the influence of Sanzenfū (Michikaze) and Seifū, subsequently became major players in the Bashō school.

Kaga Province (Ishikawa), much further south on the Japan Sea side, where Bashō spent about three weeks and which is represented by four episodes in *Narrow Road to the Interior*—on Kanazawa, Tada Shrine at Komatsu, Nata Temple, and Yamanaka Springs—proved equally fertile ground for Bashō's haikai. Bashō had looked forward to meeting Isshō (1653–88), perhaps the most prominent member of the Kaga group.[45] But when he arrived at Kanazawa, the main city in Kaga, in the Seventh Month (August), he found that Isshō had died the previous year.[46] Other talented young poets, however, flocked to Bashō such as Hokushi,[47] a sword maker in Kanazawa, who replaced Sora and accompanied Bashō as far as the Tenryūji Temple in Echizen (Fukui); Kasho (d. 1731), described in *Narrow Road to the Interior* as "a merchant commuting from Osaka"; and Otokuni, who edited *Backpack Notes* and facilitated Bashō's connections to the Ōmi (Shiga) region, where he was to reside after the journey, in 1690–91. The initial focus of the journey had been Michinoku, but it was not until Bashō had climbed west over the mountains into Dewa and faced the Japan Sea side that he reaped the most lasting fruits of his journey: a poetic dialogue that led to a new flowering of poetry, climaxing in *Monkey's Straw Coat* (1691), the most influential of Bashō's haikai anthologies.

Significantly, the text of *Narrow Road to the Interior* ends at Ōgaki, in Mino (Gifu), where his disciples in the area—Rotsū (1649–1738), Sora, Jokō (d. 1708?), Keikō (d. 1712), and others[48]—gathered to meet Bashō. After the journey Bashō remained in neighboring Ōmi, directly to the west of Mino, and for the next two and a half years, from the fall of 1689 to the autumn of 1691, he nurtured the precious seeds that he had gathered on his journey. Ōgaki—which was where *Skeleton in the Fields*, the travel account of Bashō's journey from Edo to Kamigata in 1684, came to a climax and which was closely associated with the origins of the Bashō style—now came to represent a new beginning, which would lead to *Monkey's Straw Coat*. Ōmi Province, with Lake Biwa at its center, formed a geographic nexus between northern and central Japan and became the hub of the Bashō circle, with the new Ōmi group (led by Otokuni) at the center, the Shōnai and Kaga groups to the north, the Kyoto group (with Kyorai and Bonchō) to the south, and the Sanpū group to the east in Edo.[49]

As Ogata Tsutomu has pointed out, Bashō's travel accounts, like the Bashō-school haikai anthologies, had a commemorative function, to present and commemorate the latest achievements of the Bashō circle. *Skeleton in the Fields*, which begins in a difficult, Chinese style and ends in a relaxed Japanese style, celebrates Bashō's encounter with the Owari/Nagoya group and the establishment of the Bashō style, especially the transition from the turgid Chinese-style of the early 1680s to the gentle, renga style of the mid- to late 1680s. In a similar fashion, *Narrow Road to the Interior* commemorates the emergence of a new configuration of disciples centered on Shōnai, Kaga, Ōmi (the second generation), and the Sampū group in Edo, as well as the beginning of the poetics of the unchanging and the ever-changing (*fueki ryūkō*), examined in the next chapter.

Narrow Road to the Interior, in short, embodied the inherent tension between Bashō's pursuit of the past, especially the exploration of the traces of earlier spiritual and poetic figures such as Saigyō and Nōin, *and* his pursuit of the haikai spirit, with its oppositional, inversionary movement, its roots in popular, hybrid cultures, its humor, and its discovery of new vistas and new poetic partners. According to Kyoriku's *Rhapsody on Travel* (*Tabi no fu*), Bashō once said, "One cannot have confidence in the haikai [*fūga*] of those who have not traveled on some part of the Tōkaidō, the Eastern Highway,"[50] the busy thoroughfare that connected Kyoto and Edo. Travel, in other words, opened up the variegated cultural, linguistic, and social horizons that were the mark and life of haikai. In the opening of the same essay, Kyoriku wrote: "Travel is the flower of haikai. Haikai is the spirit of the traveler. Everything that Saigyō and Sōgi have overlooked is haikai."[51] Travel was also a means, to use Bashō's own words, "of awakening to the high, returning to the low," of reaching the spiritual and poetic heights of the "ancients," while returning to and facing the everyday realities of commoner, contemporary life. It was only through this multiple process, of exploring the past, engaging in a spiritual journey, visiting poetic places, *and* of seeking out the roots of haikai, in the unbounded world of everyday, contemporary life that the poet was ultimately able to envision the new in the old, to recuperate, revive, and refigure the cultural memory as embodied in the landscape.

CHAPTER 9

Awakening to the High, Returning to the Low: Bashō's Poetics

"The changes of heaven and earth are the seeds of poetry."
—*Sanzōshi*

The popular, commoner genres of the sixteenth and seventeenth centuries such as haikai and *kana-zōshi* frequently parodied their traditional counterparts by borrowing the elegant, aristocratic forms and narratives of classical literature and giving them popular, vulgar, or erotic content. The *Preface to Young Men of Old and New* (*Kokin wakashū no jo*; 1589, published in late seventeenth c.), for example, depicted the world of pederasty, while echoing, almost word for word, the famous kana preface to the *Kokinshū*. Sometimes, the reverse phenomenon occurred: what initially appeared to be vulgar or low turned out to be refined and elegant, a process referred to as *yatsushi* (literally, the "dressing down" of a person of high station), a phenomenon that extended beyond literature to the clothing and lifestyle of the townspeople (e.g., the wearing of a colorful silk lining under a plain cotton kimono), who were officially restricted in what they could wear. Ishikawa Jun, a modern novelist and Edo scholar, regarded the popular folk tale of Otake, the lowly maid who turns out to be a contemporary incarnation of Dainichi nyorai (Skt. Mahāvairocana), the Buddha of great light, as an archetypal example of such haikai imagination. Ishikawa found the historical precedent for Otake in the Noh play *Eguchi* in which a prostitute from Eguchi turns out to be the Fugen Bodhisattva (Skt. Samantabhadra). Not only does the profane turn out to be sacred, but a Buddhist deity that had lost some of its power in the Tokugawa period takes on new life and meaning through a lowly, commoner form.

Awakening to the High, Returning to the Low

If sixteenth-century haikai comically inverted the social and religious hierarchy, lowering gods, Buddhas, and other figures of authority and power to vulgar or lesser beings, Bashō tended to work in the opposite direction: to find the subtle, the refined, the spiritual, in everyday, commoner life in a regenerative process not unlike that of the Otake narrative. This transformative movement was reflected in the notion of *sabi/shiori*, which endowed vernacular language and scenes with medieval, aesthetic overtones, and in the larger poetic ideal of *kōgo kizoku* (awakening to the high, returning to the low), which he developed toward the end of his career. According to *Sanzōshi*:

> The Master taught, "You should awaken to the high and return to the low." "You should constantly seek out the truth of poetry and with that high spirit return to the haikai that you are practicing now." (NKBZ 51: 546)

"Awakening to the high" (*kōgo*) implied spiritual cultivation, a deepened awareness of nature and the movement of the cosmos, and a pursuit of the "ancients," the noted poets of the past. "The return to the low" (*kizoku*), by contrast, implied a return to the variegated languages and everyday, material world of seventeenth-century commoners and samurai, to those topics omitted or overlooked by the traditional genres, a dimension that Bashō stressed in his later years, especially in the form of *karumi* (lightness).

Unlike classical poetry, which sought continuity in and preservation of a highly encoded and limited body of texts, haikai deliberately crossed boundaries, parodying authority and convention and seeking out new frontiers. At the same time, haikai needed, at least in Bashō's view, to forge bonds with the traditional arts, to draw

Painting, poem, and calligraphy by Bashō. 12.5 x 22.3 in. The painting, of which three similar versions exist and which are all in Bashō's late calligraphic style, attempts to capture the visual attraction of the chrysanthemums even after they have endured an autumn storm, thus echoing the hokku—*midokoro mo/are ya no/waki no nochi no kiku* (something to behold!—chrysanthemums after an autumn storm). Probably painted around 1691. Signed "Baseo." (Courtesy Kakimori Collection)

authority and inspiration from the earlier poets of Japan and China, to find a larger philosophical or spiritual base. Many of the poetic ideals, or rather, slogans, of the Bashō school—*kōgo kizoku* (awakening to the high, returning to the low), *fūga no makoto* (truth of poetic art), *zōka zuijun* (following the Creative), *butsuga ichinyo* (object and self as one), and *fueki ryūkō* (the unchanging and the changing)—reflect attempts by Bashō and his disciples to bring these two seemingly contradictory trajectories together, to create poetry that was simultaneously orthodox and unorthodox, that was sanctioned even as it was transgressive.

Bashō wrote very little on haikai, but his disciples, especially Dohō, Kyorai, and Kyoriku, who recorded their teacher's words in considerable detail, debated the interpretation of these key terms. As the following passage in *Uda Priest* suggests, Bashō's remarks came almost entirely in response to questions from his disciples.

> The Master would never volunteer to speak on matters that he was not questioned about. If a particular problem was not apparent to someone, that person did not know enough to inquire. And if that person did not inquire, the Master did not offer instruction. Undoubtedly there was much left that no one knew enough to ask about.[1]

In his teachings, Bashō was concerned primarily with practice, with the composition of haikai, rather than with any theory or systematic approach to poetry or its interpretation. He focused on the problems of the individual student, using poetic ideals and conceptions as pedagogical, corrective devices. Inevitably they had a different meaning and function for each disciple. As a consequence, there was a limited consensus among his students about what these key poetic terms meant. Nevertheless, Bashō remains one of the most important figures in the history of Japanese aesthetics and literary theory. Of the various terms—*sabi, wabi, fueki ryūkō, karumi, ada, ga/zoku*—commonly found in Japanese aesthetics and literary theory, almost all are related, some almost exclusively, to Bashō's poetics. More significantly, the debates surrounding these critical terms provide an important context for understanding the nature of Bashō's haikai and its relationship to contemporary discourse.

The Truth of Poetic Art

The notion of the "truth of poetic art" provided the foundation for the idea that haikai could become part of the larger poetic tradition even as it diverged from or remapped that tradition. Bashō used *fūga* to refer to cultural practice of the highest order: in a broad sense it included tea ceremony and painting, and in a narrow sense it meant haikai as poetic art. (Bashō's first reference to the "truth of poetic art" appears in a letter to Kyokusui in the Second Month of Genroku 5 [1692].) According to *Sanzōshi*, "Chinese poetry, waka, renga, and haikai are all *fūga*" (NKBZ 51: 524). In the seventeenth century, a sharp distinction existed between the traditional, elite (*ga*) genres such as waka (classical Japanese poetry) and *kanshi* (Chinese poetry), and the new popular (*zoku*) arts such as haikai, *jōruri*, and kabuki. To call haikai *fūga*, or poetic art, as Bashō began to do in the early Genroku period, was thus a deliberate contradiction in terms.

Bashō used the term *makoto* (Ch. *ch'eng*)—which had a range of meanings that included sincerity, absence of fault, and seriousness—to refer to a truth, or higher dimension, that could be realized in or through *fūga*, through haikai as poetic art, and that he believed was lacking in earlier haikai.[2] In *Sanzōshi*, Dohō explained.

> Since the emergence of haikai, generations of poets have amused themselves with witty expressions, and as a consequence, our predecessors never understood *makoto*, poetic truth. In the more recent past, Nishiyama Sōin of Naniwa gave haikai freedom of expression, and this approach has gained a wide following, but the result has been average in quality at best, and even today haikai is known mainly for its clever use of words.[3]
>
> Over thirty years have passed since the late Master Bashō entered the way of poetry: haikai first attained *makoto*, or poetic truth, at that point. The Master's haikai bore the same name as in the past, but it was the haikai of *makoto*, of poetic truth. How could haikai have passed on, uselessly, for so many generations without poetic truth?
>
> The Master also noted, "In the way of haikai there are no ancients." He repeated, "When one looks back at the poetry of the ancients, it is easy to follow what they did. In the future, someone will no doubt

emerge and examine what I am doing now in a similar fashion. I have only fear for those who are to come."

Since ancient times, there have been many masters of Chinese and Japanese poetry. They have all emerged out of *makoto*, poetic truth, and have followed the path of *makoto*. Our Master gave *makoto* to poetry that never possessed *makoto*, thus becoming a guide for endless generations to come. (NKBZ 51: 521–22).

According to Dohō, "the ancients," the recognized masters of Japanese and Chinese poetry, had attained *makoto*, poetic truth or the truth of poetic art, but Bashō was the first to do so with haikai, implicitly making it part of the larger poetic tradition and giving it a stature that it had never possessed. The statement also suggests that haikai poets should study the ancients who had realized *makoto*. "Those who devote themselves to *makoto* seek out the spirit of the ancients in poetry" (*Sanzōshi*, NKBZ 51: 547).[4] At the same time, however, Bashō also noted that "the way of haikai has no ancients" ("kono michi ni kojin nashi"). Haikai cannot look to the past for its poetic models. This paradox, which lies at the heart of Bashō's poetics, was embodied in the poetics of "awakening to the high, returning to the low" and of "the unchanging and the ever-changing," two polarities that, as we shall see, became one in the pursuit of *fūga no makoto*, the truth of poetic art.

Following the Creative

The notion of pursuing the "truth of poetic art" was closely related to *zōka zuijun*, "following the Creative," an ideal found in Chinese painting theory. *Zōka* (Ch. *tsao hua*), the Creator or the Creative, sometimes misleadingly translated as "Nature," was not a transcendent, anthropomorphic deity (as usually suggested by the term "creator") but a creative spirit or force that constantly shaped and transformed landscape and nature. In the Taoist context of *Chuang-tzu*, a text that Bashō was deeply influenced by, *tsao hua* implied *tsao wu che* (J. *zōbutsusha*, literally, "that which makes things"), the creative force that gave birth to and governs the movement of all things in the universe, and in the Neo-Confucian context it implied *t'ai-chi* (J. *taikyoku*), the Great Ultimate, which maintained order in the universe amidst constant change. At the beginning of *Backpack Notes*, which commemorated Bashō's journey of 1687–88 (Jōkyō 4–5) but which was probably not written until around 1690 (*Genroku* 3),[5] Bashō wrote with regard to *zōka*, the Creative.

> The fundamental spirit that stands at the root of Saigyō's poetry, Sōgi's linked verse, Sesshū's paintings, and Rikyū's practice of tea is one and the same. Those who practice such arts follow the Creative and make the four seasons their friends. What one sees cannot but be cherry blossoms; what one thinks cannot but be the moon. When the shape is not the cherry blossoms, one is no more than a barbarian; when the heart is not the cherry blossoms, one is no different from an animal. Leave the barbarians, depart from the animals, follow the Creative, return to the Creative! (NKBZ 41: 311)

Here the way of art (*fūga*), the way of the inner spirit (*kokoro*), and the way of the cosmos (*zōka*) become inseparable. Saigyō, Sōgi, Sesshū (1420–1506), and Rikyū (1522–91), the great medieval masters of waka, classical renga, painting, and tea ceremony respectively, of *fūga* or art in the broad sense, are united by a common spirit, that of following the Creative. According to Chou Tun-i's (1017–73) *Explanation of the Diagram of the Great Ultimate* (*T'ai-chi-t'u shuo*), a fundamental Neo-Confucian text published with commentary in Japan in 1678, the Great Ultimate (*t'ai-chi*, J. *taikyoku*), which reins over all things in the universe, consists of material or vital force (*ch'i*, J. *ki*), the physical dimension of the Great Ultimate, which gives life to and creates all things, and of principle (*li*, J. *ri*), the metaphysical dimension of the Great Ultimate, which governs and regulates the movement of the vital force, causing constant motion or change. All things and all human beings are equally endowed with principle, the essence of which is *ch'eng* (J. *makoto*), which the sage is able to realize within himself. In this context, the pursuit of the truth of poetic art is not simply to be sincere—as Onitsura (1661–1738), one of Bashō's haikai contemporaries, used the term—but to follow the fundamental movement of nature and the universe and to realize the creative force of the universe within oneself. If, as *Backpack Notes* observes, the artist follows the Creative and "makes a friend of the four seasons," a movement governed by *zōka*, the artist will respond to the movement and rhythm of nature, especially of the seasons, which provide constant inspiration for poetry and art.

According to *Backpack Notes*, when the poet follows *zōka*, "what he or she sees" (*miru tokoro*), which represents the human senses, and "what one thinks" (*omou koto*), which represents human feeling and thoughts, become the "moon" (*tsuki*) and "cherry blossoms" (*hana*), which represent the beauties of nature. "Seeing" is as much an internal matter, of realizing the *zōka* within, as it is an external matter. The "cherry blossoms" do not exist by themselves in nature, nor do they exist solely as a figment of the poet's imagination. Instead, they come into being only when they are "seen" by and fuse with the *zōka* within the poet. The poet who follows or "returns to the Creative" implicitly engages in a process of spiritual cultivation that allows the *zōka* within to join the *zōka* of the cosmos. Bashō here drew on Taoism, especially the chapter in the *Chuang-tzu* entitled "All Things are Equal" (J. "Seibutsuron"), and on the seventeenth-century Neo-Confucian philosophy put forward by such scholar-officials as Hayashi Razan, who argued that the "way of heaven" (*tendō*) and the "way of humans" (*jindō*) were ethically one, that to leave *zōka* was to reduce oneself to the non-human.

Spiritual cultivation is also implied in Bashō's notion of *butsuga-ichinyo* (object and self as one), as explained in Dohō's *Sanzōshi*.

> When the Master said, "As for the pine, learn from the pine; as for the bamboo, learn from the bamboo," he meant cast aside personal desire or intention. Those who interpret this "learning" in their own way end up never learning.
>
> The phrase "learn" means to enter into the object, to be emotionally moved by the essence that emerges from that object, and for that movement to become verse. Even if one clearly expresses the object, if the emotion does not emerge from the object naturally, the object and the self will be divided, and that emotion will not achieve poetic truth [*makoto*]. The effect will be the verbal artifice that results from personal desire. (NKBZ 51: 547–48)[6]

The phrase "learn from the pine" means that the poet must cast away personal, self-oriented desire and enter into the object and draw out its subtle essence, or *mono no bi* (literally, the "faintness or depth of the thing").[7] This "self" (*ga*) in *butsuga ichinyo* is not the modern notion of the "self" but a selfless state free of personal desire (*shii*). Only such a selfless "self"—one that "follows the Creative"— can enter into the object. If the poet's feelings are not sincere, the heart of the subject and that of the object will not be united, and the result will be "verbal artifice" (*sakui*).

The notion of "entering into the object" appears in earlier medieval treatises on waka and renga—Kyōgoku Tamekane's (1254–1332) poetics is perhaps the most salient example—but Bashō and his haikai contemporaries faced a world different from that of their classical or medieval counterparts. In contrast to the natural imagery found in classical poetry, which was refined, nuanced, rich in associations, the nature that Bashō confronted, especially at the bottom half of the seasonal pyramid, was more uncultivated, variegated in character, and often vulgar and mundane. Without realizing the Creative within, what the poet "sees" in such a world cannot become the "moon" and "cherry blossoms"; the new material culture and its heterogeneous languages and voices cannot be transformed into poetry. Instead, they remain vulgar, like an "animal." Without spiritual cultivation and the ability to enter into objects, the haikai poet will not have the power to discover the high in the low, to find beauty in the mundane. In contrast to the world of classical poetry, which was heavily encoded with emotional and conceptual associations, the haikai poet faced a world of unrefined language or objects that tended to be divorced from human emotions. The poet's task, at least for one pursuing "the truth of poetic art," was to internalize these external objects, to transform *haigon* into language with subtle overtones and sentiments—a task that implicitly required "awakening to the high, returning to the low."

"Object and self as one" and "following the Creative" implied an approach that did not depict the external world or express an internal state so much as explore the relationship between the two. In *kibutsu chinshi* (literally, "expressing one's thoughts through things"), a poetic technique that can be traced to the *Man'yōshū* and to Chinese poetry, the poet expresses his or her thoughts metaphorically, through "external things" (*butsu* or *mono*), especially natural images. Bashō, particularly from the late 1680s and early 1690s, pushed this technique to the point where the external became internal and the internal external.

> a wild sea—
> stretching out to Sado Isle
>   the Milky Way
>
> araumi | ya | Sado | ni | yokotau | amanogawa
> rough-sea | : | Sado | to | lay | River-of-Heaven

In this example, "rough seas" (*araumi*, a *haigon*) or the "River of Heaven / Milky Way" (amanogawa) do not represent abstract conceptualizations. Instead, the dark seas and the Milky Way function as the immediate scene or landscape and as a projection of the poet's emotive state. The objects of nature, which exist only insofar as they are implicitly seen by the poet, become indistinguishable from the poet's inner state. Only the poet who "follows the Creative" can make this kind of connection between the *zōka* within and the *zōka* without.

The Unchanging and the Ever-changing

The notions of the "truth of poetic art," "following the Creative," and "awakening to the high, returning to the low" were ultimately related to that of *fueki ryūkō* (the unchanging and the ever-changing), a notion that Bashō developed during his *Narrow Road to the Interior* journey in 1689.[8] As with many of his other poetic concepts, Bashō never directly wrote about *fueki ryūkō*. Instead, his disciples, especially Dohō, Kyorai, and Kyoriku, extensively debated the notion after his death, leaving conflicting interpretations. As the following passage in *Sanzōshi* reveals, Dohō, Bashō's disciple from

Iga, saw *fueki* (the unchanging) and *ryūkō* (the ever-changing) as two sides of the same poetic principle.

> Bashō's poetry has both the eternal unchanging and the momentary ever-changing. These two aspects become one at the base, which is the truth of poetic art. If one does not understand the unchanging, one cannot truly understand Bashō's haikai. The unchanging does not depend on the new or the old and is unrelated to change or trends; it is firmly anchored in the truth of poetic art.
>
> When one observes the poetry of successive generations of classical poets, one can see that poetry changes with each generation. And yet there are many poems that transcend the old and the new, that appear no differently now from when they appeared in the past, and that are deeply moving. One should consider these poems the unchanging.
>
> It is the law of nature that all things undergo infinite change. If one does not seek change, haikai cannot be renewed. When one does not seek change, one becomes content with the current fashion and one does not pursue the truth [*makoto*] of haikai. If one does not seek the truth or guide the spirit in that pursuit, one cannot know change based on truth. These people are only imitating others. Those who pursue truth, by contrast, will move one step ahead, not being content to tread on the same ground. No matter how much haikai may change in the future, if it is change based on truth, it will be the kind of haikai advocated by Bashō.
>
> Bashō said, "One should never, even for a moment, lick the dregs of the ancients. Like the endless changes of the seasons, all things must change. The same is true of haikai."
>
> As the Master lay dying, his disciples asked him about the future of haikai. The Master answered, "Since I have entered upon this path, haikai has changed a hundred-fold. And yet of the three stages of calligraphy—the "stopping" [*shin*], the "walking" [*gyō*], and the "running" [*sō*]—haikai has yet to move beyond the first and the second stages. While he was alive, the Master would occasionally say in jest, "My haikai has yet to untie the opening of the straw bag." (NKBZ 51: 545–46)[9]

Haikai, Dohō implied, embodies the same dynamics of the universe as conceived by Neo-Confucian and Taoist philosophers: the "ever-changing" suggests the material force, the physical part of the Great Ultimate, and the "unchanging" suggests the principle, the metaphysical element of the Great Ultimate that sustains the constant motion of the material force. In "Praise to Portraits of Three Saints" ("Sanseizu no san"; 1692–93) Bashō wrote: "The ever-changing nature of poetic art [*fūga*] changes together with heaven and earth. One respects the fact that the changes are never exhausted" (NKBZ 41: 539). As Bashō observed in *Sanzōshi*, "The changes of heaven and earth are the seeds of poetry" (NKBZ 55: 551).[10] In a philosophy that echoes the *Book of Changes* (*I-ching*), the permanence of haikai is found in its constant change (*ryūkō*). The "ever-changing" becomes the "unchanging" essence of haikai.

The idea of change in poetry is not particularly unique in Japanese poetics and appears as early as Fujiwara Shunzei's *Collection of Old and New Poetic Styles* (*Korai fūtei shō*; 1197), an influential waka treatise. Bashō, however, singled this notion out as the most salient characteristic of haikai. In the postscript to "Poetry Contest at Tokiwaya" ("Tokiwaya no kuawase"; 1680), in one of his few direct statements on the unchanging and the ever-changing, Bashō wrote:

> It is said with regard to Chinese poetry that from the time of Han to that of Wei, for over four hundred years, there have been many talented poets, and the style of poetry has changed three-fold. The way of Japanese poetry has also changed from generation to generation. Haikai changes from year to year; each month it becomes something new. (NKBZ 41: 406)

Bashō's own poetic career was marked by constant change, as he moved rapidly through the Teimon style, the Danrin style, the Chinese style, the renga style, and the Genroku landscape style. In Bashō's opinion, changes in haikai had just begun. At the same time, he held that "unchanging" poems move us as deeply now as they did the audiences of the past. This "unchanging" dimension, however, was not a fixed or permanent state but rather the result of constant change, of the ever-changing, which haikai, with its freedom and open expanse of language and topics, both encouraged and depended on. Dohō warned the reader to distinguish between superficial *ryūkō* (the ever-changing), which simply followed current trends and did not lead to the unchanging, and true *ryūkō*, which emerged from the pursuit of the truth of poetic art and resulted in poetry that moves us as deeply now as it did audiences in the distant past.[11]

The complex relationship between the unchanging and the ever-changing is reflected in the debate among Bashō's disciples about the place of the "ancients" (*kojin*), the noted poets of the past. According to *Sanzōshi* (NKBZ 51: 521), Bashō stated that "the way of haikai has no ancients," but in "Kyorai's Treatise for Fugyoku" ("Fugyoku ate Kyorai ronsho," 1694), Kyorai noted:

> When Bashō said there were no ancients, he did not mean that nothing had been accomplished in the past. He meant, rather, that in haikai it is difficult to compose in the style of the ancients. The style of haikai changes with each new day; everyday it moves in a new direction. As a consequence, it is as if there were no great ancients.[12]

This paradox of seeking out and ignoring the ancients is embodied in "On Sending Off Kyoriku" ("Kyoriku o okuru kotoba"), an essay written in the Fifth Month of 1693 (Genroku 6) in which Bashō drew on a famous statement by Kūkai (d. 835), the founder of Shingon Buddhism: "Do not seek the traces of the ancients, seek what they sought" ("Kojin no ato o motomezu, kojin no motome-taru tokoro o motomeyo"; NKBZ 41: 542). One should seek inspiration from the ancients, particularly with regard to the "truth of poetic art" and the spiritual ideals of "object and self as one" and of "following the Creative," but one should not imitate their style, form, or techniques, the "traces" of their art. As the famous opening, quoted above, to *Backpack Notes* implies, the haikai poet should share in the spirit of the medieval masters—Saigyō, Sōgi, Sesshū, and Rikyū—but cannot imitate their forms.

Bashō began speaking of the unchanging and ever-changing to his disciples during his journey to the Interior in the winter of 1689—when he sought out *utamakura*, the poetic places of the ancients, which embodied the "unchanging" (*fueki*) and yet which had physically decayed and disappeared, becoming constant reminders of the "ever-changing"—and it became a major point of discussion among his disciples in the Lake Biwa area and in Kyoto, where he stayed after his long journey. In the *fūkyō* poetics that Bashō developed in the mid-1680s, the *fūkyō* poet or persona, whose pursuit of poetic beauty is so intense as to appear insane, approached classical topics—such as cherry blossoms, winter snow, autumn moon, and winter showers—from a haikai-esque, eccentric, unconventional angle. The notion of the unchanging and the ever-changing, by contrast, offered a paradigm that did not depend on either a particular poetic persona or a particular aesthetic. In contrast to *fūkyō*, which turned its back on or transcended contemporary society, this notion was rooted in contemporary, popular culture and languages and possessed a self-critical stance, a readiness to reject even one's own accomplishments, which, in the larger perspective, were regarded as temporary and ephemeral. The notion of unchanging and the ever-changing was also a teaching strategy, a pedagogical tool for remedying bad habits or tendencies. *Ryūkō* (the ever-changing), for example, served as a warning to disciples such as Kyorai, a conservative poet, not to adhere too closely to the "poetic essences" of the classical tradition, whereas *fueki* (the unchanging) served as a reminder to those such as Bonchō, an experimental contemporary poet, not to be consumed by the latest fashions in poetry.

The ideal of the unchanging and ever-changing, like the pursuit of the truth of poetic art, sought to make haikai, hitherto regarded as light entertainment, part of the larger poetic and cultural tradition, one that had its roots in the union of spiritual and poetic paths. At the same time, it meant seeking the new, stressing the need for constant change and renewal, the source of which was ultimately to be found in everyday, contemporary life. Indeed, in its emphasis on the ever-changing present, *fueki ryūkō* also marked the beginnings of *karumi* (lightness), the commoner poetics of Bashō's last years. In Dohō's view, these two creative vectors, the unchanging and the ever-changing, came together in the pursuit of the "truth of poetic art."

Bashō did not invent the notions of the truth of poetry, following the Creative, object and self as one, and the unchanging and the ever-changing, which were drawn from a variety of sources—

Neo-Confucianism, Taoism, and Zen Buddhism. Bashō's skill lay instead in the use of these familiar notions as a means of defining and legitimizing haikai within the context of orthodox Neo-Confucian ideology, as a way of coming to terms with the paradox of haikai as *fūga*, or poetry of the highest order, and as a way to approach the complex relationship between the pursuit and the rejection of the ancients. Bashō sought common ground for haikai and the traditional genres, even as he sought, particularly through the metaphor of the ever-changing, to distinguish haikai from classical poetry. It was this latter aspect that Bashō—well aware that haikai must be justified and understood, not by its shared qualities, but by its unique qualities—pursued to the fullest and which ultimately led to the notion of *karumi*, or lightness.

Lightness

When Bashō strove to transform haikai into poetry of the highest order in the early 1680s, during the Tenna era, he borrowed heavily from Chinese and Japanese classical texts. In the postscript to *Empty Chestnuts* (1683), for example, Bashō defended the poetic merit of haikai in the name of poets such as Tu Fu, Li Po, and Saigyō. But as Bashō absorbed elements of Chinese and Japanese recluse poetry into his haikai, thereby expanding its base, his poetry began to lose some of its haikai spirit, particularly its roots in popular culture and language. During his journey to the Interior in 1689, Bashō became acutely aware of this problem, which he referred to as "oldness" (*furubi*) and "heaviness" (*omomi*), and began advocating the notion of the unchanging and the ever-changing. Of the two poles, it was the "ever-changing" and the related notion of "newness" (*atarashimi*) that Bashō believed were the most seriously lacking in his poetry at this time and that led to the notion of lightness. This movement, which began during the journey to the Interior, culminated in the compilation of two key haikai anthologies, *Gourd* (1690) and *Monkey's Straw Coat* (1691), which represented a mixture of the "lightness" and "heaviness," of the "unchanging" and "ever-changing."

Like so many of Bashō's critical terms, *karumi* defies easy defini-
tion. In its most general form, as a salient characteristic of Japanese
art from cooking to painting, "lightness" is a minimalist aesthetic,
stressing simplicity and leanness. For Bashō, it meant a return to
everyday subject matter and diction, a deliberate avoidance of ab-
straction and poetic posturing, and relaxed, rhythmical, seemingly
artless expression. Serving a variety of functions, *karumi* represented
a poetic principle, a particular style, as well as a pedagogical device
for resolving compositional problems.

Prewar modern Japanese scholars such as Ebara Taizō and Naka-
mura Shunjō assumed that the notion of *karumi* emerged in the last
years of Bashō's life, while he was in residence in Edo from the end
of 1691 to the end of his life in 1694, and that it surfaced in reaction
to the "heavier," eremitic, *sabi* poetics of *Monkey's Straw Coat*, a
haikai anthology edited in Kyoto and published in 1691. These
scholars saw *karumi* as Bashō's reaction to an earlier overemphasis
on the "unchanging" in *Monkey's Straw Coat*.[13] But as postwar schol-
ars such as Ogata Tsutomu have pointed out, *Monkey's Straw Coat*
included a number of poems that Bashō later singled out as examples
of *karumi*, and Bashō began using the term as early as 1689
(Genroku 2), during the *Narrow Road to the Interior* journey.[14] At
the risk of oversimplifying a complex historical situation, Bashō's
conception of *karumi* can be divided roughly into two major stages.
The first was from the *Narrow Road to the Interior* journey in 1689,
when he began to react against "oldness," through the period of
Monkey's Straw Coat, when he stressed internal rhythm and aimed
for "newness." The second stage occurred in the last years of Bashō's
career, after his return to Edo, from around 1691 to the end of his
life in 1694, during which time he sought to find poetry in the midst
of everyday, commoner language and life.

In perhaps the most important document on *karumi*, "Kyorai's
Treatise for Fugyoku"—dated the Third Month of 1694 (Genroku 7)
but thought to record Bashō's comments primarily from 1690-91—
Kyorai notes that "lightness [*karumi*] is valued now because it is the
expression of today's ever-changing [*ryūkō*]."[15] Kyorai regarded this

"lightness" as a counterbalance to "heaviness," for which he gave the following example.[16]

> Etsujin of Biyō wrote:
>
> > spring of the lord—
> > forever the yellow-green
> > of the mosquito nets
>
> kimi|ga|haru|kaya|wa|moyogi|ni|kiwamarinu[17]
> lord's|spring|mosquito-net|as-for|yellow-green|to|remain
>
> The Master commented, "The first five syllables should be something like "The light of the moon." The existing first five syllables cause both the content and the expression to be heavy."[18]

Kimi ga haru (spring of the lord) is a seasonal phrase for the New Year (*shinnen*). In a haikai twist, Etsujin substituted the "yellow green" of the "mosquito nets" (*kaya*), a *haigon* and commoner image, for the usual evergreen of the pines, the classical symbol of everlasting glory, thereby implying that the glory of the lord (*kimi*) remains unchanging, like the color of the mosquito nets that hang in every home. Bashō criticized Etsujin's poem for being too "heavy," too allegorical or symbolic. In Bashō's opinion, the first five syllables should be something like "The light of the moon—" (*tsukikage ya*), which would present a natural scene while still suggesting everlasting glory.

The corrections that Bashō made to his own poems when writing the text of *Narrow Road to the Interior*, in 1693–94, are equally revealing.

> On the first of the Fourth Month, we paid our respects to the holy mountain. In the distant past, the name of this sacred mountain was written with the characters Futarayama, Two Rough Mountain, but when Priest Kūkai established a temple here, he changed the name to Nikkō, Light of the Sun. Perhaps he was able to see a thousand years into the future. Now this venerable light shines throughout the land, and its benevolence flows to the eight corners of the earth, and the four classes—warrior, samurai, artisan, and merchant—all live in peace. Out of a sense of reverence and awe, I put my brush down here.

awe-inspiring!
on the green leaves, budding leaves
light of the sun

ara│tōto│aoba│wakaba│no│hi│no│hikari
ah│awesome│green-leaf│young-leaf│'s│sun│'s│light

The first version, which Bashō wrote during the journey, was:

awe-inspiring!
reaching the darkness beneath the trees
light of the sun

ara│tōto│ko│no│shitayami│mo│hi│no│hikari
ah│awesome│tree│'s│lower-darkness│also│sun│'s│light

By incorporating the name of the place into the poem—*hi no hikari* (light of the sun) is the Japanese reading for Nikkō—the hokku becomes a salute to the spirit of the mountain, to the divine insight of Kūkai, to the "venerable light" of the Tōshōgu (literally, Eastern Shining Shrine), which was dedicated to Tokugawa Ieyasu, the founder of the Tokugawa shogunate, whose "light" implicitly brought peace to the land. In the first version the "light of the sun" *(hi no hikari)* reaches down to the "darkness beneath the trees" *(ko no shitayami)*, to the people. The revised version, by contrast, eliminates this "heaviness," the overt allegory and symbolism, focusing instead on the poet's sense of awe before nature, on the sight of the sun shining on a rich mixture of dark green leaves *(aoba)* and lighter-colored young leaves *(wakaba)*, with the divine presence emerging only in the overtones. The distinctive assonance and cadence that result from the repeated "a" and "i" vowels also make the revised version infinitely superior.

In contrast to the "heavy" poem, which is conceptual or leaves little room for alternative interpretations, the poetics of lightness leaves a space for the reader to become an imaginative participant, producing what Roland Barthes calls a writerly as opposed to a readerly text. In *Great Transmission of the Methods of Japanese Painting* (*Honchō gahō daiden*, 1690) the contemporary Edo painter Tosa Mitsuoki (1617–91) noted:

The essence of painting can be summarized in one word: lightness. In all respects, when creating a painting, one should paint lightly—a rule that applies not only to ink painting but also to multicolored painting as well. The overall design of the painting should be left incomplete. Only one-third of the smaller additions should be painted in. In illustrating poetry, one should not attempt to depict the entire contents. One should paint in such a way that there are overtones. Since blank space is part of the larger design, it should be endowed with meaning.[19]

Mitsuoki related lightness to the notions of understatement, overtones, and open space, which enable the viewer to participate actively in the completion of the painting. According to "Kyorai's Treatise for Fugyoku," Bashō—reflecting the same kind of discourse as Mitsuoki—selected the following spring poem by Shadō in *Monkey's Straw Coat* as an example of *karumi*.

Shadō of Zeze wrote:

> rays of the sun—
> on top of the garbage
> parents of the sparrow

hi | no | kage | ya | gomoku | no | ue | no | oyasuzume
sun | 's | rays | : | garbage | 's | top | 's | parent-sparrow

Several young disciples laughed at the verse, "The subject matter is so mundane, it would be hard to call it a hokku." The Master responded, "You laugh because you still have not reached the stage of understanding. You should study this poem to find out why you should favor lightness and avoid heaviness."[20]

Oyasuzume, "parent sparrows," a seasonal word for spring, implies that the sparrows are searching through the "garbage" (*gomoku*) for food for their young. The combination of *oyasuzume* and *gomoku* suggests the parents' affection for their offspring, which is echoed by the implied warmth of the spring sun. *Karumi* is evident in the use of the word *gomoku*, a *haigon* taken from the Kamigata dialect, and in the manner in which the hokku leaves the rest of the scene to be filled out by the reader's imagination.

Karumi also implies rhythm and attention to the poetry of the ear, what Ezra Pound referred to as melopoeia, especially those sound patterns that generate emotional connotations. One of Bashō's first comments on *karumi*, in the spring of 1690 (Genroku 3), was with regard to the following poem, which Dohō cited in *Sanzōshi.*

> beneath the trees
> in the soup, the salad, everywhere
> cherry blossoms!

ko | no | moto | ni | shiru | mo | namasu | mo | sakura | kana[21]
tree | 's | base | at | soup | also | pickled-fish | also | cherry-blossom | ! |

When the Master composed this verse, he commented: "Grasping the rhythmic mood [*kakari*] of a verse on viewing cherry blossoms, I gave it lightness." (NKBZ 51: 565)

Bashō used two vernacular words—*shiru* (clear soup) and *namasu* (pickled fish)—to suggest, not the gazing at the cherry blossoms found in classical poetry but the festivity of eating and drinking. Bashō's hokku starts slowly with four successive "o" vowels (*ko, no, mo, to*) and then plunges into a strong consonantal beat, with each new syllable seeming to pick up speed, and then ends on the emotive, exclamatory *kana*, thus suggesting the festive, inebriated mood of a cherry blossom party.

Traditional Japanese poetry is thought to be based on syllabic meter without accent or stress, but this is true only in a very narrow sense of lacking the kind of regulated beat found in iambic pentameter. When one or more phonetic qualities—pitch, loudness, length, and timbre (fuzziness, hoarseness, sharpness, etc.)—are emphasized, as they frequently are in Bashō's poetry, the syllable is stressed or accented, creating a rhythm. Equally important are the patterned or melodic variations or repetitions of sound.

> stillness—
> sinking deep into the rocks
> cries of the cicada

shizukasa | ya | iwa | ni | shimiiru | semi | no | koe
stillness | : | rock | in | penetrate | cicada | 's | voice

The vowels in this famous hokku are:

    i u a a a
  i a i i i i u
    e i o o e

The penetrating screech of the cicadas is suggested by the repetitive vowel "i" in the middle *ku: iwa ni shimiiru.* At the same time, the paradoxical sense of stillness is connoted by the slow succession of "a"s and the recurrent soft "s" (*sagyō*) consonants: *shi, sa, shi, se.*[22]

In the *karumi* of Bashō's last years in Edo, this kind of rhythm was frequently generated through onomatopoeic vernacular phrases and words, as in the following hokku in *Charcoal Sack* (1694).

    sadness of the high voice
    trailing in the dark—
        night deer

    bii|to|naku|shirigoe|kanashi|yoru|no|shika
    bii|"|cry|trailing-voice|sad|night|'s|deer

The poetic essence of the deer in the classical tradition was its mournful, lonely voice, which was closely associated with the sadness of autumn. Bashō represented this sound onomatopoetically for the first time through the phonemes *bii.*[23] According to Kyorai's *Travel Lodging Discussion,* Bashō's disciples were so impressed by Bashō's onomatopoeic use of the vernacular that they began indiscriminately using haikai words such as *kitto* and *sutto.* The overtones in the above example are generated by rhythm and sound rather than by allegory or abstract concepts, and in this sense they represent the antithesis of heaviness.[24]

Karumi, particularly in the early 1690s, was also associated with *ada,* with the playful spirit of a child. Bashō's comments on the following hokku (in *Monkey's Straw Coat*) by Tekishi (1673–1729), a disciple from Iga Province, appear in *Kyoraishō.*

    don't let the spring wind
    knock it over—
        doll palanquin bearers

harukaze|ni|kokasu|na|hina|no|kago|no|shū
spring-wind|in|knock-over|no!|doll|'s|palanquin|'s|bearer

The Master commented: "The poet from Iga has created an *ada*-style poem. What fond memories it brings!" Jōsō replied, "You gave the appearance of not being involved in the *ada* style of the Iga poets, and yet it was you who encouraged that poetic style." (NKBZ 51: 425)[25]

The poem captures a scene from the doll's festival day in the Third Month (Sekku), when young girls made miniature palanquins with doll riders and bearers, all of which were borne by a messenger to relatives. The child warns the messengers, or palanquin bearers, not to let the spring wind "knock over" (*kokasu*, a colloquial word) her newly made doll. Although Bashō does not further define *ada*, which usually means "frivolous" or "empty," the example suggests that he is using it as an adjective (*adanai*) to mean "childish," "ingenuous," or "artless."[26] In *Travel Lodging Discussion*, Kyorai observed:

> In the year that the Master passed away, he stopped at Owari, on his way to the Western Provinces. When his disciples there asked him about the new poetic style, he told them, "You should simply pay attention to the way children act."[27]

The action of the child, who sees the world with new eyes, without preconceived notions, here becomes a metaphor for the haikai spirit. The notion of returning to the spirit of a child or the related idea of returning to the spirit of a beginner (the "shallows") after formal mastery of the art ("the depths")—a notion that appears in medieval waka and Noh drama treatises[28]—implies the recovery of youthful playfulness, spontaneity, naturalness, and fresh perspective, all of which are part of *karumi*.

The second stage in Bashō's conceptualization of karumi, from the time of his return to Edo in 1691 to his death in 1694, represents both an extension of and a further deepening of his ideas of the previous period. Significantly, Bashō moved from the Kyoto area, closely associated with the classical tradition, to Edo, the new city of *chōnin* (townspeople), of commoner culture and society. In a letter from Sanpū, a Bashō disciple, to Biji, another disciple, in the Sixth Month of 1695 (Genroku 8), Bashō is quoted as saying, "One should not depend on history or classical literature. One cannot call such poetry one's own verse."[29] The poetry written in 1690–91 (Genroku 3–4), when Bashō first began mentioning *karumi*, alludes to such classics as *The Tale of Genji* and occasionally to historical events. But by 1694 (Genroku 7), *karumi* had evolved to the point where it no longer depended on a knowledge of classical texts. In *Monkey's Straw Coat* (1691), verses were often linked by *omokage-zuke*, by the "shadow" (*omokage*) of an event or character from classical literature or history, which was an integral part of the larger poetics of scent (*nioi-zuke*). By contrast, the haikai sequences in *Charcoal Sack* (1694) and *Sequel to Monkey's Straw Coat* (1698) in Bashō's last years almost never allude to history or the literary classics, nor do they give the appearance of doing so. Instead, the focus is on the commoner landscape, everyday subject matter, and vernacular language. According to Sanpū's 1695 letter to Biji, Bashō stated:

> As the form of one's verse gradually becomes heavier, it falls into the trap of logic and reason, and one creates difficult, overly intricate verse. When that happens, one should abandon the poetic style that one has used until that point and compose lightly and gently, with ordinary words. That will give the poetry a sense of immediacy.[30]

Bashō urged poets to avoid difficult words or classical diction with fixed associations and conceptions and compose with "light," "gentle," "ordinary words" (*fudan no kotoba*), which were unencumbered. "Ordinary words" alone, however, cannot create poetry. The poet must transform these words, internalize them by various means, through the pursuit of the "truth of poetic art," "following the Creative," "becoming one with the object," or the poetics of *sabi* and *shiori*, which imbued vernacular words with subtle overtones (such as pathos and loneliness). As Bashō stated in *Sanzōshi* (NKBZ 51: 604), "The virtue of haikai is that it rectifies everyday language" ("Haikai no eki wa zokugo o tadasu nari"). A good example is the following, which Bashō composed in 1692 (Genroku 5).

> salted sea breams
> their gums too look cold—
> the fishmonger's shelf

shiodai | no | haguki | mo | samushi | uo | no | tana
salted-sea-bream | 's | gum | too | cold | fish | 's | shop

Bashō's verse appeared in Kikaku's *Verse Siblings* (*Ku kyōdai*, published 1694), where it was paired with the following poem by Kikaku.

> in a hoarse voice
> the monkey cries, teeth white—
> moon over the peak

koe | karete | saru | no | ha | shiroshi | mine | no | tsuki
voice | hoarse | monkey | 's | teeth | white | peak | 's | moon

Avoiding the imaginary Chinese world of Kikaku's poem, Bashō draws poetry out of contemporary vernacular: *shiodai* (salted sea bream), *haguki* (gums), *uo no tana* (fishmonger's shelf). The hokku reflects the poet's feelings of old age—a connection made explicit in the headnote "Thoughts on old age"—but these emotions are only suggested. Instead, in the manner of "becoming one with the object," the poet implicitly enters into the "salted sea breams"—here emphasized by the particle *mo* ("too/also")—thereby fusing the internal and the external and transforming Edo commoner language into *fūga*, or poetic art.

Karumi ultimately was associated with Bashō's notion of "awakening to the high, returning to the low," attaining the spiritual, artistic, or poetic heights achieved by the ancients, while returning to the everyday languages and worlds of the present—a movement reflected in the notion of "the unchanging and the ever-changing" and embodied in hokku such as the following, which Bashō wrote in the autumn of 1694 (Genroku 7), shortly before he died. According to *Backpack Diary*, which preserves this hokku, Bashō was invited to a poetry session but, thwarted by his illness, sent the following poem.

autumn deepening—
my neighbor
　　how does he live, I wonder?

aki | fukaki | tonari | wa | nani | o | suru | hito | zo
autumn | deep | neighbor | as-for | what | (acc.) | do | person | ?

The power of the hokku comes from the juxtaposition of "autumn deepens" (*aki fukaki*) or "autumn past its peak"[31]—a seasonal word associated in classical poetry with the quiet, "deep" loneliness, with the sorrow of late autumn—with the thoughts of the speaker, perhaps lodging on a journey, who wonders about his neighbor, whom he does not see or know. The questions of the speaker—Who is the person next door? What does that person do? How does that person make a living?—suggest the loneliness and isolation of the individual, of a traveler implicitly seeking out companionship, or the loneliness of those who live together and yet apart in urban society; or more broadly, the loneliness of life itself, particularly in one's last years—a loneliness that resonates with that of late autumn. "Awakening to the high" was associated with "following the Creative," with "object and self as one," with the ability to understand the rhythm and spirit of nature and the cosmos, a process explored by the ancients and reflected here in the image of the "deepening autumn," which functions both as the external scene and as an implicit metaphor for the internal state of the speaker, who is in the late autumn of his life. By contrast, "returning to the low" implied a return to the social and linguistic roots of haikai, to the mundane but not trivial aspects of everyday human life, to the kind of questions that the speaker asks of his neighbor. The hokku, like many others by Bashō, embodies not only this double movement, which joins nature and the human, the external and the internal, the spiritual and the mundane, classical diction (*aki fukaki*) and highly colloquial language (*tonari wa nani o suru hito zo*), but the arc of "Bashō style," which began by "awakening to the high," by exploring classical, medieval, and Chinese poetics, and which, in Bashō's last years, "returned to the low," to the exploration of various aspects of Tokugawa commoner life and language.

Parting of the Ways

> sick on a journey
> dreams roam about
> on a withered moor
> —Bashō

Whenever Bashō felt that his haikai was stagnating, he embarked on a journey and sought out new poets who could stimulate him. Like other traditional Japanese arts, haikai demanded years of training, but Bashō welcomed young or new disciples, who brought a fresh and flexible perspective.[1] The overwhelming number of poets who appear in *Haikai Seven Anthologies* (*Haikai shichibu shū*)—Yasui, Kakei, Jūgo, and Tokoku in *Winter Days* (*Fuyu no hi*; 1684), Etsujin in *Desolate Fields* (*Arano*; 1689), Shadō and Kyokusui in *Gourd* (*Hisago*; 1690), Yaba, Kooku, Taisui, Rigyū in *Charcoal Sack* (*Sumidawara*; 1694)—were in fact unknown before their appearance in these publications.[2] These anthologies were composed and edited by different poets in different places, giving each collection a distinctive mood and style: Kakei edited *Winter Days* at Nagoya; Shadō compiled *Gourd* at Konan (southern Lake Biwa); Kyorai and Bonchō edited *Monkey's Straw Raincoat* at Kyoto; and Yaba, Kooku, and Rigyū put together *Charcoal Sack* in Edo. The anthologies reveal Bashō's various regional bases, but they also reflect a process in which Bashō, in his constant search for new haikai frontiers, left behind or was abandoned by disciples who had earlier played a central role, much as the added verse (*tsukeku*) pushed off or shifted from the penultimate verse (*uchikoshi*) in linked verse.

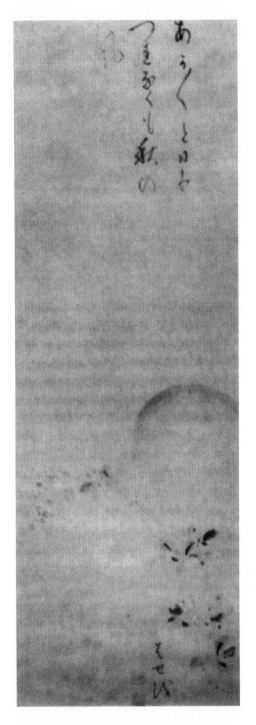

Painting, calligraphy, and poem by Bashō, probably composed around 1691–92. 32.3 x 11.4 in. The hokku—*akaaka to hi wa/tsurenaku mo aki no/kaze* (bright red, the sun shining without mercy—wind of autumn)—captures the feeling of lingering summer heat (*zansho*), an early autumn topic, and was originally written in 1689, during the journey to the Interior, on the road between Echigo and Kanazawa. Here Bashō has drawn the setting sun in light red and the blossoms of the bush clover (*hagi*), bending slightly in the wind, in light black ink. Signed "Baseo." (Courtesy Tenri University Library)

"Experienced Poets Have a Disease"

Perhaps the two most salient examples of defections occurred in the Owari (Aichi) / Nagoya region, where Kakei, the editor of *Winter Days*, the first of the Bashō school anthologies, turned against Bashō, and in the Ōmi (Shiga) / Konan region, where Shōhaku (1650–1722) and Senna (1651–1723), who were largely responsible for establishing Bashō's literary and social base at Ōmi in the mid-1680s, fell out with their teacher.[3] Bashō developed a great affection for Ōmi and for the area around Lake Biwa, particularly to the east (Hikone) and south (Ōtsu, Zeze, and Katata), which became one of Bashō's primary base camps and where he eventually asked to be buried. (His grave is at Yoshinaka Temple in Zeze.) Shōhaku and Senna became Bashō disciples after meeting him at Ōtsu, during his *Skeleton in the Fields* journey in 1685. Bashō composed the famous *Karasaki no matsu wa hana yori oboro nite* (The pine at Karasaki is mistier than the cherry blossoms) hokku, which appears in *Skeleton in the Fields*, at Shōhaku's residence in Ōtsu, in the spring of 1685. However, when Bashō resided in the Ōmi region after his *Narrow Road to the Interior* journey, during 1690–91 (Genroku 3–4), devoting himself to a new style of haikai that emerged from his long journey and that would lead to *Monkey's Straw Coat*, he worked with a new group of young Ōmi poets—Shadō, Kyokusui, Masahide, Otokuni, and others. The fruit of this new movement was *Gourd*, the Bashō-school haikai anthology edited by Shadō (also known as Chinseki), who became a disciple in the winter of 1689 (Genroku 2). Significantly, neither Shōhaku nor Senna appear in *Gourd*, nor do any of the Owari/Nagoya poets (except for Etsujin, a late recruit). By the time Bashō left the Ōmi and Kyoto area for Edo in 1691 (Genroku 4), both Shōhaku and Senna had left him. Shōhaku apparently parted with Bashō in an emotional argument over Senna's preface to *Forgotten Plum Blossoms* (*Wasureume*; edited 1691, published 1777 by Chōmu), an anthology that he was editing, but the deeper reason was no doubt the fact that he, like Senna, no longer fit into Bashō's new poetic movement.[4]

A similar problem occurred with Bashō's best disciples in the

Owari/Nagoya region, the poets with whom Bashō had composed the *Withering Gusts (Kogarashi) kasen* in 1684—Kakei, Yasui, Tokoku, Jūgo, Shōhei—and who had been the primary force in first establishing the Bashō style (*Shōfū*). From around 1690 (Genroku 3), the Nagoya group—which also included Uritsu and Etsujin—quickly faded from Bashō's circle, and after the publication in 1691 of *Monkey's Straw Coat*, which included only a limited number of poems by the Nagoya group (Etsujin has five, Kakei and Yasui have only two), they turned their backs on Bashō. According to *Biographies of Successive Haikai Poets (Rekidai kokkei den*; published 1715), a haikai history written by Kyoriku, "Rotsū, Kakei, Yasui, Etsujin, Bokuin, and others were disowned disciples."[5] Kakei, the leader of the Nagoya group and the editor of *Winter Days*, *Spring Days*, and *Desolate Fields*, went so far as to insult his former mentor. In the winter of 1693 (Genroku 6), he edited and published *Sequel to Desolate Fields (Arano kōshū*; 1693), which deliberately looked back to an earlier style of haikai—including poems from Yūsai (1534–1610) to Sōin—at a time when Bashō was advocating lightness (*karumi*) and which can be taken as an anti-Bashō manifesto. Although Kakei included 71 of his own hokku, he chose to select only four of Bashō's. Bokuin, a poet and patron from Ōgaki in Mino (Gifu) and the main host to Bashō during the *Skeleton in the Fields* journey in 1684, when Bashō met Kakei and the other Nagoya poets, encountered a similar fate. At the end of Bashō's journey through the Interior in the Eighth Month of 1689, Bokuin met Bashō at Ōgaki and took him by boat to Ise, but significantly his name does not appear in *Narrow Road to the Interior*. By the time *Narrow Road to the Interior* was written around 1694 (Genroku 7), Bokuin, along with almost all of the Owari/Nagoya poets, had become estranged from Bashō.[6]

The compilation and publication of *Monkey's Straw Coat* in 1691 (Genroku 4) had at least two larger, if not contradictory, objectives: like earlier anthologies, it was intended to be a showcase for the latest developments in the Bashō school; but, in contrast to *Gourd*, which had been limited to the new group of Ōmi disciples at Zeze, it was meant to be a conciliatory, unifying gesture, to heal the serious rifts that had opened up between Bashō and some of his older disciples and to show the regional spread of the Bashō school. The editors, Kyorai and Bonchō (15 and 41 hokku each), under the strict guidance of Bashō (41 hokku), selected a number of hokku from the Ōmi area, including some by Shōhaku (14 hokku), who had earlier been excluded from *Gourd*. The preface was written by Kikaku (15 hokku), one of the oldest of Bashō's disciples and a longtime resident of Edo, and the postface was given to the priest Jōsō (12 hokku), one of the newest and still unknown members, who had joined the Bashō school in 1689 (Genroku 2).[7] Bashō's main interest at the time was in *karumi*, which he developed with those disciples at Ōmi and Kyoto with whom he was in close contact with in 1690– 91 (Genroku 3–4), but he also wanted to accommodate as many of his disciples as possible, including a large number, particularly those in the Edo and Owari/Nagoya areas, who were no longer capable of following this latest movement. As a consequence, *Monkey's Straw Coat* is a mixture of the old and the new, literally, the *Kokinshū* (Anthology of old and new poetry) of haikai.

Bashō constantly struggled to maintain harmony between his older disciples, particularly those who had been faithful to him or who had served as his patrons, and his new disciples, to whom he looked for inspiration and new energy. *Monkey's Straw Coat* represented an attempt to achieve these contradictory objectives. For the most part, however, Bashō had great difficulty in balancing the relationship between his old and new followers; and he inevitably gave preference to his new students, who provided the stimulus and vehicle for new poetry. In *Sanzōshi*, Dohō commented:

> Experienced poets have a disease. The Master stated, "When it comes to haikai, one should let a small child compose it. The verse of a beginner is most promising." The Master repeated these comments in order to reveal the disease carried by experienced poets. (NKBZ 51: 548)

Once a group of disciples had succeeded in establishing a particular style of poetry, they usually found it difficult to break out of that mold. In Bashō's eyes, this was tantamount to having a "disease." New poetry was far more likely to emerge out of a new location with new poets, who had not been extensively exposed to or trained in the existing Bashō style. One consequence was that Bashō lost or abandoned disciples who had played a major role in the development of his haikai but who were no longer able to contribute to Bashō's latest movement. The defections became a particularly acute problem in Bashō's last years, when many disciples, including some of his most powerful supporters, refused to follow or failed to appreciate his new *karumi* style.

Bashō had the uncanny ability to find talent and bring out the best in young aspiring poets. But many of these poets, who were initially unknown, faded as quickly as they had emerged. Such was the fate of Shadō, the leader of the second Ōmi group (succeeding that of Shōhaku) that surrounded Bashō after his journey to the Interior in 1689. Shadō, for whom Bashō wrote the *haibun* "Pure Heart Dwelling" ("Sharakudō no ki"), edited and published *Gourd*, which embodied Bashō's new ideal of *karumi* and which became one of the *Haikai Seven Anthologies*. Shadō visited and stayed with Bashō at Fukagawa, after Bashō's return to Edo in the winter of 1691 (Genroku 4), but not long afterward he moved to Osaka and quickly faded from the Bashō circle. Once considered the central pillar of the new Bashō style, Shadō did not appear at Bashō's deathbed or the funeral. A similar fate awaited Bonchō, a doctor in Kyoto and the brilliant young star and editor of *Monkey's Straw Coat*, which contains 41 hokku by Bonchō (more than any other contributor). Together with Kyorai and Bashō, Bonchō, who became known for his sensitive landscape (*keiki*) poetry, participated in the noted *kasen*—such as *In the Town* (*Ichi naka wa*)—that formed the heart of *Monkey's Straw Coat*, which was published in the Seventh Month of 1691 (Genroku 4). But after Bashō's return to Edo in the winter of the same year, Bonchō's creative drive waned precipitously, and he joined the ranks of the disillusioned and disgruntled at Nagoya and even contributed to Kakei's *Arano kōshū*, the anti-Bashō manifesto. The image of the lonely traveler that appears in Bashō's literary travel diaries can be taken as a metaphor of the fate of the haikai master who yearns for companionship, indeed requires it for his art,

and yet must move on, leaving behind those who had earlier sup-
ported or inspired him. In the late autumn of 1694 (9.26.Genroku 7;
Oct. 13, 1694), at the end of his life, Bashō wrote the following
hokku, which appears in *Backpack Diary* (*Oi nikki*; 1695).

> this road—
> no one goes down it
> autumn's end

> kono|michi|ya|yuku|hito|nashi|ni|aki|no|kure
> this|road|:|go|person|none|as|autumn|'s|end

This hokku, which was composed at a large haikai gathering, can be
read as a straightforward description of the scene before the poet, as
an expression of disappointment that, at the end of his life, in the
autumn of his career—*aki no kure* can mean either "autumn's end"
or "autumn evening"—he is alone, or that life is lonely, *and* as an
expression of disappointment at the lack of sympathetic poetic part-
ners (*renju*), that is, as an expression of desire for those who can en-
gage in the poetic dialogue necessary to continue on this difficult
journey. Significantly, on Bashō's last journey in the summer of
1694, from Edo to Iga, he deliberately stopped at Nagoya, to try to
heal the breach with his former poetry companions, those surround-
ing Kakei, and then he departed for Osaka, where he would die, in
an attempt to mediate a territorial dispute between two disciples,
Shadō and Shidō (1659–1708).

Travel as Metaphor

Ultimately, travel in Bashō's work becomes a metaphor for the
haikai imagination. George Abbeele opens his book *Travel as Meta-
phor*, a study of Montaigne and other French writers, with the fol-
lowing observation:

> When one thinks of travel, one most often thinks of the interest and ex-
> citement that comes from seeing exotic places and cultures. Likewise,
> the application of the metaphor of travel to thought conjures up the im-
> age of an innovative mind that explores new ways of looking at things
> or which opens up new horizons. That mind is a critical one to the ex-

tent that its moving beyond a given set of preconceptions or values also undermines those assumptions. Indeed, to call an existing order (whether epistemological, aesthetic, or political) into question by placing oneself "outside" that order, by taking a "critical distance" from it, is implicitly to invoke the metaphor of thought as travel.[8]

As Bashō's poetics of the "unchanging and ever-changing" (*fueki ryūkō*) suggests, the pursuit of what he called the "truth of poetic art" (*fūga no makoto*) required unceasing forward movement. Travel meant a constant effort to explore new territory and new languages as well as the perpetual search for new perspectives on nature, the seasons, and the landscape, the carriers of poetic and cultural memory. The same can be said of reclusion, the other central topos of Bashō's literature. In the Chinese and Japanese poetic traditions, the recluse distances himself from the established in order to gain a critical distance on it. At the same time, however, travel for Bashō, as for his medieval poet-priest predecessors, was a movement through time, a retracing of the steps of the ancients (*kojin*), who became the source not only of spiritual and poetic inspiration but of cultural authority. Travel was a means of both expanding and acquiring cultural identity.

The cultural implications of *angya*, the journey of a renga or haikai master through the provinces, were complex. In the Zen Buddhist tradition, *angya* meant travel as an ascetic practice and as a means of seeking spiritual masters or companions; and in the Pure Land Buddhist Ji sect (Jishū) tradition founded by Priest Ippen in the Kamakura period, *angya*—or *yugyō* (spiritual wandering) as it was called—meant a proselytic journey for the purposes of preaching to and enlightening the populace in the countryside. In the course of the medieval period, another tradition emerged—one that was eventually identified with Sōgi and Bashō himself—in which the spiritual journey, the "life of no home" (*issho fujū*), of wandering like the clouds, became the ultimate poetic way. In this *angya*, the poet dressed like a mendicant priest, shaved his head in Buddhist fashion, carried a *zudabukuro*, a mendicant priest's bag, and visited poetic places. (Bashō is frequently portrayed in this fashion in paintings by his disciples and descendants.) Instead of preaching the Buddhist law, these travelers taught poetry and conducted linked verse sessions.[9] In exchange for their instruction and guidance, they received food and other offerings and were materially supported by their lay followers or patrons, who were often wealthy or powerful. Unlike most Genroku haikai masters, whose base was in one of the three great cities—Kyoto, Osaka, and Edo—Bashō was sustained by groups of disciples in various provinces. By the mid–eighteenth century, the number of traveling haikai masters had vastly increased, and the journeys were often purely commercial in orientation, literally bringing the profits of the country back to the city. The spiritual or ascetic implications of *angya* disappeared to the point where it simply referred to sightseeing by haikai poets.[10]

All these dimensions of *angya*—spiritual, cultural, social, and commercial—are relevant for understanding Bashō's life and literature. For Bashō, travel became a means of spiritual and ascetic discipline, of exploring the cultural landscape and communing with the ancients, of discovering new poetic partners and communal settings, of finding and returning to the necessary patrons, many of whom were scattered in the provinces. It was the continued *angya* of his ambitious and talented disciples that eventually gave the Bashō school a national following and that first canonized and deified Bashō.

Although Bashō mapped himself on to the medieval *angya* tradition, following in the footsteps of medieval renga masters such as Sōgi, he did so in a highly haikai-esque, Tokugawa manner, parodying and recontextualizing classical texts even as he drew on them for inspiration and authority. Travel, like reclusion, thus emerged in a seemingly contradictory fashion in Bashō's literature: on the one hand, the poet-traveler deliberately sought out poetic places that were landmarks of cultural memory, while on the other hand he took a critical, outsider's stance toward the past and toward the ancients. This apparent paradox emerged in an extremely subtle form in the constant need to seek out, retrace, and transform the poetic essences (*hon'i*) of seasonal topics as well as those of poetic places, of the landscape broadly conceived. At the same time, Bashō and other haikai poets also expanded the canon, composing on new haikai places (*haimakura*), which reflected the actual topography, and on new seasonal topics, which embodied the interests and perspectives of seventeenth-century commoners and samurai. In either case, the haikai poet had to discover new viewpoints, to go against or revision established associations: there could be no haikai without "newness" (*atarashimi*), and of all modes of existence, it was travel, with its constant motion and release from fixed perspectives, that encouraged and stimulated such "newness."

Bashō's haikai, like his travel, moved fundamentally in two directions, linking participants together and linking them with the past, with a sense of tradition. The term *za*, which originally meant to sit together in one place, referred to the place or site (*ba*) of the linked verse sessions, the participants (*renju*) of those haikai session, and the process of creating, exchanging, and appreciating poetry. In a broader sense, *za* implied a sense of group cohesion, a sense of bonding among individuals of different social backgrounds, unrelated by blood or family. *Za* in this sense enabled heteroglossia, the interplay of different social voices, languages, and subcultures, on which haikai thrived. Ogata Tsutomu has widened this sense of *za* to include the sense of cohesion among writers and readers not present at the original place or site of the haikai session, which was, by nature, transitory and semi-oral in nature.[11] This sense of a larger poetic and cultural community was made possible, most immediately, by the publication and distribution of haikai collections and anthologies—the first widely distributed print literature of Japan—which could be read by a wide range of participants in different parts of the country who gained a sense not only of a larger community but of an imagined, shared past with which they could identify.

Sōgi, while considered the great master of linked verse and the inspiration for generations of Tokugawa haikai poets, had banned haikai, its language and its topics, from linked verse, which he transformed into a form of classical poetry and high culture, and his journeys to famous places in classical poetry—such as the Shirakawa

Barrier—served to deepen his ties to the classical past. Bashō and other Tokugawa haikai travelers, by contrast, helped to absorb and transform these famous places and seasonal topics into a wider popular culture, transforming and vernacularizing these nodes of cultural memory into a cultural commodity that could be consumed by large numbers of people, particularly those wealthy merchants and samurai eager to acquire a sense of culture. In fact, Sōgi, who himself was of extremely low social origins, had, two centuries earlier, also shaped and transmitted to his clients, the powerful provincial lords, a sense of cultural identity that they lacked but craved, but it was a sense of high culture unsullied by haikai or its lowly associations.

Indeed, by the Genroku period, haikai, despite its popular, antiestablishment origins, had increasingly become a transmitter of literary and social orthodoxy to the point that the distinction between haikai and classical linked verse had almost disappeared—a phenomenon epitomized by the emergence of the renga style in the mid-1680's. Bashō worked to assimilate the Chinese and Japanese poetic traditions into haikai and to appropriate the authority and aura of the ancients—whose importance grew in the late seventeenth century, as exemplified by the ancient studies of Confucian texts by Itō Jinsai (1627–1705) and the ancient studies of the *Man'yōshū* by Keichū (1640–1701). As we have seen, Bashō incorporated orthodox Neo-Confucian thought into haikai poetics, hoping to raise the status of haikai, give it a spiritual and cosmological backbone, and make it part of the larger poetic and cultural tradition. The result of this late-seventeenth-century movement was not the creation of an oppositional culture that attempted, in the manner of Muromachi haikai, to invert the social and literary hierarchy, but rather a commoner culture that existed largely within and sometimes became indistinguishable from the cultural orthodoxy. One consequence was that, particularly from the Genroku period onward, one stream of haikai, which eventually paved the way for modern haiku, tended to gravitate toward those very elements, traditionally considered to be of high cultural value, that earlier haikai had mocked or playfully degraded, while another stream continued to move in the direction of comic, satirical verse, the seventeen-syllable *senryū*, which required neither a seasonal word nor a cutting word, base elements of haikai. Bashō, who stood at this critical point in haikai history, composed poetry that had the spiritual, aesthetic, and social implications of classical Japanese and Chinese poetry while retaining much of haikai's anticonventional, popular character. The result was a literature that was multivoiced, profoundly paradoxical in tone and nature and in ideological implication—transgressive yet traditional, humorous yet sorrowful, spiritual yet mundane—a mixture of classical culture and the new popular cultures. As we have seen, Bashō managed to give value and voice to everyday, contemporary life, but that value was attained through subtle associations with those high cultures—classical, medieval, and Chinese—that Bashō and other haikai masters consolidated for a new commoner and samurai audience. In effect Bashō helped to establish and widen the authority of these newly reconstructed cultural traditions, to which he himself would soon become affiliated, even as he moved in haikai-esque, anti-traditional directions. In the dialogic world of Bashō's haikai, to compose poetry was implicitly to answer the previous verse or earlier texts and voices, and to anticipate a poetic response, which could radically recontextualize or completely alter the meaning of the existing text, giving it new life. In this sense, the essential movement of haikai was the unceasing search for new poetic associations, new languages, new perspectives, and new styles, but it was a newness that existed in relationship to established associations and worlds, which were reconstructed and transmitted by Bashō and other haikai masters and which were embodied most concretely in the landscape, the ultimate bearer of cultural memory and the primary ground for haikai re-visioning.

Reference Matter

Glossary of Literary Terms

ada あだ A humorous, ingenuous, seemingly artless poetic mood or style that emerges from a childish, un-self-conscious approach or attitude. Kyorai considered *ada* to be the epitome of *karumi*.

ageku 挙げ句 Closing, fourteen (7/7) syllable verse in a linked verse sequence, required to be auspicious.

aisatsu 挨拶 Poetry as a performative act, especially as a greeting, expression of gratitude or respect or a prayer. A modern term first elaborated by Yamamoto Kenkichi (1907–88).

angya 行脚 Journey of a renga or haikai master through the provinces or such a traveler.

bashō 芭蕉 Japanese banana or plantain, traditionally planted in temple courtyards and gardens. Seasonal word for early autumn. Unlike the banana, which grows in the tropics and bears fruit, the *bashō*, which grows as high as four meters, can tolerate cold weather, does not require a hot, humid climate, and rarely bears fruit, at least not in Japan. The oblong green leaves grow vigorously in the summer, extending as far as two meters, but are easily torn, especially by the autumn wind and rain, creating a pitiable appearance. In the poetic tradition, the torn leaves became a metaphor for impermanence. In a haibun called "On Transplanting the Plantain," Bashō, who took his haikai name from the plant, made the *bashō* a symbol of uselessness, of freedom from utilitarian value systems.

bashōzuka 芭蕉塚 Bashō gravestones (*tsuka*). Erected around the country as branches of Bashō's grave at Gichūji Temple, generally engraved with "Bashō the Elder" (Bashō ō 芭蕉翁) and a hokku by Bashō. Close to 1,000 erected by the end of the Tokugawa period.

butsuga ichinyo 物我一如 Object and self as one. Poetic idea in which the poet becomes selfless in order to enter into the object and become one with it.

dai 題 Poetic topic on which the poet was expected to compose.

daisanku 第三句 Third verse (17 syllables) in a linked verse sequence.

dokugin 独吟 Solo composition of linked verse.

fueki ryūkō 不易流行 The unchanging and the ever-changing. Haikai poetic ideal, which Bashō began advocating during his journey through the Interior, that haikai must constantly change (*ryūkō*), find the new (*atarashimi*), shed its own past, even as it seeks qualities that transcend time.

fūga 風雅 Poetic art. Used by Bashō to refer to cultural practice of the highest order, especially that of haikai.

fūkyō 風狂 Poetic madness. The behavior and thought of a poetic persona so devoted to the pursuit of poetic beauty and ideals that he or she appears mad to the outside world.

ga/zoku 雅俗 Classical, elegant culture or language versus popular, contemporary, commoner culture or language. Traditionally, waka and renga were associated with the former, and haikai with the latter.

haibun 俳文 Haikai prose. Prose written with haikai spirit. Usually accompanied by hokku.

haiga 俳画 Haikai painting or sketch. Usually illustrates or accompanies a haikai verse. In a wider sense, any visual form that reveals haikai spirit, especially humor, brevity, suggestiveness, resistence to convention, a feeling of lightness, commoner sensibility (as opposed to decorous, intricate, refined, rich taste).

haigon 俳言 Haikai words. Includes vernacular Japanese, colloquial phrases, Chinese compounds, Buddhist terminology, and popular sayings, all of which were banned from classical Japanese poetry.

haii 俳意 Haikai spirit. Originally referred to a sense of the comic (*kokkei*), but later used by Bashō in a broader sense to mean the antitraditional, anticonventional character of haikai, including its freedom and unceasing search for new worlds, languages, and perspectives.

haikai 俳諧 Originally the abbreviation for *haikai no renga*, or comic, commoner-based, popular linked verse, as opposed to refined, aristocratically rooted, classical linked verse. Broadly used to refer to genres deriving from *haikai* such as the *hokku*, *haiku*, *renku*, *haibun*, and *haikai*-related travel accounts and narrowly used to refer to *haikai* linked verse.

haikaika 誹諧歌 Haikai poem. Unorthodox, witty, humorous 31-syllable waka, included in the Miscellaneous (*zō*) volume of *Kokinshū*.

haikaishi 俳諧師 Haikai masters, also called *haikai sōshō* or *haikai tenja*, who made a living by teaching students, conducting (*sabaku*) haikai linked verse sessions, and giving marks (*hyōten*).

haiku 俳句 Modern term for the autonomous, seventeen-syllable hokku.

haimakura 俳枕 Haikai places. Noted poetic places discovered and used by haikai poets, in contrast to *utamakura*, famous places in classical poetry.

The term first appears in the title to Yūzan's haikai anthology *Hai-makura* (published 1680).

hibiki ひびき Reverberation. Type of link in haikai in which the dramatic tension, strong rhythm, or intense emotion of the previous verse reverberates in the added verse.

hiraku 平句 Any verse of a linked verse sequence except for the first three and the last.

hokku 発句 Seventeen-syllable (5/7/5) opening verse, may come at the beginning of linked verse sequence or exist independently.

hon'i 本意 Essential nature, poetic essence. The established associations of a particular topic, derived from classical precedent and commonly recognized as the most appropriate for and essential to that particular topic.

honkadori 本歌取 Allusive variation on a classical poem (*waka*) or foundation poem (*honka*).

honzetsu (*honsetsu*) 本説 Allusive variation on some aspect of an earlier *monogatari* (Japanese tale), Chinese poem, Chinese prose, or historical event.

hyakuin 百韻 Hundred-verse sequence of linked verse.

ichibutsu shitate 一物仕立 To compose a hokku or verse using only one subject or topic, as opposed to a *toriawase*, or combination poem.

jibokku 地発句 An independent hokku as opposed to a *tateku*, a hokku that starts a linked verse sequence.

kaiseki 会席 Seating arrangement and setting for a linked verse session.

kaishi 懐紙 Poetry sheet or record for linked verse.

kanshibun-chō 漢詩文調 Chinese style of haikai poetry and prose that became popular in the Tenna era (1681–84) and that culminated in *Empty Chestnuts* (*Minashiguri*). Also referred to as the Tenna style (*Tenna-chō*) and the *Empty Chestnuts* style (*Minashiguri-chō*).

karumi かるみ Lightness. Poetic ideal advocated by Bashō in his last years. Stress on everyday, commoner subject matter; on the use of familiar, vernacular language; and on relaxed, rhythmical, seemingly artless expression.

kasen 歌仙 36-verse linked verse sequence, standard for haikai in Bashō's day.

keiki 景気 Landscape style. Found in waka, renga, and haikai. Style of verse (*ku*) or linkage that focuses on nature "as it is." Became the dominant style of haikai in the Genroku period.

keijō 景情 Scene (*keiki*) and emotion (*jō*). The fusion of the two was regarded as one of the ideals of Genroku haikai.

kidai 季題 Seasonal topic, usually centered on a cluster of fixed associations, on which poets were required to compose.

kigo 季語 Seasonal word, a requirement of the hokku, indicating the season of the verse.

kireji 切字 Cutting word in a hokku.

kiyose 季寄 Seasonal almanac, compilation of seasonal topics (*kidai*) and seasonal words (*kigo*), categorized by the seasons, without poetry examples.

kōgo kizoku 高悟帰俗 Awakening to the high, returning to the low. Haikai ideal advocated by Bashō. To attain the spiritual, artistic, or poetic heights achieved by the ancients and to give that new life and expression in the everyday language and world of haikai.

kōgyō 興行 Linked verse performance or session, requiring a master (*sōshō*), scribe (*shuhitsu*), host, and participants (*renju*).

kokoro-zuke 心付 Link between the previous verse and the added verse through content or meaning (*kokoro*). Sometimes used to refer to a link by *honkadori* or *honzetsu*, through allusive variations on classical poetry or prose.

kotoba-zuke 詞付 Word link. See *mono-zuke*.

kurai 位 Status link. Link in which the added verse reflects the socioeconomic connotations of a figure or image in the previous verse.

kyōka 狂歌 Comic waka. Written in the same 31-syllable form as classical *waka* but uses wit, parody, satire, or vulgar language to induce laughter.

maeku 前句 Previous verse, either fourteen or seventeen syllables in length, in a linked verse sequence.

maeku-zuke 前句付 Verse-capping, in which a previous verse (*maeku*), functioning as a set topic (*dai*), is capped by an added verse (*tsukeku*) to create a two-verse sequence. From the latter half of the seventeenth century, it became a popular form of competition in which multiple composers submitted entries, using a middle man who passed the submissions to a haikai master who then judged and offered prizes to the winners.

makoto 誠 Truth, sincerity, absence of fault, seriousness. Used in Bashō's poetics to refer to a truth that was realized in or through *fūga*, or haikai as poetic art, and that Bashō believed was lacking in earlier haikai.

mitate 見たて A visual or an iconographic allusion. Double vision. Often a witty, contemporary twist on a familiar image from the classical or medieval world.

mono-zuke 物付 Lexical links. Linking by established classical associations (*yoriai*), by word associations (*engo*) that include vernacular words, or by homophonic associations (*kakekotoba*).

nioi にほひ Link by scent. Type of link advocated by Bashō in which the connotations of the previous verse (*maeku*) drift imperceptibly to the added verse (*tsukeku*) like the fragrance of a flower in a breeze.

Noh or *nō* 能 Major dramatic form that flourished from the eleventh through the fifteenth centuries and that became a popular source of allusion in haikai.

renga 連歌 Linked poetry of various types. Used in this study to refer to classical linked verse, which flourished in the medieval period and derived its diction and conventions from classical waka.

renju 連衆 Participants in a linked verse session.

renku 連句 Modern linked verse. Also modern term for haikai linked verse

ryōgin 両吟 Linked verse composed by two poets.

sabaku 捌く To conduct or preside over a haikai session. Carried out by a *sōshō*, or haikai master.

sabi さび Aesthetic, poetic ideal cultivated by medieval waka and renga poets and incorporated into haikai by Bashō. A sense of beauty and spiritual depth in loneliness and tranquillity, especially in natural images, generating a subtle sentiment that emerges quietly in the overtones of the poem.

saijiki 歳時記 Seasonal almanac. Gives seasonal topics and words, along with appropriate examples of poetry, in seasonal order. Includes *kiyose*.

senryū 川柳 Seventeen-syllable poetic form not requiring a seasonal word or cutting word and humorously reflecting on the human condition.

shasei 写生 Sketch from life, a poetic ideal first advocated by Masaoka Shiki (1867–1902).

shiori しほり Implied a sensitivity toward weak or delicate objects, particularly a feeling of pathos (*aware*), which quietly emerges in the overtones of a poem. *Shiori* derives from the verb *shioru*, which was written in two ways, 湿ほる *shihoru*, "to be moist, heavy, or quiet" and 萎をる *shiworu*, "to shrivel or wilt," both of which suggest the restrained tone of *shiori*.

Shōfū 蕉風 Haikai style established by Bashō and his school. Broadly divided into three periods: (1) the Jōkyō (1684–88) era, highlighted by *Winter Days* (1684) and *fūkyō* poetics; (2) the period from Bashō's journey through the Interior in the spring of 1689 to the publication of *Monkey's Straw Coat* in 1691, marked by the fusion of classical and everyday worlds; and (3) the period from Bashō's return to Edo in the winter of 1691 to his death in 1694, focusing on lightness (*karumi*) and the poetry of commoner life and language.

Shōmon 蕉門 Bashō's immediate disciples. First emerged in Edo around

1680 and then spread during Bashō's travels from 1684 onward. Also used to refer to successive generations of followers led by such disciples as Kikaku, Ransetsu, Shikō, Yaba, and Rosen.

shuhitsu 執筆 Scribe. Checks the rules and records the poetry at a linked verse session.

shukō 趣向 Allusive innovation. Contemporary counterpoint, particularly a new twist created by superimposing the contemporary Edo world onto a familiar classical, medieval, or Chinese world so that the two co-exist. A literary technique found in haikai, kabuki, ukiyoe, and other Edo arts. *Mitate* is a visual subcategory.

sōshō 宗匠 Haikai master. Presides over the linked-verse session.

tateku 立句 Hokku at the beginning of a linked verse sequence, as opposed to a *jibokku*, an autonomous *hokku*.

tenja 点者 Marker. A professional haikai master hired to give marks or points (*ten*) to haikai compositions in exchange for a fee (*tenryō*). Led to point-garnering haikai (*tentori haikai*).

tentori haikai 点取俳諧 Point-garnering haikai in which the participants compete with each other to see who can earn the most points (*ten*) from the professional marker (*tenja*) for their compositions.

toriawase 取り合せ Combination poem. A hokku that combines two or more different topics or images so that they resonate.

tsukeai 付合 Joining of the added verse to the previous verse to create a new world. Can also mean, as with *yoriai*, the use of an established lexical association to join successive verses.

tsukeku 付句 Added verse. Verse added to and read together with the *maeku*, or previous verse.

uchikoshi 打越 Penultimate verse, the verse before the previous verse, from which, in the Bashō style, the added verse should push off.

utamakura 歌枕 Famous places in Japanese poetry. Originally referred to classical poetic diction (*kago*), or a handbook of such diction.

utsuri うつり Transference, reflection. Used to describe a particular type of link in Bashō's haikai. When the graph 移り is used, it means the transference of connotations or associations from the previous verse to the next verse. With the graph 映り, it means mutual reflection of associations between the previous verse and the added verse.

wabi わび An aesthetic and spiritual ideal first developed by medieval poets and tea masters and later advocated by Bashō. Rejects external, sensory beauty and finds spiritual and poetic depth in material poverty, in modest, simple, unadorned objects, in an ascetic lifestyle.

waka 和歌 Classical Japanese poem consisting of 31-syllables in a 5/7/

5/7/7 syllabic pattern. The same form in the modern period is generally referred to as *tanka*.

wakiku 脇句 The 14-syllable (7/7) second verse in a linked verse sequence.

yosei or *yojō* 余情 Overtones. A poetic style found in both waka and linked verse that suggests emotional overtones or sentiments without directly expressing them, leaving only a lingering echo, trace, or mood to be savored by the reader. *Yosei-zuke* (link by overtone), of which Bashō's *nioi* (scent link) can be considered a subcategory, depends on such overtones to link one verse to the next.

yoriai 寄合 Established lexical associations (such as pine and crane) derived from classical poetry, classical tales (*monogatari*), and other early sources, and used to link successive verses in classical renga.

zōka zuijun 造化随順 Following the Creative (Creator). Advocated by Bashō in the opening to *Backpack Notes*: "Those engaged in art [*fūga*] should follow the Creative and make friends of the four seasons." In Neo-Confucian cosmology, following (*zuijun*) the Creative (*zōka*), or the Creator, implied following the creative force of the universe, especially the ceaseless movement of the seasons, as well as the Creative within.

za 座 The site of the linked verse session and/or the participants (*renju*) of such a session. More broadly, it means the dialogue and communal sense that arises from linking verses together.

Notes

BOOK EPIGRAPH SOURCES: Bloom, p. 99; Greene, p. 46; Sklovsky, p. 17.

Chapter 1

1. Sato, *One Hundred Frogs: From Renga to Haiku in English*.
2. Benjamin, "On Some Motifs in Baudelaire," in his *Illuminations*. Benjamin defines "aura" as "the associations which, at home in the *mémoire involontaire*, tend to cluster around the object of a perception," p. 186.
3. Anderson, *Imagined Communities*.
4. Before 1590, almost no printing existed except in Buddhist monasteries. But within a century, well over 10,000 books were in print, sold, or rented by more than 700 bookstores.
5. *Zoku yama no i*, p. 625.
6. *Bashō shichibu shū*, pp. 232–33.
7. In reference to the *mitate-e* (painting) by Suzuki Harunobu (1725?–70), a successor of Moronobu, the art historian Kobayashi Tadashi notes two types: "In one, a modern interpretation is superimposed over the original subject; figures and animals familiar to everyone as characters from famous events, narratives, and paintings from the classical past are converted into stylish young men and women of the present. In the other, . . . they attempt to amuse by abbreviating, inflecting, or adapting the tone and meaning of the classical poem to current customs and manners" (Jenkins, p. 87).
8. Burke, *Perspectives by Incongruity*, pp. 94–99.
9. *Renju gappeki shū*, p. 118.
10. Sōkan's hokku appears in *Arano* (1689); in *Bashō shichibu shū*, p. 92.
11. *Buson zenshū*, 1: 115.
12. A modern commentary notes that the "floating leaf" is probably a lotus leaf. *Kawazu awase* (Frog competition), in *Genroku haikai shū*, p. 3.
13. *Ryōkan zenshū*, 2: 314.
14. In Ross, p. 47.

15. Bashō's given name was Kinsaku, his family name was Matsuo. But he is usually referred to by his haikai names, of which the most frequently used are Sōbō, Tōsei, and Bashō. Bashō is thought to have lived in a family of eight, with one elder brother, one elder sister, and three younger sisters.

16. See Glossary, p. 293, on the *bashō* plant.

Chapter 2

EPIGRAPH: Pound, *Personae*, p. 108.

1. Contemporary publications such as *Genroku hyakunin ikku* (One hundred Genroku haikai poets, one poem each; 1691) and *Hanami-guruma* (Flower-viewing carriage; 1702) suggest that only about 10 percent of the haikai population in the Genroku period had any affiliation with the Bashō school. Other groups in fact published far more than Bashō and his followers.

2. Shikō and Yaba were direct disciples, but Otsuyū never studied with Bashō.

3. In the course of the Kyōhō era (1716–36), the Shibaku School, referred to disparagingly by Revival poets as "the provincial Bashō school" (*inaka shōmon*), managed to spread its sphere of influence throughout the country. Meanwhile, the large cities were dominated in the early eighteenth century by such urban haikai movements as Fukaku's *kechō* style and the Edoza—an Edo movement represented by the witty, playful "stylish" (*share-fū*) haikai of Sentoku (1662–1726) and Kikaku (1616–1707), and by the "metaphoric style" (*hiyutai*) of Senshū (1670–1737). The term *Edoza* originally referred only to Kikaku's Edo group, which was located in the Kanda/Nihonbashi area of Edo, but the term is now used to refer to the entire phenomenon of *tentori* (point-garnering) haikai masters in Edo from around the Kyōhō era.

4. The names of the ten disciples differ according to the source.

5. In 1739, Kajaku edited and published *Bashō kusen* (Selected poetry by Bashō), which presented 671 of Bashō's hokku arranged by season, with notes and commentary. The *Bashō kusen*, which became a standard edition for subsequent readers, combined over 560 hokku found in *Hakusenshū* (1698, edited by Fūkoku) with hokku gleaned from other published collections.

6. *Buson zenshū*, 1: 592.

7. Riichi is probably best known for *Oku no hosomichi sugagomoshō* (1778), one of the earliest and best premodern commentaries on Bashō's *Narrow Road to the Interior*. Rankō wrote the preface for and helped to publish Dohō's *Sanzōshi* (compiled 1702) in 1776, one year after Kyōtai had published Kyorai's *Kyoraishō*. In 1786 Rankō edited *Shō ō shōsoku shū*,

the letters of Bashō. The peak of the Revival period also produced more comprehensive biographical studies, including *Shō ō zenden* (Complete biography of Bashō the Elder; 1762) by Chikujin (d. 1764), Dohō's disciple, and then Chōmu's *Bashō ō ekotobaden* (Illustrated Life of Bashō the Elder; 1792).

8. Early records indicate that Bashō memorials, or *Bashōzuka*, were built at seven locations around the country on the seventh anniversary of Bashō's death in 1700, and on the seventeenth anniversary, another seven *tsuka* were erected at noted temples throughout Japan.

9. Tōsei was one of Bashō's earlier haikai names.

10. Ogata, "Bashō o dō miru ka," in idem, *Bashō hikkei*, p. 8.

11. The proselytism of the Shikō school was modeled on that of the Ji sect which sent individual priests through the countryside to work with local groups. Annual memorial services for Bashō's spirit were held at Ji Temples, and Shikō built a Bashō *tsuka* in the Sōrin Temple, the head temple of the Ji Sect.

12. Masaoka Shiki, *Shū*, pp. 146–89.

13. Shiki gives "A wild sea—/ stretching out to Sado Isle, / the Milky Way" (araumi ya Sado ni yokotau amanogawa) as an example of "sublimity and grandeur."

14. "Bashō zōdan," in Masaoka Shiki, *Shū*, p. 177.

15. In "Jojibun" (Descriptive prose), an essay written in 1900 (Meiji 33), Shiki wrote: "For now, I call transcribing actual things the way they are *shajitsu*. It can also be called *shasei*" (*Shū*, p. 367).

16. The notion of *shasei*, which gained wide currency, was later taken over by the so-called Japanese Romantic poets, including Shimazaki Tōson, who subsequently became a pioneer of "realistic" (*shajitsuteki*) writing of the kind adapted by the Naturalist school.

17. In "Reading Bashō at Matsushima" ("Matsushima ni oite Bashō o yomu"), a poem in essay form in the journal *Jogaku zasshi* (1892), Tōkoku describes a journey to Matsushima, one of the high points of *Oku no hosomichi*, where he meets the spirit of Bashō and realizes that Bashō had not composed any poetry at Matsushima because, in a "sublime" moment, the beautiful landscape had completely consumed Bashō, fusing his spirit with that of nature. For Tōson, who wrote extensively about Bashō, Bashō's life became an ideal that he himself attempted to emulate. The symbolist poets (*shijin*) Kanbara Ariake (1875–1952) and Miki Rofū (1889–1964), who were first inspired by French Symbolist poetry, also found a Japanese counterpart in Bashō. In the preface to his symbolist poetry collection *Shunchōshū* (1905), Kanbara Ariake wrote that Bashō was "the most symbolist writer in Japanese literature."

18. Hirai Shōbin, "Kindai no haijintachi."

19. *Haikai manwa* (Haikai casual talk), Shinseisha, 1903.

20. Matsui Toshihiko, "Kindai hairon to Bashō," p. 279.

21. Ibid., pp. 282–83. Kyoshi gives Bashō's "Exhausted, / looking for a place to stay—/ hanging wisteria" (kutabirete yado karu koro ya fuji no hana) as an example.

22. Kaneko Tōta (b. 1919), who emerged under the influence of the Ningen tankyū (Pursuit of humanity) group, became one of the leaders of the Shakaisei (Social character) haiku movement (from around 1954) and then of the Zen'ei (Avant-garde) haiku movement, both of which were deeply influenced by Western trends. In the 1960s, however, another group of haiku poets—Iida Ryūta (b. 1920), Mori Sumio (b. 1919), Kusama Tokihiko (b. 1920), and others—under the influence of Shūson and Hakyō, took an interest in re-examining the haikai tradition—especially such premodern notions as *haii* (haikai spirit), *karumi* (lightness), *asobi* (play), and *kokkei* (comic)—with the primary focus on Bashō.

23. Taupin, p. 127.

24. Pound, "A Few Don'ts by an Imagiste." Pound goes on to note: "It is the presentation of such a 'complex' instantaneously which gives a sense of sudden liberation; that sense of freedom from time limits and space limits; that sense of sudden growth, which we experience in the presence of the greatest works of art."

25. Cited by Pratt, p. 22.

26. "The only way of expressing emotion in the form of art is by finding an 'objective correlative'; in other words, a set of objects, a situation, a chain of events which shall be the formula of that particular emotion; such that when the external facts, which must terminate in sensory experience, are given, the emotion is immediately evoked" (Eliot, "Hamlet and His Problems," in idem, *Selected Prose*, p. 48).

27. Pound, "Vorticism," p. 465.

28. It was also in 1958 that Nippon Gakujutsu Shinkōkai's *Haikai and Haiku*, the first serious introduction to haikai in English, was published.

29. Blyth, *History of Haiku*, 1: 25, 28.

30. Blyth, *Haiku*, 1: iii.

31. Ibid., 2: vii.

32. For Blyth, haiku is not a particular genre but a perspective and consciousness that can be found scattered throughout English literature as well as in Western philosophical writings, including that of Emerson.

33. Hackett, *Way of Haiku*, p. ix.

34. K. Yasuda, p. 24.

35. Ibid., p. 41.

36. Ibid., pp. 49–51.

37. Yu, pp. 17–19.

38. Henderson, p. 18.

39. The first edition (1974) contains about 200 haiku, the second edition, published in 1986, adds about 500 more haiku and related forms.

40. van den Heuvel, p. 261.

41. Ibid., p. 272.

42. Eliot, "Tradition and the individual talent," in idem, *Selected Essays*, pp. 42–43.

43. Fowler, p. 12.

44. On this problem, see Tomi Suzuki, *Narrating the Self*.

45. One version has "escaping" (*nogarekeri*) instead of "hiding" (*kakurekeri*).

46. Riffaterre, p. 2.

Chapter 3

EPIGRAPHS: Bakhtin, *Dialogic Imagination*, p. 272; Bergson, "Laughter," p. 123.

1. This study explores the ramifications of two different aspects of what the Russian critic Mikhail Bakhtin (*Dialogic Imagination*; *Rabelais and His World*) refers to as the dialogic: heteroglossia, the interaction of socially inscribed diverse languages, and addressivity, the text as the product of a reciprocal relationship between addresser and addressee.

2. *Teimon haikai shū I*, in KHT 1: 44.

3. *Haikaika* (haikai classical poetry) appears in the latter half (nos. 1011–68) of vol. 19 ("Miscellaneous Styles") of the *Kokinshū*.

4. In the preface to *Haikai gosan* (Haikai umbrella; 1651), Teitoku stated: "In the beginning there was no difference between haikai and classical renga. Those verses that used only elegant words came to be called 'classical renga'; those that did not reject popular words were called 'haikai.'"

5. *Shinzō inu tsukuba shū* (New dog Tsukuba collection), p. 196.

6. In the middle of the Keichō era (1596–1615), Teitoku and his friend the Neo-Confucian scholar Hayashi Razan (1583–1657) gave public lectures on the Japanese classics for commoners—a radical move in the age of secret transmissions—and from the Kan'ei period (1624–44), Teitoku and his disciples opened up private schools to educate commoners.

7. Teitoku, for example, published commentaries on *Tsurezuregusa* and *Hyakunin isshu*, and Kigin wrote commentaries on *The Tale of Genji*, *The Pillow Book* (*Makura no sōshi*), and the *Hachidai shū* (First eight imperial waka anthologies)—to mention only the most prominent.

8. *Haikai yōi fūtei*, pp. 194–95.

9. Saikoku (*Indōshū*, p. 393) observes that it is easy to combine deer

with mountain but that it takes ingenuity to make the sea lions and whales swim in the waves of flowers at the mountain peak.

10. In *Haikai mōgyū* (1675), Ichū (1639–1711) noted: "One should attempt to do two things: one should make ordinary language bloom and change a romance or ancient affairs into something that cannot possibly exist, thereby creating falsehood." Ichū and others claimed that Danrin haikai, like the *Chuang-tzu*, disrupted commonly held perceptions through humor, parody, and allegory. In *Ukiyo monogatari* (1666), Asai Ryōi (d. 1691) defined *gūgen* as "writing in such a way that what did not exist seemed to exist."

11. Muromachi renga masters such as Nijō Yoshimoto and Sōgi composed a form of linked verse in which the participants were required to include a Chinese compound in each verse of the sequence. Teitoku considered these Chinese insertions, which were normally banned from classical renga, to be *haigon* and a distinguishing feature of haikai.

12. Interestingly, the Chinese style appeared in Kyoto and Edo but not in Osaka, which did not have the *shi* (poetry in Chinese) poets found in the other major cities.

13. The passage is from a poem "Sung Chang shanjen kuei Songyang" (Bidding farewell to the hermit Chang on his return to Songyang) by Po Chü-i (J. Hakurakuten).

14. Bashō here parodied a noted phrase in a Chinese poem in *Enki kappō*: "The bell at Rich Temple rings when the frost appears," replacing Rich Temple (*hōzan*) and bell (*kane*) with Poor Temple (*hinzan*) and kettle (*kama*), respectively.

15. The association of the fragile leaves of the plantain with impermanence and the loneliness of the recluse is evident in the following poem by Tu Mu (803–52) entitled "The Plantain."

> The plantain was
>   washed away by the rain.
> So I planted another
>   in front of my window.
> I am deeply stirred
>   by the sound of the raindrops,
> Which leaves me
>   with a dream of returning home;
> But the dream fades into the distance,
>   and there is no return.
> I awake
>   and roll over with a start.

16. A similar twist occurs in the following hokku by Kikaku, Bashō's leading disciple at the time, which appears in *Inaka no kuawase* (published in 1680).

> planting a potato
> listening to the rain
> in a windy lodge!

imo | o | uete | ame | o | kiku | kaze | no | yadori | kana
potato | (acc.) | planting | rain | (acc.) | listen | wind | 's | lodging | !
(KHT 7: 369)

Instead of planting a banana plant in front of his window, the recluse plants a potato, and in keeping with poetic convention, the speaker listens to the rain and wind, even though the potato plant will obviously make no sound.

17. The title of the first major "Chinese-style" anthology, *Minashiguri* (Empty chestnuts; 1683), derives from a hokku by the editor Kikaku, which embodies this new aesthetics.

> winter gusts—
> empty chestnuts that the world
> cannot gather

kogarashi | yo | yo | ni | hirowarenu | minashiguri
winter-gusts | ! | world | in | can-not-gather | empty-chestnuts
(KHT 6: 49)

18. Ogata Tsutomu (*Matsuo Bashō*, Nihon o tsukutta hito, p. 19) goes so far as to argue that *Kōshoku ichidai otoko* (Life of an amorous man), Saikaku's first *ukiyo-zōshi*, which he wrote in 1682 and which describes the pleasure-oriented ways of the *chōnin* in the 1660s-1670s, should be regarded not as a realistic depiction of contemporary times but as a nostalgic elegy to the former *chōnin* culture.

19. Shiraishi Teizō. "Shōmon no keisei to tenkai," in idem, *Bashō*, p. 181.

20. Moreover, the recluse was only one of the many personae that Bashō experimented with at this time. Of the forty or so hokku that Bashō composed in the Tenna period (1681–84), only a handful—those most often anthologized—in fact describe the life and emotions of a "beggar." The haikai composed by Bashō after his "retreat" to Fukagawa in fact reveal a poet deeply interested in the material culture around him.

21. Cited by Inui Hiroyuki, "Jōkyō rengatai," in idem, *Bashō monogatari*, p. 67.

22. *Oi nikki* (1695, edited by Shikō) gives the following version.

At Hōgetsu's residence

ichibito ni	to the market shoppers
ide kore uran	I shall go and sell this:
kasa no yuki	a hatful of snow
	(KHT 6: 477)

23. Bashō's fondness for winter topics is reflected in the unusual number of poems on such topics as *fuyu no hi* (winter days), *fuyugomori* (winter hibernation), *kogarashi* (withering gusts), *ochiba* (fallen tree leaves), *shimo* (frost), *kōri* (ice), *kareno* (withered fields), *kareobana* (withered eulalia), *yuki* (snow), *shiwasu* (Twelfth Month), and *toshi no kure* (year's end).

24. *Shigure* became a symbol of uncertainty as a result of poems such as the following in the *Gosenshū* (951; Winter, no. 445):

kannazuki	In the Tenth Month
furimi furazumi	falling, not falling,
sadamenaki	the uncertain
shigure zo fuyu no	winter showers marking
hajime narikeri	winter's start.

25. In *Shinsen tsukuba shū*, p. 312.

26. In this hokku, which Bashō composed around 1683 and placed in *Empty Chestnuts* with the headnote "Crafting a poor rain hat by myself" ("Tezukara ame no wabigasa o harite"), Bashō changed only one word, replacing winter showers (*shigure*) with "Sōgi" (KHT 6: 45).

27. The same kind of movement is exemplified by the following hokku, which Bashō composed in 1687 and which appears at the beginning of *Oi no kobumi*.

In the beginning of the Tenth Month, the skies appeared uncertain, and I felt like the leaves scattering in the breeze, destination unknown.

"Traveler"
I shall be called—
    first winter showers

tabibito | to | waga | na | yobaren | hatsushigure
traveler | so | my | name | will-be-called | first-winter-shower

once more taking sasanquas
for my lodging

mata | sazanka | o | yado | yado | ni | shite
again | sasanqua | (acc.) | lodging | lodging | for | making

The host at Iwaki, a person called Chōtarō, composed the second verse and gave us a farewell dinner at Kikaku's residence. (NKBZ 41: 312–3)

The first hokku has frequently been read as an expression of the poet's resolve to travel, to endure the loneliness and uncertainty of travel symbolized by the winter showers. Read in the *fūkyō* mode, however, the poet simultaneously looks forward to and revels in winter showers, which allows him to enter the company of those "ancients" who were travelers. The prefix *hatsu* (first) in *hatsu-shigure* (first winter showers), like the *hatsu* in *hatsu-yuki* (first snow) or *hatsu-hana* (first cherry blossoms), implies excitement and anticipation, thereby transforming winter showers (*shigure*) from a medieval metaphor of impermanence into an object of *fūkyō* delight. The phrase "I shall be called 'traveler'" (*tabibito to wagana yobaremu*) also echoes the words of the *waki* priest who introduces himself at the beginning of the Noh play as a "traveler" before journeying to another world, particularly to meet the spirits of the dead. One manuscript version of the hokku is in fact accompanied by a text from a Noh play.

28. The following waka by Priest Jichin appears in the *Fubokushō* (Vol. 27. Msc. 9, Animals):

On hearing the wrenching voice of the monkey in the night rain

ko no shita no	Sadder than the
ame ni naku naru	monkey I hear crying
mashira yori mo	in the rain
waga sode no ue no	beneath the trees
tsuyu zo kanashiki	is the dew on my sleeves.

29. *Renju gappeki shū*, p. 115.

30. Origuchi Shinobu has defined *inja* (recluse) as someone who lives freely, standing outside society and its values, and sees three types—(1) those of high position who live a reclusive life, (2) priests, and (3) those of extremely low station, including prostitutes, outcasts, and *rōnin* (masterless samurai). Bashō turned this notion of the outsider into a new haikai ideal, with roots in Chinese and classical Japanese poetry.

31. Hori Nobuo, "Kyō," in *Sōgō Bashō jiten*, pp. 121–22.

32. According to a letter from Sanpū, one of Bashō's Edo disciples, to Biji, another disciple, on the 1st of the Sixth Month of Genroku 8 (1695), Bashō once said: "Even when it comes to the ancient poets, those categories of classical poetry such as the celebrations [*ga*] are not interesting. Without the landscape [*keiki*] of the lowly mountain dweller, the farmer, or the mountain hermit, there would be no deeply moving poems. Haikai is the same" (*Shōmon haijin shokan shū*, p. 203).

33. The *Renga entokushō* (ca. 1490–91), a renga handbook by Kensai, lists two kinds of *keiki* (landscape) poems, those that simply depict the landscape and those that are imbued with subjective emotion.

34. *Haikai jūron.* In Minami Shin'ichi, *Sōshaku Shikō no hairon,* pp. 771–72.

35. Ibid., p. 767.

36. The extant writings suggest that *sabi* had at least three fundamental, overlapping implications. On a physical or visual level, *sabi* (in a fashion that echoes the modern word *sabi,* "rust") meant the sense of depth that results when something implicitly brilliant is covered by subdued, muted colors or material. On a more psychological level, *sabi* implied a quiet beauty or depth in loneliness (*sabishisa*). *Sabi* also represented a general principle of emotional connotation in imagery, of *jō* (human emotion) submerged in *kei* (landscape/scene).

37. The hokku appears in *Komojishi shū,* a collection published in Genroku 6 (1693).

38. A similar passage appears in Kyorai's *Haikai mondō,* in the "Letter to Kyoriku" section. See Minami Shin'ichi, *Sōshaku Kyorai no hairon,* 1: 160–61.

39. The following passage appears in Kyorai's *Haikai mondō* (ca. 1687) (KHT 10: 107). "*Sabi* and *shiori* do not mean quiet loneliness in the conception [*shukō*], diction [*kotoba*], or contents [*utsuwa*] of the verse. *Sabi* and a verse of quiet loneliness [*sabishiki ku*] are different. *Shiori* does not mean pathos in the conception/design, diction, or subject matter. *Shiori* and a verse on pathos [*aware naru ku*] are different. *Sabi* and *shiori* are simply rooted within and manifested without. It is difficult to explain in words. If one must explain, one could say that *sabi* is the complexion [*iro*] of the verse. *Shiori* is the overtones [*yosei*] of the verse." According to this passage, *sabi* implied *sabishisa* (loneliness) and *kanjaku* (quietude); and *shiori* implied a state of *aware* (pathos or sorrow). But *sabi* and *shiori* are not necessarily found in the "conception," the "words," or the "subject matter" of the verse. A similar passage appears in *Kyoraishō* (NKBZ 51: 513–14).

40. The word *shiori,* which is written both *shihori* and *shiwori,* comes, in the former case, from the verb *shihoru,* which means "to be moist or wet," and in the latter, from the verb *shiworu,* which means "to shrivel, to wither." Both suggest an aesthetic of weakness and extreme sensitivity. According to *Kyoraishō,* "*Shiori* emerges in the *sugata* of the verse" (NKBZ 51: 513). In classical poetry treatises, *sugata* generally meant the connotations or overtones caused by the rhythm of the words, but Kyorai, following Shikō, used the term to mean poetic expression or imagery with emotional connotations.

41. Kyoriku's hokku appears in *Zoku sarumino* and *Infutagi*, where it is prefaced by the headnote, "Upon passing Utsu Mountain." Horikiri Minoru, *Shōmon meika kusen*, 2: 201–2.

42. *Kakyō.* In *Rengaron shū, Nōgakuron shū, Hairon shū*, p. 302.

43. *Yamanaka mondō*, KHT 10: 23. See Minami Shin'ichi, *Sōshaku Shikō no hairon*, p. 1055. In a similar vein, Kyorai writes in *Haikai mondō* (p. 107): "Generally speaking, *sabi* and *shiori* are critical for *fūga*. One must not forget them" (in Minami Shin'ichi, *Sōshaku Kyorai no hairon*, p. 223).

Chapter 4

1. Gefin, p. xii.

2. Cited in Kenner, *The Poetry of Ezra Pound*, p. 90.

3. *Sanzōshi* makes a similar observation: "The Master said, 'Haikai should be based on links by scent, reverberation, shadow, transference, or conjecture, on links that emerge from no particular form'" (NKBZ 51: 577).

4. The hokku appears under the topic of Ganjitsu (New Year's Day), in the spring section of *Enokoshū*. p. 67.

5. The following hokku, which Bashō composed in 1675 during his Teimon phase, reveals the same kind of structure.

in the mouths
of everyone crimson leaves
from the tree base

hitogoto | no | kuchi | ni | aru | nari | shitamomiji
each-person | 's | mouth | in | has | is | tongue-autumn-leaves

The two parts of the hokku—*kuchi* (mouths) and *momiji* (crimson autumn leaves)—are bridged by the intermediary homonym *shita*, which means both "tongue" and "lower" (lower leaves of a tree).

6. *Kokoro-zuke* can also mean a link based on a historical or literary allusion.

7. *Jūron'i benshō*, p. 591. The *Kyoraishō* elaborates on the scent link: "In the linked verse of the Bashō school, one avoids added verses that draw directly on the content of the previous verse. Instead, after carefully assessing the scene, the person, the person's occupation and circumstances, one should let go of the previous verse" (NKBZ 51: 508). These scent links, or links by "overtones" (*yosei*), differ from those found in classical renga in that they avoid *yoriai*, the established lexical associations based on classical precedent. Instead, the poet must link through new, non-conventional associations, often using haikai words. In the Genroku period, these scent links—along with the content links—were referred to as "distant links"

(*soku*) as opposed to word links, which were considered "close links" (*shinku*).

8. Jakobson, "Linguistics and Poetics" and "Two Aspects of Language and Two Types of Aphasic Disturbances," in idem, pp. 62–120.

9. The hokku appears in *Sarumino* under Bonchō's name.

10. The poem appears in *Arano*. The *Azuma nikki* version, which is slightly earlier, is *Kareeda ni karasu no tomaritaru ya aki no kure*.

11. See Buson's letter to Otofusa around An'ei 3 (1774); quoted in Ogata Tsutomu, "Haiga," in *Haibungaku daijiten*, pp. 665–66.

12. From a *kasen* (*Arigata ya yuki o kaorasu kaze no oto*) composed in 1689 (Genroku 2), during Bashō's journey to the Interior. Sora composed the previous verse, Bashō the added verse.

13. *Yamanaka sangin hyōgo*, which records Bashō's activities in 1689, gives the following example:

shiba karikokasu	chopping down brushwood
mine no sasamichi	on a bamboo path at the peak
matsu fukaki	deep amidst the pines—
hidari no yama wa	a thatched temple
suge no tera	on the mountain to the left

The Master said, "As a reflection [*utsuri*] of 'Chopping down brush-wood,' one should have 'Hailstones pouring down' in the first five syllables of the added verse."

The added verse subsequently was changed in accordance with Bashō's advice. In the revised version, "Hailstones pouring down" (*arare furu*), a violent winter image, "reflects" the brute action suggested in the previous verse. When defined as mutual reflection, *utsuri* becomes synonymous with link by scent in the broad sense. Indeed, in *Kyoraishō*, Bashō uses *utsuri* and *nioi-zuke* together as if they referred to the same phenomenon. The entire cluster of links could in fact be referred to as the poetics of reflection.

14. The seventh and eighth verses by Yaba and Bashō respectively, in a *kasen* (*Furiuri no gan aware nari ebisukō*) anthologized in *Sumidawara*.

15. *Uwaoki* (literally, topping) is a seasoning. *Uwa-no-sora* (literally, sky above) is a state in which one cannot concentrate due to an absorption with something else.

16. A large number of hokku, including those by Bashō, end with either *keri*, an exclamatory auxiliary verb, or the exclamatory particle *kana*, both of which initiate this circular pattern.

17. According to Ueno Yōzō ("Kireji danshō," p. 398), as many as one-third of the poems in the *Enokoshū* fall into this pattern.

18. Ogata Tsutomu, *Matsuo Bashō*, Nihon shijinsen 17, pp. 24–31.

19. The discussion of *toriawase* appears in the form of two debates between Bashō's disciples, one between Kyoriku and Kyorai and another between Kyoriku and Yaba. The earliest statements by Kyoriku, the foremost proponent of *toriawase* in the Bashō school, appear in the "Jitoku hatsumeiben" (Describing one's discoveries) section of *Haikai mondō* and in *Hentsuki* (co-authored with Riyū), both written in 1698 (Genroku 11). Kyorai responded to Kyoriku's position the following year in *Tabineron* (written in 1699). Kyoriku, apparently in response to Kyorai's response, returned to the subject in *Uda no hōshi* (published 1702), also written with Riyū. The debate between Kyoriku and Kyorai also appears in Kyorai's *Kyoraishō*. The debate between Kyoriku and Yaba appears in Kyoriku's *Kyoya shōsoku* (1714), and Kyoriku's *Rekidai kokkei den* (1715). In contrast to Kyoriku, who argued that all Bashō's hokku were *toriawase* and that one part must fall outside the sphere of the main "topic," Kyorai and Yaba believed that it represented only one, albeit important, form of the hokku.

20. Kyoriku composed this hokku in the winter of Genroku 5 (1692), when he visited the Bashō Hut at Fukugawa (Horikiri Minoru, *Shōmon meika kusen*, 2: 190).

21. In the "Jitoku hatsumeiben" section of *Haikai mondō*. For commentary, see Minami Shin'ichi, *Sōshaku Kyoriku no hairon*, pp. 241–42. Kyoriku makes similar observations in *Hentsuki*.

22. In the words of Kyorai, the poet must "leap beyond the circumference of the topic" (*Kyoraishō*, NKBZ 51: 498).

23. For commentary, see Minami Shin'ichi, *Sōshaku Kyoriku no hairon*, p. 735.

24. The cutting word is the adjectival ending *shi* in *ososhi* (late).

25. Freud, p. 11.

26. For commentary, see Minami Shin'ichi, *Sōshaku Kyoriku no hairon*, pp. 242–43.

27. The lowest tides of the year occurred on the Third Day of the Third Month and on the Eighth of the Fourth Month in the lunar calendar.

28. Another example of an "intermediary" that Kyoriku gives in *Haikai mondō* is the following hokku, which Bashō composed in 1694 and which also appears in *Separate Parlor (Betsuzashiki)*.

> hidden in the trees
> even the tea-leaf pickers must
>   be listening to the cuckoo!

kogakurete | chatsumi | mo | kiku | ya | hototogisu
hidden-in-tree | tea-picker | also | hear | ! | cuckoo

Although one could say that this is simply a combination of two sea-
sonal words, the cuckoo and the tea-leaf pickers, it is a notable poem
because the poet created the intermediary "hidden in the trees."

The opening phrase *kogakurete* (hidden in the trees) serves as an intermedi-
ary between two seasonal words for early summer, *hototogisu* (cuckoo) and
the *chatsumi*, the women who pick the tea leaves. The sound of the *hototo-
gisu* is so beautiful, it is implied, that the speaker feels certain that even the
chatsumi, whom he cannot see, are also listening to the cries of the *hototo-
gisu* as it flies overhead. (*Chatsumi* is now categorized as late spring.)

29. For commentary, see Minami Shin'ichi, *Sōshaku Kyorai no hairon*, 2:
340–41.

30. Composed by Bashō in the winter of Genroku 6 (Oct. 1693–Jan.
1694) and anthologized in *Zoku sarumino*.

31. Bashō's hokku, which was composed in the middle of the First
Month of Genroku 6 (Feb. 1693), appears in Bashō's hand on part of a
painting by Kyoriku, a disciple and professional artist.

32. For commentary, see Minami Shin'ichi, *Sōshaku Kyorai no hairon*, 1:
391–92.

33. In one of the central haiku debates of the Taishō period, Ōsuga
Otsuji argued for "niku isshō" (two phrases, one sentence) in a letter writ-
ten in 1914 to Usuda Arō (1879–1951), who later responded that the cut-
ting word was not necessary and instead advocated "ikku isshō" (one
phrase, one sentence).

34. Yamaguchi introduced the term *nibutsu shōgeki*, "collision of two
objects," which he borrowed from Eisenstein's notion of montage and ap-
plied to haiku.

35. In *Chōshi* (*Eldest Son*), which takes its title from this poem; see
Nakamura Kusatao, *Shū*, p. 18.

Chapter 5

EPIGRAPH: Barthes, *Roland Barthes*, p. 93.

1. The *yukiyō* or *sanku no watari* movement may have been influenced
by the Chinese poetic form of the *chüeh-chü* (J. *zekku*), which is divided in-
to four parts or lines: the "introduction" (J. *ki*), the continuation or exten-
sion (*shō*), the turn or twist (*ten*), and the conclusion (*ketsu*). The *wakiku*,
the second verse of a haikai sequence, follows the hokku, the opening
verse, much as the *shō* follows the first line of the *chüeh-chü*, that is, by
supporting and extending the opening verse; and the *daisanku*, the third

verse, boldly moves away from the hokku, much like the *ten* in the *chüeh-chü*. In haikai, however, there is no *ketsu* or "concluding verse" (J. *kekku*).

2. *Yamanaka mondō*, pp. 23–25.

3. *Minashiguri* (1683), one of the earliest anthologies to include Bashō's poetry, contains only *kasen*.

4. As the *Kyoraishō* (NKBZ 51:510) notes:

The late Master said, "A sequence that is uniform in tone from the front of the first sheet to the back of the second sheet is unsightly."

Kyorai commented, "The front [*omote*] of a haikai sequence should be composed quietly. The back of the first sheet through the middle of the front of the second sheet should contain verses that are special or unusual. From there to the back of the second sheet should be composed lightly, without effort. When one arrives at the end of a sequence, the participants will begin to tire of each other, and if one continues to compose outstanding verses, the sequence will bog down and be incomplete. But if the participants remain enthusiastic to the very end and an excellent verse emerges, one need not stop it. One should simply not feel the need to compose an excellent verse at the end."

5. In the *kasen*, autumn and spring are usually restricted to three successive verses.

6. The moon had to appear in the fifth verse on the front of the first sheet, the seventh verse on the back of the first sheet, and the eleventh verse on the front of the second sheet. In later periods, the second moon verse tended to appear in the eighth verse rather than in the seventh verse of the back of the first sheet.

7. Cherry blossoms appeared in the eleventh verse on the back of the first sheet and in the fifth verse on the back of the second sheet.

8. The scribe made sure that the participants followed the rules, reminding the participants, for example, when a "moon" or a "cherry blossom" verse was approaching.

9. In the *degachi*, the haikai master, in selecting the verses, would attempt to maintain variety and balance so that the same participant did not go twice in a row or dominate the rest.

10. *Ōsaka dokugin shū* (Osaka solo sequences collection; published 1675), which established the reputation of Sōin's Danrin school, for example, consisted of ten solo sequences by ten different Osaka poets, including Saikaku, who eventually took the form to a new extreme in his *yakazu* (countless arrow) thousand-link solo performances.

11. Japanese recluses (*inja*) can be divided into two broad categories, those that left the secular world, usually taking the tonsure and devoting themselves to the Buddhist path (referred to as *hijiri*, *intonsha*, or *tonseisha*), and those who abandoned their secular professions and escaped into the world of art or poetry. Kamo no Chōmei (1153–1216), who retreated to a ten-foot-square hut after taking the tonsure, is the first type of recluse (*inja*), for whom the grass hermitage (*sōan*) came to represent a step toward the Buddhist Pure Land. In the course of the medieval period, however, the *sōan* also evolved into a place for assembly (*yoriai*) where people could practice linked verse, tea ceremony, and other communal arts. When Bashō left his profession as a haikai master (*haikaishi* or *haikai tenja*) in Edo to retire to Fukagawa, on the bank of the Sumida River, he became a recluse (*inja*) in the second sense, and the Bashō Hut became a gathering place for haikai composition.

12. *Winter Days* contains five linked verse sequences, of which the first is *Withering Gusts*, and differs from the later Bashō-school haikai anthologies in that it does not contain any hokku, perhaps reflecting the importance that the Nagoya poets placed on linked verse.

13. Before the arrival of the participants (*renju*), the host, who was chosen in advance and played an important role, would place an inkstone box (*suzuribako*)—which included brushes, water, inkstone, and gimlet—and poetry sheets (*kaishi*) on a low writing table (*bundai*) and leave them on the alcove or altar (*toko*), which was decorated with a divine image, often that of Sugawara Michizane, the god of poetry, whose spirit functioned as a muse and protector. (In the eighteenth century, haikai poets frequently replaced Michizane with an image of Bashō.) The host would also place inkstones (*suzuri*) at the seat of each participant. Arriving before the others, the scribe would place the low writing table in front of the alcove, where he recorded the verses, directly facing the other participants. At the end, the scribe would write the date and place on the poetry sheets, which he would bind and place before the divine image. This formal procedure, which was developed by classical renga poets, was followed, usually in a more relaxed, freer fashion, by haikai poets.

14. In a *hyakuin*, with five participants, each participant went every fifth time, leaving a four-verse interval between appearances, but in the *kasen*, this created an imbalance, which was remedied by the arrangement mentioned in the text.

15. The text of *Kogarashi* is based on that in *Bashō shichibu shū*, SKBT 70, pp. 3–7.

16. *Kyōku* and Chikusai are haikai words.

17. The most reliable of the older commentaries on this sequence is the

Etsujin Commentary (*Etsujin chū*) by Etsujin, a poet from the Nagoya area, who became a Bashō disciple around this time.

18. Some commentators read the word *kyōku* as a prefatory statement, and others see it as part of the hokku. Bokuin wrote the following hokku when Bokuin left Ōgaki together with Bashō:

> gone mad with poetry—
> two of them
>   in the withering gusts

uta | monogurui | futari | kogarashi | sugata | kana
poetry | madness | two | winter-gust | appearance | !

19. The phrase *kogarashi no mi* may come from a Fujiwara Teika poem in the *Shinkokinshū* (Love, no. 1320)—*kiewabinu utsurou hito no aki no iro ni mi o kogarashi no mori no shitatsuyu*—in which the word *kogarashi* means both "withering gusts" (*kogarashi*) and "to burn oneself" (*mi o kogasu*) from excessive love.

20. *Sazanka* (sasanqua), a haikai word, belongs to the *tsubaki*, or camellia family. In the Bashō school, the *kasa*, a large hat that provided protection from rain, snow, and sun, became a symbol of the traveler, especially the *fūkyō* traveler.

21. Ogata Tsutomu has pointed out to me that the explosive sound, particularly the "t" syllables in *taso ya tobashiru*, directly echoes the strong "k" alliteration in *kyōku kogarashi*, in the previous verse.

22. A miscellaneous, non-seasonal verse is normally inserted between one season and the next, but it is not unusual in the *omote* (first six verses) of the *kasen* to move directly from one season to another in preparation for the moon verse, which must appear in the fifth verse of the front of the first side.

23. Another widely held interpretation is that the Master of Early Dawn with sasanqua in his hat is opening up a wine shop (*sakaya*), which sells liquor.

24. *Chirichiri* and *kome* are haikai words.

25. The last verse of the *omote*, called *orihashi*, and the first verse of the *ura*, the *oritate*, were supposed to be the same season. This verse, the first of the *ura*, is a miscellaneous verse (no season), and thus a violation, but since the previous four verses were autumn, one more than normally allowed, the non-seasonal verse creates the necessary change.

26. *Hayasu* (to grow) is a haikai word.

27. Or it could be someone taking refuge in the grass hut of the recluse.

28. *Shinobu* here means "to hide" rather than "to long for," but it nevertheless remains a love word.

29. According to Ogata Tsutomu (*Bashō no sekai*, p. 109), in the Edo period, when a woman of low birth became involved with a man of some means and bore him a son, she was often stripped of her child, particularly if the man had no other heirs, and abandoned. Such a woman could not divorce or remarry until she had served for three years as a nun in a temple.

30. *Sotoba* and *sugosugo* are haikai words.

31. *Kagebō*, a haikai word, is an abbreviation for *kagebōshi* (shadow).

32. *Karaie* (empty house) and *hin* (poverty) are haikai words.

33. *Tanaka* may be the name of a place (Koman of Tanaka), but most commentators believe that it means simply "middle of the rice field" (*tanaka*).

34. The use of the verb "to drop" (*otsuru*) rather than the standard "to scatter" (*chiru*) is haikai-esque.

35. A "shadow link" may in fact suggest a figure or event that never existed.

36. The erotic overtones have caused some commentators to call this verse and the previous verse, both of which are spring verses, "love verses" (*koi no ku*).

37. *Norimono* (palanquin) is a haikai word.

38. Ogata Tsutomu, *Bashō no sekai*, p. 132.

39. *Ika* and *urakata* are haikai words.

40. It is not clear if the original Japanese is *tokeji* (I can not solve) or *tokeshi* (it was solved).

41. *Shūsui itto* is a haikai phrase.

42. In the Heian period the *mukuge* was often confused with the *asagao*, or morning glory, which faded the same day that it bloomed and consequently became a symbol of impermanence.

43. *Mi* and *konoshiro* are haikai words.

44. *Haramu* is a haikai word.

45. It could also be another woman (other than the woman with the basket on her head) who is praying.

46. Ueno Yōzō (*Bashō shichibu shū*, Koten kōdoku siriizu, p. 73) argues that the *mayukaki* was held to celebrate the birth of a child.

47. *Oriyu* and *koshite* are haikai words.

48. Almost all Bashō's sequences end with spring, which was considered a felicitous season.

49. Cited by Hattori Sachio, "Haikai to kabuki," in *Haibungaku daijiten*, pp. 696–97.

50. Kira Sueo, "Genroku Kyōto haidan no kōsei," in idem, *Genroku Kyōto haidan kenkyū*, pp. 3–20. See also Kon Eizō, "Haikai keizai shakaigaku."

51. *Maeku-zuke* actually took various forms. The most popular form in the Genroku period was the *goku-zuke*, in which five *maeku*, or "topics" (*dai*) were presented at one time, with the participants composing *maeku-zuke* or verse caps for each.

52. Suzuki Katsutada, "Tōdai haikaishi no jittai to Bashō," p. 170.

53. Teishitsu, for example, began training with Teitoku at the age of eighteen and became a *tenja* at age 42, in 1651 (Keian 4). The Danrin school was far less strict, apparently requiring only the presentation of a *manku* (ten thousand verses).

54. Kira Sueo, "Ten," in *Sōgō Bashō jiten*, p. 173.

55. In a letter addressed to Fugyoku, Kyorai describes an episode in which he corrected a *kasen* sequence sent to him by Ranyū and Rayō but for which he did not receive compensation. Kyorai, who did not want to be considered a professional marker, had another poet, Shadō, write down the comments and collect the fee. The episode appears in a letter from Kyorai to Fugyoku. For the letter, see Minami Shin'ichi, *Sōshaku Kyorai no hairon*, 1: 38–41.

56. According to an anecdote in *Ishijari* (1725), when Tōrin asked the master if he could become a marker, Bashō responded: "Do you want to give up haikai? Haikai and the profession of the marker do not go together. It is better to become a beggar" (cited in Suzuki Katsutada, "Tōdai haikaishi no jittai to Bashō," p. 180).

57. Bashō vehemently attacked *tentori haikai* and lamented its popularity in a series of letters to his Kamigata disciples (Chinseki, Kyokusui, and Kyorai) from the Second Month to the Fifth Month of Genroku 5 (1692) and again in a letter to Kyoriku in the autumn of the same year.

58. *Bashō bunshū*, pp. 208–11. For text and commentary, see Muramatsu Tomotsugu, *Bashō no tegami*, pp. 136–42.

59. The *tentori haikai* that Bashō severely criticized here and in other letters to his Kamigata disciples apparently referred not to the marking of *kasen* and *hyakuin*, of extended linked verse, but to the marking of *maeku-zuke*, a practice that Bashō never engaged in and that he found repulsive.

60. *Kyō habutae*, a haikai handbook and record of Kyoto haikai poets published in 1691, divides haikai poets into three categories: the markers (*tenja*), who were professionals and who made a living based on fees for points (*tenryō*); haikai teachers (*haikaishi*), who either did not have as much experience as markers or composed haikai as a hobby while they pursued other professions and whose status was lower than that of a marker; and composers (*sakka*), who were amateurs and who were the lowest in prestige. Bashō and his Kyōto disciples are listed in the middle category (Kira Sueo, *Genroku Kyōto haidan kenkyū*, p. 23).

61. Ogata Tsutomu and Matsuzaki Yoshio, "Maeku-zuke and karumi," in Ogata, *Bashō hikkei*, pp. 174–79.

Chapter 6

EPIGRAPH: Volosinov, pp. 85–86 (Bakhtin is thought to have co-authored this book).

1. Yonetani Iwao ("Bashō aisatsu ku no suikō ni tsuite," pp. 54–61) claims that 46 percent of Bashō's hokku in his travel literature are greetings or expressions of gratitude.

2. Kidō, *Rengaron shū II*, p. 446.

3. As Dohō's *Sanzōshi* reveals, Bashō followed the tradition established by his renga and haikai predecessors:

> From long ago it has been said that the host composes the second verse, although that depends on the circumstances. From the distant past, the hokku—called the guest's opening verse—was always composed by the guest as a greeting to be answered by the author of the second verse. In the words of the Master, "The second verse is composed by the host and is, in this regard, a greeting." He taught us that even verses strictly on snow, the moon, or cherry blossoms should include the spirit of greeting. (NKBZ 51: 536–37)

4. The hokku, which appears in *Nozarashi kikō*, was composed by Bashō in the Fourth Month of Jōkyō 2 (May 7, 1685). *Unohana* (deutzia) is a seasonal word for summer.

5. *Shohon taishō Bashō haibun kubun shū*, p. 534.

6. *Uete* (planting) is the continuative form of the *shimo nidan* verb *uu* (to plant).

7. *Haikai shogaku shō*, p. 362.

8. Scholars are uncertain whether the second line of the poem should be *umi ni iretaru* (pouring into the sea) or *umi ni iritaru* (entering into the sea). Grammatically, the second version is more logical, but both variants exist.

9. *Hotaru* (firefly) is a seasonal word for summer.

10. Another famous haibun greeting to a host is "Pure Heart Dwelling" ("Sharakudō no ki"), which was written in the Third Month of 1690 while Bashō stayed at the home of Shadō, or Chinseki (d. 1737), a young doctor in Zeze in Ōmi and the editor of the *Gourd* (*Hisago*; 1690).

> The mountain is still and nurtures the spirit; the water moves and consoles the heart. Between this stillness and movement lies the dwelling of Chinseki of the Hamada family. Here one can gaze forever at the beautiful landscape, compose poetry, and be cleansed

of the dust of the world. Hence, the name Pure Dwelling. At its gate hangs a warning, "Worldly knowledge may not enter," which is better and more refined than Sōkan's comic poem, "The best guest never comes, the next best comes but doesn't stay, the worst lodges for two nights." The extremely simple dwelling has two small tea rooms, where Chinseki practices the *wabi* spirit of Sen Rikyū and Takeno Jōō without being preoccupied with their complex rules of tea. The Bay of Omono, wearing Seta on its left and Karasaki on its right like two sleeves, embraces Lake Biwa and faces Mount Mikami. Lake Biwa appears in the shape of a lute, causing the wind in the pines to harmonize with the sound of the waves. From an angle, one can see Mount Hiei and the high peak of Hira, while Otowa Mountain and Mount Ishiyama rest on one's shoulder. In the spring, the Pure Dwelling wears the cherry blossoms of Nagara in its hair; and in the autumn, it dresses in front of the moon of Mirror Mountain. The setting is like the makeup of a beautiful woman, light one day and heavy the next, causing the admiring heart to change with the scenery.

> cherry blossoms
> blowing in from all directions—
>   waves of the grebes

shihō | yori | hana | fukiirete | nio | no | nami
four-directions | from | blossom | blowing-in | dabchick | 's | waves
(KBZ 6:452–53)

The "waves of the grebes" (*nio no nami*) refers to Lake Biwa, known for its *nio* (grebes), which float up and down between the waves.

11. This *kaishi*, or rectangular poetry sheet, is not to be confused with the *kaishi* that was the paper record of a haikai sequence.

12. In the medieval period, classical renga masters frequently traveled great distances, visiting powerful and wealthy provincial patrons, who invited, treated, and supported their favorite poetry teachers in exchange for their company, judgment, and instruction. It was customary for a renga master to write about his journey and to send the travel journal to the provincial host as an expression of gratitude for his patronage and hospitality.

13. The text and the illustrations of *Kasshi ginkō emaki* can be found in *Kōhon Bashō zenshū*, special volume (*bekkan*), pp. 180–99.

14. For evidence that *Nozarashi kikō* was written for Bokuin, see Yonetani Iwao, "*Nozarashi kikō* ni okeru Bashō," pp. 76–85; and Ogata Tsutomu, "Nozarashi, sutego," in idem, *Za no bungaku*, pp. 102–19.

15. Yonetani Iwao ("*Nozarashi kikō* ni okeru Bashō") argues that *Nozarashi kikō* was written in two stages: the first stage was up until this poem, and the second stage was a kind of sequel.

16. The version in *Hakusenshū* ends with *fuji no yuki.*

17. Ogata Tsutomu, "Chinkon no ryojō."

18. An earlier variation of this passage was:

Tokoku had encountered misfortune and was living at Irago Point, where I visited him. As we were speaking, I heard the voice of a hawk.

a hawk in the flesh
is more reliable than
one in a dream

yume | yori | mo | utsutsu | no | taka | zo | tanomoshiki
dream | than | also | reality | 's | hawk | ! | reliable

The headnote suggests that Bashō had constantly been dreaming of Tokoku, represented here by the hawk, and was now overjoyed to be finally with him.

19. On the composition of *Oi no kobumi,* see Takahashi Shōji, "*Oi no kobumi* no yōkyoku kōsei ni tsuite"; Ogata Tsutomu, "Chinkon no ryojō"; and Abe Masami, "*Oi no kobumi* no seiritsu." All three scholars argue, for different reasons, that *Oi no kobumi* was written long after the actual journey and that the death of Tokoku was the primary motive for composition.

20. In the original version the first line was *ana muzan ya* ("Ah, how piteous!"), which had excess syllables.

21. The Sanemori hokku is part of a sequence of six hokku in *Oku no hosomichi* on the sorrow of autumn in the Hokuriku region, beginning with the lament on Isshō's death and ending with three poems on the "autumn wind" (*akikaze*).

22. *Zōtanshū*, p. 43.

23. In the following hokku in *Oi no kobumi*, for example, the traveler, who is visiting Yoshino, a place well known for its cherry blossoms, envisions himself as a *shite* (protagonist) in a Noh play attending a sake party beneath the cherry blossoms.

in the shadow of a tree
scooping sake with a fan—
scattering cherry blossoms

ōgi | nite | sake | kumu | kage | ya | chiru | sakura
fan | with | wine | scoop | shadow | = | scatter | cherry-blossom

24. The following passage appears immediately after Bashō's visit to Shirakawa Barrier in *Narrow Road to the Interior*:

Beside this dwelling stood a large chestnut tree. A monk who had turned his back on the world had taken shelter under the shade of this tree. I was quietly reminded of Saigyō's poem about gathering chestnuts. In my notebook, I jotted down:

The Chinese character for chestnut consists of the graphs for "tree" and "west" and must have some connection to Amida's Western Paradise. They say that throughout his life Priest Gyōki used the wood of this tree for his cane and the pillar of his hut.

> flowers overlooked
> by the people of this world—
> chestnut tree by the eaves

yo | no | hito | no | mitsukenu | hana | ya | noki | no | kuri
world | 's | person | 's | not-find | flower | : | eave | 's | chestnut
(NKBZ 41: 352)

The unobtrusive but attractive flower of the chestnut tree (*kuri*), a seasonal word for summer, is now blooming under the eaves. As with many of Bashō's greetings to living hosts, Bashō praises the virtues of the spiritual figure by showing his affection and admiration for the person's reclusive lifestyle and dwelling.

25. For an English translation of *Yugyō yanagi, The Priest and the Willow*, see Keene, *Twenty Plays*, pp. 220–36.

Chapter 7

EPIGRAPHS: Bloom, p. 19; *Sanzōshi*, NKBZ 51: 550.

1. *Renju gappeki shū*, p. 118.

2. Bashō appears to have used *Mountain Well* (*Yama no i*) or its revised version *Zō yama no i* or *Zoku yama no i* extensively.

3. Baisei's *Ruisenshū*, which provides extensive lists of lexical associations, both of classical and haikai origin, is indispensable for appreciating the word links in Teimon and Danrin haikai.

4. The *kiyose*, which lists seasonal words and topics but gives no examples, is generally considered a subcategory of the *saijiki*, which gives both seasonal words and poetry examples.

5. *Renga shihōshō*, pp. 233, 234.

6. *Yama no i*, p. 421.

7. The hokku by Kyūho (1594–1656) appears in the spring section under the topic of *yanagi* (willow) in the first volume of *Enokoshū*, p. 71.

8. *Renju gappeki shū*, p. 94.

9. *Chikuenshō*, p. 426.

10. *Shōtetsu monogatari*, p. 176. For an English translation of *Shōtetsu monogatari*, see Brower and Carter, pp. 77–78.

11. Listed in the section on Suruga Province in *Haimakura*, p. 425.

12. "Fox trap" (*kitsune wana*) refers to a word in the previous verse (*maeku*).

13. *Kyoraishō* notes: "The former Master said, 'Generally speaking, hokku written on a painting or on a famous place should be composed in such a way that it appears to be a poem on that painting or on that particular place'" (NKBZ 51: 487).

14. As the opening verse, the hokku served as a greeting to the host of the haikai session and required a seasonal word that would reflect the occasion of the gathering. Bashō never broke this rule. A passage in *Sanzōshi* reveals, however, that he allowed for non-seasonal hokku—on topics such as travel, famous places, and love—when there was no need for a poetic greeting. Bashō appears to have made this exception because hokku on poetic places (*utamakura*), travel, or love contained their own poetic essence that might conflict with that of the seasonal topic.

15. For these texts, see the bibliography.

16. *Yatsururu* modifies both *mugimeshi* and *koi*, meaning "emaciating barley and love."

17. For text and commentary, Minami Shin'ichi, *Sōshaku Kyorai no hairon*, 1: 337–38.

18. The *take uuru* (bamboo-planting) poem may have been composed in the summer of 1688 (Jōkyō 5), but the date is uncertain.

19. *Daikonhiki* appears in some early Teimon handbooks such as the *Haikai shogaku shō* but not in *Zō yama no i* (Expanded *Mountain Well*).

20. *Sanzōshi* (NKBZ 51: 567) gives this hokku as an example of a poem on the topic of *zansho*. The difficulty of identifying the implied topic is evident in a passage in *Oi nikki* that reveals that Shikō, one of Bashō's best disciples, had to confirm the seasonal topic with Bashō himself.

21. In *Bashō ō gyōjō ki* (Memorial to Bashō the Elder; 1695), Rotsū, Bashō's disciple, observes: "[Bashō] stopped at the hermitage in Awazu, rested there for a while, and composed on the topic of lingering heat." In *Hakusenshū*, the hokku is mistakenly placed in the summer section rather than in the autumn section, suggesting the difficulty of identifying the seasonal topic.

22. *Sanzōshi* (NKBZ 51: 567) gives this hokku as an example of the *yokan* topic.

23. A letter from Kyorai to Dohō indicates that Fūkoku's poem was composed in the autumn of 1695 (Genroku 8).

24. Kyorai's corrected version suggests that with the approach of evening, the noisy crowds have left the temple and the poet is left with a feeling of loneliness, which is diminished or obscured by the sound of the evening temple bells, which give him emotional strength.

25. For text and commentary, see Minami Shin'ichi, *Sōshaku Kyoriku no hairon*, p. 411. An almost identical passage appears in Kyoriku's "Jitoku hatsumei ben" section of *Haikai mondō*, KHT 10: 158.

26. Kyorai took exception to Kyoriku's assessment of Kikaku's poem, which he felt stressed the unusual at the expense of the traditional *hon'i*. As Kyorai observed in *Tabine ron*, "A bush warbler that inverts its body is a playful warbler. A playful warbler is not found in early spring" (KHT 10: 197). In *Kyoraishō*, Kyorai elaborated:

uguisu no	bush warbler
mi o sakasama ni	turning its body upside down—
hatsune kana	first song of the year
	—Kikaku

uguisu no	bush warbler
iwa ni sugarite	clinging to a large rock—
hatsune kana	first song of the year
	—Sokō

Kyorai: "In Kikaku's verse, a bush warbler, excited by the warm spring weather, has gone mad. I find nothing interesting in the notion of a young [first] bush warbler that has inverted its body. It is difficult to understand the phrase, 'The first song of the year.' Sokō's verse does not present an image of the singing warbler. If a warbler is clinging to a crag, it means that it has been frightened and has flown there for safety, or that it is gathering food, or that it is flying about, using the crag as a resting place. Generally speaking, in composing on a topic, one must grasp the heart [*honjō*] of the object. If one does not do that, one will be distracted by the novelty of the subject or by new words, and one will miss the essence. Becoming overly attached to the object can be distracting. This is what they call losing the poetic essence. Even a veteran like Kikaku sometimes fails. Needless to say, a beginner must be cautious." (NKBZ 51: 454–55)

27. *Renju gappeki shū*, p. 104, lists the following *yoriai*, or classical associative words, under the entry for *hototogisu*: "deutzia [*unohana*], orange

blossoms [*hanatachibana*], mountain, passing showers [*murasame*], moon, amid the clouds, one voice, crying endlessly, the Fifth Month, first song, waking up, dewdrops from the forest, don't add tears."

28. The version that appears in *Zoku minashiguri* is *Hototogisu nakinaki tobu zo isogawashi.*

29. Another possible pre-text is the following poem in the *Kokinshū* (Travel, no. 409), attributed to Hitomaro.

honobono to	Faintly,
Akashi no ura no	in the morning mist
asagiri ni	on Akashi Bay,
shimagakureyuku	it disappears behind an island,
fune o shi zo omou	the boat I long for.

In Bashō's hokku, the flight of the disappearing *hototogisu*, which the poet implicitly longs to see, becomes the path of the ship, which "disappears behind" Awajishima, the "one island."

30. In the Heian period, *yokotau* (to lay sideways) was a transitive *shimo nidan* verb, but Bashō appears to use *yokotau* here as an intransitive verb.

31. Ogata Tsutomu, *Matsuo Bashō*, Nihon shijinsen, pp. 95–100.

32. Gombrich, p. 66.

Chapter 8

EPIGRAPHS: Walter Benjamin, "The Work of Art in the Age of Mechanical Reproduction," in idem, p. 223; Bloom, p. 30.

1. The area now called Tōhoku (the Northeast) was formerly called Dewa, on the Japan Sea side, and Michinoku, on the Pacific Ocean side. Michinoku was also called Mutsu as well as Ōshū or Oku, from which *Oku no hosomichi* takes its name.

2. The authorship of the *Tōkan kikō* is uncertain—it is sometimes thought to be Minamoto Mitsuyuki (d. 1244) or his son Chikayuki (d. 1272–77?)—but in the Genroku period both were attributed to Kamo no Chōmei, the noted author of the *Hōjōki* (Ten-foot square hut; 1212). *Tōkan kikō* (1242?) was published as *Chōmei michi no ki* (Chōmei's travel account) and *Kaidōki* (1223) as *Kamo no Chōmei kaidōki* (Kamo no Chōmei's travels on the seaboard). The following passage in *Backpack Notes* reveals that Bashō had the same view.

As for travel diaries, ever since Tsurayuki, Chōmei, and Nun Abutsu excelled in describing in detail the emotions of travel, the work that has followed has all been imitation; no one has been able to escape from the dregs of their predecessors. Needless to say, someone with my lack of talent cannot match those writers. Anyone can write,

"On that day it rained; in the afternoon it cleared. At that place was a pine; over there flowed a river with such and such a name." But unless one has the unusualness and newness of Su Tung-p'o and Huang T'ing-Chien, one has nothing to say. (NKBZ 41: 313–14)

While revealing his admiration for Tsurayuki, Chōmei, and Abutsu as model authors of the travel genre, Bashō expresses profound dissatisfaction with existing travel diaries and a determination to give new life to the form. Travel literature, he noted, should have the "unusualness and newness of Su Tung-p'o and Huang T'ing-chien," which suggests a concern not with the recording of external facts but with internal truth, with what stimulates the heart, and with travel literature as a form of poetry.

3. *Honchō bunkan*, pp. 1–2.

4. *Honchō monzen*, pp. 14. Also Minami Shin'ichi, *Sōshaku Kyoriku no hairon*, p. 951.

5. Also Minami Shin'ichi, *Sōshaku Kyorai no hairon*, 2: 293.

6. Burton Watson has translated *Genjūan no ki* as "The Hut of the Phantom Dwelling," in Watson and Sato, pp. 292–95. Donald Keene has translated *Genjūan no fu*, another variant, as "Prose Poem on the Unreal Dwelling," in his *Anthology of Japanese Literature*, pp. 374–76.

7. *Oku no hosomichi* may also represent an extension of *Oi no kobumi*. In the preface to the version of *Oi no kobumi* published in 1709 by Otokuni, the Ōmi disciple entrusted with the unfinished manuscript, Otokuni noted: "The Master gathered together the short records of the road, which he had made during his pilgrimage to the Kamigata area, and called them *Backpack Notes*. They have gradually accumulated into a large number of written pieces." Otokuni probably compiled and edited a number of haibun that Bashō wrote or rewrote around 1690–91 (Genroku 3–4), long after the *Oi no kobumi* journey in 1687–88, and that reflect his thinking when he began to write *Oku no hosomichi*, which incorporated many of the elements of *Oi no kobumi* and accomplished what it may have aimed at but failed to do: successfully combine the traditional travel diary genre with a new haibun ideal.

8. Also Minami Shin'ichi, *Sanzōshi sōshaku*, p. 59.

9. In writing his new haibun, Bashō drew heavily on Chinese prose models, particularly Six Dynasties parallel prose (*p'ien-wen*)—which used four- and six-word parallel phrases, emphasized verbal parallelism, and stressed tonal euphony and allusion—*and* the Ancient Style (*ku-wen*), which emerged in the T'ang period in reaction to the *p'ien-wen* style and which often generated a rhythm based on the four-character line.

10. In "On Parting from Kyoriku" ("Kyoriku ribetsu no kotoba"; NKBZ 41: 451), Bashō wrote: "I made painting my master, and poetry my

disciple." The pairs—painting and poetry, master and disciple—are not binary opposites so much as reflections or extensions of each other. As Horikiri Minoru (*Haibun kenkyū josetsu*, p. 212) has pointed out, this particular style offers a bird's-eye view of the landscape, a multi-angle, shifting lens.

11. Other examples include the contrast between the colorful shrine of the Shiogama deity, which appears in the front and which sparkles in the bright morning light, and the Kehi Shrine at Tsuruga, in the back, which is enshrouded by clouds and darkness, under the light of the evening moon. The lantern in front of the Shiogama Shrine brings back the memory of Izumi Saburō, a warrior who earned fame 500 years earlier, whereas the sand-carrying ceremony at Kehi Shrine reminds Bashō of an equally distant past.

12. Matsushima appears in 52 poems in *Matsuba meisho waka shū*, another well-used handbook for poetic places.

13. A reference to the famous tidal bore on the Ch'ien-t'ang River in Che-chiang.

14. *Shiogoshi* (literally, "tide crossings") refers either to the shallows at the entrance of the bay or to a place in the bay by that name or both.

15. Kisagata become associated with Nōin as a result of the following poem (*Goshūishū*, Travel, no. 519).

On the way to Dewa Province, he composed this poem at a place called Kisagata.

yo no naka wa	My life has been
kakute mo hekeri	spent this way:
Kisagata no	making the grass hut
ama no tomaya o	of the fisherfolk at Kisagata
waga yado ni shite	my lodging.

The other famous poem on Kisagata, a *Shinkokinshū* (Travel, no. 972) poem by Fujiwara Akinaka, is:

During the reign of the retired emperor Horikawa, this poem on travel was offered as part of a hundred-poem collection.

Sasurauru	Since it is my fate
waga mi ni shi areba	to wander,
Kisagata ya	I lodge again and again
ama no tomaya ni	in the grass hut of the fisherfolk
amata tabinenu	at Kisagata.

16. The poem does not appear in *Sankashū*, the standard collection of Saigyō's poems.

17. Hori Nobuo, "*Haibunshū* toshite no *Oku no hosomichi*," p. 54.

18. A copy of an early draft of *Oku no hosomichi* in the hand of Sora is extant and referred to as the Sora text. Soryū, a Bashō disciple and a skilled calligrapher, produced two exquisitely penned copies of the final version, now called the Kakimori (Shiei) and the Nishimura texts. Bashō chose the Nishimura text for his final text and bound it with a cover that bears the words *Oku no hosomichi* in his own hand. Bashō carried the Nishimura text during his last journey in 1694 (Genroku 7) and left it with his brother Matsuo Han'zaemon, who, following Bashō's deathbed instructions, turned it over to Kyorai, his chief Kyoto disciple. Kyorai had it published by Izutsuya Shōbei in Kyoto a number of years after Bashō's death. The earliest printed version is from 1702 (Genroku 15). Some scholars consider the Sora text to be closer to the original than the Nishimura text, which was the basis for the printed versions circulated in the Tokugawa and modern periods. The translations in this study are based on the Nishimura (Soryū) text, the base text for *Matsuo Bashō*, NKBZ 41, which gives the Sora and Kakimori variations in the headnotes. In late 1996, it was announced that an original manuscript in Bashō's hand, with his own corrections, had been discovered in an Osaka used-book store.

19. These notes are referred to as *Haikai kakidome*, or *Haikai Notes*, which is part of *Sora tabi nikki* (Sora's Travel Diary). KBZ 6, pp. 240–77. Also printed in Hagiwara Yasuo, *Bashō Oku no hosomichi*, pp. 131–152.

20. Imoto Nōichi, "*Oku no hosomichi* ron," and "*Oku no hosomichi* no watakushi shōsetsusei," in idem, *Bashō no bungaku no kenkyū*.

21. Joseph Kitagawa (pp. 127–36) has distinguished three major types of pilgrimages in early Japan—to sacred mountains, to temples and shrines, and to sacred places based on a faith in certain holy men who are believed to have hallowed those places by their visits—all of which appear in *Narrow Road to the Interior*.

22. The first version was recorded in Sora's travel diary, the second was preserved in *Hatsusemi* and *Hakusenshū*. The third and last version, in *Oku no hosomichi*, was probably composed in 1694.

23. *Tsuki* (moon) homophonically implies both the verb *tsuku*, "to exhaust" or "to be gone" (with regard to the clouds), and the verb *tsuku* (to build up), suggesting the emergence of the mountain. The verb *kuzuru* (to collapse) inverts the usual association of "clouds" (*kumo*) with the verb *tachinoboru* (to rise up).

24. Some scholars believe that the hokku is an allusive variation on the following waka in the *Shinchokusenshū* (Love 1, no. 657).

koi no yama	Mountain of Love:
shigeki osasa no	as I soon as I make my way
tsuyu wakete	through the dew
irisomuru yori	of the bamboo grass,
nururu sode kana	I wet my sleeves.

25. Hirai Shōbin, *Oku no hosomichi nyūmon*, pp. 107–10.

26. Sakurai Takejirō, "*Oku no hosomichi* shippitsu ni kansuru ichi shiron," p. 49.

27. *Utamakura*, the basic building block of the traditional Japanese travel diary, appears in two basic forms: a static form in which an entire prose section is devoted to a single *utamakura* and a fluid form, sometimes referred to as a *michiyuki*, or poetic journey, in which the text moves quickly from one *utamakura* to the next, generating a path of poetic associations in the reader's mind. Of the 40 different *utamakura* that appear in *Oku no hosomichi*, about a third are of the static type, forming the focal point of an extended prose passage. Among the most prominent of the static type are Muro no yashima, Yugyō Willow, Shirakawa Barrier, Asaka Mountain / Shinobu Village, Kasajima (Bamboo Hat Island), Takekuma no matsu (Pine at Takekuma), Tsubo no ishibumi (Tsubo Stone Inscription), Sue no matsuyama / Shiogama no ura (Tip-of-the-Pine Mountain/Shiogama Bay), Matsushima, Mogami River, Kisagata, and Nōin Island.

28. Fujiwara Suemichi's poem in the *Senzaishū* (1188, Summer, no. 142) joined Shirakawa (White River) Barrier with the white *unohana* (deutzia).

mide suguru	Since no one passes
hito shi nakereba	without looking
unohana no	at the shrub fence
sakeru kakine ya	blooming with white deutzia,
Shirakawa no seki	it must be Shirakawa Barrier.

29. The same poem appears on a *tanzaku*, or poetry sheet, with the headnote, "On Passing the Shirakawa Barrier."

30. Shiraishi Teizō, "Mō hitotsu no *Hosomichi*," in idem, *Bashō*, pp. 46–73.

31. *Ruiji meisho waka shū* contains 94 poems on Shinobu and *Matsuba meisho waka shū* 29 poems.

32. Bashō in fact composed a poem here, which suggests that this passage, like many others, was part fiction, perhaps part poetic stance.

33. In the following poem (*Kokinrokujō*, no. 1553), the Koromo River represents an unreliable woman.

mi ni chikaki	The intimate name
na wo zo tanomishi	I have come to rely on,
michinoku no	Robe River
koromo no kawa to	of the Interior,
mite ya wataran	why are you flowing away?

Saigyō (*Sankashū*, no. 1131) also wrote on Koromo River, playing on the homophones *kitaru* ("to wear"/"to come") and *shimu* ("to penetrate"/"to dye").

When I arrived at Hiraizumi on the twelfth of the Ten Month, snow was falling, and there was a fierce storm. I had been anxious to see the River of the Robe, and when I arrived at the bank of the river, the walls of the castle on the River of the Robe seemed unusual. The edge of the river was frozen, and it was particularly cold.

toriwakite	Extra cold,
kokoro mo shimite	it freezes even my heart,
sae zo wataru	the Robe River
koromogawa mi ni	that I came to see,
kitaru kyō shimo	to wear today.

Another *utamakura* at Hiraizumi, albeit a very minor one, was Tabashine Mountain, which was famous for its cherry blossoms, especially as a result of a poem by Saigyō (*Sankashū*, no. 1442).

I went to Hiraizumi in the Interior, where there is a mountain called Tabashine. The mountain was covered, as far as the eye could see, with cherry trees, as if there were almost no other kind of tree. Seeing the flowers in bloom, I wrote:

kiki mo sezu	I had never heard
Tabashineyama no	of such cherry blossoms
sakurabana	outside Yoshino,
Yoshino no hoka ni	as beautiful as these
kakarubeshi to wa	of Tabashine Mountain.

34. The hokku by Tōrin, who was a relative of Bashō, appears in *Mutsuchidori* (1697), a haikai travel account and collection edited by Tōrin. Gikū's hokku appears in his *Ushiran* (1717), a haikai travel account.

35. Hirota Jirō, "*Oku no hosomichi* to utamakura," in idem, *Bashō to koten: Genroku jidai*, pp. 532–84.

36. Andō Tsuguo, *Teihon Bashō*, p. 354.

37. Ogata Tsutomu, "Haimakura," in idem, *Haiku no shūhen*, p. 39.

38. *Renga shihōshō*, p. 235.

39. The original version had *sumi | kawaru | yo | ya* instead of *sumi | kawaru | yo | zo*.

40. *Oku no hosomichi sugagomoshō*, the best of the premodern commentaries, notes that *hina no ie* (doll's house) means a container for dolls, but modern scholars generally believe it is a house with dolls on display.

41. Bashō's first poem on the actual journey, preserved in *Zoku Sarumino*, was an allegorical parting poem in which the *ayu* (baby sweetfish), representing the disciples, send off the *shirauo* (white fish), the elder master.

> baby sweetfish
> sending off a whitefish—
> parting!

ayu | no | ko | no | shirauo | okuru | wakare | kana
sweetfish | 's | child | 's | white-fish | send-off | parting | !

When writing *Oku no hosomichi*, however, Bashō revised the poem to stress both the cyclical movement of the seasons and spatial movement: time becomes personified.

42. Seifū followed the Kamigata style of Shintoku and Gonsui.

43. The hokku on "evening cool" (*yūsuzumi*) at Atsumiyama in the Sakata section of *Oku no hosomichi* is a greeting to Fugyoku (1648–97), a doctor from Sakata and Bashō's host at the time.

44. Rogan took the notes for *Kikigaki nanukagusa* (Seven day grass notes; 1716–36), which includes Bashō's earliest recorded comments on "the unchanging and the ever-changing" and which was edited by Chikudō, Rogan's disciple.

45. Of the many Kaga poets included in Shōhaku's anthology *Hitotsu matsu* (One pine; 1687), Isshō had the most (194 verses).

46. Bashō paid tribute to the memory of Isshō in the hokku "Grave mound, move too! my weeping voice is the autumn wind" (*Tsuka mo ugoke waga naku koe wa aki no kaze*).

47. Hokushi was the author of *Yamanaka mondō*.

48. Jokō and Keikō were two Ōgaki samurai.

49. The difference between Genroku 2 (1689), when Bashō took the journey, and Genroku 6–7 (1693–1694), when he wrote the text, is noticeable in the depiction of Bashō's Edo disciples, which, by the time Bashō was writing the manuscript, had split into two groups, an urban group led by Kikaku and Ransetsu and a Fukagawa group centered on Sanpū. Upon his return to Edo, Bashō avoided Kikaku's urban group, which he found involved with *tentori*, point-garnering haikai, and worked almost exclusively with Sanpū's group, who remained "amateurs" and rejected the

commercialization of *tentori haikai*. Bashō, in short, wrote *Oku no hoso-michi* at a time when he was divorcing himself from Kikaku's group in Edo, and as a consequence they were eliminated from *Oku no hosomichi*, as was Bokuin, who had welcomed Bashō at Ogaki and taken him to Ise. At the end of the Matsushima passage in *Oku no hosomichi*, Bashō "greeted" his friends and fellow poets in Edo, with whom he shares poems on Matsu-shima, but although he included Sanpū and others he made no mention of Kikaku's group—Rosen (1655–1733), Sentoku, Kikaku, Ransetsu—despite the fact they had earlier formed the core of his Edo disciples.

50. *Infutagi*, p.291. Also *Honchō monzen*, p. 409.

51. *Infutagi*, p. 289. Also *Honchō monzen*, p. 408.

Chapter 9

EPIGRAPH: *Sanzōshi*, NKBZ 55: 551.

1. *Uda no hōshi*, p. 245.

2. The graph for "sincerity" was also closely connected to the Neo-Confucian notion of *li* (J. *ri*), or principle, which was thought to govern all things, both nature and human beings.

3. "Predecessors" (*sendatsu*) refers to Teitoku, the founder of Teimon haikai, and haikai poets before Teitoku. Sōin brought "freedom" with re-gard to diction, subject matter, and form (for example, breaking the 5/7/5 rule for the hokku).

4. In another section of *Sanzōshi*, Dohō noted: "Those who devote themselves to *makoto* seek out the spirit of the ancients in poetry. In more recent times, they have a profound understanding of the spirit of the Mas-ter. If one does not understand the spirit of the ancients or that of the Mas-ter, one cannot follow the way of *makoto*. To understand that spirit, one should follow the traces of the Master's writings and come to know them well. Having done that, one should rectify one's spirit until it achieves the level of that of the ancients or of the Master. To devote oneself to achiev-ing that spirit is to devote oneself to *makoto*" (NKBZ 51: 546–47).

5. An almost identical passage, which argues that the *fūga* of Saigyō, Sō-gi, and others are joined by a "common thread" (*kandōsuru mono*), appears in a version of the *Genjūan no ki* dated the Seventh Month of 1690 (Gen-roku 3), which strongly suggests that this part of *Oi no kobumi* was written about the same time.

6. The *Sanzōshi* (NKBZ 51: 546–47) also notes: "As for those who are always immersed in haikai [*fūga*], when the color of the heart, of the thoughts and emotions within, becomes the object, the verse is created. As a consequence, the object is naturally grasped, and there is no interference.

If the color of the heart is not pure, the words become superficial and decorative. This is the result of a heart that is vulgar and does not devote itself to the truth of poetry [*makoto*]."

7. This view resembles the poetic approach to waka found in such medieval treatises as *Kōun kuden* (1408) and *Tamekane kyō waka shō* (1285).

8. In *Kyoraishō* (NKBZ 51: 494), Kyorai observed that Bashō began expounding the notion of *fueki ryūkō* in the winter of 1689 (Genroku 2). While staying at Haguro Mountain during his *Narrow Road to the Interior* journey, Bashō also spoke of *fueki ryūkō* to Rogan, a host and student whose notes are preserved in *Kikigaki nanoka gusa*, and to Hokushi, a disciple at Kanazawa, who wrote about their discussion in *Yamanaka mondō* (Genroku 2, 1689).

9. Kyorai makes a similar statement in *Haikai mondō* (pp. 101–2), in a "Letter to Kikaku" ("Zō shinshi Kikaku sho"). "I have heard the following. 'In verse, there is the form [*sugata*] of the unchanging [*fueki*] and the form of the ever-changing [*ryūkō*].' The Master taught us that they represented two extremes, but the two are rooted in the same source. The two become one since they both possess, at their root, the truth of poetry [*fūga no makoto*]." The "Letter to Kikaku" from Kyorai is the first part of *Haikai mondō* (compiled 1697–98), a series of epistolary exchanges between Kyorai and Kyoriku on problems of haikai.

10. In *Yamanaka mondō*, which records some of Bashō's teachings during his journey to the Interior, Hokushi wrote: "Those who intend to follow the proper Bashō style should not lose themselves in worldly concerns or be caught in vulgar language. Instead, they should place heaven and earth to the right, not forgetting the poetic essence [*honjō*] of all things, of the mountains and rivers, of the grass and trees, of human relations. They should play in the scattering flowers and the falling leaves. If they do, they will reach across the past and the present, without losing the principle of the unchanging [*fueki no ri*], and participate in the change of the ever-changing [*ryūkō no hen*]" (p. 21).

11. In contrast to Dohō, who saw the changing and the unchanging as two sides of a single principle or phenomenon, Kyorai attributed the difference between the two to specific rhetorical techniques. *Kyoraishō* explains:

> Rochō asked, "What kind of expression [*sugata*] does an unchanging verse have?"
> Kyorai answered, "An unchanging verse is a style of haikai. It is a verse that does not depend on a special expression [*monozuki*] and consequently is suitable for all ages. Take, for example, poems such as the following:

stick a handle
in the moon:
makes a good fan
                    —Sōkan

tsuki|ni|e|o|sashitaraba|yoki|uchiwa|kana
moon|in|handle|stick|good|fan|!

"this and this . . ."
all I could say—
cherry blossoms at Mount Yoshino
                    —Teishitsu

kore|wa|kore|wa|to|bakari|hana|no|Yoshinoyama
this|as-for|this|as-for|saying|only|flower|'s|Mount-Yoshino

winds of autumn—
the cemetery at Ise
still frightening
                    —Bashō

aki|no|kaze|Ise|no|hakahara|nao|sugoshi
autumn|'s|wind|Ise|'s|cemetery|still|frightening

Rochō asked, "Isn't comparing a moon to a fan a special expression?"

Kyorai answered, "Direct expression of feelings [*fu*], allegory [*hi*], and metaphor [*kyō*] are not restricted to haikai. They emerge naturally in poetic composition. Virtually everything that appears in poetry is related to these three. Therefore, one cannot call this a special expression."

Rochō said, "What is a changing verse like?"

Kyorai replied, "A changing verse is one that has a special expression and becomes fashionable. It is like those things—from appearance to clothes to utensils—that become fashionable from time to time. For example,

like sultry weather—
heat from a rice pot
in summer

musu|yō|ni|natsu|ni|koshiki|no|atsusa|kana
steam|like|as|summer|in|rice-cooker|'s|heat|!
                    (NKBZ 51: 491–92)

The ever-changing as defined by Kyorai meant verses that used "special expressions" (*monozuki*), fashionable or popular rhetorical techniques, in contrast to the unchanging, which did not. Kyorai's examples of unchanging verse suggest that he saw the unchanging in the poetic essence (*hon'i*) of classical topics. The poem by Sōkan humorously captures the poetic essence of summer moon (*natsu no tsuki*), which was coolness amid the summer heat. Teishitsu's hokku likewise embodies in haikai fashion the traditional associations of Yoshino, an *utamakura* known for its beautiful cherry blossoms. Bashō's poem, which expresses sorrow and desolation, captures the traditional association of autumn wind (*aki no kaze*). In each case, the haikai poet uses ever-changing language or contemporary approaches to give new expression to the unchanging topics and associations of classical poetry.

12. "Kyorai's Treatise for Fugyoku" ("Fugyoku ate Kyorai ronsho"). KBZ 7: 452–53; also Minami Shin'ichi, *Sōshaku Kyorai no hairon*, 1: 31.

13. See Ebara Taizō, "'Karumi' no shingi," in idem, *Chosakushū*, 10: 119–44.

14. Ogata Tsutomu, "Karumi e no shikō," in idem, *Za no bungaku*, pp. 127–47; also Shimazu Tadao, "*Sarumino* no ichi kōsatsu," in idem, *Rengashi no kenkyū*, pp. 218–32.

15. "Kyorai's Treatise for Fugyoku" takes the form of a letter to Fugyoku, a Bashō disciple, in which Kyorai answers a series of questions posed by Fugyoku. According to modern textual scholarship, this letter was written in the Third Month of Genroku 7 (1694). Details in the letter reveal, however, that Kyorai was citing comments that Bashō made from late 1689 (Genroku 2) to early 1691 (Genroku 4). On the problem of dating and *karumi*, see Imoto Nōichi, "Bashō no karumi no kōsatsu," in idem, *Bashō to haikai no kenkyū*, pp. 9–10. For the text, see KBZ 7: 446–57; also Minami Shin'ichi, *Sōshaku Kyorai no hairon*, 1: 36–38.

16. In advocating this notion of *karumi*, Bashō was probably reacting against the kind of conceptualization found in Kyoto haikai at the time.

17. The word *miyo*, or imperial reign, appears in most versions of this poem instead of *kimi* (sovereign).

18. KBZ 7: 449. Also Minami Shin'ichi, *Sōshaku Kyorai no hairon*, 1: 16. A similar passage appears in *Kyoraishō* (NKBZ 51: 427–28).

19. The passage cited in Ebara Taizō, "'Karumi' no shingi," in idem, *Chosakushū*, 10: 141. For the text, see Yasuda Akio, *Nihon no geijutsuron*, pp. 235–36.

20. KBZ 7: 451. Also Minami Shin'ichi, *Sōshaku Kyorai no hairon*, 1: 25–6.

21. From a *kasen* in *Hisago*.

22. Many of the popular *kigo* have similar rhythmical or melodic quali-

ties: for example, *hototogisu* (cuckoo), with its successive "o"s and "t"s. *Kirigirisu* (cricket), which is associated with its sharp cries in autumn, has four successive "i" vowel syllables as well as the repetitive "r" consonant.

23. R. H. Blyth (*Haiku*, 1: 366–71) distinguishes three types of onomatopoeia: the direct representation of sound, the representation of movement and physical sensations other than sound, and the representation of "soul states," psychological or emotional movement, all of which appear in Bashō's haikai.

24. Rhythm and melody were extremely important throughout Bashō's haikai career. The following hokku, which Bashō composed in 1687 and which is often cited as an example of *fūkyō* poetics, would be mediocre, if not meaningless, without the aural effect.

> well, then,
> let's go snow-viewing
> until we tumble over

iza | saraba | yukimi | ni | korobu | tokoro | made
well | then | snow-viewing | for | tumble | place | until

The four successive "a" vowels in the opening line—*iza saraba*—give the upper five syllables an emphatic rhythm, which is lacking in the earlier version *iza yukamu*. This is followed by the three "i" vowels in *yukimi ni*, and then by five rolling "o" vowels in *korobu tokoro*. Together, they create a dance-like movement, which embodies the sense of *fūkyō* excitement and anticipation. This kind of resonance became a central factor in Bashō's last years, when he advocated *karumi*.

25. Also Minami Shin'ichi, *Sōshaku Kyorai no hairon*, 2: 30–33.

26. On *ada*, see Ogata Tsutomu," Ada naru fū ni tsuite," *Kokugo to kokubungaku* (August 1955); reprinted in idem, *Haikaishi ronkō*, pp. 251–70.

27. *Tabine ron*, p. 207; also Minami Shin'ichi, *Sōshaku Kyorai no hairon*, 1: 401.

28. Ebara Taizō, "'Karumi' no shingi," in idem, *Chosakushū*, 10: 143.

29. *Shōmon haijin shokan shū*, p. 203.

30. Ibid.

31. Kigin's *Zō yama no i* lists *aki fukashi* (deepening autumn) as a seasonal word for the Ninth Month, the last month of autumn.

Epilogue

EPIGRAPH: tabi | ni | yande | yume | wa | kareno | o | kakemeguru (journey | on | ailing | dream | as-for | withered-field | (acc.) | go-around). Dictated by Bashō to his student Donshū in the early morning of Nov. 25, 1694

(10.8.Genroku 7), shortly before his death, and recorded in Shikō's *Tsuizen no nikki* (Requiem journal), with the headnote "During Illness."

1. Most of the editors of the Bashō-school anthologies, particularly those in the *Haikai shichibu shū*, were either young or newly inducted students. Kakei, while an experienced poet, had been with Bashō for less than a year before he was asked to edit *Fuyu no hi* (1684). Most of the other poets at Nagoya, who were virtually unknown before their appearance in *Fuyu no hi*, were young: Yasui was 27 and Tokoku in his twenties. Shadō was only 23 at the time he compiled *Hisago*.

2. Tomiyama Susumu, "Shōfū haikai no itansei."

3. Bashō's disciples at Ōmi can be divided into two geographical areas: those to the east of Lake Biwa, centered at Hikone, and those to the south of Lake Biwa (Konan), based at Ōtsu, Zeze, and Katata (Katada). (All these places are now in Shiga Prefecture.) Morikawa Kyoriku was from Hikone; Shōhaku, Chigetsu, Otokuni, and later Jōsō were at Ōtsu; Kyokusui, Masahide, Shadō (Chinseki), and others were at Zeze; and Senna was at Katata.

4. For the details of the relationship between Bashō and the Ōmi schools, see Ogino Kiyoshi, "Ōmi Shōmon no bunretsu to Bashō," in idem, *Haibungaku no sōsetsu*, pp. 75–94.

5. *Rekidai kokkei den*, p. 348.

6. It is no accident that a number of Bashō's founding disciples—Kakei and Yasui from Owari, Shōhaku and Senna of Ōmi, and Bonchō from Kyoto—were never counted as part of the "Ten Disciples of Bashō" (*Shōmon jittetsu*).

7. A total of 118 poets (108 in the hokku section) are represented in *Sarumino*. Except for Sengin (Bashō's deceased master), Rosen, and some others, almost all are Bashō-school poets. The anthology includes poets from Kyoto, Konan, Iga, Edo, Owari, Mino, Nagasaki, and Kaga, including those who had joined him during his *Oku no hosomichi* journey. The older generation of poets—Ransetsu, Sanpū, Etsujin, Kakei, Kyokusui, etc.—are represented by only two to five hokku each.

8. Abbeele, p. xiii.

9. Medieval renga masters such as Sōgi taught daimyō, provincial lords, while haikai masters such as Bashō taught samurai and wealthy commoners.

10. "Angya," in *Haibungaku daijiten*, p. 30.

11. Ogata Tsutomu, *Za no bungaku*.

Selected Bibliography

Works in Western Languages

Abbeele, George. *Travel as Metaphor: From Montaigne to Rousseau*. Minneapolis: University of Minnesota Press, 1992.

Anderson, Benedict. *Imagined Communities*. London: Verso, 1983. Rev. and extended ed., 1991.

Bahktin, Mikhail. *The Dialogic Imagination*. Trans. Caryl Emerson and Michael Holquist. Austin: University of Texas Press, 1981.

———. *Problems of Dostoevsky's Poetics*. Trans. Caryl Emerson. Minneapolis: University of Minnesota Press, 1984.

———. *Rabelais and His World*. Trans. Helene Iswolsky. Reprinted—Bloomington: Indiana University Press, 1984.

Barthes, Roland. *The Pleasure of the Text*. Trans. Richard Miller. New York: Hill and Wang, 1975.

———. *Roland Barthes by Roland Barthes*. Trans. Richard Howard. New York: Hill and Wang, 1977.

Benjamin, Walter. *Illuminations*. New York: Harcourt, Brace & World, 1968. Paperback ed.—New York: Schoken, 1969.

Bergson, Henri. "Laughter" (Le Rire, 1912). In *Comedy*, ed. Wylie Sypher, pp. 61–190. Baltimore: John Hopkins University Press, 1980 (1st ed. 1956).

Bloom, Harold. *The Anxiety of Influence*. New York: Oxford University Press, 1973.

Blyth, Reginald H. *Haiku*. 4 vols. Tokyo: Hokuseidō Press, 1949–52.

———. *A History of Haiku*. 2 vols. Japan: Hokuseidō Press, 1963, 1964.

Britton, Dorothy, trans. *A Haiku Journey*. Tokyo: Kōdansha International, 1974.

Brower, Robert, and Steven Carter, trans. *Conversations with Shōtetsu*. Ann Arbor: University of Michigan, Center for Japanese Studies, 1992.

Burke, Kenneth. *Language as Symbolic Action: Essays on Life, Literature, and Method*. Berkeley: University of California Press, 1966.

————. *Perspectives by Incongruity.* Ed. Stanley Edgar Hyman. Bloomington: Indiana University Press, 1964.

Carter, Steven. *The Road to Komatsubara.* Cambridge, Mass.: Harvard University, Council on East Asian Studies, 1987.

Chamberlain, Basil Hall. "Basho and the Japanese Poetical Epigram." *Transactions of the Asiatic Society of Japan* 30 (1902): 241–362. Reprinted in idem, *Japanese Poetry,* pp. 145–260. London: John Murray; Yokohama, Kelly and Walsh, 1910.

Coffman, Stanley, Jr. *Imagism: A Chapter for the History of Modern Poetry.* Norman: University of Oklahoma Press, 1951.

Corman, Cid, and Kamaike Susumu, trans. *Back Roads to Far Towns.* New York: Grossman, 1968. Reprinted—Hopewell, N.J.: Ecco Press, 1996.

Eliot, Thomas Stearns. "Hamlet and His Problems." 1919. In *Selected Prose of T. S. Eliot,* ed. Frank Kermode, pp. 45–49. New York: Harcourt Brace Jovanovich, 1975.

————. *Selected Essays.* 3d ed. London: Faber and Faber, 1951 [1919].

Fenollosa, Ernest. *The Chinese Written Character as a Medium for Poetry.* Ed. Ezra Pound. San Francisco: City Lights Books, 1936.

————. "The Logic of Art." *The Golden Age* 1 (May 1906).

Fowler, Edward. *The Rhetoric of Confession.* Berkeley: University of California Press, 1988.

Freud, Sigmund. *Jokes and Their Relationship to the Unconscious.* New York: Norton, 1960.

Gefin, Laszlo. *Ideogram: History of a Poetic Method.* Austin: University of Texas Press, 1982.

Gombrich, E. H. *Art and Illusion.* Princeton: Princeton University Press, 1960.

Greene, Thomas M. *The Light in Troy: Imitation and Discovery in Renaissance Poetry.* New Haven: Yale University Press, 1982.

Hackett, J. W. *The Way of Haiku.* Tokyo: Japan Publications, 1969.

————. *The Zen Haiku and Other Zen Poems.* Tokyo: Japan Publications, 1983.

Haiku Society of America, ed. *A Haiku Path: The Haiku Society of America, 1968–1988.* New York: Haiku Society of America, 1994.

Hass, Robert. *Twentieth Century Pleasures: Prose on Poetry.* Hopewell, N.J.: Ecco Press, 1984.

Hass, Robert, ed. *The Essential Haiku.* Hopewell, N.J.: Ecco Press, 1994.

Henderson, Harold G. *An Introduction to Haiku: An Anthology of Poems and Poets from Bashō to Shiki.* Garden City, N.Y.: Doubleday, 1958.

Higginson, William J. *The Haiku Handbook.* New York: McGraw-Hill, 1985.

Hughes, Glenn. *Imagism and the Imagists*. New York: Humanities Press, 1960.

Hutcheon, Linda. *A Theory of Parody*. New York: Methuen, 1985.

Jakobson, Roman. *Language in Literature*. Ed. Krystyna Pomorska and Stephen Rudy. Cambridge, Mass.: Harvard University Press, 1987.

Jenkins, Donald, ed. *The Floating World Revisited*. Portland, Ore.: Portland Art Museum, 1993.

Keene, Donald. *Travelers of a Hundred Ages*. New York: Henry Holt, 1989.

———. *Twenty Plays of the Nō Theatre*. New York: Columbia University Press, 1970.

———. *World Within Walls: Japanese Literature in the Pre-Modern Era, 1600–1867*. New York: Grove Press, 1976.

Keene, Donald, ed. *Anthology of Japanese Literature*. New York: Grove Press, 1955.

Kenner, Hugh. *The Poetry of Ezra Pound*. London: Faber and Faber, 1951. Reprinted—Lincoln: University of Nebraska Press, 1985.

———. *The Pound Era*. Berkeley: University of California Press, 1971.

Kerouac, Jack. *The Dharma Bums*. 1958. New York: Penguin, 1986.

Kitagawa, Joseph. "Three Types of Pilgrimage in Japan." In idem, *On Understanding Japanese Religion*. Princeton: Princeton University Press, 1987.

Matejka, Ladislav, and Krystyna Pomorska, eds. *Readings in Russian Poetics: Formalist and Structuralist Views*. Cambridge, Mass.: MIT Press, 1971.

Nippon Gakujutsu Shinkōkai. *Haikai and Haiku*. Tokyo: Nippon Gakujutsu Shinkōkai, 1958.

Pound, Ezra. "A Few Don'ts by an Imagiste." *Poetry* (Mar. 1913).

———. *Personae: The Collected Shorter Poems of Ezra Pound*. 1926. New York: New Directions Pub., 1926.

———. "Vorticism." *Fortnightly Review*, n.s. 92 [old series 102] (Sept. 1, 1914), pp. 461–71.

Pratt, William, ed. *The Imagist Poem*. New York: Dutton, 1963.

Ramirez-Christensen, Esperanza. *Heart's Flower: The Life and Poetry of Shinkei*. Stanford: Stanford University Press, 1994.

Riffaterre, Michael. *Semiotics of Poetry*. Bloomington: Indiana University Press, 1978.

Ross, Bruce, ed. *Haiku Moment: An Anthology of Contemporary North American Haiku*. Rutland, Vt., and Tokyo: Charles Tuttle, 1993.

Sato, Hiroaki. *One Hundred Frogs: From Renga to Haiku in English*. New York: Weatherhill, 1983.

Sklovsky, Victor. "Theory of the Formal Method." In *Readings in Russian*

Poetics: Formalist and Structuralist Views, ed. Ladislav Matejka and Krystyna Pomorska, pp. 3–37. Cambridge: MIT Press, 1971.

Suzuki, Tomi. *Narrating the Self: Fictions of Japanese Modernity*. Stanford: Stanford University Press, 1996.

Taupin, René. *L'Influence du symbolisme français sur la poésie américaine (de 1910 à 1920)*. Paris: Librarie Ancienne Honoré Champion, 1929.

Ueda, Makoto. *Bashō and His Interpreters*. Stanford: Stanford University Press, 1991.

———. *Matsuo Bashō*. New York: Twayne, 1970; Tokyo: Kōdansha International, 1982.

van den Heuvel, Cor, ed. *The Haiku Anthology*. Garden City, N.Y.: Doubleday, Anchor Press, 1974.

Volosinov, V. N. *Marxism and the Philosophy of Language*. Trans. Ladislav Matejka and I. R. Titunik. New York: Seminar Press, 1973.

Watson, Burton, and Hiroaki Sato, eds. and trans. *From the Country of Eight Islands*. New York: Doubleday, 1981.

Welsh, Andrew. *Roots of Lyric: Primitive Poetry and Modern Poetics*. Princeton: Princeton University Press, 1978.

Yasuda, Kenneth. *The Japanese Haiku: Its Essential Nature, History, and Possibilities in English*. Rutland, Vt., and Tokyo: Tuttle, 1957.

Yu, Pauline. *The Reading of Imagery in the Chinese Poetic Tradition*. Princeton: Princeton University Press, 1987.

Yuasa, Nobuyuki, trans. *Bashō: The Narrow Road to the Deep North and Other Travel Sketches*. Harmondsworth, Eng.: Penguin Books, 1966.

Works in Japanese

All primary sources in Japanese are listed by title, followed by the Japanese characters. All modern collections of primary texts or multivolume series of modern scholarship are listed by title. Unless otherwise indicated, the place of publication is Tokyo. The following abreviations are used:

HT	Haisho taikei
KBZ	Kōhon Bashō zenshū
KHT	Koten haibungaku taikei
NKBT	Nihon koten bungaku taikei
NKBZ	Nihon koten bungaku zenshū
SNKBT	Shin Nihon koten bungaku taikei
SNKS	Shinchō Nihon koten shūsei

Abe Masami. "*Oi no kobumi* no seiritsu." In *Bashō II*, pp. 134–40. Nihon bungaku kenkyū shiryō sōsho. Yūseidō, 1977.

Abe Masami, ed. *Bashō renkushō*. 8 vols. Meiji shoin, 1965–83.

Abe Masami and Asō Isoji, eds. *Oku no hosomichi: shosetsu ichiran.* Meiji shoin, 1970.

Andō Tsuguo, *Teihon Bashō.* Chikuma shobō, 1977.

Arano あら野 (Desolate fields). Published 1689. Bashō-school haikai anthology, ed. Kakei. In *Bashō shichibu shū*, ed. Shiraishi Teizō and Ueno Yōzō, pp. 59–225. SNKBT 70. Iwanami shoten, 1990.

Arano kōshū あら野後集 (Sequel to *Desolate Fields*). 1693. Haikai anthology, ed. Kakei, after his break from Bashō, stressing a return to the past. In *Shōmon haikai shū I*, ed. Abe Kimio, Abe Masami, Ōiso Yoshio, pp. 314–49. KHT 6. Shūeisha, 1972.

Atsumeku あつめ句 (Gathered verses). 1687. Hokku-haibun collection, by Bashō. In *Shohon taishō Bashō haibun kubun shū*, ed. Yayoshi Kan'ichi, Nishimura Masako, Akahane Manabu, Danjō Masataka, pp. 530–38. Shimizu kōbundō, 1977.

Bashō. Nihon bungaku kenkyū shiryō sōsho. Yūseidō, 1969.

Bashō II. Nihon bungaku kenkyū shiryō sōsho. Yūseidō, 1977.

Bashō bunshū. Ed. Toyama Susumu. SNKS. Shinchōsha, 1978.

Bashō jiten. Ed. Nakamura Shunjō. Shunjūsha, 1978.

Bashō kōza. 5 vols. Ed. Bashō kōza henshūbu. Yūseidō. 1983–85.

Bashō kushū. Ed. Kon Eizō. SNKS 51. Shinchōsha, 1982.

Bashō kushū. Ed. Ōtani Tokuzō and Nakamura Shunjō. NKBT 45. Iwanami shoten, 1962. Bashō's hokku arranged by season and topic.

Bashō no hon. 7 vols. Ed. Nakamura Yukihiko, Katō Shūson, Ogata Tsutomu, et al. Kadokawa shoten, 1970. Good collection of modern scholarship on different aspects of Bashō's life and literature.

Bashō shichibu shū. Ed. Shiraishi Teizō and Ueno Yōzō. SNKBT 70. Iwanami shoten, 1990.

Bashō zen zufu. 2 vols. Ed. Bashō zen zufu kankō kai. Iwanami shoten, 1993. Most comprehensive set of reproductions of texts and paintings in Bashō's original hand.

Binsenshū 便船集 (Timely boat). Published 1668. Haikai handbook, ed. Baisei. Not available in a printed edition.

Buson zenshū. Ed. Ogata Tsutomu and Morita Ran. Vol. 1. Kōdansha, 1992.

Chikuba kyōgin shū 竹馬狂吟集 (Hobby horse mad composition collection). 1499. In *Chikuba kyōgin shū, Shinsen inu tsukuba shū*, ed., Kimura Miyogo and Iguchi Hisashi, SNKS 77. Shinchōsha, 1988.

Chikuenshō 竹園抄 (Bamboo garden collection). 1285. Waka treatise by Fujiwara Tameaki. In *Nihon kagaku taikei*, 3: 410–28. Kazama shobō, 1956.

Ebara Taizō. *Ebara Taizō chosakushū.* 22 vols. Chūō kōron sha, 1979–84.

Enokoshū 犬子集 (Puppy collection). 1633. Ed. Shigeyori, a Teitoku disciple. In *Teimon haikai shū I*, ed. Nakamura Shunjō and Morikawa Akira, pp. 63–152. KHT 1. Shūeisha, 1970.

"Fugyoku ate Kyorai ronsho" 不玉宛去来論書 (Kyorai's essay for Fugyoku). 1694. KBZ 7: 446–57.

Fuyu no hi 冬の日 (Winter days). 1684. Bashō-school anthology, comp. Kakei. In *Bashō shichibu shū*, ed. Shiraishi Teizō and Ueno Yōzō, pp. 3–28. SNKBT 70. Iwanami shoten, 1990.

Fūzoku monzen 風俗文選. See *Honchō monzen*.

Genjūan no ki 幻住庵記 (Record of an unreal dwelling). 1690. Model haibun by Bashō, published in *Sarumino* in 1691. Revised a number of times, resulting in different variants. KBZ 6: 456–74. Fujimi shobō, 1989.

Genroku haikai shū. Ed. Ōuchi Hatsuo, Sakurai Takejirō, and Kira Sueo. SNKBT 71. Iwanami shoten, 1994.

Haibungaku daijiten. Ed. Katō Shūson, Ōtani Tokuzō, Imoto Nōichi, Ogata Tsutomu, Kusama Tokihiko, Shimazu Tadao, Ōoka Makoto, and Morikawa Akira. Kadokawa shoten, 1995.

Haikai daijiten. Ed. Ijichi Tetsuo, Imoto Nōichi, Kanda Hideo, Nakamura Shunjō, and Miyamoto Saburō. Meiji shoin, 1957.

Haikai gosan 俳諧御傘 (Haikai umbrella). Published 1651; reprinted 1659. 10-vol. handbook of haikai rules by Teitoku. HT 8: 1–142. Shunjūsha, 1928.

Haikai jūron 俳諧十論 (Haikai ten discussions). 1719. Haikai treatise by Shikō. HT 9. Shunjūsha, 1928. Also in *Sōshaku Shikō no hairon*, ed. Minami Shin'ichi, pp. 703–844. Kazama shobō, 1983.

Haikai mōgyū 俳諧蒙求. 1675. Danrin haikai treatise by Ichū (1639–1711). In *Danrin haikai shū II*, ed. Iida Masakazu, Enosaka Hirohisa, and Inui Hiroyuki, pp. 82–111. KHT 4. Shūeisha, 1972.

Haikai mondō 俳諧問答 (Haikai dialogue). Comp. 1697–98. Series of essays exchanged by Kyoriku and Kyorai on key issues in Bashō's haikai. In *Shōmon hairon haibun shū*, ed. Ōiso Yoshio and Ōuchi Hatsuo, pp. 101–70. KHT 10. Shūeisha, 1970.

Haikai shichibu shū 俳諧七部集 (Haikai seven anthologies). Seven anthologies of the Bashō school—*Fuyu no hi, Haru no hi, Arano, Hisago, Sarumino, Sumidawara, Zoku sarumino*—selected and ed. Ryūkyo (1686–1748), around 1731, as part of a movement to revive the Bashō style, published as a single set by Ryūkyo's disciple Chōsui (1701–69) around 1756, became the core of the Bashō haikai canon, and commonly referred to as the *Shichibu shū* (Seven anthologies). In *Bashō shichibu shū*, ed. Shiraishi Teizō and Ueno Yōzō. SNKBT 70. Iwanami shoten, 1990. Also KBZ 3–5. Fujimi shobō, 1989.

Haikai shogaku shō 俳諧初学抄 (Instructions for haikai beginners). 1641. By Tokugen. In *Teimon haikaishū II*, ed. Nakamura Shunjō and Morikawa Akira, pp. 358–82. KHT 2. Shūeisha, 1971. Also in *Teimon haikai shū*, pp. 479–502. HT 14. Shunjūsha, 1929.

Haikai yōi fūtei 俳諧用意風躰 (Haikai essential style). 1673. Haikai treatise by Kigin. In *Kigin hairon shū*, ed. Ogata Tsutomu, pp. 193–224. Koten bunko 151. Koten bunko, 1960.

Haiku hairon. Ed. Shiraishi Teizō and Ogata Tsutomu. Kanshō Nihon koten bungaku 33. Kadokawa shoten, 1977.

Haimakura 俳枕 (Haikai pillow). By Yūzan. In *Danrin haikai shū II*, pp. 419–70. HT 16. Shunjūsha, 1929.

Haisho taikei (HT). Also referred to as Nihon haisho taikei. All pages references are to Fukyūban haisho taikei (Popular edition of Haisho taikei). 34 vols. Ed. Kanda Hōsui and Katsumine Shinpū. Shunjūsha, 1928–30.

Hakusenshū 泊船集. Six-vol. collection of Bashō's poetry, ed. Fūkoku in 1698. The preface and the sixth volume are in *Shōmon haikai shū II*, ed. Abe Kimio, Abe Masami, and Ōiso Yoshio, pp. 534–47. KHT 6. Shūeisha, 1972.

Hanahigusa はなひ草 (Hanahi grass). 1636. Teimon haikai seasonal handbook by Shigeyori. In *Teimon haikai shū II*, pp. 321–57. KHT 2. Shūeisha, 1971.

Hanami-guruma 花見車 (Flower-viewing carriage). 1702. Portraits of Genroku haikai masters, including Bashō, by Tesshi (published anonymously). In *Genroku haikai shū*, ed. Ōuchi Hatsuo, Sakurai Takejirō, and Kira Sueo, pp. 377–491. SNKBT 71. Iwanami shoten, 1994. Also in *Haikai keifu itsuwa shū II*, pp. 81–121. HT 32. Shunjūsha, 1930.

Haru no hi はるの日 (Spring days). 1686. Bashō-school anthology ed. Kakei. In *Bashō shichibu shū*, ed. Shiraishi Teizō and Ueno Yōzō, pp. 31–56. SNKBT 70. Iwanami shoten, 1990.

Hatsukaishi hyōchū 初懐紙評注 (Commentary on the First Poetry of the New Year). 1686; published 1729. Only surviving commentary by Bashō on linked verse sequence. In KBZ 7: 405–19. Fujimi shobō, 1989.

Hentsuki 篇突. 1698. Poetic treatise ed. Riyū and Kyoriku, two Bashō disciples. In *Shōmon hairon haibun shū*, ed. Ōiso Yoshio and Ōuchi Hatsuo, pp. 171–93. KHT 10. Shūeisha, 1970.

Hirai Shōbin. "Kindai no haijintachi." In vol. 3 of *Bashō kōza*, ed. Bashō kōza henshūbu, pp. 120–32. Yūseidō, 1983.

———. *Oku no hosomichi nyūmon.* Nagata shobō, 1988.

——. *Shin saijiki: shinnen*. Kawade bunko. Kawade shobō shinsha, 1990.

Hirota Jirō. *Bashō to koten: Genroku jidai*. Meiji shoin, 1987.

Hisago ひさご (Gourd). 1690. Bashō-school haikai anthology ed. Shadō, an Ōmi disciple; the title, taken from a story in *Chuang-tzu*, symbolizes "lightness" (*karumi*). In *Bashō shichibu shū*, ed. Shiraishi Teizō and Ueno Yūzō, pp. 229–55. SNKBT 70. Iwanami shoten, 1990.

Honchō bunkan 本朝文鑑 (Prose mirror of Japan). 1717. Haibun collection ed. Shikō. In *Haikai bunshū*, ed. Iwaya Sueo, pp. 1–154. Haikai bunko 19. Hakubunkan, 1900.

Honchō monzen 本朝文選 (Prose collection of Japan). Published 1706. Ed. Kyoriku. Later retitled *Fūzoku monzen*. In *Shōmon hairon haibun shū*, ed. Ōiso Yoshio and Ōuchi Hatsuo, pp. 379–501. KHT 10. Shūeisha, 1970.

Hori Nobuo. "Haibunshū toshite no *Oku no hosomichi*." *Kokubungaku* 34, no. 6 (May 1989): 54–60.

Hori Nobuo and Imoto Nōichi. *Koten haiku o manabu*. 2 vols. Yūhikaku, 1977.

Hori Nobuo and Imoto Nōichi, eds. *Matsuo Bashō shū*. SNKBZ 70. Shōgakukan, 1995.

Horikiri Minoru. *Haibun kenkyū josetsu*. Waseda daigaku shuppanbu, 1990.

——. *Haidō: Bashō kara Bashō e*. Fujimi shobō, 1990.

——. *Hyōgen toshite no haikai: Bashō, Buson, Issa*. Perikansha, 1988.

——. *Shōfū hairon no kenkyū*. Meiji shoin, 1982.

Imoto Nōichi. *Bashō no bungaku no kenkyū*. Kadokawa shoten, 1978.

——. *Bashō to haikai no kenkyū*. Kadokawa shoten, 1984.

Indōshū 引導集 (Teachings collection). 1684. Danrin haikai handbook ed. Saikoku. Printed in Nakamura Shunjō, *Haikaishi no shomondai*. Kasama shoin, 1970.

Infutagi 韻塞. 1696. Haikai collection ed. Riyū and Kyoriku. In *Shōmon haikai shū II*, ed. Miyamoto Saburō and Kon Eizō, pp. 257–97. KHT 7. Shūeisha, 1971.

Inui Hiroyuki. *Haiku no genzai to koten*. Heibonsha, 1988.

——. *Kotoba no uchi naru Bashō*. Miraisha, 1980.

——. *Shoki haikai no tenkai*. Ōfūsha, 1968.

Inui Hiroyuki and Shiraishi Teizō. *Renku e no shōtai*. Yūhikaku shinsho. Yūhikaku, 1980.

Inui Hiroyuki and Shiraishi Teizō, eds. *Bashō monogatari*. Yūhikaku, 1977.

Inu Tsukuba shū 犬筑波集 (Dog Tsukuba collection). 1532. Thought to be edited by Yamazaki Sōkan. In *Teimon haikai shū I*, ed. Nakamura Shunjō and Morikawa Akira, pp. 44–62. KHT 1. Shūeisha, 1970.

Ishida Yoshisada. *Inja no bungaku*. Hanawa shobō, 1968.

Ishikawa Jun. "Edojin no hassō hō ni tsuite." In idem, *Bungaku taigai*. Chū-ō kōron sha, 1976.

Iwata Kurō, ed. *Shochū hyōshaku Bashō haiku taisei*. Meiji shoin, 1967.

Jūron'i benshō 十論為弁抄 (Explanation of Ten Discussions). Published 1725. Poetic treatise by Shikō, explaining the terms used in *Haikai jūron*. In *Shōmon haikai shū I*, ed. Abe Kimio, Abe Masami, Ōiso Yoshio, pp. 549–625. KHT 6. Shūeisha, 1972.

Kanbara Ariake. *Shunchōshū*. Meicho fukkoku zenshū. Nihon kindai bungakukan, 1968 (1905).

Kashima mōde 鹿島詣 (Pilgrimage to Kashima) by Bashō. In *Matsuo Bashō shū*, ed. Imoto Nōichi, Hori Nobuo, and Muramatsu Tomotsugu, pp. 303–8. NKBZ 41. Shōgakukan, 1972.

Katō Shūson. *Bashō zenku*. 2 vols. Chikuma shobō, 1975.

———. "Shinjitsu kangō no to iu hiyaku." In *Haiku hyakunen no toi*, ed. Natsuishi Banya, pp. 126–38. Kōdansha, 1995.

Kawazu awase 蛙合 (Frog competition). 1686. Poetry contest ed. Senku, beginning with the famous "old pond" hokku by Bashō. In *Genroku haikai shū*, ed. Ōuchi Hatsuo, Sakurai Takejirō, and Kira Sueo, pp. 3–19. SNKBT 71. Iwanami shoten, 1994.

Kefukigusa 毛吹草 (Fur-blown grass). Published 1645. Haikai collection and dictionary, ed. Shigeyori, a Teimon poet. In *Kefukigusa*. Iwanami bunko 3304–8. Iwanami shoten, 1943. Reissued 1971.

Kikigaki nanukagusa 聞書七日草 (Seven day grass notes). 1716–36. Notes taken by Rogan on Bashō's teaching during his journey to the Interior. Edited by Chikudō, a Rogan disciple. In *Teihon Bashō taisei*, ed. Ogata Tsutomu et al., pp. 664–77. Sanseidō, 1962.

Kira Sueo. *Genroku Kyōto haidan kenkyū*. Benseisha, 1975.

Kitamura Tōkoku. "Matsushima ni oite Bashō o yomu." *Jogaku zasshi* (1892). Reprint in *Jogaku zasshi*. Kyoto: Rinsen shoten, 1966–67.

Kobun shinpō 古文真宝 (*Ku-wen chen-pao*, True treasury of the ancient style). Anthology of classical Chinese literature extensively used by the Japanese. *Kobun shinpō*, ed. Hoshikawa Kiyotaka. Shinshaku kanbun taikei 9–10, 16. Meiji shoin, 1963, 1967.

Kōhon Bashō zenshū (KBZ). 10 vols. plus the *bekkan*, special volume. Komiya Toyotaka, general ed. Fujimi shobō, 1988–91.

Kokin waka shū 古今和歌集 or *Kokinshū* (Collection of old and new Japanese poems). Ca. 905. Ed. Ozawa Masao. NKBZ 7. Shōgakukan, 1971.

Kon Eizō. *Bashō nenpu taisei*. Kadokawa shoten, 1994.

———. "Haikai keizai shakaigaku." *Chūō daigaku kokubun* 17 (Mar. 1974): 1–8.

Kon Eizō and Miyamoto Saburō. *Matsuo Bashō*. Haiku shiriisu hito to sakuhin. Ōfūsha, 1967.

Koten haibungaku taikei (KHT). 16 vols. Hisamatsu Sen'ichi and Imoto Nōichi, general eds. Shūeisha, 1970–76. Most comprehensive edited series on haikai.

Kuriyama Riichi. *Bashō no geijutsu kan*. Nagata shobō, 1981.

———. *Haikai no keifu*. Kadokawa shoten, 1980.

———. *Haikaishi*. Hanawa sensho. Hanawa shobō, 1963.

Kuriyama Riichi, ed. *Nihon bungaku ni okeru bi no kōzō*. Yūzankaku, 1982.

Kyō habutae 京羽二重 (Kyoto silk). Published 1691. Also called *Haikai Kyō habutae*. Haikai handbook with list of haikai poets in Kyoto, ed. Rinkō. In *Haisho keifu itsuwa shū II*, pp. 123–62. HT 32. Shunjūsha, 1930.

Kyoraishō 去来抄 (Kyorai's gleanings). Comp. 1704, published 1775. Record of Bashō's teachings by Kyorai. Draws heavily on Kyorai's own letters to other disciples (such as Kikaku, Fugyoku, Rōka, Kyoriku) and from his own poetic treatise *Tabineron*. In *Rengaron shū, Nōgakuron shū, Hairon shū*, ed. Ijichi Tetsuo, Omote Akira, and Kuriyama Riichi, pp. 421–515. For text with commentary, see Minami Shin'ichi, ed., *Sōshaku Kyorai no hairon (ge): Kyoraishō*.

Kyoya shōsoku 許野消息 (Correspondence between Kyoriku and Yaba). Published 1785. Ed. Yūzan, poetic treatise consisting of essays exchanged in a debate between Kyoriku and Yaba in 1714–15. In *Shōmon hairon haibun shū*, ed. Ōiso Yoshio and Ōuchi Hatsuo, pp. 325–39. KHT 10. Shūseisha, 1970. For text and commentary, see Minami Shin'ichi, ed., *Sōshaku Kyoriku no hairon*, pp. 723–803. Kazama shobō, 1974.

Man'yōshū 万葉集 (Collection of ten thousand leaves). 759. Ed. Kojima Noriyuki, Kinoshita Masatoshi, and Satake Akihiro. NKBZ 2–5. Shōgakukan, 1971–75.

Masaoka Shiki. *Haijin Buson*. Hototogisu, 1899.

———. *Masaoka Shiki shū*. Ed. Matsui Toshihiko. Nihon kindai bungaku taikei 16. Kadokawa shoten, 1972.

Matsuba meisho waka shū 松葉名所和歌集 (Pine needle collection of Japanese poetry on famous places). 1660. In *Matsuba meisho waka shū*. Kasama sakuin sōkan 57. Kasama shoin, 1977.

Matsuda Osamu. *Nihon kinsei bungaku no seiritsu*. Hōsei daigaku shuppankyoku, 1972.

Matsui Toshihiko. "Kindai hairon to Bashō." In vol. 7 of *Bashō no hon*, ed. Konishi Jin'ichi, pp. 251–94. Kadokawa shoten, 1970.

Matsuo Bashō shū. Ed. Imoto Nōichi, Hori Nobuo, and Muramatsu Tomotsugu. NKBZ 41. Shōgakukan, 1972.

Minami Shin'ichi. *Sanzōshi sōshaku*. Rev. ed. Kazama shobō. 1980.

———. *Sōshaku Kyorai no hairon (ge): Kyoraishō*. Vol. 2. Kazama shobō, 1975.

———. *Sōshaku Kyorai no hairon (jō): Kyorai shokan, Tabineron*. Vol. 1. Kazama shobō, 1974.

———. *Sōshaku Kyoriku no hairon*. Kazama shobō, 1974.

———. *Sōshaku Shikō no hairon*. Kazama shobō, 1983.

Minashiguri みなしぐり (Empty chestnuts). 1683. Chinese-style haikai anthology comp. by Kikaku. In *Shōmon haikai shū I*, ed. Abe Kimio, Abe Masami, Ōiso Yoshio, pp. 25–52. KHT 6. Shūeisha, 1972.

Miyamoto Saburō. *Shōfū haikai ronkō*. Kasama shoin, 1974.

Moritake senku 守武千句 (Thousand verses by Moritake). 1540? In *Teimon haikai shū* I, ed. Nakamura Shunjō and Morikawa Akira, pp. 19–43. KHT 1. Shūeisha, 1970.

Muramatsu Tomotsugu. *Bashō no tegami*. Taishūkan shoten, 1985

Musashiburi 武蔵曲 (Musashi style). Published 1682. Haikai anthology ed. Chiharu, including early poetry by Tōsei (Bashō). In *Shōmon haikai shū* I, ed. Abe Kimio, Abe Masami, Ōiso Yoshio, pp. 17–24. KHT 6. Shūeisha, 1972.

Nakamura Kusatao. *Nakamura Kusatao shū*. Gendai haiku no sekai 6. Asahi shinbunsha, 1984.

Nakamura Shunjō. *Bashō no renku o yomu*. Iwanami seminaa bukkusu 16. Iwanami shoten, 1985.

———. *Haikaishi no shomondai*. Kasama shoin, 1970.

Nakamura Yukihiko. *Nakamura Yukihiko chojutsushū*. Chūō kōron sha, 1982. 11 vols.

Natsuishi Banya, ed. *Haiku hyakunen no toi*. Kōdansha gakujutsu bunko. Kōdansha, 1995.

Nihon angya bunshū 日本行脚文集 (Prose collection on travels through Japan), by Michikaze (Sanzenfū). In *Haikai kikō zenshū*, ed. Saitō Hiroshi, pp. 1–184. Haikai bunko 24. Hakubunkan, 1901.

Nihon haisho taikei. See Haisho taikei (HT).

Nihon kagaku taikei. 10 vols. Ed. Sasaki Nobutsuna. Kazama shobō, 1956–63.

Nihon koten bungaku taikei. Iwanami shoten. 1957–68. 102 vols.

Nihon koten bungaku zenshū. Shōgakukan. 1971–76. 51 vols.

Nose Asaji. "Bashō no hairon." In idem, *Nose Asaji chosakushū*. Kyoto: Shibunkaku shuppan, 1981.

———. *Sanzōshi hyōshaku*. Meichō kankōkai, 1970.

Nozarashi kikō 野ざらし紀行 (Skeleton in the fields). Travel account by Bashō of journey in 1684, from Edo to Kamigata region. Probably written late in 1684. Alternative titles include *Kusamakura, Nozarashi no shū*,

Nozarashi no kikō, and *Kasshi ginkō*. In *Matsuo Bashō shū*, ed. Imoto Nō-ichi, Hori Nobuo, and Muramatsu Tomotsugu, pp. 287–99. NKBZ 41. Shōgakukan, 1972.

Ogata Tsutomu. *Bashō Buson*. Kashinsha, 1978.

———. *Bashō no sekai*. 2 vols. Nihon hōsō shuppan kyōkai, 1978. Reissued in a significantly abbreviated version as *Bashō no sekai*. Kōdansha gakujutsu bunko 822. Kōdansha, 1988. All references are to the Kōdansha version unless noted.

———. "Chinkon no ryojō: Bashō *Oi no kobumi* kō." In *Bashō II*, pp. 122–33. Nihon bungaku kenkyū shiryō sōsho. Yūseidō, 1977.

———. *Haiku no shūhen*. Fujimi shobō, 1990.

———. *Haikaishi ronkō*. Ōfūsha, 1977.

———. *Haiku to haikai*. Kadokawa shoten, 1981.

———. *Kasen no sekai*. Kōdansha, 1986.

———. *Matsuo Bashō*. Nihon o tsukutta hito 18. Heibonsha, 1978

———. *Matsuo Bashō*. Nihon shijinsen 17. Chikuma shobō, 1971.

———. *Za no bungaku*. Kadokawa shoten, 1973.

———. *Zoku Bashō Buson*. Kashinsha, 1985.

Ogata Tsutomu, ed. *Bashō hikkei*. Bessatsu kokubungaku 8. Gakutōsha, 1980.

Ogino Kiyoshi. *Haibungaku no sōsetsu*. Akao shibundō, 1971.

Oi nikki 笈日記 (Backpack diary). Published 1695. Chronologically arranged collection of poetry related to Bashō, including account of Bashō's last days, edited by Shikō, a disciple. Written as sequel to *Oi no kobumi*. In *Shōmon haikai shū I*, ed. Abe Kimio, Abe Masami, Ōiso Yoshio, pp. 440–533. KHT 6. Shūeisha, 1972.

Oi no kobumi 笈の小文 (Backpack notes). Travel account of Bashō's journey in winter of 1687 from Edo to Kamigata region, written by Bashō, ed. Otokuni, a disciple. In *Matsuo Bashō shū*, ed. Imoto Nōichi, Hori Nobuo, and Muramatsu Tomotsugu, pp. 311–30. NKBZ 41. Shōgakukan, 1972. Also in KBZ 6: 75–94.

Okada Riei. *Bashō no hisseki*. 2 vols. Shunjūsha, 1968. Good analysis of Bashō's calligraphy.

Oku no hosomichi おくの細道 (Narrow road to the Interior), by Bashō. Literary account of Bashō's journey to Michinoku from the Third to the Eighth Month of 1689. In *Matsuo Bashō shū*, ed. Imoto Nōichi, Hori Nobuo, and Muramatsu Tomotsugu, pp. 341–86. NKBZ 41. Shōgakukan, 1972.

Oku no hosomichi sugagomoshō 奥細道菅菰抄 (Narrow road to the Interior sedge mat collection). 1778. One of the earliest and best commentaries on *Oku no hosomichi*, by Riichi (1714–83). In *Oku no hosomichi*, ed. Hagiwara Yasuo, pp. 154–243. Iwanami bunko. Iwanami shoten, 1979.

Rekidai kokkei den 歴代滑稽伝 (Biographies of successive haikai poets). Published 1715. Haikai history written by Kyoriku, a disciple of Bashō. In *Shōmon hairon haibun shū*, ed. Ōiso Yoshio and Ōuchi Hatsuo, pp. 340–54. KHT 10. Shūeisha, 1970.

Renga haikai shū. Ed. Kaneko Kinjirō, Teruoka Yasutaka, Nakamura Shunjō. NKBZ 32. Shōgakukan, 1974.

Rengaron shū. 2 vols. Ed. Ichiji Tetsuo. Iwanami bunko. Iwanami shoten, 1953, 1956.

Rengaron shū I. Ed. Kidō Saizō and Shigematsu Hiromi. Chūsei no bungaku. Miyai shoten, 1972.

Rengaron shū II. Ed. Kidō Saizō. Chūsei no bungaku. Miyai shoten, 1982.

Rengaron shū, Nōgakuron shū, Hairon shū. Ed. Ijichi Tetsuo, Omote Akira, and Kuriyama Riichi. NKBZ 51. Shōgakukan, 1973.

Renga shihōshō (Renga treasures). 1586. By Jōha. In *Rengaron shū II*, ed. Ijichi Tetsuo, pp. 231–59. Iwanami bunko. Iwanami shoten, 1956.

Renga shū. Ed. Ijichi Tetsuo. NKBT 39. Iwanami shoten, 1960.

Renju gappeki shū 連珠合璧集 (Gathered gems). 1476. By Ichijō Kaneyoshi. In *Rengaron shū I*, ed. Kidō Saizō and Shigematsu Hiromi, pp. 26–202. Miyai shoten, 1972.

Renku jiten. Ed. Higashi Akimasa, Sugiuchi Toshi, Ōhata Kenji. Tōkyōdō shuppan, 1986. Best handbook on composing modern linked verse.

Ruiji meisho waka shū 類似名所和歌集 (Classified collection of Japanese poetry on famous places). 1617. Waka on famous places arranged by provinces, used by renga and haikai poets for linking, edited by Shōtaku, used by Sora in preparation for *Oku no hosomichi* journey. In *Ruiji meisho waka shū sakuin*, ed. Senso Akio and Tanichi Yoshikazu. Kasama shoin, 1988.

Ruisenshū 類船集 (Accompanying boat). Published 1676. Haikai dictionary, giving lexical associations (*tsukeai*) for haikai linking, revised and expanded version of *Binsenshū*, written by Baisei, a Teimon poet. In *Haikai ruisenshū sakuin*, ed. Noma Kōshin, 2 vols. Kinsei bungei sōkan. Han'an Noma Kōshin sensei kankō kinen kai, 1973–75.

Ryōkan zenshū. Ed. Tōgō Toyoharu. Sōgensha, 1959.

Sakurai Takejirō. "*Oku no hosomichi* shippitsu ni kansuru ichi shiron." In *Haibungei no kenkyū*. Kadokawa shoten, 1983.

Sankashū 山家集. Collection of Saigyō's poems. Ed. Gotō Shigeo. SKBS 49. Shinchōsha, 1982.

Sanzōshi 三冊子 (Three booklets). Comp. 1702, published 1776. Collection of Bashō's teachings by Dohō, an Iga disciple, probably the most accurate record. Consists of "White Booklet" (*Shirosōshi*), "Red Booklet" (*Akasōshi*), and "Black Booklet" (*Kurosōshi*). In *Rengaron shū, Nōgakuron shū, Hairon shū*, ed. Ijichi Tetsuo, Omote Akira, and Kuriyama Riichi, pp. 519–623. For text and commentary, see Minami Shin'ichi, *Sanzōshi sōshaku*. Rev. ed. Kazama shobō, 1980.

Sarashina kikō 更科紀行 (Journey to Sarashina). 1688–89? Travel account of Bashō's journey to Sarashina in 1688, by Bashō. In *Matsuo Bashō shū*, ed. Imoto Nōichi, Hori Nobuo, and Muramatsu Tomotsugu, pp. 333–37. NKBZ 41. Shōgakukan, 1972.

Sarumino 猿蓑 (Monkey's straw coat). Published 1691. Ed. Kyorai and Bonchō. The most famous and influential of the Bashō-school haikai anthologies. In *Bashō shichibu shū*, ed. Shiraishi Teizō and Ueno Yōzō, pp. 259–355. SNKBT 70. Iwanami shoten, 1990

Shihōshō. See *Renga shihōshō*.

Shimazu Tadao. *Rengashi no kenkyū*. Kadokawa shoten, 1969.

Shinchō Nihon koten shūsei. Shinchōsha. 1976–89. 48 vols.

Shin kokin waka shū 新古今和歌集 or *Shinkokinshū*. (New collection of old and new poems). 1205. Ed. Munemura Fumito. NKBZ 26. Shōgakukan, 1974.

Shin Nihon koten bungaku taikei. Iwanami shoten, 1989–.

Shinsen Tsukuba shū 新撰筑波集 (New Tsukuba collection). 1495. Classical renga anthology edited by Sōgi, Kenzai, and Sanjōnishi Sanetaka. Selections in *Renga shū*, ed. Ijichi Tetsuo, pp. 177–340. NKBT 39. Iwanami shoten, 1960.

Shinzō inu Tsukuba shū 新増犬筑波集 (New dog Tsukuba collection). 1643. Teimon haikai anthology edited by Teitoku. In *Teimon haikai shū I*, ed. Nakamura Shunjō and Morikawa Akira, pp. 194–254. KHT 1. Shūeisha, 1970.

Shiraishi Teizō. *Bashō*. Kashinsha, 1988.

Shohon taishō Bashō haibun kubun shū. Ed. Yayoshi Kan'ichi, Nishimura Masako, Akahane Manabu, and Danjō Masataka. Shimizu kōbundō, 1977.

Shōmon haijin shokan shū (Letters by Bashō's disciples). Ed. Iida Masakazu. Ōfūsha, 1972.

Shōmon hairon haibun shū. Ed. Ōiso Yoshio and Ōuchi Hatsuo. KHT 10. Shūeisha, 1970.

Shōmon meika kusen. Ed. Horikiri Minoru. 2 vols. Iwanami bunko. Iwanami shoten, 1989.

Shōtetsu monogatari 正徹物語 (Conversations with Shōtetsu). In *Karon shū*, ed. Hashimoto Fumio, Ariyoshi Tamotsu, and Fujihira Haruo, pp. 165–234. NKBZ 50. Shōgakukan, 1975.

Sōgō Bashō jiten. Ed. Kuriyama Riichi. Yūzankaku, 1982.

Sora tabi nikki 曾良旅日記 (Sora's travel diary, 1689). Written while accompanying Bashō through Michinoku. Reveals the fictional dimension of *Oku no hosomichi.* In KBZ 6: 206–77.

Sumidawara 炭俵 (Charcoal sack). 1694. Bashō-school haikai anthology edited by Yaba, Kooku, and Rigyū in Edo. In *Bashō shichibu shū,* ed. Shiraishi Teizō and Ueno Yōzō, pp. 359–453. SNKBT 70. Iwanami shoten, 1990.

Suzuki Katsutada. *Haikaishi yō.* Meiji shoin, 1973.

———. *Kinsei haikaishi no kiso: Shōfū shūhen to zappai.* Nagoya City: Nagoya daigaku shuppankai, 1992.

———. "Tōdai haikaishi no jittai to Bashō." In vol. 2 of *Bashō no hon,* ed. Katō Shūson, pp. 163–93. Kadokawa shoten, 1970.

Tabineron 旅寝論 (Travel lodging discussion). 1699. Poetic treatise by Kyorai, written in response to *Hentsuki* (by Kyoriku and Riyu). In *Shōmon hairon haibun shū,* ed. Ōiso Yoshio and Ōuchi Hatsuo, pp. 194–217. KHT 10. Shūeisha, 1970. Also in Minami Shin'ichi, *Sōshaku Kyorai no hairon (jō): Kyorai shokan, Tabineron,* pp. 279–439. Kazama shobō, 1974.

Takahashi Shōji. "*Oi no kobumi* no yōkyoku kōsei ni tsuite: *Oi no kobumi* ron josetsu." In *Bashō II.* Nihon bungaku kenkyū shiryō sōsho. Yūseidō, 1977.

Tomiyama Susumu. "Shōfū haikai no itansei." In *Kokugo kokubun* 36, no. 11 (Nov. 1967): 23–44.

Toyama Shigehiko. "Shōryaku no bungaku: kireji ron." In vol. 4 of *Bashō no hon,* ed. Kadokawa Gen'yoshi, pp. 320–51. Kadokawa shoten, 1970.

Tsukuba shū 筑波集 (Tsukuba collection). 1356. Classical renga anthology ed. Nijō Yoshimoto. Selections in *Renga shū,* ed. Ijichi Tetsuo, pp. 39–174. NKBT 39. Iwanami shoten, 1960.

Uda no hōshi 宇陀法師 (Uda priest). Published 1702. Poetic treatise ed. Riyū and Kyoriku. In *Shōmon hairon haibun shū,* ed. Ōiso Yoshio and Ōuchi Hatsuo, pp. 231–52. KHT 10. Shūeisha, 1970.

Ueno Yōzō. *Bashō ron.* Chikuma shobō, 1986.

———. *Bashō shichibu shū.* Koten kōdoku siriizu. Iwanami seminaa bukkusu 102. Iwanami shoten, 1992.

———. *Bashō, tabi e.* Iwanami shinsho. Iwanami shoten, 1989.

———. "Kireji danshō." In *Haiku hairon,* ed. Shiraishi Teizō and Ogata Tsutomu, pp. 393–402. Kanshō Nihon koten bungaku 33. Kadokawa shoten, 1977.

Yamamoto Kenkichi. *Bashō: sono kanshō to hihyō.* Shinchōsha, 1957.

———. *Bashō zen hokku.* 2 vols. Kawade shobō shinsha, 1974.

———. *Ikite kaeru koten bungaku hyōron.* Kawade shobō shinsha, 1973.

———. *Kihon kigo gohyaku sen*. Kōdansha gakujutsu bunko. Kōdansha, 1989.

Yamanaka mondō 山中問答 (Dialogue at Yamanaka). Published 1850 or 1862. Poetic treatise by Hokushi, a Bashō disciple. The first half records what Hokushi learned from Bashō during the *Oku no hosomichi* journey, especially about *fueki ryūkō*. The second half, probably written much later and perhaps forged by Shikō or a Shikō disciple, presents Hokushi's system for linking verses. In *Shōmon hairon haibun shū*, ed. Ōiso Yoshio and Ōuchi Hatsuo, pp. 21–27. KHT 10. Shūeisha, 1970. Also in Minami Shin'ichi, *Sōshaku Shikō no hairon*, pp. 1035–72.

Yama no i 山の井 (Mountain well). Published 1647. Seasonal almanac (*kiyose*) and poetry collection ed. Kigin. In *Teimon haikai shū*, pp. 415–76. HT 14. Shunjūsha, 1929.

Yasuda Akio. *Nihon no geijutsu ron*. Sōgensha, 1957.

Yodo no watari 淀の渡 (River pool crossing). 1495. Poetic treatise by Sōgi. In *Rengaron shū II*, ed. Ijichi Tetsuo, pp. 78–85. Iwanami bunko. Iwanami shoten, 1956.

Yonetani Iwao. "Bashō aisatsu ku no suikō ni tsuite." In *Bashō II*, pp. 54–61. Nihon bungaku kenkyū shiryō sōsho. Yūseidō, 1977.

Yonetani Iwao. "*Nozorashi kikō* ni okeru Bashō." *Kinsei bungeikō* 10 (1966). Reprinted in *Bashō*, pp. 76–85. Nihon koten bungaku shiryō sōsho. Yūseidō, 1969.

Zoku goron 続五論 (Sequel to five discussions). 1699. Poetic treatise by Shikō, a Bashō disciple. In *Shōmon hairon haibun shū*, ed. Ōiso Yoshio and Ōuchi Hatsuo, pp. 218–20. KHT 10. Shūeisha, 1970.

Zoku sarumino 続猿蓑 (Sequel to *Monkey's Straw Coat*). 1698, Bashō-school haikai anthology, ed. Senbo and Bashō, with aid of Shikō. In *Bashō shichibu shū*, ed. Shiraishi Teizō and Ueno Yōzō, pp. 457–570. SNKBT 70. Iwanami shoten, 1990.

Zoku yama no i 続山井 (Sequel to *Mountain Well*). 1667. Seasonal almanac, revised and expanded version of *Yama no i*, ed. Koshun, son of Kigin. In *Teimon haikai shū I*, ed. Nakamura Shunjō and Morikawa Akira, pp. 488–626. KHT 1. Shūeisha, 1970.

Zōtanshū 雑談集 (Miscellaneous talk collection). Published in 1691. Haikai collection ed. Kikaku, an Edo disciple. In *Shōmon hairon haibun shū*, ed. Ōiso Yoshio and Ōuchi Hatsuo, pp. 28–55. KHT 10. Shūeisha, 1970.

Zō yama no i 増山井 (Expanded *Mountain Well*). 1667. Seasonal almanac by Kigin. Published with *Zoku yama no i* (Sequel to *Mountain Well*) in a 7-vol. set. In *Teimon haikai shū II*, ed. Kodaka Yoshirō, Morikawa Akira, and Inui Hiroyuki, pp. 431–87. KHT 2. Shūeisha, 1971.

Cited Hokku by Bashō, with Approximate Dates of the Earliest Variant

akaaka to hi wa tsurenaku mo aki no kaze, 17th, Seventh Month, Genroku 2 (Aug. 31, 1689), 280

akebono ya shirauo shiroki koto issun, Early Eleventh Month, Jōkyō 1 (Dec. 1684), 98, 101

aki fukaki tonari wa nani o suru hito zo, 28th, Ninth Month, Genroku 7 (Nov. 15, 1694), 278

akikaze ya yabu mo hatake mo Fuwa no seki, Late Ninth Month, Jōkyō 1 (Oct.–Nov. 1684), 201

aki no kaze Ise no hakahara nao sugoshi, Mid-or-late Ninth Month, Genroku 2 (Oct. 1689), 335

aoyagi no doro ni shidaruru shiohi kana, Mid-spring, Genroku 7 (Feb., 1694), 111

ara tōto aoba wakaba no hi no hikari, 1st, Fourth Month, Genroku 2 (May 19, 1689), 271

ara tōto ko no shitayami mo hi no hikari, 1st, Fourth Month, Genroku 2 (May 19, 1689), 271

araumi ya Sado ni yokotau amanogawa, 7th, Seventh Month, Genroku 2 (Aug. 21, 1689), 242, 263, 303

atsuki hi o umi ni iretari Mogamigawa, 14th, Sixth Month, Genroku 2 (July 30, 1689), 171

ayamegusa ashi ni musuban waraji no o, 7th, Fifth Month, Genroku 2 (June 23, 1689), 246

ayu no ko no shirauo okuru wakare kana, 27th, Third Month, Genroku 2 (May 16, 1689), 332

bashō nowaki shite tarai ni ame o kiku yo kana, Autumn, Enpō 9 (Aug.–Nov. 1681), 64

bii to naku shirigoe kanashi yoru no shika, 8th, Ninth Month, Genroku 7 (Oct. 26, 1694), 274

botan shibe fukaku wakeizuru hachi no nagori kana, Early Fourth Month, Jōkyō 2 (May 1685), 165

General Index

In this index an "f" after a number indicates a separate reference on the next page, and an "ff" indicates separate references on the next two pages. A continuous discussion over two or more pages is indicated by a span of page numbers, e.g., "57–59." *Passim* is used for a cluster of references in close but not consecutive sequence.

Kyohaku, verse by, 192
Kyōka (comic waka), 12, 73
Kyokusui (1660-1717), 87, 92, 157,
173, 258, 279, 281, 338: verse by,
6
Kyorai (1651-1704), 31, 33, 102,
157, 169, 199, 212, 252, 257, 263,
267, 319; and *Monkey's Straw
Coat*, 5, 279, 283f; on *sabi*, 77f,
310f; verse by, 78; on status
links, 96; on combination
poems, 111–14, 313; on *utama-
kura*, 193; on traditional topics
and poetic essence, 197–98, 204–
6, 325, 336; on the Unchanging
and the ever-changing, 263, 334
—*Kyoraishō* (*Kyorai's gleanings*;
comp. 1704), 33, 302; on *sabi* and
shiori, 77–79, 310f; on combina-
tion poems, 90, 111, 113, 313; on
linking, 94, 96; on cutting words,
103–4, on composing *kasen*, 168,
315; on *utamakura*, 192–93, 324;
on new seasonal words, 199, 201;
on preserving traditional poetic
essence, 204–5, 325; on haibun,
216; on *ada*, 274–75; on the
Unchanging and the ever-chang-
ing, 334–35.
—other works: *Haikai mondō* (ca.
1687), 310f, 334; *Travel Lodging
Discussion* (*Tabineron*; 1699),
112–13, 197–98, 274, 275, 313
Kyoriku (1656-1715), 33, 84, 162,
197, 215, 257, 263, 338; on
combination poems, 24, 105–13
passim, 210, 313; hokku by, 78,
105, 109–10; paintings by, 84,
186, 214; on traditional topics
and poetic essence, 198, 205–7;
on *haibun*, 215
—works: *Biographies of Successive*

Haikai Poets (*Rekidai kokkei den*;
published 1715), 282, 313; *Haikai
Dialogue* (*Haikai mondō*; 1697-
98), 105–6, 109–10, 313–14, 334;
Hentsuki (1698), 205–6, 313;
Prose Collection of Japan (*Honchō
monzen*; published 1706), 215,
219; *Rhapsody on Travel* (*Tabi no
fu*), 252; *Uda Priest* (*Uda* 1702),
124, 197, 257, 313
Kyōtai (1732-92), 33–34f, 302
Kyoto, Bashō school poets in, 20f,
251–52, 266, 279, 283, 319, 338
Kyōto habutae (Kyōto Silk; 1691),
156, 319
Kyoya shōsoku, see Correspondence
between Kyoriku and Yaba
Kyūho, verse by, 189
Kyūshū: Bashō school followers in,
31; shrine to Bashō in, 36

Landscape, broadly conceived, *see*
Classical poetry; Cultural
memory; *Haimakura*; Poetic
essence; Seasonal topics; Travel;
Utamakura
Landscape (*keiki*) style: in Genroku
poetry, 23, 51, 76–81, 191, 265,
295, 309n32; in renga, 76, 310; as
fusion of scene (*kei*) and human
emotion (*jō*), 76, 243, 310
Language: Vernacular in haikai, 7f,
10, 56, 60, 79ff, 87f, 97, 115, 120,
276ff; vernacular in haibun, 27,
212f, 215f, 220; in renga, 53, 56,
61, 306; in classical poetry, 53,
60f; in Teimon haikai, 56, 58. *See
also* Contemporary commoner
life and culture; Haikai words
Lawrence, D. H., 41
Lexical associations, for linking:
yoriai (established or classical

Library of Congress Cataloging-in-Publication Data

Shirane, Haruo
    Traces of dreams : Landscape, cultural memory, and the poetry
of Bashō / Haruo Shirane.
        p.   cm.
    Includes bibliographical references (p.   ) and index.
    ISBN 0-8047-3098-9 (cloth : alk. paper) —
    ISBN 0-8047-3099-7 (pbk. : alk. paper)
    1. Matsuo Bashō—1644–1694—Criticism and interpretation.
2. Haikai—History and criticism. 3. Haiku—History and
criticism. I. Title.

PL794.4.Z5S586   1998
895.6'132—dc21   97-29388
                                                          CIP

This book is printed on acid-free, recycled paper.

Original printing 1998
Last figure below indicates year of this printing:
07   06   05   04